"More than any of his other case studies, Freud's *Little Hans* is central to his theory of the Oedipus complex, which is at the core of his conception of neurosis and psychological development. There have been many reinterpretations of the *Little Hans* case, but there is none that even begins to match the thoroughness and cogency of Wakefield's exposition. This is so for at least two reasons: One is that Wakefield had access to evidence from the Freud Archives that was not available to other authors. The other reason is Wakefield's brilliance in bring the evidence together in the formulation of a thoroughly convincing set of theses.

A central thesis of the book for which there is overwhelming evidence is that with the participation of Freud, Hans' father, Max Graf, imposed Oedipal theory on his wife and son as a means of keeping Hans from seeking intimacy and soothing from his mother and blocking his wife's effort to provide them – all in the service of having his wife pay more attention to him than to their son. This convincing formulation is located in the context of Foucault's power/knowledge discussion of the function of theory, that is, the role of a theory in supporting society's changing values and structures.

One can dispense with all previous interpretations of the *Little Hans* case. Wakefield's characteristically compelling analysis – which is also evident in his other works, for example, his analysis of Freud as philosopher of mind - renders previous accounts essentially peripheral. Finally, two additional comments: One, reading Wakefield's new book is like reading, through the lens of examining a particular case, an overall enlightening analysis and critique of core aspects of Freudian theory; and two, reading this book provides a taste of Wakefield's brilliance and whets one's appetite for gaining familiarity with his other work."

Morris Eagle is professor emeritus at the Derner Institute for Advanced Psychological Studies, Adelphi University, and author of *Toward a unified psychoanalytic theory*

"This book is a must-read for anyone interested in Freud scholarship, psychoanalysis, psychotherapy, feminism, intellectual and social history, the philosophy of science, and the social construction of parenthood. Using previously inaccessible materials, the author critiques Freud's famously strained oedipal analysis of a young boy's fear of horses, arriving at a new understanding rooted in shifting cultural power dynamics. Wakefield's readable and fascinating book restores dignity to 'Little Hans' and to his much-bashed mother, who deserves our admiration for taking her own maternal intuition more seriously than speculations from the 'new science' of psychoanalysis."

Nancy McWilliams is visiting full professor at Rutgers Graduate School of Applied & Professional Psychology, and author of *Psychoanalytic Diagnosis*

"Revisiting Freud's illustrious case history of 'Little Hans', Wakefield shows with almost forensic precision that the father of psychoanalysis got it all wrong: in fact, it was Freud's own Oedipal theory, enforced by Hans' father within this very Freudian family, that caused the boy's anxiety in the first place! Wakefield elucidates a truly Copernican reversal that makes this book a must-read for anyone wanting to know the truth about a theory that has played such an outsized role in our culture at large."

Mikkel Borch-Jacobsen is emeritus professor of Comparative Literature at the University of Washington, and author of *Freud's Patients*

Attachment, Sexuality, Power

In *Attachment, Sexuality, Power*, Jerome C. Wakefield challenges established views of Freudian psychoanalysis by applying Foucault's concept of 'power/ knowledge' to Freud's case of Little Hans, illuminating the role that Oedipal theory has played in reorganizing intimate family relationships.

Combining close examination of the Hans case with accounts of the history of marriage and psychology of co-sleeping, this book argues that the Oedipal theory achieved prominence because its implications for family dynamics supported changing social values. Wakefield identifies a previously overlooked reason for Hans's anxiety—his father attempted to protect Hans from his supposed Oedipal desires by separating Hans from his mother. Thus, Wakefield argues, the father's exercise of power based on his belief in Oedipal theory, not an actual Oedipus complex, caused Hans's vulnerability to anxiety—revealing the theory's potential to cause harm by distancing children from their parents, even as such distancing made the theory socially appealing.

This book's novel and carefully documented articulation of the mechanisms of power by which Oedipal theory exerts its influence on family life will be of interest to psychoanalysts and psychotherapists alike, and essential for scholars in the fields of psychoanalysis, philosophy of science and the history of psychiatry.

Jerome C. Wakefield holds a PhD in Philosophy, a DSW and an MSW in Clinical Social Work, and an M.A. in Mathematics with a specialty in Logic and Methodology of Science, all from University of California, Berkeley. After pursuing postdoctoral research in feminist theory at Brown University and Cognitive Science at Berkeley, he held faculty positions at University of Chicago, Columbia University, and Rutgers University before coming to

NYU in 2003, where he is university professor, professor of social work, professor of the Conceptual Foundations of Psychiatry (2007–2019), associate faculty in the Center for Bioethics in the School of Global Public Health, and honorary faculty in the Psychoanalytic Association of New York affiliated with NYU Grossman School of Medicine, at New York University. He is an elected fellow of the National Academy of Social Work and Social Welfare and an elected member of the Rapaport-Klein Study Group in Ego Psychology. The author of over 300 publications addressing issues at the intersection of philosophy and the mental health professions that appear in journals and books in psychology, philosophy, psychiatry, psychoanalysis, and social work, he is author or editor of four books, the last being *Freud and Philosophy of Mind: Reconstructing the Argument for Unconscious Mental States* (2018, Palgrave). His coauthored book, *The Loss of Sadness: How Psychiatry Transformed Normal Sorrow into Depressive Disorder* (2007, Oxford), was named best psychology book of 2007 by the Association of Professional and Scholarly Publishers.

PSYCHOLOGICAL ISSUES

DAVID L. WOLITZKY
Series Editor

The basic mission of *Psychological Issues* is to contribute to the further development of psychoanalysis as a science, as a respected scholarly enterprise, as a theory of human behavior, and as a therapeutic method.

Over the past 50 years, the series has focused on fundamental aspects and foundations of psychoanalytic theory and clinical practice, as well as on work in related disciplines relevant to psychoanalysis. *Psychological Issues* does not aim to represent or promote a particular point of view. The contributions cover broad and integrative topics of vital interest to all psychoanalysts as well as to colleagues in related disciplines. They cut across particular schools of thought and tackle key issues, such as the philosophical underpinnings of psychoanalysis, psychoanalytic theories of motivation, conceptions of therapeutic action, the nature of unconscious mental functioning, psychoanalysis and social issues, and reports of original empirical research relevant to psychoanalysis. The authors often take a critical stance toward theories and offer a careful theoretical analysis and conceptual clarification of the complexities of theories and their clinical implications, drawing upon relevant empirical findings from psychoanalytic research as well as from research in related fields.

Series Editor David L. Wolitzky and the Editorial Board continues to invite contributions from social/behavioral sciences such as anthropology and sociology, from biological sciences such as physiology and the various brain sciences, and from scholarly humanistic disciplines such as philosophy, law, and ethics. Volumes 1-64 in this series were published by International Universities Press. Volumes 65-69 were published by Jason Aronson. For a full list of the titles published by Routledge in this series, please visit the Routledge website: https://www.routledge.com/Psychological-Issues/book-series/PSYCHISSUES

Attachment, Sexuality, Power

Oedipal Theory as Regulator of Family
Affection in Freud's Case of Little Hans

Jerome C. Wakefield

Routledge
Taylor & Francis Group
NEW YORK AND LONDON

Cover image: The Three Ages of the Woman. Klimt, Gustav (1862–1918). Galleria Nazionale, d'Arte Moderna e Contemporanea, Rome, Lazio, Italy, Luisa Ricciarini/Bridgeman Images.

First published 2023
by Routledge
605 Third Avenue, New York, NY 10158

and by Routledge
4 Park Square, Milton Park, Abingdon, Oxon, OX14 4RN

Routledge is an imprint of the Taylor & Francis Group, an informa business

Library of Congress Cataloging-in-Publication Data
A catalog record has been requested for this book

ISBN: 978-1-032-22410-7 (hbk)
ISBN: 978-1-032-22409-1 (pbk)
ISBN: 978-0-203-81712-4 (ebk)

DOI: 10.4324/9780203817124

Typeset in Times New Roman
by Taylor & Francis Books

Contents

Acknowledgments

Like the parallel volume, *Freud's Argument for the Oedipus Complex*, that is being published simultaneously with this one, this book has been in preparation for a very long time. Regrettably, I cannot thank everyone who has helped along the way; there are simply too many. My gratitude goes first and foremost to my wife Lisa N. Peters and my sons Joshua and Zachary Wakefield for their support, encouragement, and love, and their tolerance of the time away from them that my efforts on this book required. They make it all worthwhile. Lisa also provided helpful editorial feedback on some chapters.

Many illuminating discussions of psychoanalytic theory with the editor of this series, David Wolitzky, and with the brilliant psychoanalyst and philosopher Morris Eagle, improved this work immensely. As well, David Abrams offered invaluable guidance on biographical and historical questions regarding Olga Honig Graf. More distantly, in addition to my many philosophical and psychoanalytic teachers and mentors, I must particularly acknowledge the influence of my teachers in the area of Continental and Foucauldian philosophy, Hubert Dreyfus and Michel Foucault.

I am once again profoundly grateful to my indefatigable research assistant and colleague, Jordan Conrad, for help with all aspects of the manuscript. Of course, the errors and excesses that were nonetheless retained despite all this support are mine alone. I also thank the patient team at Routledge—current and past—especially the editor, Kate Hawes, her editorial assistant, Georgina Clutterbuck, as well as Hannah Wright, Charles Bath, and Kristopher Spring, for seeing me through the long process that has finally yielded this book and offering me the opportunity to share the results of my investigations with interested readers.

Chapter 1

Introduction
Oedipal Theory and Family Power

In this book, I offer a new analysis of Sigmund Freud's case of Little Hans, the case history in which Freud presented what he considered to be his best evidence for his theory of the Oedipus complex. Like the many other commentators on the case, one of my goals is to solve the puzzle of what might have caused an apparently robust boy like Hans to be vulnerable to the development of an anxiety condition, namely, a horse phobia that developed after seeing a horse fall down in the Vienna streets. In this regard, I reject Freud's Oedipal account as well as Bowlby's rival analysis and provide a novel and, I think, rather unsettling solution that is solidly anchored in a close reading of the text. I go on to argue that the solution to the Hans case has broader social implications for how Freud's theory has influenced our lives and been used in rationalizing certain forms of power within the family.

My analysis draws on attachment theory (although in a different way than Bowlby's analysis) but is ultimately primarily a "neo-Foucauldian" analysis. By this I mean that it loosely reflects certain ideas of the philosopher and historian of ideas Michel Foucault, specifically his notion of *power/knowledge*. By this term, Foucault refers to the ways in which a psychological theory of human nature can, by its very acceptance as true (whether it is in fact true or false), alter human relationships and create new forms of interpersonal power. I will argue that understanding Hans's anxiety as well as understanding the Hans case's broader social significance requires recognizing the power/knowledge implications of Freud's Oedipal theory. With regard to the Hans case, the power/knowledge implications emerge largely in the way Hans's father applied the theory to his family. In later chapters, I expand my analysis to suggest that the power/knowledge expression of Oedipal theory that one sees in the

DOI: 10.4324/9780203817124-1

Hans case history has subsequently engulfed our culture at large, and that the socio-syntonic nature of the theory's effects may explain the extraordinary influence of Freud's Oedipal theoretic construct.

My focus throughout this book is exclusively on constructing my own analysis rather than analyzing Freud's Oedipal account of Hans's difficulties or assessing the evidence Freud presents to support his claims. A thorough philosophy-of-science analysis of Freud's arguments—and why they fail to support Freud's Oedipal account of Hans's difficulties—is provided in a parallel volume to this one, *Freud's Argument for the Oedipus Complex* (Wakefield, 2022). I am concerned here only with Freud's clinical theory regarding the etiology of neurosis and have dealt elsewhere with his broader philosophical argument for the existence of unconscious mental states (Wakefield, 2018).

"Little Hans" as a Study of the First Oedipal Family

The Little Hans case (Freud, 1909/1955), as it has come to be called—formally titled "Analysis of a Phobia in a Five-Year-Old Boy"—concerns a four-year-old boy who developed a horse phobia after witnessing a horse accident in which a horse pulling a bus-wagon fell down in the streets of Vienna in 1908. (Hans was four-and-a-half at the phobia's onset, and the analysis extended to just after he reached his fifth birthday [Wakefield, 2007].) Freud interpreted the boy's subsequent intense fear of horses as resulting not from the accident itself but from the horse accident's symbolizing Hans's unconscious desires and conflicts, specifically his sexual desire for his mother and jealous anger and fear of revenge from his father, a set of interrelated mental contents that Freud called the "Oedipus complex." Freud postulated that the Oedipus complex is a universal developmental stage in which a boy sexually desires his mother and wants his father to be gone or dead, a desire in conflict with the boy's love for his father. Freud further postulated that the boy is terrified of his father's possible retribution for these desires, specifically via castration to eliminate the offending organ in which the boy's inchoate sexual desire for his mother originates. Freud's central clinical claim is that all psychoneuroses originate from failure to resolve the Oedipus complex.

"Hans's" real name, we now know, was Herbert Graf. However, I will generally stick with "Hans" for consistency with the many passages I will be quoting from the case study. Hans was the son of an eminent Viennese music critic, Max Graf, and his wife Olga Honig-Graf (with apologies, for simplicity I omit the umlaut over the "o"). Hans himself went on to a distinguished career as an opera stage director, and served for many years in this capacity at the Metropolitan Opera in New York City before returning to Europe to be general manager of the Grand Theatre in Geneva. Some relevant details of Hans's family's history and conflicts are presented in Chapter 2.

After Freud published his controversial theories concerning early child-hood sexual development in 1905 in his *Three Essays on the Theory of Sexuality* (1905/1953), Freud asked his followers to keep diaries of their children's development that might be used to support his theories, and to impose the least constraints on the children's sexual expression compatible with proper upbringing. He soon focused on the diary of Hans's develop-ment, as Freud explains at the beginning of the Hans case study:

> I have for many years been urging my pupils and my friends to col-lect observations of the sexual life of children—the existence of which has as a rule been cleverly overlooked or deliberately denied. Among the material which came into my possession as a result of these requests, the reports which I received at regular intervals about little Hans soon began to take a prominent place. His parents were both among my closest adherents, and they had agreed that in bring-ing up their first child they would use no more coercion than might be absolutely necessary for maintaining good behaviour. And, as the child developed into a cheerful, good-natured and lively little boy, the experiment of letting him grow up and express himself without being intimidated went on satisfactorily.
>
> (1909/1955, p. 6)

Hans's father, as we shall see in Chapter 4, eventually went further than just keeping a diary and additionally intervened in his family's life guided by the Oedipal theory in an effort to prevent Hans from being over-stimulated sexually. Thus, in addition to a straightforward diary of Hans's sexual development, the diary became the earliest record of the potential effects of applying Oedipal theory to a family—in effect, the first record of an "Oedipal family" reshaped by a belief in the Oedipal theory. Despite Max's theory-guided preventive efforts—or, I shall argue, partly because of them—Hans soon developed a horse phobia.

Based on his theory of the Oedipus complex, Freud claimed that the underlying source of Hans's anxieties was that he was "a little Oedipus who wanted to have his father 'out of the way', to get rid of him, so that he might be alone with his beautiful mother and sleep with her" (1909/1955, p. 111). Because his desires could not be satisfied, the suppressed sexual desire emerged in anxiety symptoms. Most commentaries on the Hans case attempt to better understand the cause of Hans's phobia, either by elaborating or amplifying Freud's Oedipal account or by putting forward an alternative theory of unconscious contents determining Hans's fear, of which there are many (Midgley, 2006; see later Chapter 10 for evaluations of four accounts of Hans's phobia). John Bowlby (1973) reinterpreted the case in terms of his attachment theory, arguing that rather than libidinal repression it was anxious attachment due to his mother's threats to leave that caused Hans to be disposed to develop an anxiety disorder. My analysis will be framed largely within Bowlby's attachment theory, which is now supported by extensive empirical evidence. However, after close examination of Bowlby's account of the Hans case in Chapter 3, I will reject the adequacy of Bowlby's specific reinterpretation of this case, opening the way for fresh exploration.

Rethinking the Case of Little Hans from a Power/Knowledge Perspective

I will offer yet another account of the likely etiology of Hans's phobia, but it is one that is quite different from those previously put forward not only in content but in its more fundamental approach. Rather than offering an alternative formulation of Hans's internal conflicts and unconscious desires and fears, I will focus on previously ignored, but evident, features of the case material that concern how Hans's father applied Oedipal theory to his family's life. I will thus approach the question of the etiology of Hans's phobia by first attempting to answer a different and, to my knowledge, previously unasked question: what impact did the application of the Oedipal theory have on Hans's family dynamics, and in particular how was it used in the exercise of the father's power within the family?

By "power" I have in mind here Foucault's very broad sense of power as any capacity for interpersonal action that intentionally influences the actions of others. In examining how the acceptance of a scientific theory of human psychology influences the power dynamics of human relationships, I am considering what Foucault termed "power/knowledge." Foucault argued that the acceptance of any theory of human nature leads us to view ourselves and others in a new way, and the theory thus becomes integrated into how people understand and react to each other. Consequently, there is an inevitable effect on the nature of human relationships that comes about as a result of believing the theory, regardless of whether the theory is true or false. The changed power dynamics that result from theory acceptance constitute the theory's form of power/knowledge. It will turn out that my analysis of Oedipal power/knowledge will lead to a surprising new insight, different from both Freud's and Bowlby's accounts, into what likely disposed Hans to develop an anxiety disorder.

Looking at the Hans case through the lens of attachment theory, what is salient about Freud's Oedipal-theoretic analysis is how he reinterprets attachment-related behaviors and desires in sexual/libidinal terms. Due to this theoretical sexualization of attachment, normal nonsexual attachment-related behaviors can be seen as dangerous and in need of control. (Precisely why this should be the reaction to sexually interpreted attachment behaviors is explored in Chapter 5.) Within the patriarchal family environment of the Hans case, the application of Oedipal theory with its sexualized interpretation of attachment needs yields a novel power dynamic within Hans's family in which Hans's father prohibits Hans from cuddling with his mother in bed in the morning, and this prohibition occurs just in the months after Hans is moved into his own bedroom and feels anxious when alone. This exercise of power by Hans's father is, I will argue in Chapter 4, a form of Oedipal power/knowledge that results from acceptance of the Oedipal theory along with some auxiliary theoretical assumptions that I excavate, all of which makes cuddling between mother and son, when sexually rather than attachment-theoretically interpreted, appear to be dangerous to Hans's health. Despite Hans's distress and his mother's protests, this persistent Oedipal-theory driven disruption by the father of their attachment bond continues, with the side benefit of allowing the father to share the bed with his wife undisturbed by Hans.

The explanation of Hans's disposition to develop a phobia when he sees a horse accident will be derived directly from my power/knowledge analysis. Max's disruption of the mother–child attachment bond denies Hans a safe haven from his anxieties and thus undermines the anxiety-regulating function of mother–son comforting and soothing. I will present textual evidence, previously unappreciated, that this disruption went on for several months prior to the onset of the phobia. The father's actions of blocking Hans's access to his mother when he was anxious almost certainly raised Hans's anxiety level and, empirical studies suggest, likely created a disposition to develop an anxiety disorder under stress, such as the stress of Hans seeing a horse accident. It may also have created some degree of separation anxiety and anxious attachment of the sort postulated by Bowlby. The analysis of Oedipal power/knowledge and how it was applied by Max yields an account of the primary cause of Hans's disposition to develop a phobia that, I believe, is better supported by textual evidence than any alternative view. Thus, I will argue that it is Max's belief in the Oedipal theory and his consequent application of the Oedipal theory to his family, and not the truth of the theory itself, that is at the root of Hans's anxiety—so that one might say it is not an Oedipus complex but rather the belief in the Oedipal theory that caused Hans's phobia.

Against the Mother Bashers: A New Perspective on Hans's Mother

Inspired by attachment theory and other object-relational theories of early development, in recent years, psychoanalytic theoreticians have tended to focus their attention away from Oedipal neurosogenesis and toward traumatic pre-Oedipal experiences that cause psychopathology. Regarding the Hans case, this turn to trauma has had a disturbing consequence that is somewhat at odds with my overall analysis of the case that focuses on the father's actions in separating Hans from his mother. Instead, the general logic of multiple analyses has been that Hans's fears were caused by early trauma, that this trauma must have come from his parents, and that, since historically mothers have primary responsibility for child raising, the likely agent of his trauma was his mother. This seems a dangerously misogynistic line of thinking unless well supported by clear evidence, as psychoanalysts learned after the "schizophrenogenic mother" debacle. We know Hans's mother suffered from a variety of psychological inhibitions and problems, and so this has made it easy to engage in rather wild unsupported yet extreme hypothesizing about the mother's level of psychopathology and how she inflicted her own troubles on Hans through physical and sexual abuse to a traumatic degree that brought about his anxiety disorder. In other words, one might say that within the Hans literature, the standard approach in recent work has been "mother bashing."

My analysis of the case as described above implies a very different perspective. Olga Graf was, along with Hans, the target of unwanted exercises of paternal power that disrupted her relationship with Hans, based on Max's belief in the Oedipal theory. Thus, in my view, Olga, like Hans, was a victim, not a perpetrator. In Chapters 6 and 7 I directly address this radical divergence of views about the role of Hans's mother in his troubles, and in doing so try to push back on the tide of misogyny I see in the way trauma theory is being applied to the Hans case. In Chapter 6, I offer a perspective on Olga, using aspects of the case history that have not been previously emphasized or brought together, that suggest that, in the context of the joint patriarchal power of Max and Freud, she heroically resisted the imposition of Oedipal power/knowledge to the degree that she could without open conflict. Then, in Chapter 7, I take on the most eminent Olga bashers one by one, challenging the strength of their evidence and the coherence of their arguments for Olga's etiological culpability.

Understanding the Social Influence of the Oedipal Theory

A further question, which I will ask and attempt to answer in Chapters 8 and 9—but only speculatively and provisionally, because the answer cannot be neatly anchored to textual evidence—concerns the role of the Oedipal theory in our culture at large. This question has two components: To what extent can the analysis of the Hans case illuminate the effects that the Oedipal theory has had more broadly on marital and family norms in our culture? And, as Foucault hypothesizes, does the impact of the theory fit with changing norms in the culture in a way that its effects on marriage and the family could be the very reason why the theory was so widely accepted and become so influential, despite a paucity of evidence?

In a companion volume to this one, *Freud's Argument for the Oedipus Complex*, I conclude that evidence for the Oedipal theory was lacking from the first. Consequently, given the lack of evidence, one must ask what made the Oedipal theory so appealing and influential. Foucault suggests that a theory's appeal is often that the theory's power/knowledge fits well with changing social values, so the appeal of the theory lies not in its evidence but in its power/knowledge. I will present a circumstantial argument, using both an analysis of background social changes in marriage presented in Chapter 8 and a case study of modern distinctively Western objections to parent-child cosleeping in Chapter 9, to show that the appeal of the Oedipal theory is likely linked to the way its power/knowledge articulates with society's changing marital and family ideals.

Freud's theoretical sexualization of attachment created a new form of power and regulation within the family. In making a natural act, the physical intimacy between mother and son, suspicious as a potentially overly stimulating sexual activity that might amplify incestuous desires in the child, the theory demanded a redistribution of family power in order to regulate mother–son affection. This new form of regulation made the theory appealing in the social environment of changing marital ideals. The acceptance of Oedipal theory thus had the social function of serving changing marital ideals, quite independently of whether the theory was true or false.

My analysis suggests that, far from being liberatory, Freud's Oedipal theory led to oppressive alterations in family power so as to limit the natural physical soothing that takes place in the parent–child relationship. This new Oedipal form of family power was reinforced by the medical profession in its warnings about the potential excesses of physical affection between mother and child and in its underscoring of the dangers of parent and child sharing a bed. This influence continues to resonate in our culture in advice still sometimes given to mothers by pediatricians and other experts about the dangers of children being allowed to sleep with the mother or cuddle extensively with her, contrary to the usual child-rearing practices in most other cultures and times. My analysis of the Hans case will show one form of harm that the Oedipal theory can inflict on a family by distancing children from parents, and my social analysis will suggest that it is that very effect, fitting with changing social marital ideals, that makes the theory so appealing to society at large.

In the course of this book, I occasionally refer to the medical anti-masturbation campaign—or "masturbation crusade"—that took place in the 18th and 19th centuries in Europe and America, up until about the time that Freud proposed the Oedipal theory. During the crusade, childhood masturbation was thought to be strongly pathogenic, justifying extreme surveillance and regulative medical interventions in order to prevent the child from masturbating. This "crusade" period is much discussed and analyzed by Foucault (1978, 2003) and other historians and is the historical contextual backdrop to Freud's Oedipal theorizing. So, I sometimes note differences in power/knowledge structures between the Oedipal theory and the masturbation crusade. In the context of analyzing the masturbation crusade, Foucault raises the question of what explains the wide influence and acceptance of the Oedipal theory at the particular historical point that it was proposed, a question I address in this book in a quite different way. Unfortunately, a consideration of Foucault's analysis could not be included here and will be presented in a separate work (see *Foucault Versus Freud*, Wakefield, forthcoming).

My central thesis is that Freud's hypothesis of the Oedipus complex played a distinctive role in redistributing family power by making a natural, biologically designed act, a mother's physical comforting of her son, suspicious as a potentially overly stimulating activity that might trigger incestuous sexual desires in the child. This yields a power dynamic in which the mother–son affectionate interaction is considered potentially dangerous and restricted in favor of a protected marital bed. Based on an examination of changes in the nature of marriage and cultural norms about whether parents should sleep in the same bed with their children, I suggest that the insights gained through the study of the Hans case can plausibly, albeit cautiously and speculatively, be generalized to our culture at large.

There is an important caveat regarding my use of a neo-Foucauldian perspective. Foucault is known for (supposedly) arguing that even rational argument and scientific theories of human nature are ultimately all about power rather than evidence. I am not at all a Foucauldian in this absurd sense that would deny the search for truth through the accumulation of evidence and the power of explanation. Rather, I adhere to a "modest Foucauldianism" that rejects any universalist claims about power as generally exerting dominant force in theory acceptance and accepts the role of rationality in the quest for evidentially supported truth, but which nonetheless embraces a critical-minded perspective on theory acceptance that acknowledges that especially within the social and psychological sciences, power considerations sometimes augment or dominate over rational considerations in theory acceptance. Consistent with this modest Foucauldianism, I borrow Foucault's power/knowledge perspective here not because of a doctrinaire belief that it must apply but rather because I think, upon reflection and evidential analysis, that in the particular instance of Freud's Oedipal theory Foucault's framework applies in a compelling and illuminating way. This seems especially likely given my conclusions in *Freud's Argument for the Oedipus Complex* (Wakefield, 2022) that the theory lacked cogent evidence from the beginning. If Oedipal theory is a prime instance of power/knowledge, the Hans case is the original laboratory in which the experiment of applying the Oedipal theory to a family was undertaken, and thus a uniquely revealing place to look for the manifestations of the theory's power/knowledge.

What is the Oedipus Complex?

Freud believed that the Oedipal theory was his central and most distinctive scientific contribution. He reaffirmed the theory throughout his work, from the earliest statements in *The Interpretation of Dreams* ("Being in love with the one parent and hating the other are among the essential constituents … determining the symptoms of the later neurosis" [Freud, 1900/1953a, p. 261]) to his last works published posthumously ("I venture to say that if psycho-analysis could boast of no other achievement than the discovery of the repressed Oedipus complex, that alone would give it a claim to be included among the precious new acquisitions of mankind" [Freud, 1940/1964, pp. 192–193]). Indeed, he insisted that acceptance of the Oedipal theory "has become the shibboleth that distinguishes the adherents of psycho-analysis from its opponents" (Freud, 1905/1953b, p. 226, n.1 [footnote added 1920]).

The Oedipal theory hypothesized a universal developmental stage of male psychosexual development at about the ages of three to six years old in which a son experiences intense sexual desire for his mother. This inchoate but specifically sexual desire—potentially involving bodily premonitions of copulatory movement—is accompanied by angry jealousy of the boy's father for possessing his mother and a resultant desire to get rid of or kill the father. The boy's sexual and aggressive fantasies cause a fear of vengeful retribution by the boy's father in the form of castration, thus removing the organ that is the origin of the pleasurable feelings that create the desire. However, the son also loves and needs the father, so he is conflicted about his jealous and murderous desires.

Note that unlike commentators who attempt to soften the Oedipal theory's blunt Oedipal formulations regarding incestuous sexuality and murderous rage by interpreting Freud's talk of sex and aggression as elliptical for broader sensual feelings or feelings related to cultural gender norms and so on, I take Freud's assertions as he clearly intended them, as statements about a child's literal sexual and murderous feelings. Of course, Freud's Oedipal theory builds on many partial truths; some normal-range sexual and aggressive feelings towards parents occur during childhood, some pathologies look like Freud's description of the Oedipus complex gone astray, and rank sexualization of parent–child relationships does occur. Moreover, there are routine developmental challenges that children must undergo that broadly fit Freud's described Oedipal stage, such as separating from one's mother, feeling safe in outdoing one's father, grappling with jealousy at others' intimacies, and negotiating the trinary relationship with one's father and mother. But, none of this is equivalent to what Freud suggested: a universal developmental phase of intense sexual and aggressive fantasies towards parents at a young age that is developmentally pivotal and the source of all psychoneuroses, with Freud maintaining that the Oedipus complex is "the nucleus of every case of neurosis" (Freud, 1924/1961b, p. 198).

According to Freud, the resolution of the Oedipus complex propels the boy's psychological development forward. Repression of Oedipal incestuous desires due to castration anxiety causes displacement of a son's sexual interest from his mother to sexual object choices outside his family, and in order to avoid the father's revenge the son identifies with his father's disapproval of his desires, yielding an internalized conscience or superego. As Eagle (2018) observes, "how the individual resolves oedipal conflicts plays a determinative role in psychological development, including sexual identity, superego formation, and the capacity to integrate love and desire" (pp. 95–96).

Note that for ease of exposition, I consider the Oedipus complex here only as it applies to the sexual desire of a son for his mother, the dyad relevant to the Little Hans case. This was the initial form of the theory, only later expanded to daughters: "The information about infantile sexuality was obtained from the study of men and the theory deduced from it was concerned with male children" (Freud, 1925/1959, p. 36, n. 1 [footnote added 1935]). Regarding that later extension, even Freud acknowledged that the theory's extension to girls, which required a convoluted ad hoc theoretical rationale based on the dubious notion of penis envy, was problematic from the start: "It was natural enough to expect to find a complete parallel between the two sexes; but this turned out not to hold. Further investigations and reflections revealed profound differences between the sexual development of men and women" (Freud, 1925/1959, p. 36, footnote added 1935). Freud struggled with the coherence of his theory of female psychosexual development to the point that even as late as 1924 he could write:

The process which has been described refers, as has been expressly said, to male children only. How does the corresponding development take place in little girls? At this point our material—for some incomprehensible reason—becomes far more obscure and full of gaps.

(Freud, 1924/1961a, p. 177)

As well, I consider only the "positive" Oedipus complex that applies to the relationship of a child to the opposite-sex parent, and not the homo-erotic feelings between a child and the same-sex parent that Freud mentions peripherally in his Hans commentary but explored more seriously later on.

Freud considered the castration anxiety component of the Oedipus complex particularly important for neurosogenesis, stating that castration anxiety "may probably be regarded as the central experience of the years of childhood, the greatest problem of early life and the strongest source of later inadequacy" (Freud, 1940/1964, p. 191). However, the logic of the Oedipus complex is such that the hypothesis of incestuous sexual desire by the child for the parent is the central thesis that leads to all the other features:

> in the Freudian account of the Oedipus complex, incestuous wishes are primary and hostile wishes are secondary. For, according to this view, in the mind of the Oedipal child, the source of hostile wishes toward the same sex parent is that that parent, as a rival, stands in the way of gratifying incestuous wishes.
>
> (Eagle, 2018, pp. 96–97)

So, the son's hypothesized spontaneous, normal, and universal incestuous sexual desire for his mother—the hypothesis purportedly tested and confirmed in Freud's case of Little Hans—was at the core of the theory and remained the necessary trigger of all the rest of the complex's features. It is this central thesis of incestuous desire on which I focus and that, I shall argue, has the most direct impact on Oedipal power/knowledge.

Dethroning Oedipal Theory

The Oedipal theory remained at the heart of Freud's clinical theory for much of a century, guiding mainstream psychoanalytic interpretations of patients' symptoms and associations. It thus reshaped patients' views of themselves, their histories, and their relationships to their family members. Moreover, the Oedipal theory captured the minds of a wider audience of intellectuals and laypersons alike, exerting a strong influence on the arts, literature, the humanities, and the popular culture of the educated lay public (e.g., Kakutani 2008; Dowd 2012). More than any other specific hypothesis, the Oedipus complex constituted the core of the "whole climate of opinion" (Auden, 1940, p. 33) that Freud became for our culture.

Despite continued fealty to Freud's signature hypothesis by some traditionalists within the psychoanalytic community, psychoanalysis is now gradually moving past the dominance of the Oedipal theory, with many questioning its developmental centrality or even abandoning entirely the hypothesis that it is a universal developmental stage (Eagle, 2018; Hartke, 2016; Kohut, 1977; Kupfersmid, 1995; Morehead, 1999; Simon, 1991). However, as psychoanalysis teaches us, it is not so easy to escape the past. The overwhelming acceptance and influence of the Oedipal theory for so long makes it difficult to dissociate psychoanalysis and its fate from the Oedipal theory. Yet, it is arguable that in order to move forward in the contemporary psychotherapeutic context, psychoanalysis must decisively part company with its Oedipal heritage.

The dethroning of Oedipal theory is not just a matter of extending the understanding of pathogenesis to vicissitudes in the pre-Oedipal mother–child dyad, as in Bowlby's (1982) attachment theory or other object relations theories. Rather, the dethroning is also about abandoning the idea that the Oedipal theory describes a universal psychosexual stage at all, and understanding why the evidence demands such a conclusion. Psychoanalysis's thorough evidence-based abandonment of the Oedipal theory's hegemonic interpretive straight jacket would allow for a greater idiographic openness to variations in patients' narratives. My arguments in this book and the companion volume, *Freud's Argument for the Oedipus Complex*, support a thorough housecleaning that refocuses psychoanalysis on idiographic unconscious meaning and liberates psychoanalysis from Freud's anachronistic Victorian-inspired sexual theory. This challenge to the Oedipal theory is pursued without questioning the broader psychoanalytic enterprise of exploring unconscious meaning, which I believe is wholly legitimate and scientifically anchored when divorced from Oedipal dogmas.

The Oedipal theory's great success and influence over so long a time raises a profound puzzle for those who accept the conclusion of my argument in *Freud's Argument for the Oedipus Complex* that the Hans case offers no serious evidential support for the Oedipal theory. The first step in a search for redemption from an error of this magnitude must be to ask the following sorts of questions with an open mind: Why was the Oedipal theory taken so seriously? What effects did the widespread acceptance of Freud's Oedipal theory have on our family relationships and on our cultural values? And, how do we extirpate the effects of the power the theory had over us for so many years?

As I have explained, a power/knowledge analysis attempts to understand a theory's appeal in terms of its social *effects* rather than its evidential support. This is a particularly important perspective if the evidence for the Oedipal theory is indeed weak. However, it is worth noting that one does not have to agree with me in rejecting the Oedipal theory to find the exploration of the theory's effects of interest. The Oedipal theory as a social phenomenon certainly had an impact on family dynamics, just as any analysis of an individual patient has an impact on that patient's family dynamics. Consequently, the analysis of the power/knowledge implications and effects of the Oedipal theory can be fruitfully considered even if one believes in the Oedipal theory and rejects the claim that the Oedipus complex was accepted *because* it had those effects.

An important caveat is that, although attachment theory is an empirically supported theory that forms a foundation for my analysis, it must be acknowledged that issues of power/knowledge can be and have been raised about various aspects of that theory as well. Power/knowledge aspects of a theory can exist for any theory, whether the theory is true or false. Foucault himself notes that his analyses of psychiatry's power/ knowledge do not imply that psychiatric theories themselves are untrue. With regard to attachment theory, there are several examples of issues of power/knowledge that have been raised at one time or another. First, there is a general inclination by theorists to accept secure attachment as a natural norm that is the way attachment is biologically designed to be and to see other attachment patterns as deviant adaptations that are risk factors for disorder or even forms of abnormality or pathology in themselves. However, this perspective has been called into question on the grounds of cultural differences in patterns of parent–child relationships and differing frequencies of attachment styles. It has thus been argued that attachment theory has been used to support the values and preferred family structures that our culture's theorists find most desirable. This leads to a second issue, namely, that the theorized preference for secure attachment is then applied, sometimes with minimal evidence, to social issues, such as concerns about whether mothers with young children should work or how much and what kind of early contact between parent and child is necessary for proper attachment bonding. As in Freud's Oedipal theory, there is a strong inclination to give primacy to a child's relationship to the mother, when in fact developmentally appropriate attachment relations may be quite flexible. Indeed, our culture's focus on the normality of one primary attachment figure, generally the mother, can be questioned based on cross-cultural data suggesting a hierarchy of multiple attachment figures available to a child in some other cultures. All of these issues remain controversial.

However, in this book, I stay neutral and steer clear of these complex issues which continue to be studied and argued intensively. I rely instead on certain core principles and agreed scientific findings of attachment theory that have a strong empirical base, such as the effects on a child's anxiety of disrupting a primary attachment relationship. These findings are scientifically well-supported whatever their power/knowledge social reverberations.

Three more minor textual caveats are worth noting. First, many of the writers I quote, including Freud, use italics liberally for emphasis. Rather than stating each time whether italics are in the original text or added by me for emphasis, I adopt the convention that any italics appearing in quoted passages are in the original, unless otherwise stated. Second, when quoted writers cite others within the quoted passage, I often eliminate the reference citations from within quoted passages without the addition of ellipses. Finally, I use the French version of the adjectival version of "Foucault," "Foucauldian" (with the pronounced "d" but silent "l" [fŭ-ˈkō-dē-ən]), because it has become the standard usage in English scholarly literature, rather than using the less common but admittedly more intuitive "Foucaultian" (where, as in "Foucault," the final "t" is silent [fŭ-ˈkō-ē-ən]).

References

Auden, W. H. (1940). In memory of Sigmund Freud. *The Kenyon Review, 2(1)*, 30–34.

Bowlby, J. (1973). *Attachment and loss (Vol. 2): Separation: Anxiety and anger.* New York, NY: Basic Books.

Bowlby, J. (1982). *Attachment and loss (Vol. 1): Attachment* (Rev. ed.). New York, NY: Basic Books.

Dowd, M. (2012, January 3). Oedipus Rex complex. *New York Times.* Retrieved from https://www.nytimes.com/2012/01/04/opinion/dowd-oedipus-rex-complex.html.

Eagle, M. N. (2018). *Core concepts in classical psychoanalysis: Clinical, research evidence and conceptual critiques.* New York, NY: Routledge.

Foucault, M. (1978). *History of sexuality (Vol. 1): An introduction* (R. Hurley, Trans.). New York, NY: Pantheon.

Foucault, M. (2003). *Abnormal: Lectures at the College de France 1974–1975.* (G. Burchell, Trans.), V. Marchetti & A. Salomini, Eds. New York, NY: Picador.

Freud, S. (1953a). The interpretation of dreams (first part). In J. Strachey (Ed. & Trans.), *The standard edition of the complete psychological works of Sigmund Freud* (Vol. 4, pp. ix–627). London, UK: Hogarth Press. (Original work published 1900).

Freud, S. (1953b). Three essays on the theory of sexuality. In J. Strachey (Ed.& Trans.), *The standard edition of the complete psychological works of Sigmund Freud* (Vol. 7, pp. 123–246). London, UK: Hogarth Press. (Original work published 1905).

Freud, S. (1955). Analysis of a phobia in a five-year-old boy. In J. Strachey (Ed. & Trans.), *The standard edition of the complete psychological works of Sigmund Freud* (Vol. 10, pp. 1–150). London, UK: Hogarth Press. (Original work published 1909).

Freud, S. (1959). An autobiographical study. In J. Strachey (Ed. & Trans.), *The standard edition of the complete psychological works of Sigmund Freud (Vol. 20 , pp. 1–74). London, UK: Hogarth Press. (Original work published 1925.)

Freud, S. (1961a). The dissolution of the Oedipus complex. In J. Strachey (Ed. & Trans.), *The standard edition of the complete psychological works of Sigmund Freud* (Vol. 19, pp. 171–180). London, UK: Hogarth Press. (Original work published 1924).

Freud, S. (1961b). A short account of psycho-analysis. In J. Strachey (Ed. & Trans.), *The standard edition of the complete psychological works of Sigmund Freud (Vol. 19 , pp. 189–209). London, UK: Hogarth Press. (Original work published 1924).

Freud, S. (1963). Introductory lectures on psycho-analysis, part 3. In J. Strachey (Ed. & Trans.), *The standard edition of the complete psychological works of Sigmund Freud* (Vol. 16). London, UK: Hogarth Press. (Original work published 1917).

Freud, S. (1964). An outline of psycho-analysis. In J. Strachey (Ed. & Trans.), *The standard edition of the complete psychological works of Sigmund Freud* (Vol. 23, pp. 141–208). London, UK: Hogarth Press. (Original work published 1940).

Hartke, R. (2016). The Oedipus complex: A confrontation at the central crossroads of psychoanalysis. *International Journal of Psychoanalysis, 97*(3), 893–913.

Kakutani, M. (2008, February 1). Who's your daddy? *The New York Times.* Retrieved from https://www.nytimes.com/2008/02/01/books/01book.html.

Kohut, H. (1977). *The restoration of the self.* New York, NY: International University Press.

Kupfersmid, J. (1995). Does the Oedipus complex exist? *Psychotherapy: Theory, Research, Practice, Training, 32*(4), 535–547.

Midgley, N. (2006). Re-reading "Little Hans": Freud's case study and the question of competing paradigms in psychoanalysis. *Journal of the American Psychoanalytic Association, 54*(2), 537–559.

Morehead, D. (1999). Oedipus, Darwin, and Freud: One big, happy family? *Psychoanalytic Quarterly, 68*(3), 347–375.

Simon, B. (1991). Is the Oedipus complex still the cornerstone of psychoanalysis? Three obstacles to answering the question. *Journal of the American Psychoanalytic Association, 39*, 641–668.

Wakefield, J. C. (2007). Max Graf's "Reminiscences of Professor Sigmund Freud" revisited. *Psychoanalytic Quarterly, 76,* 149–192.

Wakefield, J. C. (2018). *Freud and philosophy of mind (Vol. 1): Reconstructing the argument for unconscious mental states.* New York, NY: Palgrave Macmillan.

Wakefield, J. C. (2022). *Freud's argument for the Oedipus complex: A philosophy of science analysis of the case of Little Hans.* New York, NY: Routledge.

Wakefield, J. C. (forthcoming). *Foucault vs. Freud: Oedipal theory and the deployment of sexuality.* New York: Routledge.

Chapter 2

The Graf Family's Dynamics as Background to the Little Hans Case

In this chapter I provide selected background on Hans's parents, Olga Honig Graf and Max Graf, reviewing relevant aspects of the nature of their marriage and their relationships with Freud. This material will form the context for understanding the Hans case as my analysis unfolds in the coming chapters. It will also provide some additional evidence, beyond what is contained in the Hans case history, for the next chapter's evaluation of Bowlby's (1973) theory that it was anxious attachment, not Oedipal desire, that caused Hans to develop an anxiety condition.

The material presented below is largely drawn from interviews by Dr. Kurt Eissler with family members that were recorded and then transcribed. These interviews had long been held by the Sigmund Freud Collection in the Library of Congress (the "Freud Archives") but were restricted in access and unavailable to the public. The interviews were finally derestricted and made publicly available in 2005 thanks to Dr. Harold Blum, the Director of the Freud Archives. The interviews are with Max Graf, Little Hans's father (Graf, 1952); Herbert Graf, Little Hans himself (Graf, 1959); and Lise Graf, Herbert's wife at the time (Graf, 1960) who as daughter-in-law was familiar with Herbert's/Hans's mother, Olga Honig. Olga herself declined to be interviewed, for reasons explained below. The interviews are primarily in German and in translating the passages quoted below I have relied on existing translations in the literature and at the Freud Archives as well as help received from colleagues. Note that, in the absence of reasons to the contrary, I generally take the interview reports as accurate. However, given the Grafs' subsequent divorce and other tensions within the family, as well as the many years that passed between the events of the case history and the interviews, it must be kept in mind that the reports could be biased or inaccurate.

DOI: 10.4324/9780203817124-2

Olga Honig's Personality and Parenting

Olga Honig (often spelled "Hoenig" to capture the umlaut over the "o") was born in Vienna in 1877, married Max Graf in 1898, gave birth to her son Herbert in 1903 and her daughter Hanna in 1906, eventually divorced Max and remarried, and died in 1961. In understanding the Hans case and assessing Bowlby's attachment-theoretic account, a relevant issue is the nature of the mother's personality and her responses to Hans. Freud, in his commentary in the case history, is rather positive, saying that she was an "excellent and devoted" (Freud, 1909/1955, pp. 27–28) mother who cannot be blamed for Hans's phobia. In later comments to the Vienna Psychoanalytic Society (Nunberg & Federn, 1967, p. 235), Freud asserted that, other than the mother's taking Hans into the W.C. with her when he protested being left alone, the parents made no errors that can be held responsible for Hans's neurotic condition, which must be laid to Hans's sexual constitution. In the case study, both Hans's father and Freud portray Olga as having a tender, affectionate relationship with Hans. (Indeed, the father thinks it is *too* affectionate, a point we will return to in a later chapter.)

The most problematic feature of Olga's personality—and one on which all three of the Archives interviewees agree—is that Hans's mother was a highly anxious, emotional, and neurotic individual. Max says, "She is without a doubt a hysterical woman" (Graf, 1952). Herbert says, "she is a very nervous person and always was a very nervous person" (Graf, 1959). Herbert's wife, Lise, affirms, "Herbert's mother's nerves are not so good and never were" (Graf, 1960). As part of her "nervous" temperament, she seems to have been possessed of an emotional intensity that she did not hesitate to display. For example, Herbert, when describing his father's aversion to funerals and characterizing his avoidance of emotion as "wise," contrasts his father's emotional restraint with his mother's (and his own) lack of restraint: "I am not that wise because I am also my mother's son. She is not as controlled as my father was" (Graf, 1959).

Olga suffered from what appears to be a generalized social phobia or avoidant personality disorder. Max describes his wife as "a woman who, for example, did not want to socialize, or was uncertain in social situations, was restless, and didn't feel well and therefore avoided going into social situations" (Graf, 1952). He makes it clear that his wife's primary anxiety problem was neither a specific phobia like

Hans's nor agoraphobia, but more resembles a generalized social phobia or avoidant personality:

> GRAF: "She had shyness [*Hemmungen*] around people, so she didn't want to go out."
> EISSLER: "Was she also afraid [*Angst*] to go out?"
> GRAF: "No, not in that sense. At least not as something that would be really striking. No, she was just generally of an unsocial nature."
> EISSLER: "Yes. But nevertheless there was a certain similarity to the symptoms of the child?"
> GRAF: "Yes, but not from fear."
>
> (Graf, 1952)

Olga's reluctance about socializing was accompanied by difficulty getting along with people, including her in-laws. In discussing Max's regular visits to his mother on Sundays with Hans but without Olga, Max explains:

> EISSLER: "Did your wife go along, or were you alone."
> GRAF: "Usually not."
> EISSLER: "Was there a tension between your wife and ... "
> GRAF: "And my mother, Yes .... There was a tension between my wife and everybody."
>
> (Graf, 1952)

In addition to her social anxieties, we know that Olga was once described by Freud as having obsessional ideas. This occurred when she was quite a bit younger, however, over a decade before the events of the Hans case, and it is not mentioned in the interviews.

Max's Archives interview, consistently with the case history, suggests that although Olga may have been distant from Hans at times, she did not grossly neglect Hans in a way that would be likely to cause anxious attachment. Max portrays his wife as a mother who "had a good attitude toward" Hans, in contrast to her reserved attitude toward her second child, Hanna, towards whom Olga reacted negatively even at her birth, according to Max. Max suggests that Olga was self-involved and "hysterical," by which he seems to have meant highly emotional and perhaps sexually evasive. However, it should be kept in mind that Max appears to have been emotionally quite controlled in contrast. One has here a possible variant of the classic obsessive-hysterical marriage in which the opposing traits that were an attraction to the opposite partner at the outset become an irritant and a matter of blame in the long run (Barnett, 1971).

Max reports that his ex-wife did not spend as much time with Hans as Max would have thought desirable, though not at a level that one would consider neglect:

> EISSLER: "Did your wife spend much time with him?"
> GRAF: "No, she did not, she was an hysteric, and she was focused completely on herself."
> EISSLER: "She neglected him?"
> GRAF: "You really can't say 'neglected.' But did she really pay attention to him the way a mother pays attention to a child? I don't really want to say that."
>
> (Graf, 1952)

Although both Harold Blum (2007) and John Munder Ross (2007) have suggested that Olga suffered from postpartum depression after having her second child, Hanna, Max explicitly denies that Olga had postpartum depression and casts about for another explanation for her negative reaction to the birth of Hanna:

> GRAF: "She had a good attitude toward the child, but to the girl she did not .... When they brought the girl to her, she waved off and rejected the child."
> EISSLER: "Depression?"
> GRAF: "No, no she never lived well with the child. I think it was jealousy because it was a girl. She probably wanted to have a boy."
>
> (Graf, 1952)

Given the mother's favoritism for Hans and the fact that Hanna, who is said to be the brighter child, was later deprived of the educational opportunities made available to Hans (not only university, but even Gymnasium) just as Olga herself did not pursue her talents, it is perhaps not surprising that, according to Max, Hanna later "had a certain feeling of being neglected" relative to Herbert. The explanation Max offers for Olga's seeming rejection of Hanna—that Olga wanted a boy—appears to be either a disingenuous evasion or a memory lapse on Max's part, as we shall see below. But, the problem does not seem to have been postpartum depression but rather a general antipathy towards being pushed into having a second child which she did not want.

Olga's Difficult Family Background

That Olga has some emotional issues would not be surprising given her history, troubling aspects of which have emerged from the interviews and after some additional historical detective work. We know from a remark in the Hans case history that Hans's mother had been a patient of Freud's for some unspecified problem ("His beautiful mother fell ill with a neurosis as a result of a conflict during her girlhood. I was able to be of assistance to her at the time, and this had in fact been the beginning of my connection with Hans's parents" [1909/1955, pp. 141–142]), but little else about her is revealed. Max's interview adds some crucial information that allows us to infer, first, that Olga is the one who, while in treatment with Freud, introduced her suitor, Max, to Freud (Wakefield, 2007).

Secondly and more importantly, Max Graf's Archives interview reveals a staggering history of familial suicidality and death within Olga Honig's family of origin. Olga, born in 1877, attended a music conservatory as a girl. Her father, Ignaz Hönig, died when she was less than a year old, and when she was a girl her two older brothers died by suicide, each shooting himself to death, Arthur (born 1867) in 1887, and Oskar (born 1874) in 1891. We are told in the interview that one of them, presumably Arthur, was in the military and suicided after receiving a medal for saving someone's life. As well, one of her younger sisters suffered from infantile paralysis, and another attempted suicide.

Yet, it must also be said that her family showed remarkable resilience and artistic talent. One of her older sisters was a concert pianist, another an actress in Berlin, and Olga was an accomplished violinist, described as brilliant as well as beautiful. Olga's background will be discussed further in a later chapter, but I note that when she was a patient, Freud describes Olga's symptoms as pure obsessional ideas, so we can perhaps attribute to her an obsessive nature or obsessive personality disorder a decade later in addition to her social anxiety issues.

With regard to possible attachment-related implications of these discoveries about Olga's history, Bowlby (1973) postulated that knowledge of the suicide or death of others can be an independent risk factor or exacerbate the effect of parental threats on anxious attachment. In light of Olga's family history, one might speculate that the multiple tragedies that she had experienced might have come to Hans's attention in overhearing family discussions. However, this is sheer speculation and remains unknown.

One imagines that Olga's history of losing two older siblings under shocking and unexpected circumstances might have caused Olga to be anxious about her attachments, and we know from the interviews that she was ambivalent about having children. Nonetheless, the case record indicates that, even if we postulate that she was not perfectly attuned and sometimes absorbed in her own anxieties, Olga was yet neither rejecting nor hostile to Hans and displayed genuine caring and affection to him, as well as an immediate good-enough responsiveness to his anxieties and attachment needs.

The Grafs' Marital Conflicts Over Sex, Work, and Socializing

Although the case history contains no explicit report of marital disharmony, the Archives interviews with the family reveal a range of issues that divided Olga and Max. They portray a contentious marriage with intense marital disputes on a range of topics from work and socializing and sex to having children and even psychoanalytic theory.

Victorian marriage ideology emphasized patriarchy and the wife's role in creating a soothing home environment as a safe haven from the male's struggles in the world outside. At the beginning of the twentieth century, marital relationships were undergoing a period of fundamental change from this tradition towards somewhat greater symmetry in marital roles and a greater emphasis on mutual sexual and emotional satisfaction, leading to the possibility of conflict and stress in new forms and intensities. The Grafs were no exception, and their personalities were such as to amplify the marital conflicts emerging at the time. The marital conflicts between the Grafs provide a useful context for understanding the motives of the partners as they apply Oedipal theory to the intimate life of their family.

Marital conflict has often been speculated to be a factor in causing Hans's anxiety but it has not generally been a salient part of interpretations of the case simply because there is little direct evidence within the case report for such conflict. Commentators, including Bowlby (see

Chapter 3), have suggested the existence of marital disputes that influenced Hans from the mention in the report that the parents eventually divorced, assuming without evidence that the divorce was imminent at the time of the case study and thus that pre-divorce conflicts would have been present. For example, Paul Verhaeghe (2009) states that "the father does not possess the mother 'in all tranquility'; on the contrary, their divorce is on the way (see Freud's appendix on the case)" (p. 10) and Herbert Strean (1967) asserts that "When Hans, the family member with the presenting problem, improved, the parents' marriage soon after was dissolved" (p. 3).

Yet, there is no evidence in the case report to support the inference that the divorce is imminent. Freud's appendix, added to the case many years later after Hans visited Freud when he was nineteen years old, about thirteen years after the case history was published, says only that the parents divorced and offers no date for the divorce. Consequently, little could be confidently inferred about the marriage at the time of Hans's phobia, until recently.

The timing of the divorce was finally revealed in the Freud Archives interviews with Max and Herbert Graf. Max reports that the divorce occurred about eighteen-and-a-half years into the marriage, and Herbert reports that his parents separated when he was about sixteen to seventeen years old, thus about twelve or thirteen years after the occurrence of the horse phobia. The marital separation thus occurred just before Herbert's visit to Freud. This was no coincidence. The interviews reveal that it was during Hans's packing of his father's library for the father's move to a new apartment subsequent to the divorce (and perhaps in forming a new marriage: "His parents had been divorced and each of them had married again" [Freud, 1909/1955, p. 148]), that Hans came across the father's copy of the published case history, read it, recognized some of the names Freud had not changed, and realized it was about him. This led him soon thereafter to visit Freud. So, the inferences in the literature about the quality of the Grafs' marriage that were based on their supposedly imminently divorcing after the case were based on a false premise; given its timing, the divorce in itself offers no reason to postulate intense family strife at the time of the case, over a dozen years earlier.

However, one can be right for the wrong reasons. Inferences and speculation regarding the state of the Grafs' marriage closer to the time of the case history are no longer needed because the Freud Archives interviews provide a direct window into the marriage in its earlier years—albeit as recalled by one ex-spouse decades later. They reveal a striking picture of spousal conflict over a variety of issues, starting from the beginning of the marriage.

From the interviews, we learn that Max Graf, twenty-seven years old when he married, although smitten with the beauty and brains of his twenty-three-year-old bride, Olga Honig, already had serious concerns about his wife's emotional suitability prior to the marriage:

> My first wife is a very interesting, very intelligent, and very beautiful woman. She is without a doubt a hysterical woman, something I was not able as a young man to judge. Even in those moments when she was hysterical, she was attractive and interesting. Before I made the decision to marry this woman, I went to Professor Freud, [who] .... said to me, "Marry her, and you'll have your fun." Well, I didn't really have fun, but it was possible that I was too young. It was possible that if I had been older, that I really would have laughed.
>
> (Graf, 1952)

Max describes Olga as "very interesting, very intelligent, and very beautiful," yet observes that his wife is "without a doubt a hysterical woman," by which he presumably refers to her emotional volatility and anxious intensity combined with sexual ambivalence. We have seen that Max's wife-to-be, Olga, was in treatment for neurotic symptoms with Freud at the time that Max and Olga were courting and that Olga was the one to introduce Max to Freud. Max thus sought Freud's approval of the marriage given his knowledge of Olga's emotional issues. Despite this precaution and Freud's reassurance, Max's concerns unfortunately turned out to be amply warranted. With regard to Freud's dubious advice, "Marry her, and you'll have your fun," Max can only lament, "Well, I didn't really have fun."

It is clear that Max's disappointment with his wife is in part tied to the way that Olga's social anxieties, described above, thwarted his social and professional ambitions to be part of Viennese high society and attend social and musical events linked to his work as an increasingly recognized and prominent music critic. Olga apparently would not accompany him to such events. Explaining why his marriage was problematic, Max says:

> On the one hand, I was at the beginning of a career, I wanted to advance, I had the ambitions of a talented person, I had already published two

books. On the other side was a woman who, for example, did not want to socialize, or was uncertain in social situations, was restless, and didn't feel well and therefore avoided going into social situations.

So you have a beautiful young woman, with whom one is shut up into an apartment. That was one of the reasons. Another reason was that the woman suddenly became jealous of my writings and that she tore them up.

(Graf, 1952)

Max reports that during the first year of marriage—long before Hans was on the scene—Olga "suddenly became jealous of my writings and that she tore them up" (Graf, 1952). No doubt the needs of an ambitious writer can easily lead a spouse to feel abandoned and can cause conflict in a family. In the first year of the marriage in 1898, when this argument took place, Max had managed to publish two books while constantly writing music reviews as well (he later recalls that "After a short time I was sitting as a music critic in the office of one of the greatest newspapers of Vienna and writing my reviews day by day" [Graf, 1946, p. 24]). On top of this, he was pursuing his social and professional obligations in the evening. Olga's frustrations, although due partly to her own inhibitions, are understandable.

On her part, Olga may have become frustrated watching the intense work habits of her ambitious writer-husband while her own talents languished. She came from an accomplished family in which, as noted, one of her older sisters was a concert pianist and another was an actress in Berlin. Watching her husband work all day and attend events without her at night in search of his further success might well have rankled her. If Olga did tear up some of Max's papers in the course of a heated argument, this occurred at an early point in the marriage well before Herbert's birth. We do not know whether the conflicts over work continued; there is no mention of intense fights later on in the marriage, either in the case study or in the interviews. However, we do know that having a child was an apparent attempt to save the marriage from these conflicts, as we shall shortly see.

The couple also had sexual problems that were an additional source of marital conflict and dissatisfaction on Max's part. At one point in the interview with Eissler, Max hints of sexual problems but modestly backs away from the topic: "There were other things about which I don't wish to speak any further which did not fit well into a young marriage in which one would have some erotic pleasure." Later, he returns to the topic and explains: "The circumstances of the depression, to the extent that she had them, were always after sex .... I only know that after each night of lovemaking [*Liebesnacht*], that early in the morning she would have some outburst or other" (Graf, 1952). This sounds more like distress or anger than depression. In this area it is Max who clearly felt abandoned and frustrated and longed for greater physical intimacy with a wife that he repeatedly described as beautiful. His wife's ambivalence about sex may be one of the main reasons Max described her as "hysterical," given that her sexual allure followed by coldness would be perceived as a classic hysterical pattern.

In fairness, it should be kept in mind that Max's wife wanted to avoid having further children. At the time, the available birth control methods were of limited effectiveness, and pregnancy and childbirth in themselves were still quite dangerous to the woman. (See Chapter 6.)

Olga and Max's Marital Conflicts over Children and Psychoanalysis

At the time of these early marital conflicts over work, socializing, and sex, Max seriously considered ending the marriage. He again sought Freud's advice:

> In short, after a year, I went to Professor Freud. And I said to him, "Herr Professor, this marriage isn't working." He was very surprised, and I made another effort. I thought, maybe children will change the circumstances. But that didn't happen, and nevertheless I lasted eighteen and a half years in this marriage until the children were so big that I could easily leave the marriage without disturbing their development. Only later did I have doubts if it wouldn't have been better if I'd left sooner. I don't know what would have been the right thing.
>
> (Graf, 1952)

Freud apparently did not support ending the marriage, and the passage suggests Freud's acquiescence in Max's plan to have children to fix the situation. Whether Olga was consulted is not stated. However, the idea that in a patriarchal spirit Max took Freud's advice on important and sensitive matters of family life such as this seemingly without consulting his wife is suggested as well by an account in the interview of Max's consultation with Freud on whether Herbert should be raised to be Jewish in the virulently anti-Semitic atmosphere of Vienna:

> When my son was born, I had to decide whether to let him grow up as a Jew, or I wondered if to make life easy for him, I should have him baptized. I went to Freud and asked his advice; he said raise him as a Jew, because the boy will gain a lot from having to do twice as much as anyone else.
>
> (Graf, 1952)

Olga was reluctant to have children, although she eventually acquiesced, and continued to try even after an initial miscarriage until she succeeded. Her primary reason for not wanting children appears to be her awareness of her own emotional limitations—Herbert reports his mother resisted having children because "for her it [i.e., having children] was too much of a burden on her mind" (Graf, 1959)—and perhaps her still-latent artistic aspirations. She was consequently resentful of her husband's and Freud's pushing her into having not only Hans but also a second child. One wonders if the logic of the solution of having children to save the marriage was simply to cement the marriage with a child, or if it might have been that Olga was deemed to be in need of her more womanly form of creativity, children, so as not to be jealous of her husband's creative success in the world of the arts.

Due to Freud's involvement, the couple's tension around enlarging their family translated into Olga's resentment of Freud. Herbert reports that "My mother still has complaints, saying that Freud was not good in her life, and advising father to have children, and so forth, etc. It ultimately more or less broke up the marriage" (Graf, 1959). Whatever the reasons behind Max and Olga's disagreement over having children, the outbursts and associated arguments about sex could easily have impacted Hans, if indeed they were ongoing and he witnessed them, which we do not know.

It appears that Freud may have relied on this very possibility of Hans witnessing such arguments in inferring how it was that Hans arrived at a sadistic theory of coition. In his paper on the sexual theories of children (Freud, 1908/1959), which is largely about the Graf case although not identified as such, Freud observes that children may pick up the notion that sex is violent from observing marital interactions:

In many marriages the wife does in fact recoil from her husband's embraces, which bring her no pleasure, but the risk of a fresh pregnancy. And so the child who is believed to be asleep (or who is pretending to be asleep) may receive an impression from his mother which he can only interpret as meaning that she is defending herself against an act of violence. At other times the whole marriage offers an observant child the spectacle of an unceasing quarrel, expressed in loud words and unfriendly gestures; so that he need not be surprised if the quarrel is carried on at night as well.

(pp. 221–222)

Given what the interviews reveal about the Graf's quarrel-filled marriage, intense conflict over sex, and Olga Honig's reluctance to have children, this description seems likely to be Freud's reconstruction of Hans's experiences given what he knew of the marriage, although it does not correspond to the parents' insistence that Hans never witnessed a primal scene. While some of the couple's disputes are known to have occurred early in the marriage before Hans's birth, the disagreement over whether to have a second child would have occurred during Hans's early childhood—but still long before the time of his phobia.

In any event, having Hans did not resolve the marriage's overall tensions. Yet, Max and Olga stayed in the problematic marriage for many years before finally divorcing. They both went on to marry again more happily.

The interview also reveals that to the couple's considerable conflicts was eventually added a theoretical divergence over psychoanalysis. At the very time that Freud and Alfred Adler were joined in an intense conflict over the future of psychoanalysis, Olga—despite her earlier analysis with Freud—turned against Freudian doctrine and embraced Adler's rival view that the feeling of inferiority rather than repressed sexuality is at the heart of neurosis. Max left Freud's circle over the Freud-Adler split due to his divided sympathies and refusal to swear fealty to Freud, although he never ceased being primarily a Freudian.

Olga's friendship with Adler is mentioned by Herbert in his interview:

H.G.: "My mother had later a very great personal friendship with Alfred Adler. She didn't like Professor Freud because of what she felt was bad advice to my father. But she was a great personal friend of Alfred Adler .... And she is full of psychoanalysis and studying *now* .... She is quite experienced, I mean, and reads about it. But she did not *ever* speak to me about it, in particular .... My mother still has complaints, saying that Freud was not good in her life, and advising father to have children, and so forth, etc. It more or less ultimately broke up the marriage."

K.E.: "She thinks she should not have had children?"

H.G.: "She should, maybe one, maybe still me, but not then the sister who has in the meantime died. But that it was too much of a burden on her mind, and so this went on and so forth, and it was not good for their private living. I have no way of judging it. I would think all these things develop rather normally and it was a different cause why this marriage broke up."

(Graf, 1959)

Although in his Archives interview Max does not quite state explicitly that Freud recommended having children, Olga's claim, reported by Herbert, that Freud recommended having children has a factual basis in the consultation that Max describes between himself and Freud after a year of marriage about how to proceed with the marriage. Herbert also reports that his mother is still steeped in psychoanalytic theory, but Adlerian, not Freudian. He sensibly observes that the notion that Freud broke up his parents' marriage is likely exaggerated: "I would think all these things develop rather normally and it was a different cause why this marriage broke up" (Graf, 1959). But Herbert also says of his parents' relationship to Freud that "it was not good for [his parents'] private living" (Graf, 1959).

Herbert's wife, Lise Graf (denoted in the interview transcript by *F.G.* for *Frau Graf*), in her interview also describes these allegiances of her mother-in-law's as continuing decades later:

F.G.: "My mother[-in-law] had broken with Freud, and then she went to Adler. And whenever you see her, she still talks about Freud and Adler."

K.E.: "But against Freud?"

F.G.: "Against Freud!"

K.E.: "Yes. And what had turned her against Freud? Do you know that?"

F.G.: "No, I don't know that. I didn't want to know it."

K.E.: "Why?"

F.G.: "Because we are Freudians to our core. And Herbert's mother's nerves are not so good and never were. She exaggerates and somehow we never really wanted to go into it with her."

(Graf, 1960)

Lise's statement that "we are Freudians to our core" appears to be the case from the interviews. For example, as an adult, Herbert Graf continued to accept the Oedipal-theoretic approach to his own life story presented in his case history. In his Archives interview (1959), he notes that Plutarch says that a king's son was not allowed to enter the king's bedroom with a sword because such fear existed between father and son as pretender to the throne. Yet, in his own case, "For the first time in the history of the world, a little boy told his father: 'I'll have to kill you!' And the father didn't become upset" (Graf, 1959).

Lise portrays Olga as still highly emotional. She says she does not know why her mother-in-law Olga turned away from Freud, whereas we saw above that Herbert offers the startling explanation that it was partly due to the bad advice Freud gave to Max about having children, or at least a second child.

In a letter that Olga wrote to Kurt Eissler in 1953 that was hand-carried to him by her son Herbert, in which she refused Eissler's request to interview her, Olga refers sarcastically to how "noble" it was of her ex-husband Max to refer her to Eissler for an interview concerning Freud, apparently quoting something Adler had said long before about Max being noble at other people's expense (Adler died in 1937). In the note to Eissler, Olga also says of her marriage to Max that Freud "wreaked havoc on us" and that the relationship with Freud did not work, and suggests that an interview might open up old wounds (specifically, she mentions battling insomnia) (Mikkel Borch-Jacobsen, personal communication, 2021; Ross, 2007).

Lise Graf (Herbert's wife) speaks of her and her husband meeting Freud many years before and then of losing contact with him. Freud's interest in Herbert seems to have waned once Freud had obtained the evidence he desired of Herbert's continued health to show that psychoanalysis had not harmed a child. She notes, however, that she and Herbert nonetheless remained admirers of the "awfully kind, humble" Professor (Graf, 1960, as quoted in Ross, 2007, p. 786). I note in passing that Lise Graf was herself troubled and abused alcohol and drugs, and engaged in a long-term affair. She died of an overdose, possibly a suicide, some years after the interview with Eissler. Herbert appears to have achieved greater happiness in a later marriage.

In sum, the Grafs' marriage was characterized prior to the case record by marital conflicts over sex, work, socializing, family life (e.g., due to her social anxiety and tensions she had with Max's mother, Olga generally refused to accompany Max and Herbert to visit Max's mother in Lainz on Sunday), and childbearing. The conflict extended to psychoanalytic theory itself, in which the Freud/Adler split that eventually led to Adler's defection from Freud's circle was reflected in the marriage. These marital conflicts were addressed in part through occasional patriarchal consultations between Max and Freud about Olga and regarding momentous decisions, apparently without her involvement.

Was Olga a Charity Case of Freud's?

In a paper offering his reminiscences of his relationship with Freud, Max Graf (1942) notes: "Freud took the warmest part in all family events in my house; this despite the fact that I was still a young man and Freud was already aging" (p. 474). Max goes on to say that Freud "knew how to live with people; he was a person with social feelings," and he illustrates this characterization as follows: "It was his fundamental rule always to treat at least one patient without compensation. It was his way of doing welfare work" (p. 474).

This revelation about Freud's charity cases is left at a wholly abstract, intellectual level, suggesting that it is secondhand knowledge gleaned from conversations with Freud. However, the Archives interview suggests a surprising personal background to this statement that may explain why Max associated from the topic of his family's personal relationship with Freud to the issue of charity cases. Max's knowledge of Freud's charitable practices may have been obtained not from Freud but from his future wife, Olga Honig.

Max's discussion in the 1952 interview of Freud's "welfare" cases is as follows:

> Well, I'll tell you something personal [Personliches] because it will illustrate the character and personality of Freud. So, Professor Freud, there was a session every day, and then there came a time when the

family of this lady [dieser Dame] felt resistance against the things that the girl had apparently told them, and the mother declared that she would no longer pay for the treatment. As a consequence, this young lady went to Freud and said, "Professor Freud, unfortunately I can no longer continue the treatment—no?—I ask, I no longer have the money for it," and told him the story. And Freud said to her: "No, and you cannot make up your mind to continue treatment as a poor girl?" She accepted that—he treated her without any fee. He told me later, occasionally, that he treated one patient for free every week. That is the kind of charity he can practice and that he practices habitually.

(Graf, 1952)

Max's use of the demonstrative "this" in dieser Dame indicates that there very likely was a reference to this woman earlier in the interview. Since the only such person referred to in the interview thus far was the one described as having introduced Max to Freud, and she turned out to be Olga, the phrasing suggests that it was Olga who at some point was treated for free, as a welfare case, by Freud. Max says that the story is "personal," and this could be what is so personal about it. Max presents this account from the perspective of one intimately familiar with the young lady under discussion, describing her interaction with her family, what she said to Freud, and what Freud said back to her in vivid detail. He hints at the patient's internal conflict in being "treated as a poor girl." The gratitude that Freud's actions would have engendered in Max and Olga makes it more understandable why a physician treating an occasional patient who was unable to pay—a practice that is not at all so unusual—should garner such effusive praise.

The story fits Olga's situation in two ways. First, Max says the family of the lady objected to what she was reporting of the analysis's insights. Olga started analysis when Freud believed that actual seductions explained conditions such as hers, and thus the interpretations communicated to her mother would likely have involved claims about incest committed by her suicided brothers. Such interpretations surely would have horrified Olga's mother, plausibly causing her to end family financial support of her daughter's treatment with Freud. Second, the family's decision and authority over expenses is said to reside with the patient's mother, not the father, an oddity for that time and place. We know that Olga lost her father when she was an infant, thus the mention of the mother as in charge of the family's financial decisions also fits Olga's situation. In sum, it is likely that Olga Honig was the woman described by Max as Freud's charity patient, and that Max's story was obtained from his wife-to-be in her reports about her analysis.

This insight can reshape how one sees the relationship between Olga and Freud. If Olga was treated for free after her family refused to pay Freud's fees, this introduced a need for reciprocity into the relationship between Olga and Freud. Perhaps the meticulous journal of Herbert's early years that the Grafs kept in response to Freud's request for more information about child sexual development might have been partly motivated by the desire to repay Freud. Additionally, Olga's rather subtle and restrained resistance to Freud's Oedipal-theoretic approach to Hans's phobia despite her changing psychoanalytic views may have been out of a desire to show respect for someone who, whatever his errors, had been generous to her at one time.

Psychoanalytic Politics and Marital Conflict: Why did Max Graf Leave Freud's Circle?

Max Graf left Freud's psychoanalytic meeting group, the "Wednesday Circle," within a couple of years after the Hans case was published, at around the time of Alfred Adler's defection or ejection from the Circle in 1911. In later writings, Max cites the growing medicalization of the Wednesday Circle and Freud's dispute with Adler and, above all, Freud's forceful insistence on a with-me-or-against-me orthodoxy, as the causes of his withdrawal:

> Freud would not listen. He insisted that there was but one theory, he insisted that if one followed Adler and dropped the sexual basis of psychic life, one was no more a Freudian. In short, Freud—as the head of a church—banished Adler; he expelled him from the official church. I did not feel able to decide to take part in the strife between Freud and Adler's group.
>
> (Graf, 1942, pp. 471–472)

In that paper, Max portrays himself as a passive observer who, despite acknowledging that Adler was no match for Freud ("Freud's best pupil cannot be compared to [Freud's] creative imagination and real genius" [Graf, 1942, p. 474]), did not want to be forced to take sides in the conflict between Adler and Freud and felt forced to withdraw when Freud presented him with an ultimatum: "I was unable and unwilling to submit to Freud's 'do' or 'don't'—with which he once confronted me—and nothing was left for me but to withdraw from his circle" (Graf, 1942, p. 474).

Max's 1952 interview offers a different perspective on Max's role. Rather than acting as a passive observer, Max emerges as having taken an active and even relentless role in debating Adler's theory and its merits with Freud, not only at the Circle meetings but also, and especially, in Freud's frequent visits to his home. It appears that Max's insistence that Freud could incorporate some of Adler's ideas, rather than an arbitrary impulse of Freud's, triggered Freud's demand that Max make a choice:

> Every time Adler started discussing inferiority, he got resistance from Professor Freud, who always got the last word .... I tried [to find common ground] in my conversations with Professor Freud, and above all in conversations in my house, because I was a friend of Professor Freud's. I had always invited him to us; Professor Freud often came to an evening meal at our house, although he'd already had a hard work day and was tired and would much rather have been at home. And we frequently talked about the opposition between his and Adler's points of view .... It is my nature to find the good in everything, and in different opinions to find the kernel of truth, so I made the effort to also find some merit as well in the opinions of Dr. Adler, with whom I was very friendly. But I was unable to reach a decision because I did not have the knowledge .... When I made the effort in a conversation with Professor Freud to find a bridge between his theories and the theories of Professor Adler, he very vigorously corrected me, and said to me, "Either you accept or not." That gave me the feeling that my time was past, right? ... I did not really want to take part in these "guilt"/penance discussions that reminded me of the council discussions of early Christianity. So I no longer went to sessions of the psychoanalytic association.
>
> (Graf, 1952)

Nevertheless, in the long run Max stayed a Freudian. Olga, on the other hand, became an embittered anti-Freudian and went over to Adler's side.

This divide likely added to their marital burdens. The simultaneously intellectual and personal nature of the split between Max and Freud— presumably Freud took no more dinners at the Grafs—explains Freud's comment at the end of the case report that regarding Little Hans (and, therefore, also regarding his father) "about two years after the end of his analysis I had lost sight of him and had heard nothing of him for more than ten years" (1909/1955, p. 148).

Max's Anxiety about Death

As will be detailed in the next chapter, the case history reveals that Hans attended his first funeral at Gmunden the summer before he developed his phobia. Given the anxieties about parent loss that awareness of death might bring, this experience could fit with Bowlby's (1973) anxious-attachment interpretation of Hans's anxiety. In light of information about the family revealed in the Archives interviews, there is a further speculative point worth making about Hans's reaction to that funeral that concerns his father. For Hans to experience anxiety as a result of the funeral he attended would not be surprising, but it would be particularly expectable if a parent had unusual anxieties about death and funerals. We learn from the Archives interviews that Hans's father appears to have had such anxieties.

According to Herbert, his father had a remarkably intense aversion to funerals (Herbert describes it as a "wonderful ability ... to push things away") that kept him even from attending his own daughter's funeral after her suicide. Hans's sister Hanna committed suicide after the breakup of a relationship while living in America. Max was visiting America at the time, and Herbert was there as well. Max's report of this event in his interview is heartrending:

> I lost the daughter. She died here in America. She committed suicide in America. She had married and lived in an unhappy marriage, and my god somehow she wanted to replace that with other men, and then she came across a man with whom she experienced the same thing as with the other one whom she divorced, and that seems to have been decisive. And the tragic part was that three days after this event, a letter from her man came in which he asked me if I could bring about a reconciliation. It was already too late.
>
> (Graf, 1952)

When the topic of Hanna's death is discussed in the interview with Herbert, it yields additional insight into Max's personality:

HG: "My sister, in this country, unfortunately committed suicide. Father was here when this happened and I don't know how he could really manage that situation! It was amazing! But he wouldn't go to the cemetery, even so!"

KE: "And to the funeral?"

HG: "No!"

KE: "Also like Goethe .... was only at one funeral."

HG: "So!? A very wise man! I am not that wise because I am also my mother's son. She is not as controlled as my father was."

(Graf, 1959)

Herbert makes similar comments about his father's reaction to the death of his second wife:

HG: "Father had this wonderful ability ... to push things away. ... I remember when his second wife died when he was still rather young, in his best age, and I came to him. I was horrified at the idea of going to him at that moment and seeing him alone. He was sitting there, with a smiling face. He said, she died so beautifully, so wonderfully! And this was a good trait. He had enormous strength to turn things to the positive, or to forget them ... put them aside."

(Graf, 1959)

In his interview, Max says of himself that "It was my nature to find the good in everything." This admirable trait does seem to characterize Max. When taken to an extreme, however, it can become a form of denial that could be communicated as anxiety to his son Hans.

References

Barnett, J. (1971). Narcissism and Dependency in the Obsessional-Hysteric Marriage. *Family Process, 10,* 75–83.

Blum, H. P. (2007). Little Hans: A centennial review and reconsideration. *Journal of the American Psychoanalytic Association, 55(3),* 749–765.

Bowlby, J. (1973). *Attachment and Loss (Vol. 2): Separation: Anxiety and anger.* London, UK: Hogarth Press.

Freud, S. (1955). Analysis of a phobia in a five-year-old boy. In J. Strachey (Ed. & Trans.), The standard edition of the complete psychological works of Sigmund Freud (Vol. 10, pp. 1–150). London, UK: Hogarth Press. (Original work published 1909).

Freud, S. (1959). On the sexual theories of children. In J. Strachey (Ed. & Trans.), *The standard edition of the complete psychological works of Sigmund Freud* (Vol. 9, pp. 205–226). London, UK: Hogarth Press. (Original work published 1908).

Graf, H. (1959). Interview [of Herbert Graf] by Kurt Eissler. Box R1, Sigmund Freud Papers, Sigmund Freud Collection, Manuscript Division, Library of Congress, Washington, D.C.

Graf, L. (1960). Interview [of "Frau" Graf] by Kurt Eissler, Box R1, Sigmund Freud Papers, Sigmund Freud Collection, Manuscript Division, Library of Congress, Washington, D.C.

Graf, M. (1942). Reminiscences of Professor Sigmund Freud. *Psychoanalytic Quarterly*, *11*, 465–476.

Graf, M. (1946). *Composer and critic: Two hundred years of musical criticism*. New York: W.W. Norton & Company.

Graf, M. (1952). Interview [of Max Graf] by Kurt Eissler. Box 112, Sigmund Freud Papers, Sigmund Freud Collection, Manuscript Division, Library of Congress, Washington, D.C.

Graf, O. (1953). Letter to Kurt Eissler, *August 8, 1953*. Sigmund Freud Papers. Sigmund Freud Collection, Manuscript Division, Library of Congress, Washington, DC.

Nunberg, H., & Federn, E. (Eds.). (1967). *Minutes of the Vienna Psychoanalytic Society (Vol. 2): 1908–1910*. New York, NY: International Universities Press.

Masson, J. M. (1985). *The complete letters of Sigmund Freud to Wilhelm Fliess, 1887–1904*. Cambridge: Harvard University Press.

Ross, J. M. (2007). Trauma and abuse in the case of Little Hans: A contemporary perspective. *Journal of the American Psychoanalytic Association, 55(3)*, 779–797.

Strean, H. S. (1967) A family therapist looks at "Little Hans." *Family Process, 6*, 227–234.

Verhaeghe, P. (2009). *New studies of old villains: A radical reconsideration of the Oedipus complex*. New York, NY: Other Press.

Wakefield, J. C. (2007). Max Graf's "Reminiscences of Professor Sigmund Freud" revisited. *Psychoanalytic Quarterly, 76*, 149–192.

Chapter 3

Little Hans and Attachment Theory
Bowlby's Interpretation Reconsidered

In this chapter, I consider John Bowlby's (1973) attachment-theory account of the etiology of Little Hans's phobia. Bowlby argues that Hans had a disposition to develop an anxiety disorder due to his being anxiously attached to his mother, a known risk factor for anxiety disorder. The anxious-attachment account of Hans's tendency to anxiety disorder has become the main psychoanalytic rival to Freud's (1909/1955) Oedipal theory. My own approach that I will develop in later chapters also rests on elements of attachment theory but applies the theory to the Hans case in a way different from Bowlby's account, although elements from both approaches could coexist. I thus consider Bowlby's views at some length in this chapter, identifying both its strengths and the shortcomings that call for further investigation, before moving on to focus on my own attachment-theoretic analysis in Chapter 4. I also spell out in this chapter an underappreciated eclectic undercurrent in Bowlby's work that incorporates both behavioral and attachment-theoretic elements and will prove to be a useful framework later in this book. Note that throughout this chapter, given the context of the Hans case, I use "mother" or "caregiver" and feminine pronouns as a shorthand for the attachment figure and use masculine pronouns for the child.

Attachment Theory as a Challenge to Oedipal Theory

Based on a searching theoretical critique of Freud's theory of sexuality, Bowlby published a trilogy of articles (Bowlby, 1958, 1959, 1960) presenting the elements of attachment theory to the psychoanalytic community, provoking considerable criticism by mainstream psychoanalysts (Freud, 1960; Schur, 1960; Spitz, 1960). Attachment theory explained major forms

DOI: 10.4324/9780203817124-3

of childhood distress in terms of real external events of loss, separation, and inadequate parenting that interfered with the child's natural attachment relationship to a caregiver, rather than attributing such troubles to the child's Oedipal sexual fantasies. Thus, attachment theory seemed to many psychoanalysts to be a throwback to Freud's early seduction theory of the neuroses in which early actual trauma was postulated as the etiology of the psychoneuroses. The birth of psychoanalysis is generally considered to coincide with Freud's rejection of the seduction theory and development of the Oedipal theory focusing on spontaneous childhood fantasy rather than real relationships and events as pathogenic. So, attachment theory's focus on the effects of real disruptions in the parent–child relationship as the major cause of emotional problems seemed to some to be an attack on the essence of psychoanalysis rather than a welcome theoretical advance. Moreover, Bowlby postulated that attachment to a caregiver involves a distinct instinctual system not reducible to a form of sexuality, contrary to Freud's view. Bowlby thus took a major step toward object relations theory, which holds that nonsexual aspects of relating to people are more crucial than sexuality per se in a child's development and in the explanation of some forms of psychopathology.

Propelled by Bowlby's masterful three-volume exposition of his theory (Bowlby, 1973, 1980, 1982) and an impressive empirical research program that supported his claims, attachment theory overcame initial resistance by the psychoanalytic community and has since become accepted as a vital part of modern psychoanalytic thought. Eagle (1997) opened the way to some degree of reconciliation by arguing that even if an individual's internal working model of the attachment relationship is based on real events as Bowlby claimed, it need not be a strictly veridical representation of early parenting because psychodynamic factors could influence the representation's formation.

According to attachment theory, the child is biologically designed to possess an instinctual motivational system that causes the child to develop a special bond to a primary caregiver or other "attachment figure" (or perhaps a set of primary and secondary figures). This motivational system was naturally selected to keep the relatively defenseless and vulnerable human child in proximity to the caregiver to protect the child from predation and other dangers such as getting lost or aggression by conspecifics. If the child becomes separated from the caregiver, instinctual mechanisms cause the child to urgently seek the caregiver, and this is especially so when potential danger threatens. In an infant, attachment-related behaviors might include crawling toward the caregiver as well as signals that alert the caregiver to come to the infant, such as crying, and signals of satisfaction with proximity, such as smiling. Older children use more direct methods such as walking toward or verbally engaging the caregiver until proximity and emotional responsiveness are achieved. The child's initial distress when danger threatens is relieved both by a sense of safety that comes from proximity to the caregiver and by the caregiver's mental and physical soothing of the child, including physical skin contact (e.g., Duhn, 2010; Main & Stadtman, 1981). As the child gets older and more exploration of the environment takes place, the child uses the caregiver as a "secure base" from which to mount forays out into the world with a relative sense of safety given the caregiver's continued attention and availability; and when anxiety occurs, the child uses the attachment figure as a "safe haven" to which to return for emotional refueling through soothing and a sense of safety that creates the confidence to explore further.

As the child develops, the attachment figure as secure base becomes mentally represented and physical proximity becomes less essential. The nature of the attachment figure's relationship to the child becomes internalized as a representation or "working model" identifying attachment figures, where to access them, and how they are likely to respond. The initial working model influences later intimate attachments.

If the attachment figure is physically unavailable or emotionally unresponsive to the child over time, the child may develop a working model that renders the child insecure about the attachment figure's future availability or responsiveness when needed. Such insecure attachment can trigger chronic "separation anxiety" or "anxious attachment" in the young child manifested in overdependency and clinging behavior. Bowlby considers anxious attachment to be essentially excessive attachment behavior, or as he wryly puts it, "attachment behaviour more frequently and more urgently than the clinician thinks proper" (1973, p. 212). In addition to occurring when apart from the caregiver, such anxiety may continue in the presence of the caregiver due to the child's uncertainty about the caregiver's continued availability. Additionally, anxiety about lack of caregiver availability or responsiveness may cause the child to develop defensive strategies of avoiding expression of distress and need for the caregiver.

The attachment instinctual system's motivational mechanisms tend to be activated when the child's "security comfort level" deviates from some set-point that varies with circumstances and over developmental time, causing situational attachment distress and attachment-motivated behavior such as proximity seeking. These are all normal, expectable, adaptive components that are part of the attachment system's naturally selected workings. In contrast, chronic separation anxiety due to an anxiety-provoking working model is an apparently maladaptive form of attachment distress.

Subsequent to Bowlby, the focus of attachment theory shifted to discovering, classifying, and understanding the causes of different styles of child attachment behavior. The existence of such a typology is not immediately obvious given that Bowlby's theory appears to predict that separation of a child from his caregiver will cause distress and trigger the attachment system's motivational components, causing the child to seek proximity to the caregiver and show relief and independent exploratory behavior when the caregiver is close and available. A history of separation or other attachment threats or disruptions might cause unusually intense and persistent attachment-motivated behavior, but the same pattern of behavior might be expected to prevail at a more severe level.

This prediction led to a series of pivotal studies of attachment behavior by Mary Ainsworth and her colleagues (Ainsworth, 1979; Ainsworth & Wittig, 1969; Ainsworth, Blehar, Waters, & Wall, 1978; see also Duschinsky, 2015). The child was first observed playing with its caregiver present in an unfamiliar laboratory environment and then subjected to a brief period of separation followed by a reunion (the "Strange Situation"). The child's reactions before, during, and after separation were recorded and analyzed.

Instead of one universal pattern of proximity-maximizing attachment behavior, the Ainsworth Strange Situation studies revealed three patterns of attachment-related behaviors. The most common pattern was the Bowlby-predicted "secure" pattern in which the infant explored the room when the caregiver was present, showed distress at the caregiver's leaving, hastened to be close to the caregiver and showed relief when the caregiver returned, and then continued playing. However, a smaller group of children failed to show distress either at the caregiver's leaving or return. These children were classified as "avoidant" due to their lack of attachment distress. The "avoidant" label reflected Ainsworth's assumption that underneath the child's cool reaction the attachment motivational system was activated and the child was suppressing natural attachment distress. Another group of children were classified as having an "ambivalent/resistant" pattern of attachment behavior because they were not easily comforted and showed distress even when the caregiver was present, as if they did not trust the caregiver's continued availability.

Ainsworth argued that the avoidant and ambivalent-resistant attachment patterns were due to the child learning to suppress the natural attachment response due to previous experiences of how the attachment figure responded to the child's distress. If the child's distress triggered rejection and the caregiver's retreat, then the child might adopt the avoidant approach of not expressing distress so as to keep the caregiver from withdrawing. This view received some empirical support, for example in measures of increased heart rate in infants that on the outside seemed nondistressed by separation (Sroufe & Waters, 1977). On the other hand, if the child had learned to distrust the caregiver's continued availability and to expect random disruptions in responsiveness, the child might become ambivalent/resistant and continue to display distress preventively even when the caregiver is present and even when being comforted so as to continue to engage the caregiver's response. Mary Main (1979, 1981, 1990) reframed these patterns as adaptive "conditional strategies" for achieving the greatest possible proximity to the caregiver, given the nature of the caregiver's likely reactions to the child's needs.

Attachment theory is unique among psychoanalytic theories in its degree of empirical support by methodologically sophisticated studies of child development. Moreover, recent neurobiological evidence tends to support the notion, basic to Bowlby's conception, that there are distinct sexual and attachment motivational systems involving different brain circuits and neurotransmitters (Fisher et al., 2002). Given its ample research base, attachment theory has gained sufficient scientific respectability to have adherents among child psychologists who are not otherwise psychoanalytic. Bowlby's argument that the attachment system is a naturally selected mechanism for protecting the child from predators and other dangers confers the advantage of anchoring his theory in the broader discipline of evolutionary psychology. Moreover, the fundamental ideas about child development and parent–child relations that are put forward in attachment theory seem consistent with what most parents commonsensically know and observe of their children's development.

Bowlby on the Roots of Anxious Attachment

For Bowlby, anxious or insecure attachment is a chronic condition of insecurity in which a child feels excessive distress and anxiety ("separation anxiety") about being away from the attachment figure even when there is no threat. The child may continue to feel needy of reassurance and clingy even when the attachment figure is present or easily available.

Bowlby put forward three basic propositions regarding the development of anxious versus secure attachment. First, Bowlby claimed that "when an individual is confident that an attachment figure will be available to him whenever he desires it, that person will be much less prone to either intense or chronic fear" (1973, p. 202). Conversely, disrupted or anxious attachment predisposes to developing anxiety conditions such as animal phobias, school refusal, and agoraphobia. Without a well-functioning attachment relationship, the child will experience more frequent and persistent anxiety and, when frightening incidents occur, is more likely to experience traumatic levels of fear that can produce phobias. Second, the working model of attachment develops during a sensitive period during childhood and remains relatively constant after that. Third, the child's attachment security reflects in a roughly accurate way the actual attachment experiences during the sensitive period. In contrast to Freud's emphasis on fantasy, Bowlby cautions that one should not try to explain childhood fears in terms of unconscious wishes until explanations in terms of the child's actual experience have failed.

On the basis of the research literature and clinical experience, Bowlby identified several particularly potent factors in the child's real experiences that may bring about anxious attachment and consequently dispose the child to develop an anxiety disorder. First, Bowlby argued that actual separations from the mother have the most substantial effects on attachment security, and that after a period of separation small children tend to be anxious and cling to the attachment figure. Bowlby cites evidence that lengthy real separation is the most common etiology of anxious attachment in which children exhibit overdependency and fear of separation. For example, Newson and Newson (1968) studied the fears of four-year-old children and concluded: "Most of these children's separation fears are reality-based, in that they or their mothers have been hospitalized or some other hurtful separation has already taken place" (1968, pp. 198–199).

Second, Bowlby holds that a major risk factor for anxious attachment is when the attachment figure threatens to abandon the child, generally in order to control or discipline the child. For example, a parent might say that the child will be sent away somewhere if behavior does not improve, or that the child's mother will go away and leave the child. Bowlby suggests that it is likely that many children experience such threats and, rather speculatively, asserted that "there is reason to believe that ... such threats play a far larger part in increasing a person's susceptibility to separation anxiety than has yet been realized by psychiatrists" (1973, p. 199).

A third factor promoting anxious attachment is intense parental arguments. Bowlby holds that children understand that such arguments could cause a parent to depart. Indeed, overheard spousal arguments may involve explicit threats of a parent leaving, and, Bowlby observes, children often hear more than parents think they do.

These are general considerations that dispose to anxious attachment, according to Bowlby. His case for his reinterpretation of the Hans case in attachment-theoretic terms depends on placing the case within this general framework.

Separation Anxiety Versus Situational Attachment Distress

There is an important ambiguity in Bowlby's first proposition above that if a child is confident that the attachment figure will be available when the child desires contact, then the child will be less susceptible to either intense or chronic anxiety. Bowlby is primarily referring here to the child's relatively stable long-term sense of confidence in the attachment figure likely being accessible and responsive that is built up over time. As the other two propositions make clear, this sense of confidence is based on a working model of attachment formed slowly over years of early childhood experience that provides the expectation that the attachment figure will likely on average be available when needed, even if this expectation is occasionally disappointed. A less confident working model can give rise to chronic separation anxiety or anxious attachment.

However, the same proposition could apply to the reaction to a specific situation rather than a stable disposition. If a child is afraid or feels lack of adequate proximity to the attachment figure in a specific instance, this triggers normal situational attachment anxiety that causes the child to want to be near the attachment figure. If access is blocked or the figure is otherwise unavailable, the child's situational attachment distress will naturally increase. This is a normal response to a situation, not a stable disposition, and is entirely compatible with secure attachment and with a benign working model. Such distressing occasions need not influence the child's working model that has been formed over years, although of course if serious difficulty gaining proximity to the attachment figure occurs often enough over a long enough period of time, this may start to reshape the child's working model. However, situational attachment anxiety is intrinsic to the normal adaptive functioning of the secure attachment system that causes the child to be motivated to seek proximity to the attachment figure under a variety of threatening or anxiety-provoking circumstances.

Bowlby makes clear that situational attachment distress can be intense irrespective of the nature of an individual's working model and is of the utmost importance in understanding the attachment system's workings:

> [N]o fear-arousing situation is missed or camouflaged as often as is fear that an attachment figure will be inaccessible or unresponsive …. [T]he degree to which each of us is susceptible to fear turns in great part on whether our attachment figures are present or absent …. [O]f the many fear-arousing situations that a child, or older person, can foresee, none is likely to be more frightening than the possibility that an attachment figure will be absent or, in more general terms, unavailable when wanted …. Intimately linked to the type of forecast a person makes of the probable availability of his attachment figures, moreover, is his susceptibility to respond with fear whenever he meets any potentially alarming situation during the ordinary course of his life.
>
> (1973, pp. 200–203)

Although they can be described in similar terms, the distinction between anxious attachment and situational attachment distress will turn out to be pivotal for my analysis. I will argue in the next chapter that Bowlby missed an obvious immediate source of Hans's heightened anxiety prior to the phobia's onset, namely, repeated situations in which he experienced heightened attachment distress due to his father's blocking his access to his mother's soothing.

Was Hans Attached to His Mother?

Before addressing Bowlby's claim that Hans was anxiously attached to his mother, there is a preliminary point that to my knowledge is not controversial: Hans's primary attachment object was indeed his mother.

It is true that several authors (e.g., Frankiel, 1992; Juri, 2003), including me (Wakefield, 2007a), have pointed out that Hans's analysis by his father brought Hans and his father closer together and to some extent provided Hans with a secondary attachment figure in addition to his mother. As Freud observed, as a result of the analysis Hans "got on to rather familiar terms with his father" (1909/1955, p. 144). However, the increasing closeness between Hans and his father should not obscure the fact that, as Bowlby recognizes, the case report clearly indicates that Hans was primarily attached to his mother.

Hans's attachment to his mother is most directly evidenced by the fact that it is his mother that Hans consistently seeks out for soothing when he is anxious. When Hans is anxious upon awakening alone in his bedroom in the morning, he generally goes into his parents' bedroom to cuddle with his mother; when he feels afraid of horses while out with his nursemaid, he wants to go home and "coax" (cuddle) with his mother ("in the street he had begun to cry and asked to be taken home, saying that he wanted to 'coax' with his mother" [1909/1955, p. 23]). Indeed, Freud's Oedipal interpretation of Hans's condition is based on the observed fact that Hans primarily wants to have access to and physical contact with his mother. Interpreted attachment-theoretically rather than Oedipally, that indicates that she was his primary attachment figure.

Hans's mother is not only Hans's safe haven when he is anxious but also the secure base allowing him to explore while anticipating the ability to retreat to her if necessary. To take a revealing example from Hans's fantasy life, one day Hans is outside his house watching carts go into and out of a loading dock across the street, and he imagines the fun of climbing onto a cart while it is stopped, but then anxiously imagines that it might drive away with him ("I'm afraid of ... the cart driving off quick, ... and my driving off in the cart"). His father asks: "Perhaps you're afraid you won't come home any more if you drive away in the cart?" Hans answers, "Oh no! I can always come back to Mummy, in the cart or in a cab. I can tell him the number of the house too" (1909/1955, pp. 47–48). Although he is with his father and his mother is not present and has not been mentioned, Hans's fantasy about safely reuniting with his family after being carried off is exclusively about getting home to his mother. Moreover, Hans assumes that if he should travel away on a cart, not only could he get home to his mother but there is no question that she would still be there; no anxiety about her possibly leaving while he is away is evident.

Bowlby's Argument that Hans Was Anxiously Attached to His Mother

So, what does Bowlby have to say about Hans's attachment and his phobia? If attachment theory reveals a truth about human nature, then it should be able to provide new insights into past cases, including the very cases used to support the classic psychoanalytic theory that it disputes. Just such a demonstration of the retrodictive usefulness of attachment theory was attempted by Bowlby in offering an attachment-theoretic reinterpretation of Freud's (1909/1955) case of Little Hans. Freud presented the case as his most direct evidence for the Oedipus complex, arguing that Hans's horse phobia was due to longings of a specifically sexual, even inchoately genital, nature for his mother, along with resultant fears of castration anxiety and aggressive impulses towards his father. Bowlby argued instead that Hans's phobia is explained by heightened nonsexual separation anxiety brought about by a combination of Hans's actual separation from his mother during her confinement when giving birth to Hans's sister, Hanna, a year before and Hans's mother's tendency to use threats of leaving the family to control Hans's misbehavior.

Bowlby recognized that Freud's study of four-year-old Little Hans's horse phobia was not only a key paper in the overall development of psychoanalytic theory but specifically the basis for the subsequent psychoanalytic theory of phobias. He proposes to provide an alternative explanation of Hans's anxiety based on anxious attachment, maintaining that this factor has been overlooked by previous commentators. Observing that Freud's interpretation construes Hans's fear of horses as symbolic fear of castration by his father, Bowlby asks: "What evidence, we may now ask, is there that anxiety about the availability of attachment figures was playing a larger part in Hans's condition than Freud realized?" and he answers: "Most of his anxiety, it is suggested, arose from threats by his mother to desert the family" (Bowlby, 1973, p. 283). He says this claim is supported by Hans's own statements, by the sequence of emergence of his symptoms, and by evidence that Hans's mother did threaten to abandon him.

Bowlby holds that childhood animal phobias are caused by anxious attachment, and anxious attachment is caused by a history of real triggering experiences in the attachment relationship that undermine the perceived availability of the mother. Thus, to support his claim that Hans's phobia is due to anxious attachment, Bowlby argues that: (1) Hans displays anxious attachment in his statements and symptoms prior to the phobia's onset; and (2) known anxious attachment-triggering experiences—in the form of an actual separation when Hans's sister was born and, especially, threats of abandonment by Hans's mother when disciplining Hans—preceded his displays of anxious attachment.

Turning first to Bowlby's claim that Hans displays anxious attachment in his statements and symptoms prior to the phobia's outbreak, Bowlby recounts how, at the age of four and three-quarters, Hans developed a fear that a horse would bite him in the street, and was afraid to go on his usual walks. Bowlby observes that Hans expressed some anxiety about his mother in the week before the phobia's onset and also one time some months before. Bowlby refers here to the incidents reported in the Hans case record as follows:

'Hans (aged four and three-quarters) woke up one morning in tears. Asked why he was crying, he said to his mother: "When I was asleep I thought you were gone and I had no Mummy to coax with." ['Coax' was Hans's term for cuddling.]

'An anxiety dream, therefore.'

'I had already noticed something similar at Gmunden in the summer. When he was in bed in the evening he was usually in a very sentimental state. Once he made a remark to this effect: "Suppose I was to have no Mummy", or "Suppose you were to go away", or something of the sort; I cannot remember the exact words.

(1909/1955, p. 23)

So, Bowlby's evidence for anxious attachment based on the emergence of Hans's symptoms and his statements comes down to two points. First, shortly before the onset of his horse anxieties, Hans expressed attachment-related anxieties about his mother going away or not being available for cuddling. Second, six months before the onset of symptoms, Hans had also expressed concern that his mother might not be available. Consequently, "Hans's own statements make it clear that, *distinct from and preceding any fear of horses*, Hans was afraid that his mother might go away and leave him" (1973, p. 284).

Bowlby next argues that a background of chronic anxious attachment is a plausible hypothesis because features that are risk factors for anxious attachment are present in the case history. This argument is circumstantial because such causes do not generally produce anxious attachment but only increase its probability.

One such possible causal factor mentioned by Bowlby is that Hans was separated from his mother for some time when his sister Hanna was born. Bowlby observes that Hans's father suggests that Hans's separation from his mother at the time his wife was giving birth to Hanna could be responsible for Hans's later anxiety, and Freud seems to agree. However, Bowlby places little weight on this actual separation in terms of evidence for causation of anxious attachment. One obvious reason is that it occurred a year-and-a-quarter before Hans's phobia. There is no case evidence of any reaction of attachment anxiety by Hans following the mother's confinement, and the earliest expression of insecurity noted by Bowlby occurred just one time six months before the phobia, so the birth separation does not fill in the causal chain in a persuasive way. Moreover, whereas Bowlby emphasizes that it is "very prolonged or repeated separation" (1973, p. 12) that has an impact on attachment, Hans's separation appears to have been brief: "At five in the morning, labour began, and Hans's bed was moved into the next room" (Freud, 1909/1955, p. 10). Hans was not permanently moved into his own room until half a year later, when the family moved into a new flat, so he did not stay in his separate bedroom at that point. Hans's father, Max, mentioned in his interview that Hans at some point was sent to stay at his paternal grandparents' house for a visit with his loving grandmother (Graf, 1952), but there is no evidence that Hanna's birth was the occasion for that visit nor that the visit was lengthy, and the case report indicates that Hans was at home to examine the bloody washbasins immediately after Hanna's birth.

Instead, Bowlby proposes that "Most of his anxiety, it is suggested, arose from threats by his mother to desert the family" (1973, p. 284) that caused anxious attachment. Bowlby thus hypothesizes that the Hans case fits one of the typical family patterns (pattern B) that he identifies as the causes of animal phobias and school refusal, in which the child fears that something bad will happen to the mother while the child is at school and thus tries to remain at home to prevent it from happening. Bowlby claims that "buried deep in the 'analytic' record, Hans lifts the curtain" (1973, p. 284) on the mother's threats, and that the case record yields evidence that Hans's mother used threats of abandonment to discipline Hans.

Bowlby refers here to an interchange between Hans and his father.

> "Hans: 'When you're away, I'm afraid you're not coming home.' I: 'And have I ever threatened you that I shan't come home?' Hans: 'Not you, but Mummy. Mummy's told me she won't come back.' ... I: 'She said that because you were naughty.' Hans: 'Yes'."
>
> (1909/1955, pp. 43–45; see below for further discussion of this passage)

The father then speculates that Hans's desire to stay at home is due to fear of his not finding his parents at home because they have gone away. Bowlby concludes that "it is not implausible to believe" (1973, p. 287) that Hans's symptoms are an expression of his fear of his mother leaving while he is away.

In addition to the earlier actual separation from his mother and her threats of abandonment, Bowlby tentatively suggested that perhaps Hans also overheard marital arguments that created anxiety about the continued presence of his mother. The case history contains no explicit report of marital disharmony. However, when Hans visited Freud many years later, he revealed that his parents had since divorced. The case history says nothing about when the divorce occurred, so one cannot really tell whether the process and its likely associated arguments were going on at the time of Hans's phobia, leaving any inferences quite risky. Nonetheless, Bowlby speculates that there might have been intense pre-divorce spousal conflict at the time of the phobia onset at a level that may have led to threats of leaving and caused Hans increased attachment anxieties.

How Persuasive is Bowlby's Argument that Hans Was Anxiously Attached to His Mother?

Bowlby understands that his case is suggestive but inconclusive. Thus, to the question of whether anxiety about the availability of his mother for attachment contact played a larger part in Hans's condition than Freud realized, Bowlby answers that on the basis of "clear presumptive evidence ... it seems probable that anxious attachment was indeed contributing a great deal to Little Hans's problem" (1973, p. 284). The guardedness of Bowlby's language ("reason to believe," "not implausible," "presumptive," "probable") is appropriate because risk factors offer only statistical associations and in addition the temporal relationship to the proposed factors is speculative. The fact that Hans's mother made some threats at some time does not resolve the question of whether in Hans's case the threats of abandonment actually caused anxious attachment and anxious attachment actually contributed to the development of Hans's phobia.

However, Bowlby does not adequately address a more basic question that should be resolved before such speculation: *Was Hans indeed anxiously attached to his mother as Bowlby hypothesizes?* After all, we have ample evidence in the case history of Hans's behavior, and if he was anxiously attached in the chronic way Bowlby infers, then there ought to be persuasive evidence of this in Hans's behavior other than the few incidents of anxiety Bowlby mentions.

Bowlby's argument for Hans being anxiously attached is highly problematic given the limited evidence about Hans's relationship with his mother he cites from the case history. As we saw, this essentially consists of two incidents six months apart. First, Bowlby notes that the father reports an expression of insecurity by Hans that occurred one time six months before. The father cannot recall Han's precise words, and there is no context provided to evaluate whether Hans's anxiety in that instance might be explained in terms of transient circumstances rather than chronic anxious attachment. For example, we know from the case report that during that summer Hans attended his first funeral, and that he subsequently brought it up often. His saying around that time something like "Suppose I were to have no Mummy" seems understandable as a transient reaction to the funeral or to talk about death that Hans may have overheard.

Second, Bowlby refers to the expression of anxiety about the mother's availability that occurred just before the phobia's onset. This also occurred just once and lacks context. The fact that it occurred just days prior to the recognition of Hans's phobia yields a suggestive but still invalid "post hoc ergo propter hoc" force to the argument. The fact that the form of words used by Hans regarding whether he would have a Mummy to coax with seems to express anxiety about the availability of the attachment figure is not conclusive. Bowlby himself indicates that when a child has becomes afraid of some external threat and the availability of the child's attachment figure for soothing is uncertain, the child may express anxiety about access to the attachment figure using the same words that can indicate anxious attachment: "whenever our attachment behaviour is aroused ...

but for some reason we are unable to find or reach our attachment figure, … we might say, 'I was afraid you were gone', or 'I was frightened when I could not find you', or 'Your long absence made me anxious'" (1973, p. 92).

In a companion volume (Wakefield, 2022), I argue on the basis of a detailed analysis of the case data that Hans likely already had his horse phobia in these days before he admitted the phobia to his parents. So, it may not be a matter of his attachment needs being activated in the days before the horse fear appeared, but of Hans already being afraid of horses—although as yet unwilling to admit it—and thus needing his mother's soothing. If this is the case, then Hans's concern about his mother's availability was a manifestation of a normal attachment need for soothing in the face of an external fear of horses. Moreover, a crucial flaw in Bowlby's analysis is that Hans had immediate reason to believe that his access to his mother would be blocked by his father and so his anxieties were an expression of a situation of lack of access, an issue addressed in the next chapter.

A deeper problem for Bowlby's argument is that he embraces the thin evidence of the two incidents of Hans's anxiety without considering the potential counterbalancing or disconfirmatory evidence that appears to go against his hypothesis. The fact is that, on an open-minded reading, the evidence of Hans's behavior in the Hans case study does not indicate ongoing separation anxiety or anxious attachment on Hans's part in any generalized or substantial way. Bowlby describes anxious attachment as a pronounced condition in which a child is "exceptionally demanding and intolerant of frustration" (1973, p. 238), clingy, overly dependent and preoccupied with the attachment figure, and making continual attempts to retain proximity to her. In anxious attachment, the child is not only anxious when the caregiver is not present but also tends to demand continuous proximity and remains concerned about loss of the figure's availability or responsiveness even when the figure is present. Consequently, when anxious, the child is often not adequately calmed down or reassured by the caregiver's soothing. To this extent, anxious attachment in Bowlby's sense most resembles Ainsworth's "ambivalent-resistant" category. Anxious attachment is also often accompanied by the child not freely exploring on his own due to insecurity about the availability of his "secure base" and "safe haven." Being distressed whenever apart from the attachment figure ("separation anxiety"), he lacks outside relationships and friendships. So, the question is whether the case evidence places Hans within this category. In answering this question, it should be kept in mind that children's behavior can vary for many circumstantial or idiosyncratic reasons, so it is useful to observe the principle that the behaviors characteristic of a given attachment pattern must be displayed at a substantial level of intensity and consistency to justify classifying a child's pattern within that category (Granqvist, et al., 2017).

Bowlby certainly had in mind such pronounced and consistent behaviors when writing of anxious attachment. As a comparison point, here are descriptions by their mothers of two such overly dependent anxiously attached children, to which Bowlby refers as exemplars. These descriptions were obtained in a research study in which the mothers—who are from working class backgrounds, one a miner's wife and the other a lorry-driver's wife who is separated from her husband—were asked whether their children, both around Hans's age, liked to be cuddled:

Ever since I left her that time I had to go into hospital (two periods, 17 days each, child aged 2 years), she doesn't trust me any more. I can't go anywhere—over to the neighbours or in the shops—I've always got to take her. She wouldn't leave me. She went down to the school gates at dinner time today. She ran like mad home. She said, 'Oh, Mum, I thought you was gone!' She can't forget it. She's still round me all the time.

(Newson & Newson, 1968, p. 100)

Yes, all the time just lately—only since he left …. she's continually clinging round me, she keeps saying, 'Do you love me? You won't leave me, Mummy, will you?'—and so I sit down and try to talk to her about it, you know; but I mean, at her age [about four], really you can't explain. And she used to dress herself; but since my husband's been gone, she's relied on me for—well, every mortal thing I've had to do for her …. I did put her in a nursery just after he went, because I thought it might take her mind off things, you see, but anyhow the matron asked if I'd mind taking her away, because she said she just sat and cried all day long. I think she'd got it into her head that because her Daddy's gone, and me taking her there and leaving her all day, she p'raps thought I'd left her too, you see. So she was only there a fortnight, and then I took her away. But she's afraid of being left on her own, I mean, if I go to the toilet, I have to take her with me, she won't even stay in the room then on her own. She's frightened of being left.

(Newson & Newson, 1968, p. 100)

The Hans case report makes clear that this sort of description does not even approximately fit Hans as a general characterization. Prior to and even after the onset of the phobia, Hans is portrayed in the case history as being generally cheerful, inquisitive, and exploratory, and not as complaining, whiney, clingy, or needy. He readily makes friends and happily goes off and plays with them and explores on his own. For example, prior to the phobia: "In the summer of 1906 Hans was at Gmunden, and used to run about all day long with our landlord's children" (Freud, 1909/1955, p. 12); "During the last few days Hans has been playing parlour games and 'forfeits' with our landlord's children" (1909/1955, p. 20). And, just a few months before the phobia's onset,

> we moved to Gmunden for the summer holidays. In our house there his playmates were our landlord's children: Franzl (about twelve years old), Fritzl (eight), Olga (seven), and Berta (five). Besides these there were the neighbour's children, Anna (ten), and two other little girls of nine and seven
>
> (1909/1955, p. 16).

As Freud notes of Hans, "in the country his affections had been divided among a number of playmates and friends of both sexes" (1909/955, p. 26). Nor did the children stay close to the adults: "'Used you to play at horses with the children at Gmunden?' He: 'Yes.' ... I: 'Who was the horse?' He: 'I was; and Berta was the coachman .... When Berta said 'Gee-up', I ran ever so quick; I just raced along .... Fritzl was the horse once, too." (1909/1955, p. 58); "you and the others were often in the stables" (1909/1955, p. 60). In Vienna, when his mother is not around and Hans is in the nanny's charge, he plays happily with her:

> On March 3rd we got in a new maid, whom he is particularly pleased with. She lets him ride on her back while she cleans the floor, and so he always calls her 'my horse,' and holds on to her dress with cries of 'Gee-up'.
>
> (1909/1955, p. 30)

The evidence is that this was not a child clinging to his mother!

Moreover, when Hans does feel anxious and gains access to his mother for cuddling, this successfully calms him down instead of initiating endless anxiety about further availability or triggering ambivalence, detachment, or resistance. For example, here are descriptions of three different evenings in the anxious days immediately following the onset of Hans's phobia when Hans sought soothing physical cuddling ("coaxing") from his mother: "Till the evening he was cheerful, as usual. But in the evening he grew visibly frightened; he cried and could not be separated from his mother, and wanted to 'coax' with her again. Then he grew cheerful again, and slept well"; "In the evening he seems to have had another attack similar to that of the previous evening, and to have wanted to be 'coaxed' with. He was calmed down"; "That evening his attack of nerves and his need for being coaxed with were less pronounced than on previous days" (1909/1955, pp. 24, 31). In sum, looking at Hans's behavior as a whole and considering both supportive and disconfirmatory evidence, there is decidedly insufficient support for the claim that Hans's behavior manifests a substantial level of anxious attachment and much evidence suggesting the contrary.

On the crucial topic of Hans's mother's behavior towards Hans, the negatives pointed out by Bowlby must be placed in context. Although Olga was clearly emotionally fragile and anxious, and she did use dramatic threats at times to try to control Hans, both Hans's father and Freud portray Olga as having an affectionate relationship with Hans. Max says that she had "a good attitude toward" Hans and that, although self-absorbed, she did not neglect him. In terms of documented behavior, the mother's response to Hans as described in the case history appears to be by and large exactly what Bowlby suggests, namely, a "natural and comforting expression of motherly feeling" (1973, p. 287), that she manages to provide despite her personal inhibitions and anxieties. For example, she lets Hans come into her bed for cuddling in the morning when he is anxious and seeks soothing, she personally bathes both Hans and his sister when she might easily have left this to a nursemaid, she personally takes Hans out on a walk to see what is bothering him when his anxiety is first reported by the nursemaid ("On January 8th my wife decided to go out with him herself, so as to see what was wrong with him" [1909/1955, p. 24]), she spends the entire morning talking to him trying understand what is bothering him after the night in which he has his disturbing giraffe dream ("My wife had in fact examined him all the morning, till he had told her the giraffe story" [1909/1955, p. 38]), she offers him helpful advice about how to deal with his fear of horses ("He managed all this, looking hurriedly away whenever any horses came along, for he was evidently feeling nervous. In looking away he was following a piece of advice given him by his mother" [1909/1955,p. 33]), and she writes multiple times to Freud to thank him when Hans's symptoms finally subside ("In the course of the next few days Hans's mother wrote to me more than once to express her joy at the little boy's recovery" [1909/1955, p. 99]). Of note, after her divorce from Max, Olga subsequently remarried and stayed married to her husband for many years until death did them part, suggesting some capacity for emotional stability despite her emotionally intense nature.

Some elements in Hans's behavior suggest a possible mild level of anxious attachment. In particular, Hans desires to cuddle with his mother in the morning and sometimes in the evening when, he says, he experiences fear. This could be normal situational attachment distress due to his being frightened by waking up alone after being recently moved to his own bedroom, or once the phobia begins it could be due to fear of horses ("He said, crying: 'I know I shall have to go for a walk again tomorrow.' And later: 'The horse'll come into the room' [1909/1955, p. 24]). However, Hans's desire for cuddling mostly in the mornings before the day gets underway is a quite minimal indicator when compared to Bowlby's examples of how anxious attachment usually presents. Moreover, there is no hint of any longer-term problems with attachment or overdependency in the reports of the parents on Hans's development prior to the time of the phobia. Even during the phobia the case history is clear that, other than the phobic anxiety, Hans remains normally cheerful and not insecure:

> "Apart from his being afraid of going into the street and from his being in low spirits in the evening, he is in other respects the same Hans, as bright and cheerful as ever."
>
> (p. 22)

The morning cuddling desires in the context of Hans's overall behavior are not by themselves strongly indicative of anxious attachment to any substantial extent.

As Bowlby observes, the case evidence does indicate that Hans's mother at some point threatened to leave if he did not behave himself.

Given that the threat (or threats) remained on Hans's mind, we can reasonably assume with Bowlby that it caused Hans some anxiety. Moreover, Hans acknowledges that in coming into his parents' bedroom in the morning for cuddling, he is afraid not just of being alone in bed but also of his parents not being there. The problem is that there is no evidence as to the frequency, recency, or precise nature of such threats, so it is impossible to evaluate the plausibility of this hypothesis as an explanation for Hans's phobia. Moreover, a careful examination of the context of this interchange suggests alternative possible meanings (see below).

There are three further concerns one might have about Bowlby's emphasis on the mother's threats of abandonment as the sole grounds for Hans's development of anxious attachment. First, the research literature strongly supports the role of actual separation in the genesis of anxious attachment, but it does not address the causal potency of occasional threats. As Bowlby acknowledges, such threats have not been systematically studied, so their significance remains unknown. Consequently, Bowlby's belief in the strong causal efficacy of threats remains speculative.

Second, it appears that the threat or threats of leaving that occurred were infrequent and were not accompanied by actual separations. Occasional use of such threats is very common in the heat of the moment when trying to control a child. Bowlby reports that 30% of the parents in some studies report use of such threats, and he speculates that many more do so but do not recall using them or are embarrassed to admit that they have. One current parental-advice website states frankly, "At some point of parenthood, we all have used threats. Parents use threats to keep their children under check" (Goidani, 2020). Bowlby suggests that the impact of threats on a child's working model is greatest when real separations follow multiple threats, so that the impact is due to a combination of "the high incidence of such threats" and "the cumulative effects of actual separations" (1973, p. 235). In Hans's case, there are no actual separations from his mother immediately prior to the phobia and no demonstrable high incidence of the threats themselves, so the potential impact is unclear. By way of comparison, in Bowlby's review of the literature, most of the clear cases of anxious attachment he cites have more severe triggering factors, including lengthy actual separations.

Third, the potential for abandonment threats to trigger anxious attachment depends on how seriously the child takes the threats. Bowlby notes that of course such threats vary both in the seriousness with which they are made and how seriously they are taken by the child, and this matters for their effects. The one earlier episode in the case history that Bowlby mentions as an example of the mother's threats seems to indicate that from a young age Hans took his mother's threats with a grain of salt. When Hans's mother made her "castration threat" to stop him from touching his penis (i.e., that otherwise she would call Dr. A to cut it off), instead of crying, displaying anxiety, or begging her not to, Hans calmly banters with his mother and responds that then he will widdle with his bottom. Hans treats the mother's threat so nonchalantly that Freud feels compelled to defend his view that castration threats are traumatic, given this seeming disconfirmation. He offers the ad hoc explanation that Hans had a deferred reaction and his anxiety in response to his mother's threat emerged a year later in another context that reminded him of the earlier incident. A less convoluted explanation is that Hans, an intellectually precocious boy, understood that his mother's threats were empty.

Regarding Bowlby's reference to Hans's parents' divorce, we now know what Bowlby did not know, that the parents were not about to divorce at the time of Hans's phobia and that the divorce occurred more than a decade after the time of the case history. We know from the Archives interviews that the parents had intense arguments about a range of subjects early in their marriage, before having children. However, we do not know whether these arguments continued in this way several years later or the spouses instead eventually fell into a calmer state of discontent after having Hans. Neither the case history nor the Freud Archives interviews offers any support for the contention that intense arguments with threats of leaving that might have been overheard by Hans were still occurring prior to Hans's phobia.

Bowlby is certainly correct that Hans had experiences that *might* lead to attachment-related anxieties. In emphasizing threats by Hans's mother, Bowlby overlooked or did not know about many other relevant risk factors for anxious attachment that one might identify (Wakefield, 2007a). These include, for example, Hans having attended a funeral a few months before and being bothered by it afterwards, Hans having been moved into his own bedroom, Hans having been moved to a new apartment, the socially anxious nature of Hans's mother, the negative attitude of Hans's mother towards his sister Hanna, and the father's apparent anxieties about death. However, all of these remain speculative, without direct evidence to support their causal role. Most importantly, the existence of such presumed risk factors does not change the fact that the case evidence simply does not indicate pronounced anxious attachment on Hans's part.

Perhaps the weaknesses and limitations in Bowlby's argument for Hans's anxious attachment are part of the reason for Bowlby's notable caution in stating his conclusions while avoiding direct rejection or even criticism of Freud's account. He concluded merely that the attachment-theoretic approach is at least as plausible as the Oedipal account: "There it must be left since there is no way of knowing which of the alternative constructions is nearer the truth …. The hypothesis advanced here seems no less plausible than the one adopted by Freud" (1973, p. 287). This conclusion suggests that Bowlby's arguments are aimed not at establishing the anxious-attachment explanation of Hans's horse phobia but rather at showing merely that attachment theory could be deployed in such a way as to do as well as Freud's sexual theory in explaining Hans's phobia, and thus that Freud's account of the Hans case is no objection to the possible superiority of Bowlby's theory.

Further Thoughts about Hans's Report of His Mother's Threat to Leave

As Bowlby says, Olga did use dramatic threats at times to try to control Hans when he misbehaved. Interestingly, so did Hans's father. In recounting Hans's policeman fantasies, Max notes that when Hans wondered why he could not go under a rope into a closed off space at the zoo, Max told him there was a policeman to take away little boys who did that. Max also notes that he had used similar threats on other occasions: "I replied that a policeman might come along and take one off. There is a lifeguardsman on duty at the entrance of Schönbrunn; and I once told Hans that he arrested naughty children" (1909/1955, pp. 40–41). As well, Max implies that Hans being naughty might be grounds for his mother to stop loving him: "Perhaps it was because you'd been naughty and thought she didn't love you any more?" (1909/1955, p. 67). There is no evidence that these sorts of occasional and rather unlikely threats had much impact on Hans.

The specific threat that Bowlby takes seriously, Olga's threat to leave unless Hans stopped misbehaving, does not itself occur in the case history but is referred to by Hans when speaking with his father. Given the enormous emphasis Bowlby places on this threat in his interpretation of the case, it is worth closely examining the text:

On April 3rd, in the morning he came into bed with me, whereas for the last few days he had not been coming any more and had even seemed to be proud of not doing so. "And why have you come today?" I asked.

HANS: "When I'm not frightened I shan't come any more."

I: So you come in to me because you're frightened?"

HANS: "When I'm not with you I'm frightened; when I'm not in bed with you, then I'm frightened. When I'm not frightened any more I shan't come any more."

I: "So you're fond of me and you feel anxious when you're in your bed in the morning? and that's why you come in to me?"

HANS: "Yes. Why did you tell me I'm fond of *Mummy* and that's why I'm frightened, when I'm fond of you?" ….

I: "When you're alone, you're just anxious for me and come in to me."

HANS: "When you're away, I'm afraid you're not coming home."

I: "And have I ever threatened you that I shan't come home?"

HANS: "Not you, but Mummy. Mummy's told me she won't come back."(He had probably been naughty, and she had threatened to go away.)

I: "She said that because you were naughty."

HANS: Yes."

I: "So you're afraid I'm going away because you were naughty; that's why you come in to me."

(1909/1955, pp. 43–45)

The threat that is supposedly on Hans's mind thus emerges after a long sequence of interactions that make its mention seem more tactical than an expression of something emotionally urgent. Indeed, there is a reading of this interchange in which Hans is mainly trying to placate his father. First, a bit of context is necessary. We know that Max scolded Hans for trying to come into the marital bed ("What do I really scold you for?" [1909/ 1955, p. 82]), and that Hans concluded from this that his father was mad at him for wanting to be with his mother ("You're cross. I know you are. It must be true" [1909/1955, p. 83]). On April 3, having held back for a few days due to his father's objections, Hans likely came into his parents' bedroom in the morning looking for his mother, but she was already gone. To avoid his father's scolding, Hans explains that he is coming into the room because he feels anxious: "When I'm not frightened I shan't come any more." His father's response focuses the discussion on Hans's relationship to Max: "So you come in *to me* because you're frightened?" (emphasis added).

Hans sees an opening to reassure his father that he is not interested only in his mother, and thus escape a scolding:

> When I'm not *with you* I'm frightened; when I'm not in bed *with you*, then I'm frightened .... Why did you tell me I'm fond of *Mummy* and that's why I'm frightened, when *I'm fond of you*?
>
> (emphasis added)

His father responds by asking for an explanation of why Hans is anxious for his father when alone. Hans, thinking quickly, says that he is anxious about his father being away: "When you're away, I'm afraid you're not coming home." Yet, Hans's father has not been away recently, and there is no evidence in the case record suggesting that Hans actually experienced anxiety about his father not returning when he did go away, as the father had during the previous summer. If Hans had expressed such anxiety, surely it would be mentioned as evidence of an Oedipal conflict. It seems instead that in the interchange above Hans made up or exaggerated such anxiety to placate his father and provide the demanded explanation for why he felt anxious when not with his father.

However, Max then challenges the rationality of such a fear: "And have I ever threatened you that I shan't come home?" At this point, Hans, caught in his own web of misleading statements, says that not his father but his mother had threatened to go away. This is a *non sequitur* that does not address his father's question, yet remarkably the ploy works. Max points out that as far as Olga goes, the fear of being left is irrational because Olga made the threat only to control Hans when he was being naughty. He then shifts the point back to himself ("So you're afraid I'm going away because you were naughty; that's why you come in to me"), just as Hans had hoped. The entire interchange about the mother's threat has more the feel of a convoluted rationalization that might placate Hans's father—I'm really fond of you, and Mummy once threatened to leave, so I'm afraid that you might leave, and that's why I need to come into your bed—than of the expression of a traumatic experience that is causing Hans chronic anxiety. It seems a stretch to place as much burden on this passage as Bowlby places on it.

Hans from the Perspective of Contemporary Attachment Theory Categories

Post-Bowlby attachment researchers have greatly expanded the options for labeling attachment patterns beyond Ainsworth's categories of avoidant attachment, in which the child appears emotionally detached and ignores the mother upon reunion, and ambivalent-resistant attachment, in which the child might approach the mother upon reunion but then resists her soothing and perhaps expresses anger. Notably, the resistant-ambivalent pattern is a risk factor for anxiety disorders (Bradley, 2000; Cassidy & Berlin, 1994). Both types of insecure children tend to display exaggerated concern about the attachment figure's availability, yet have difficulty being soothed when the figure is available, and are reluctant to explore when away from the figure's secure base. Additionally, Main and her colleagues (e.g., Main & Solomon, 1986) presented evidence for a more chaotic insecure state, disorganized/disoriented attachment, in which there exists no consistent strategy for coping with separation and reunion. Like many recent writers, I will use "anxious" or "insecure" attachment to refer to any of these Ainsworth-Main categories and other deviations from secure attachment.

Of course, it is impossible to know how Hans might have reacted to the Strange Situation. However, his parents, who were keeping a detailed diary of his sexual development including his relationship to his mother, do not report any unusual anxiety, clinginess, or detachment on Hans's part prior to the case report. Instead, Hans is reported to be a normal, cheerful, robust, and curious boy. Hans is not ambivalent about his mother's soothing, not detached from her, not resistant to affection in her presence or dismissive of her once she offers to hold him, and not overly dependent and without friends. Nor does the case history offer evidence to support the notion that Hans possessed a naturally inhibited temperament, a risk factor for insecure attachment (Kagan, Reznick, & Gibbons, 1989;

Kagan, Snidman, Zentner, & Peterson, 1999). Nor does the evidence suggest that Hans possessed a disorganized pattern to any pronounced degree; his described behavior in seeking his mother's soothing appears well-organized, coherent, purposeful, unambivalent, and thoughtfully defended against his father's objections. Hans actively and with neither ambivalence nor resistance seeks his mother's soothing, engages in cuddling when she is available, and once cuddled is generally calmed down. He is not excessively preoccupied with or dependent on his mother's constant availability, and he readily explores the world and makes friends with whom he plays enthusiastically without her being present. The overall picture is of a child that is both secure and autonomous. In sum, Hans's behavior as portrayed in the parents' diary and in the case study does not offer evidence that Hans's attachment behavior fits any of the above Ainsworth-Main insecure categories.

Although attachment theory was initially applied to infants and very young children, research extended attachment measures to preschool and school-age children (e.g., Cassidy & Marvin, 1992; Crittendon, 1992; Main & Cassidy, 1988; Waters & Deane, 1985). In this work, additional more complex attachment strategies were observed in children Hans's age. In particular, the child may try to control the parent's attention by assuming a judgmental punitive-hostile or cheerful-caregiving role that is more appropriate for a parent than a child (Main & Cassidy, 1988; Moss, Cyr, & Dubois-Comtois, 2004). There is no evidence of a controlling-punitive approach in Hans's reaction to his mother, but Hans's fantasies late in the case history of his caring for children might be interpreted in controlling-caregiving terms. However, the controlling interpretation of Hans's attachment to his mother runs into insuperable problems. A controlling-caregiving strategy is generally a response to failure of the usual attachment soothing-seeking behaviors, leading to a compromise formation: the child does not get direct soothing but gets to stay close to the attachment figure by offering caregiving, and thus receives indirect soothing without explicitly seeking it. Yet, Hans manifests a normal capacity for soothing-seeking and a potentially responsive mother, and when he avails himself of her soothing he gets direct and willing cuddling from her rather than needing to engage in his own caregiving strategy to maintain closeness.

In the last chapter, we saw that Hans's mother suffered from anxiety problems. Research indicates that caregiver anxiety is a risk factor for various forms of insecure attachment and anxiety conditions in the child

(Manassis, 2001; Manassis et al., 1994, 1995), and that if parental anxieties are accompanied by distracted, self-involved states of consciousness, this can confuse or frighten a child as to the parent's availability for protective attachment functions, yielding disorganized attachment behaviors (Hesse & Main, 2006; Main & Hesse, 1990; Main & Solomon, 1986, 1990). However, again, a risk factor is not equivalent to the condition for which it is a risk factor, and the case history contains no evidence of disorganized attachment on Hans's part. Research also indicates that the caregiver's thoughtful perspective on her past influences whether these anxieties are transmitted to the child (Main, 2000a, 2000b), and one must keep in mind that Olga had been in analysis with Freud. Similarly, Hans's actual behavior is inconsistent with a variety of other classifications of insecure attachment (Brennan, Clark, & Shaver, 1998; Main, 2000a, 2000b; Main, Kaplan, & Cassidy, 1985; Shamir-Essakow et al., 2005). Overall, Hans's attachment behavior seems to best fit the secure-autonomous category, perhaps with some relatively mild anxiety and insecurity issues nibbling around the edges.

Bowlby's Integration of Attachment Theory and Behavioral Theory in the Explanation of Childhood Animal Phobias

Bowlby's name is indelibly associated with attachment theory and its empirically supported explanations. It thus may be surprising to learn that, even as Bowlby put forward his revolutionary theory, he was willing to acknowledge the complexity of psychological reality and the limits of his theory and to allow a role for learning theory.

Although Bowlby allowed that "true and limited animal phobia" (1973, p. 289) in the learning-theory sense surely exists, he held that for most cases "the principal source of anxiety lies in the home" (1973, p. 289) and he placed Hans in this category. But, in acknowledging that true cases of conditioned animal phobia exist, Bowlby opens the door to additional theoretical accounts, including of Hans.

Writing in 1973 about the Hans case, Bowlby was aware of the powerful behaviorist critique of Freud's Oedipal account that had been put forward by Wolpe and Rachman (1960), and the one-trial conditioning theory of Hans's anxiety that they had proposed as an alternative. The justification for Wolpe and Rachman's behaviorist analysis of Hans's phobia was the fact, emerging late in Hans's analysis, that Hans had developed his fear of horses immediately after a terrifying experience in which he saw an accident in which a horse that was pulling a buswagon fell down in the street, kicking and whinnying:

> HANS: "I'm most afraid too when a bus comes along."
> I: "Why? Because it's so big?"
> HANS: "No. Because once a horse in a bus fell down."
> I: "When?"
> HANS: "Once when I went out with Mummy ... "
>
> (This was subsequently confirmed by his mother.) ...
>
> I: "You had your nonsense already at that time?"
> HANS: "No. I only got it then. When the horse in the bus fell down, it gave me such a fright, really! That was when I got the nonsense."
> (1909/1955, pp. 49–50)

Freud dismissed the horse accident as a mere "precipitating cause" that was not traumatic in itself and that got its phobia-triggering power from symbolic links to Hans's Oedipus complex:

> We have learned the immediate precipitating cause after which the phobia broke out. This was when the boy saw a big heavy horse fall down; ... Hans at that moment perceived a wish that his father might fall down in the same way—and be dead.
> (1909/1955, pp. 51–52)

Wolpe and Rachman (1960) rejected Freud's Oedipal theory as being without persuasive evidence and elevated the horse accident into the prime and virtually sole cause of Hans's phobia, along with some preparatory incidents that had sensitized Hans to horse danger. Their theory of Hans's one-trial fear conditioning had a major influence on subsequent behavioral theorizing about phobias.

Bowlby was well aware that transient animal phobias like Hans's are so common in children that it is highly unlikely that anxious attachment is linked to them all. He summarized his review of the literature on the frequency of childhood animal phobias by observing that in one major study animals were commonly reported by parents to elicit fear in children of all age groups, that rates of such fears at Hans's age were over 40% in that study and approaching 30% in other studies, and that in experimental situations animals are the most fear-arousing stimulus in children. Bowlby acknowledged that behavioral learning-theory approaches can help in understanding some animal phobias, and he thus accepted that anxious attachment is not necessary for development of a phobia, citing evidence that there are some individuals who have intense fear of some kind of animal but who do not have any other form of emotional disturbance.

Bowlby takes an eclectic view of the etiology of animal phobias in two ways. First, he recognizes behavioral pathways to phobias other than just traumatic frights. These include modeling on someone else's fear, such as when a child's parent or other adult habitually react with fear to a particular type of animal, being warned about a danger, or just hearing a frightening story.

More fundamentally, for some animal phobias Bowlby accepted learning-theory explanations of the type proposed by Wolpe and Rachman (1960) in their analysis of the Hans case, and explicitly rejected the claim that attachment anxieties are always involved in phobias: "There is no disposition to argue here that every case of animal phobia ... is but the tip of an iceberg ... which comprises intense fear of losing an attachment figure" (1973, p. 289). Some cases, he acknowledged, result from a particularly frightening experience, such as being attacked by an animal.

Bowlby cites evidence that in many cases when an individual is unusually afraid of a specific situation, the fear can be traced back to a particular incident of a similar nature. For example, Newson and Newson (1968) state that when one explores a child's previous experiences, a fear that initially seems inexplicable is often seen as reasonable even if exaggerated. Bowlby cites examples from other authors as well that are cases of one-trial fear conditioning of the kind that Wolpe and Rachman attribute to Hans. These include, for example, a child afraid of mud after her feet got trapped in mud; a child afraid of water after falling in a river; and a child afraid of balloons after an operation with a gas balloon used for the anesthetic. Bowlby allows that such cases are simply a matter of overgeneralizing. However, with regard to why some individuals become phobic after a fright while others do not, Bowlby speculates that a frightening experience will have more phobic potential if a child is without access to his attachment figure: "compound situations of which one component is being alone seems especially likely" (1973, p. 197). Bowlby held that the ongoing availability of an attachment figure after a frightening incident modulates the child's response: "when an individual is confident that an attachment figure will be available to him whenever he desires it, that person will be much less prone to either intense or chronic fear" (1973, p. 202).

These observations of Bowlby's will provide what I will argue in the next chapter is a more evidentially supportable explanation of Hans's vulnerability to anxiety. Hans was with his mother when the frightening incident with the horse occurred, but he was alone with his fear when sent to his bedroom at night and, as we shall see in the next chapter, he had to contend with obstacles to his seeking soothing from his mother. Recall Hans's later anxious plea, after being initially calmed down by coaxing with his mother, that "The horse'll come into the room" (1909/1955, p. 24). Freud takes this as a clue that the horse symbolism must refer to the father who, unlike a horse, can indeed come into Hans's room. Yet, at night Hans is alone in his bedroom, and his fear increases. "The horse'll come into the room" is an expression of his increased horse fear when alone in his bedroom without the availability of his mother—and knowing that if he goes to his mother for comforting, his father will not allow it.

In sum, rather than rejecting behaviorist notions out of hand as inconsistent with attachment-theory doctrine, Bowlby adopted an eclectic understanding of the sources of anxiety, admirably resisting the tendency to claim the universal applicability of his own theory. Bowlby's eclectic understanding that emphasizes anxious attachment in the etiology of phobias but also allows for behavioral determinants opens up possibilities for multitheoretical explanations of Hans's phobia that may better fit the data of the case record than any unicausal theory.

Is the Function of Hans's Phobia to Stay Close to His Mother?

Surprisingly, there is one aspect of the explanation of Hans's phobia that Bowlby and Freud share. They both claim that the real purpose of the phobia was to keep Hans close to his mother. For Freud, the "closeness-to-mother" understanding of Hans's phobia allows Hans to partially satisfy his Oedipal yearning and thus allows Freud to defend his theory of symptoms as compromise formations in which repression yields both symptoms and offsetting gratification.

The content of his phobia was such as to impose a very great measure of restriction upon his freedom of movement, and that was its purpose .... [H]owever clear may have been the victory in Hans's phobia of the forces that were opposed to sexuality, nevertheless, since such an illness is in its very nature a compromise, this cannot have been all that the repressed instincts obtained. After all, Hans's phobia of horses was an obstacle to his going into the street, and could serve as a means of allowing him to stay at home with his beloved mother. In this way, therefore, his affection for his mother triumphantly achieved its aim. In consequence of his phobia, the lover clung to the object of his love.

(1909/1955, pp. 139–140)

For Bowlby, the "closeness-to-mother" hypothesis allows Hans to achieve soothing proximity to his mother that assuages his anxious attachment. This approach to childhood animal phobias derives from Bowlby's analysis of school phobia or "school refusal." Bowlby argued that the underlying problem in school refusal was worry about the mother being safe and present at home when the child returns, so that the child's anxiety about going to school is not a fear of school per se but rather a fear of leaving home and leaving mother. So, for Bowlby, school refusal is generally about staying close to mother.

Bowlby—perhaps too hastily, in my view, and without the evidential support that is available in regard to school refusal—took the function of animal phobias to be analogous to school refusal. He thus interpreted Hans's reluctance to leave home due to his fear of horses as really a fear of being away from his mother. Bowlby thus approvingly quotes Hans's father saying of Hans that Hans's motive is his fear of not finding his mother at home. This interpretation strengthens Bowlby's case because on its face a horse phobia does not seem to be about attachment.

The "closeness to mother" hypothesis in both Bowlby's and Freud's cases is devoid of direct evidential support. Testing this hypothesis against the manifest case evidence, one quickly sees that the thesis is contradicted in two directions.

On the one hand, when Hans is out with his mother and there are horses around, he experiences full-blown fear despite being in her presence: "Next day his mother took him with her into town and he was very much frightened in the streets" (1909/1955, p. 31). Bowlby ignores this anomaly. Freud recognizes the problem and tries to explain why this should be the case. He is forced to suggest a convoluted ad hoc hypothesis that the anxiety has now become independent of the libidinal goal of being with his mother, even as he continues to insist that the neurosis's function is closeness to the mother:

> He wanted to stay with his mother and to coax with her; his recollection that he had also been separated from her at the time of the baby's birth may also, as his father suggests, have contributed to his longing. It soon became evident that his anxiety was no longer reconvertible into longing; he was afraid even when his mother went with him.
>
> (1909/1955, p. 114)

On the other hand, when Hans is out with his father and without his mother and there are no horses around, he is okay and able to travel anxiety-free with his father to visit his grandmother in Lainz:

> [H]e could not be induced to go out, or at any rate no more than on to the balcony. Every Sunday he went with me to Lainz, because on that day there is not much traffic in the streets, and it is only a short way to the station.
>
> (1909/1955, p. 29)

> Hans had promised to go with me to Lainz .... He resisted at first, but finally went with me all the same. He obviously felt all right in the street, as there was not much traffic, and said: 'How sensible! God's done away with horses now'.
>
> (1909/1955, p. 31)

The hypothesis that the function of Hans's anxiety is to keep him close to his mother thus fails the evidential test at the most elementary level. This conclusion is consistent with Bowlby's acceptance of the behavioral notion that extreme fright can yield a phobia with no need for further meaning such as closeness to mother.

There is a problem here of correlation being confused with causation. When one's mother is generally at home, there is bound to be an initial correlation between being afraid of going out because one is afraid of horses and staying near to one's mother. Moreover, when a child is frequently afraid because of what was at that time a common stimulus such as horses, the child will often seek the comfort and soothing of its mother, so there will be a correlation between the fear and being close to her. However, correlation is not causality. The evidence is that Hans is afraid of horses, not of being away from his mother, except of course that he wants to know that when he is anxious and needs soothing she will be available. Recall that Bowlby accepts that behavioral theory is correct that there is sometimes one-trial conditioning of fear. This implies that Bowlby's extension of the "derived fear" explanation of school refusal to animal phobias is unwarranted. Sometimes, a horse phobia is just a horse phobia.

Conclusion: The Need for Further Explanation of Hans's Disposition to Anxiety

Applying attachment theory to the Hans case, Bowlby hypothesizes that Hans's anxiety disorder was a manifestation of anxious attachment due to his mother's threats to leave when he was naughty, rather than suppressed Oedipal sexual desire for his mother. In getting us to see the Hans case through the lens of attachment theory, Bowlby provides a fresh view of the case that is both more plausible on its face than the Oedipal theory and illuminating of myriad details overlooked or underemphasized by Freud.

However, Bowlby's evidence is modest and there are gaps in his explanation of Hans's phobia. Direct evidence of Hans's anxious attachment is minimal, at best consisting of Hans's persistent visits to his mother's bed in the morning. However, Hans's desire to cuddle with his mother upon waking up alone in his newly separate bedroom could also be an expression of normal-range situational attachment distress when afraid. No generalized anxious-attachment problem of significant magnitude is at all manifest in Hans's overall behavior in the case report—quite the contrary. So, the explanation of Hans's disposition to an anxiety disorder based on attachment theory remains elusive, based on the evidence Bowlby provides.

As to Bowlby's "threat" theory of the genesis of Hans's anxious attachment, evidence regarding the frequency, recency, and nature of such threats, as well as how seriously Hans took them, is lacking. The timing of the phobia remains unexplained because the threats appear to have started long before. Most problematically, threats are quite common and at most are a risk factor for, not a pathognomonic indicator of, anxious attachment.

The overall evidence of the case record and the Archives interviews together suggests that Olga's sensitivity to Hans was at least approximately "good enough," within the evolved boundaries of an "average expectable mother" who provides an environment that allows for her son's normal maturation, even if not an exceptional mother. It is thus understandable that Hans, whatever incipient anxieties he may have had, did not display a classic pattern of overdependent or anxious attachment in the case history, and nothing in the Archives interviews hints at such a problem. Contemporary research suggests that caregiver sensitivity and responsiveness is central to a child's attachment security, and such features have been found to be stable over time (Goldberg et al., 1994). To the degree that the case history indicates a predominance of secure attachment on Hans's part, this suggests that the mother had offered good-enough mothering in the attachment-theoretic sense to Hans for some time.

Despite the presence of risk factors that *might* cause Hans to have anxious attachment and thus to have a disposition to develop an anxiety disorder, the actual presence of anxious attachment is not supported by the case data. There thus remains an explanatory gap that justifies a search for missing pieces of an attachment-theoretic explanation for Hans's phobia. I will explore the possibility that Hans's experiences within his family at the time of the phobia's onset yielded not a problematic working model of attachment, as Bowlby assumes, but rather direct disruption of the attachment relationship, yielding substantial situational attachment distress and predisposing Hans to react as severely as he did to the horse accident. As Bowlby implicitly suggests in his comments on behavioral theory, these predisposing attachment-theoretic factors likely interacted with the process of one-trial conditioning in response to Hans's stressful witnessing of the horse accident, forming the basis for a plausible combined account of the genesis of Hans's intense phobia.

Bowlby's view allows for four potential causal factors at work in creating a child's anxiety or distress: (1) normal situational anxiety in response to an external danger or stressor; (2) one-trial behaviorally conditioned phobic-level anxiety in response to an overwhelming external stressor or danger, perhaps facilitated by anxious attachment; (3) normal attachment anxiety or what I am calling "situational attachment distress" when a child is trying to gain access to his attachment figure and finds the figure is unavailable or the pathway blocked, precluding the soothing that reduces anxiety; and (4) separation anxiety that is part of chronic anxious attachment due to a problematic working model. Further examination of the Hans case that draws on this multifaceted perspective will, I believe, help to resolve the remaining puzzles about Hans's phobia.

References

Ainsworth, M. D. S. (1979). Infant-mother attachment. *American Psychologist, 34*, 932–937.

Ainsworth, M. D. S., Blehar, M. C., Waters, E., & Wall, S. (1978). *Patterns of attachment: A psychological study of the strange situation.* Hillsdale, NJ: Erlbaum.

Ainsworth, M. D. S., & Wittig, B. A. (1969). Attachment and exploratory behaviour of one-year-olds in a strange situation. In B. A. Foss (Ed.), *Determinants of infant behaviour* (Vol. *4*). London: Methuen.

Bowlby, J. (1958). The nature of the child's tie to his mother. *International Journal of Psycho-Analysis, 39*, 350–373.

Bowlby, J. (1959). Separation anxiety. *International Journal of Psycho-Analysis, 41*, 89–113.

Bowlby, J. (1960). Grief and mourning in infancy. *The Psychoanalytic Study of the Child, 15*, 3–39.

Bowlby, J. (1973). *Attachment and loss (Vol. 2): Separation: Anxiety and anger.* New York, NY: Basic Books.

Bowlby, J. (1980). *Attachment and loss (Vol. 3): Loss, sadness and depression.* New York, NY: Basic Books.

Bowlby, J. (1982). *Attachment and loss (Vol. 1): Attachment* (Rev. ed.). New York, NY: Basic Books.

Bradley, S. (2000). *Affect regulation and the development of psychopathology.* New York, NY: Guilford.

Brennan, K. A., Clark, C. L., & Shaver, P. R. (1998). Self-report measurement of adult romantic attachment: An integrative overview. In J. A. Simpson & W. S. Rholes (Eds.), *Attachment theory and close relationships* (pp. 46–76). New York, NY: Guilford Press.

Cassidy, J., & Berlin, L. J. (1994). The insecure/ambivalent pattern of attachment: Theory and research. *Child Development, 65*, 971–991.

Cassidy, J., & Marvin, R. (1992). *Attachment organization in 3- and 4-year-olds: Procedures and coding manual.* Unpublished manuscript, Attachment Working Group, Department of Psychology, University of Virginia, Charlottesville.

Crittendon, P. M. (1992). Quality of attachment in the preschool years. *Development and Psychopathology, 4*, 209–241.

Duhn L. (2010). The importance of touch in the development of attachment. *Advances in Neonatal Care, 10*(6), 294–300.

Duschinsky R. (2015). The emergence of the disorganized/disoriented (D) attachment classification, 1979–1982. *History of psychology, 18*(1), 32–46.

Eagle, E. (1997). Attachment and psychoanalysis. *British Journal of Medical Psychology, 70*, 217–229.

Fisher, H. E., Aron, A., Mashek, D., Li, H., & Brown, L. L. (2002). Defining the brain systems of lust, romantic attraction and attachment. *Archives of Sexual Behavior, 31*, 413–419.

Frankiel, R. V. (1992). Analysed and unanalysed themes in the treatment of Little Hans. *International Review of Psycho-Analysis, 19*, 323–333.

Freud, A. (1960). Discussion of John Bowlby's paper. *The Psychoanalytic Study of the Child, 15*, 53–62.

Freud, S. (1955). Analysis of a phobia in a five-year-old boy. In J. Strachey (Ed. & Trans.), *The standard edition of the complete psychological works of Sigmund Freud* (Vol. *10*, pp. 1–150). London, UK: Hogarth Press. (Original work published 1909.)

Goidani, N. (2020). How threats damage your child's personality and self-esteem. *Wow Parenting*,April 24, 2020. Accessed 10/3/20 at https://wowparenting.com/blog/parents-use-threats-harm-children/.

Goldberg, S., MacKay-Soroka, S., & Rochester, M. (1994). Affect, attachment, and maternal responsiveness. *Infant Behavior and Development, 17*, 335–340.

Granqvist, P., Sroufe, L. A., Dozier, M., Hesse, E., Steele, M., van Ijzendoorn, M., … Duschinsky, R. (2017). Disorganized attachment in infancy: a review of the phenomenon and its implications for clinicians and policy-makers. *Attachment & Human Development, 19*(6), 534–558.

Hesse, E., & Main, M. (2006). Frightened, threatening, and dissociative parental behavior in low-risk samples: Description, discussion, and interpretations. *Development and Psychopathology, 18*, 309–343.

Juri, L. J. (2003). Revisiting Freud in the light of attachment theory: Little Hans' father – Oedipal rival or attachment figure? Cortina, M., & Marrone, M. (Eds.), *Attachment Theory and the Psychoanalytic Process* (pp. 227–241). New York, NY: Wiley & Sons.

Kagan, J., Reznick, J. S., & Gibbons, J. (1989). Inhibited and uninhibited types of children. *Child Development, 60*, 838–845.

Kagan, J., Snidman, N., Zentner, M., & Peterson, E. (1999). Infant temperament and anxious symptoms in school age children. *Development and Psychopathology, 11*, 209–224.

Main, M. (1979). The ultimate causation of some infant attachment phenomena: Further answers, further phenomena, and further questions. *Behavioral and Brain Sciences, 2*, 640–643.

Main, M. (1981). Avoidance in the service of attachment. In K. Immelman, G. Barlow, L. Petrinovitch, & M. Main (Eds.), *Behavioral development* (pp. 651–693). Cambridge, UK: Cambridge University Press.

Main, M. (1990). Cross-cultural studies of attachment organization: Recent studies, changing methodologies, and the concept of conditional strategies. *Human Development, 33*, 48–61.

Main, M. (2000a). The adult attachment interview: Fear, attention, safety and discourse processes. *Journal of the American Psychoanalytic Association, 48*, 1055–1095.

Main, M. (2000b). The organized categories of infant, child, and adult attachment: flexible vs. inflexible attention under attachment-related stress. *Journal of the American Psychoanalytic Association, 48*, 1055–1096.

Main, M., & Cassidy, J. (1988). Categories of response to reunion with the parent at age 6 predictable from infant attachment classifications and stable over a 1-month period. *Developmental Psychology, 24*, 415–426.

Main, M., & Hesse, E. (1990). Parent's unresolved traumatic experiences are related to infant disorganized/disoriented attachment status: Is frightened and/or frightening parental behavior the linking mechanism? In M. Greenberg, D. Cicchetti, & E. M. Cummings (Eds.), *Attachment in the preschool years: Theory, research, and intervention* (pp. 161–182). Chicago, IL: University of Chicago Press.

Main, M., Kaplan, N., & Cassidy, J. (1985). Security in infancy, childhood, and adulthood: A move to the level of representation. In I. Bretherton & E. Waters (Eds.), *Growing points of attachment theory and research* (pp. 66–104). Chicago, IL: Chicago University Press.

Main, M., & Solomon, J. (1986). Discovery of an insecure-disorganized/disoriented attachment pattern. In T. B. Brazelton & M. Yogman (Eds.), *Affective development in infancy* (pp. 95–124). Norwood, NJ: Albex.

Main, M., & Solomon, J. (1990). Procedures for identifying infants as disorganized/disoriented during the Ainsworth strange situation. In M. Greenberg, D. Cicchetti, & E. Cummings (Eds.), *Attachment in the preschool years: Theory, research, and intervention* (pp. 121–160). Chicago, IL: University of Chicago Press.

Main, M., & Stadtman, J. (1981). Infant response to rejection of physical contact by the mother: Aggression, avoidance, and conflict. *Journal of the American Academy of Child Psychiatry, 20*, 292–307.

Manassis, K. (2001). Child–parent relations: Attachment and anxiety disorders. In W. K. Silverman & P. D. Treffers (Eds.), *Anxiety disorders in children and adolescents: Research, assessment and intervention* (pp. 255–272). New York, NY: Cambridge University Press.

Manassis, K., Bradley, S., Goldberg, S., Hood, J., & Swinson, R. P. (1994). Attachment in mothers with anxiety disorders and their children. *Journal of the American Academy of Child and Adolescent Psychiatry, 33*, 1106–1113.

Manassis, K., Bradley, S., Goldberg, S., Hood, J., & Swinson, R. P. (1995). Behavioral inhibition, attachment and anxiety in children of mothers with anxiety disorders. *Canadian Journal of Psychiatry, 40*, 87–92.

Moss, E., Cyr, C., & Dubois-Comtois, K. (2004). Attachment at early school age and developmental risk: Examining family contexts and behavior problems of controlling-caregiving, controlling-punitive, and behaviorally disorganized children. *Developmental Psychology, 40*, 519–532.

Newson, J. & Newson, E. (1968). *Four years old in an urban community.* London: Allen & Unwin.

Schur, M. (1960). Discussion of John Bowlby's paper. *The Psychoanalytic Study of the Child, 15*, 63–84.

Shamir-Essakow, G., Ungerer, J. A., & Rapee, R. M. (2005). Attachment, behavioral inhibition, and anxiety in preschool children. *Journal of Abnormal Child Psychology, 33*, 131–143.

Spitz, R. (1960). Discussion of John Bowlby's paper. *The Psychoanalytic Study of the Child, 15*, 85–94.

Sroufe, A., & Waters, E. (1977). Attachment as an organizational construct. *Child Development, 48*, 1184–1199.

Wakefield, J. C. (2007a). Little Hans and attachment theory: Bowlby's hypothesis reconsidered in light of new evidence from the Freud Archives. *The Psychoanalytic Study of the Child, 62*, 61–91.

Wakefield, J. C. (2007b). Attachment and sibling rivalry in Little Hans: The 'phantasy of the two giraffes' reconsidered. *Journal of the American Psychoanalytic Association, 55,* 821–849.

Wakefield, J. C. (2022). *Freud's argument for the Oedipus complex: A philosophy of science analysis of the case of Little Hans.* New York: Routledge.

Waters, E., & Deane, K. (1985). Defining and assessing individual differences in attachment relationships: Q-methodology and the organization of behavior in infancy and early childhood. In I. Bretherton & E. Waters (Eds.), *Growing points in attachment theory and research. Monographs of the Society for Research in Child Development, 50* (1–2, Serial No. 209), pp. 41–65.

Wolpe, J., & Rachman, S. (1960). Psychoanalytic "evidence": A critique based on Freud's case of little Hans. *Journal of Nervous and Mental Disease, 131(2),* 135–148.

Chapter 4

Oedipal Power/Knowledge

The Sexualization of Attachment and the Regulation of Mother–Son Affection

In this chapter, I ask: When the Oedipus complex was introduced into Little Hans's family system by Hans's father, Max Graf, what role did it come to play in the Graf family's day-to-day interactions and how was it exploited for purposes of marital and family power? In particular, how did the intrusion of Oedipal theory influence the relationship between Hans and his mother, Olga Honig Graf? And, how do these effects on family relations intersect with an understanding of the etiology of Hans's phobia?

I will argue that careful analysis of the case material reveals a previously unrecognized but crucial detail: Hans's father, Max, motivated by his Oedipal-inspired concerns about Hans and Olga's cuddling, started disrupting Hans's attachment relationship to his mother several months *before* the onset of Hans's phobia, causing Hans considerable anxiety. This discovery provides a plausible and entirely novel explanation for why Hans was disposed to develop an anxiety disorder, and opens the case to a radical reinterpretation solidly anchored in the text.

Forms of Power in the Hans Case

In exploring Oedipal power/knowledge in the Graf family, it is important to distinguish this form of power that is due to the acceptance of Oedipal theory from other forms of power operating in the family due to various roles associated with psychoanalysis. For example, there is Freud's power over Hans's father, based on the relationship of famous expert and mentor to his follower. This power is expressed by Freud's direct instructions to Max on how to conduct the analysis, by Max's submitting his case notes to Freud for Freud's judgment but not the other way around, and by Freud's right to override Max's judgment in his position as the originator,

DOI: 10.4324/9780203817124-4

and thus unquestioned authoritative interpreter, of the Oedipal theory's implications.

Another source of power is Max's power due to his position as analyst of Hans and thus a privileged mediator between Hans's statements and the analyst's interpretation whose associations to Hans's material can shape the direction of analysis. For example, Max interprets Hans's giraffe dream or fantasy—in which Hans approaches a crumpled giraffe and takes it away from a protesting large giraffe—in terms of an Oedipal bedroom scene in which Hans approaches his mother in bed despite Max's protests. I (Wakefield, 2007) have argued that the dream might also be interpreted in terms of a common situation in which a parent looks on with concern as an older child approaches and grasps a baby. However, Max would likely not have witnessed such a common domestic scene. Because Max is the analyst, Max's interpretation is based on *his* associations to Hans's fantasy, which partly defines the space of possible interpretations. Olga is not heard from, even though Olga may know more about the scenes of Hans's everyday life than Max does.

There are many other forms of power impinging on the Graf family. I will be concerned in the remainder of this chapter with the one particular form of power that Foucault calls *power/knowledge*. This is a form of power that is constituted by the acceptance of a certain scientific theory as true. In this case, the theory is the Oedipal theory. Oedipal power/knowledge refers specifically to the effect of the acceptance of the theory on potentially reformulating power structures in family relationships. I will argue that the issue of Oedipal power/knowledge most clearly manifested in the Hans case and most momentous for understanding Hans's phobia is the struggle between Max and Olga over whether Hans should be allowed to cuddle in bed in the morning or evening with his mother when he is anxious.

The Graf Family's Struggle Over Hans's Access to Max and Olga's Marital Bed

One of the most remarkable things about the clash between Bowlby and Freud over the Hans case is that they, along with subsequent interpreters of the case, share a crucial and inexplicable blind spot in their accounts. They fail to identify or even mention the fact that Hans's phobia develops during a period when Hans's father, Max, was actively and regularly attempting to block Hans's access to his mother for soothing when he was anxious. Max does this primarily by stopping Hans from entering into bed with his mother for affection when he is anxious in the morning or evening. I first look in this section at Max's actions after the phobia's onset as documented in the case report, and then in the next section argue that we can infer that such actions were occurring before the phobia's onset, as well.

Such protection of the marital bed from intrusion by children was not part of the doctrines of the nineteenth-century anti-masturbation campaign. The fear then was that a child might masturbate when left alone in bed at night, a fear still played out in the Hans case in the parents' attempts to stop Hans from masturbating at night by placing him in a restraining sack. However, the masturbation campaign included no prohibition of parent–child cosleeping and intimacy, and in some cases physicians even advised parents to sleep with their children to prevent masturbation. If there is a novel exercise of power that could be considered Oedipal power/knowledge in the sense that it is a form of power made possible by the acceptance of the Oedipal theory, Max's protection of the marital bed from Hans would seem to be it.

We know that from around the time of Hans's phobia's onset, Hans sometimes went into his mother's bed in the morning for some cuddling before the day began: "On about January 5th he came into his mother's bed in the morning" (Freud, 1909/1955, p. 23). (Note that sometimes Max refers to the parents' bed as "our" bed and sometimes he distinguishes the mother's bed versus his bed. It was common at that time for a couple's bed to consist of two single beds pushed together, so assuming this was the case, either description could be appropriate.) The practice of Hans coming into his parents' bed, and specifically Olga's "too frequent readiness to take [Hans] into her bed" (1909/1955, p. 28), is also mentioned by Freud as one reason why Max blames Olga for Hans's neurosis. So, Max already at the time of the phobia's onset saw Hans's coming into bed to cuddle and his wife's willingness to provide such comforting to Hans as potentially pathogenic.

Some way into the case record it becomes clear that Max not only disapproves but persistently attempts to prevent bed-cuddling contact between Hans and Olga. As a consequence, there was an ongoing struggle between Max on one side and Olga and Hans on the other over whether Hans should be allowed to cuddle with his mother in bed in the morning when he felt anxious, even for a few minutes. A moment particularly revealing of the ongoing struggle over Hans's time in bed with his mother is the interpretation of a dream (or possibly a fantasy) of Hans's that causes him to come into his parents' bedroom at night. He describes the dream as follows:

> In the night there was a big giraffe in the room and a crumpled one; and the big one called out because I took the crumpled one away from it. Then it stopped calling out; and then I sat down on top of the crumpled one.
>
> (Freud, 1909/1955, p. 37)

Max interprets the dream as reproducing a frequent event:

> 'The big giraffe is myself … and the crumpled giraffe is my wife ….
>
> 'The whole thing is a reproduction of a scene which has been gone through almost every morning for the last few days. Hans always comes in to us in the early morning, and my wife cannot resist taking him into bed with her for a few minutes. Thereupon I always begin to warn her not to take him into bed with her ('the big one called out because I'd taken the crumpled one away from it'); and she answers now and then, rather irritated, no doubt, that it's all nonsense, that after all one minute is of no importance, and so on. Then Hans stays with her a little while. ('Then the big giraffe stopped calling out; and then I sat down on top of the crumpled one.')
>
> (Freud, 1909/1955, p. 39)

Freud agrees with the father's interpretation: "His father recognized the phantasy as a reproduction of a bedroom scene which used to take place in the morning between the boy and his parents" (1909/1955, p. 121). For Freud, this struggle between Hans and his father over access to his mother's bed expresses the sexual desire that underlies Hans's anxiety:

> But the whole thing was a phantasy of defiance connected with his satisfaction at the triumph over his father's resistance. 'Call out as much as you like! But Mummy takes me into bed all the same, and Mummy belongs to me!'
>
> (1909/1955, pp. 39–40)

The critical point for present purposes is the revelation that "almost every morning" there is a struggle of this kind between Max on one side and Olga and Hans on the other over the issue of whether Hans can crawl into bed and get a bit of cuddling with his mother before the day starts, especially when he is feeling anxious. It is not clear exactly why Hans felt anxious in his bedroom in the morning, but he had recently been moved into his own bedroom from his parents' bedroom, and waking up alone in his own bed in his own room was a relatively new experience for him. The interpretation of the giraffe dream reveals that it was not only Hans coming into his parents' bed but also Max's attempts to stop him from doing so that were frequently occurring during the time of the treatment.

After the giraffe dream in late March, there was a period during which Hans within weeks was ill with the flu and had an operation to remove his tonsils, so not much occurred in the analysis. The reports for the month of April which are the heart of the analysis reveal a constant ongoing struggle over Hans coming into the parents' bed, even when—or perhaps especially when—he feels frightened. For example: April 3, "in the morning he came into bed with me ... 'And why have you come today?' I asked. 'Hans: 'When I'm not frightened I shan't come any more'" (1909/1955, p. 43); April 5th, "Hans came in to our bedroom again, and was sent back to his own bed. I said to him: 'As long as you come into our room in the mornings, your fear of horses won't get better.' He was defiant, however, and replied: 'I shall come in all the same, even if I am afraid'" (1909/1955, p. 47); and April 11, "This morning Hans came into our room again and was sent away, as he always has been for the last few days" (1909/1955, p. 65).

As in the giraffe dream interpretation, Max's singular focus on his struggle with Hans over the marital bed is evidenced in his interpretation of Hans's "borer" fantasy:

'Later on, he began: "Daddy, I thought something: *I was in the bath, and then the plumber came and unscrewed it. Then he took a big borer and stuck it into my stomach*."' Hans's father translated this phantasy as follows: '"I was in bed with Mummy. Then Daddy came and drove me away. With his big penis he pushed me out of my place by Mummy."'

(1909/1955, p. 65)

On April 21, Max observes that Hans becomes afraid when two horses pull-ing a carriage are "proud," that is, they are strutting under tight reins with heads high, which makes Hans afraid they will fall down. The ensuing interchange reveals that Hans, not unreasonably, believes that his father must be angry at him when the father stops Hans from coming into bed to cuddle with his mother. This implies that the father's attempts to keep Hans from coming into the parents' bed were continuing. It also makes clear that the father's blocking of Hans's efforts to be with his mother triggers Hans's fear as well as anger and aggressive fantasies toward his father:

I asked him who it really was that was so proud.

> HE: "You are, when I come into bed with Mummy."
> I: "So you want me to fall down?"
> HE: "Yes .... then I'll be able to be alone with Mummy for a little bit at all events ....
> I: "So you'd like to go to Mummy?"
> HE: "Yes."
> I: "What do I really scold you for?"
> HE: "I don't know."(!!)
> I: "Why?"
> HE: "Because you're cross."
> I: "But that's not true."
> H: "Yes, it *is* true. You're cross. I know you are. It must be true."

Evidently, therefore, my explanation that only *little* boys come into bed with their Mummies and that *big* ones sleep in their own beds had not impressed him very much.

(1909/1955, pp. 82–83)

One might speculate about any ulterior motives Max might have in exer-cising Oedipal power/knowledge to keep Hans from cuddling with Olga. As has been observed by others, Freud completely ignores what we now call the "Laius complex," the father's jealousy of the little boy's place in the heart and attentions of his wife, and the father's resentment of not having his wife to himself. As marital happiness has become more focused on the partners' mutual emotional and sexual satisfaction, the constraints posed by children have come to feel more burdensome, for children detract from marital freedom. In Max's case, we know from the Archives interview that he was resentful of his wife's conflicts about sex, so protecting the marital bed to attain some privacy and the sexual possibilities that it might bring may have seemed particularly important to him. However, beyond such speculations and the facts of his actions in keeping Hans from Olga's bed, there is no broader case to be made from the Hans case materials that Max was particularly jealous of Hans. It is only clear that his actions of imposing his will on Olga and Hans against their wishes were rationalized by Oedipal theory and driven at least in part by his fear of the Oedipal nature of Hans's longing for Olga.

Despite Hans repeatedly linking his need to see his mother to reducing his fear, not once in the entire case history does Freud consider whether the father's blocking of Hans's access to his mother might itself be etiologically relevant to Hans's anxiety. He and Max focus on the mother's affection as pathogenic despite the fact that a major outlet for such affection has been blocked. Freud approvingly says of the father's actions that, despite Hans's desire to cling to the object of his love, "steps had been taken to make him innocuous" (1909/1955, p. 140). When Freud totes up all the challenges to Hans's erotic needs that ultimately yield the phobia— including loss of friends from Gmunden when the family returns to Vienna, loss of friends where he used to live before his family moves to a new apartment, being moved from his parents' bedroom into his own room, his privations due to the arrival of his little sister and the degree of deprivation of his mother's attention that brings about, and other such factors—Freud does not mention the father's attempts to prevent Hans from sharing intimate moments with his mother as a candidate factor. This might make sense if, as it might seem from the case study and from the discussion so far, the father's efforts occurred as a reaction to the phobia and were aimed at treating a problem that had already been caused by other factors. In the next section, I will argue that in fact Max's actions in this regard started several months before the phobia occurred, making it a candidate cause of Hans's heightened vulnerability to anxiety and thus a potential causal factor in Hans's phobia.

The Bedtime Struggle Began Before the Onset of the Phobia

I am now going to argue that Max's application of Oedipal power/ knowledge by blocking Hans's access to his mother's soothing was not just something that occurred during the course of the phobia but is likely one of the causes of Hans's phobia due to the situational attachment distress it created. By "caused" here, I mean not merely that it sustained and amplified the phobia when it already existed by adding to Hans's distress, but that, as an efficient cause, it contributed to creating a disposition to develop the phobia in the first place.

However, causes cannot come after effects. So, in order to argue that the father's control of Hans's cuddling with his mother in bed was a cause of Hans's intensifying anxiety and disposition to develop a phobia, I must first show that the father's practice of such control over Hans's relationship with his mother started prior to the phobia. This is not immediately obvious from the case record. The father's efforts after the phobia begins are explicitly noted, but what was occurring prior to the phobia's outbreak is not as well documented and must be inferred. Alternative hypotheses would be that Max only came to disapprove of Olga's time cuddling in bed with Hans and saw it as pathogenic after the onset of the phobia in reaction to it, or that Max disapproved of and was concerned about Olga's cuddling with Hans prior to the phobia's onset and thus immediately blamed her for the phobia but took no direct action to stop the practice until the phobia developed and he saw his fears realized. The evidence will allow us to reject both of these rival hypotheses.

Note that arguing for a causal hypothesis is not to say that Max's prohibitions were not harmful or problematic after the phobia began. It is ironic and sad that during Hans's phobia the Oedipal theory caused Hans's father to believe that Hans's cuddling with his mother in bed would make Hans's anxiety worse. So, he protected the marital bed from Hans and thereby blocked the major source of soothing and reduction in anxiety that was available to Hans. The father's actions may well have contributed to the maintenance of the phobia by increasing Hans's distress. In the face of his father's frustratingly absurd logic, Hans, who is coming into his mother's bed *because* he is afraid, can only answer with equal absurdity, "I shall come in all the same, even if I am afraid" (1909/1955, p. 47). But, the father's intervention during the phobia's course does not imply that the same intervention was occurring prior to the phobia and so is largely irrelevant to evaluating the hypothesis that Max's actions may have partly caused Hans's phobia.

So, is there reason to believe that Max was already interfering in Hans's attachment behaviors in the time before the phobia appeared, and preferably at a time reasonably close to the phobia's outbreak? The case study's detailed portrayal of events begins after the phobia emerged, so what was happening prior to the phobia regarding the family's bedtime practices must be inferred. Yet, there is enough information in the remarks in the case history about the emergence of the phobia and what preceded it that a solid conclusion can be reached. In evaluating such a hypothesis, I ask: Was Olga's cuddling with Hans in bed an issue of concern prior to the phobia? Was Hans even sleeping in his own bedroom away from his parents prior to the phobia? I will start by focusing on these preliminary questions before then directly addressing the primary question: was Max actively attempting to block cuddling between Olga and Hans when Hans attempted to seek out his mother's comforting prior to the onset of the phobia? I focus on the period during which the family was at their summer home in Gmunden because the best pre-phobia information is available about that period and it occurred only a few months before the phobia's onset.

First, can we be sure that Hans was not sleeping in his parents' bed or bedroom prior to the phobia's onset? Before the birth of his sister Hanna when he was three-and-a-half, Hans slept in his parents' room and so had easy access to his mother. The birth of his sister was one of Hans's earliest experiences of not being able to access his mother due to being moved out of his parents' bedroom: "Hans's bed was moved into the next room. He woke up there at seven, and, hearing his mother groaning, asked: 'Why's Mummy coughing?'" (1909/1955, p. 10). It is not clear how long this separation continued, but it was likely brief because we know that Hans was not permanently moved into his own room until about half a year later, around the age of four, when the family moved into a new flat: "When Hans was four years old we moved into a new flat" (1909/1955, p. 15) and "Hans was about four years old when he was moved out of our bedroom into a room of his own" (1909/1955, p. 99). (Freud had mis-stated Hans's age at the time as four-and-a-half years old in the case history, and Max's note corrected Freud that it had been a bit earlier.) That would have been just before the summer in Gmunden before the phobia's onset. Strachey, too, infers that "The sleeping-arrangements may have been changed at the time of the move into the new flat" (1909/1955, p. 133, n. 1).

Granting that Hans started sleeping alone in Vienna prior to the summer and prior to the phobia, do we know whether Hans slept in a separate bedroom when the family was at the summer home at Gmunden? We do know this based on the following passage in which Hans asks whether a friend can sleep with the family:

> He was fond, too, of the fourteen-year-old Mariedl—another of our landlord's daughters—who used to play with him. One evening as he was being put to bed he said: 'I want Mariedl to sleep with me.' On being told that would not do, he said: 'Then she shall sleep with Mummy or with Daddy.' He was told that would not do."
>
> (1909/1955, p. 16)

This passage confirms that Hans was sleeping apart from his parents at Gmunden, for he fantasizes Mariedl sleeping with him or Mariedl sleeping with his parents as two exclusive alternatives. We saw that shortly before the summer Hans had been moved into his own bedroom in the family's new Vienna flat. The above passage confirms that this new arrangement was continued during the family's summer stay in Gmunden.

Given that Hans had recently been moved into his own room and was likely seeking his mother's comforting in her bed, is there evidence that during the time at Gmunden Max was already disapproving of Olga and Max's affectionate cuddling in bed and may have been interfering with Hans's attachment soothing? A first observation is that one might see the parents' disapproving reply in the "Mariedl" passage above, "that would not do," as not only a rejection of the suggestion that Mariedl sleep with Hans or the parents but also an indirect way of reinforcing to Hans that his sleeping with parents is inappropriate. We know from a remark later in the case study that this is a point that Max was making to Hans: "Evidently, therefore, my explanation that only *little* boys come into bed with their Mummies and that *big* ones sleep in their own beds had not impressed him very much" (1909/1955, p. 83). Max likely had been making this point from the time Hans started sleeping alone, to shame him into returning to his own bed when Hans tried to circumvent the new situation.

Further evidence that there was ongoing concern by Max about Olga and Hans's cuddling prior to the onset of the phobia emerges from a close reading of Max's note to Freud. At the first sign of trouble with Hans, and before any evidence has emerged from the analysis and prior to any new consultation with Freud, Max blames Hans's problem on Olga's affectionate response to Hans:

No doubt the ground was prepared by sexual overexcitation due to his mother's tenderness; but I am not able to specify the actual exciting cause. He is afraid a *horse will bite him in the street* ... I cannot see what to make of it .... Or is the whole thing simply connected with his mother?

(Freud, 1909/1955, p. 22)

The use of the obscure phrase "overexcitation due to his mother's tenderness" without further explanation and the assertion that "no doubt" this was the cause suggests that the problem of Hans's bedtime behavior had been discussed by Max and Freud and was an agreed concern before the phobia appeared.

Freud concurs with Max's linking Hans's newly emerging phobia to Olga's affectionate behavior toward Hans, and characterizes the behavior to which Max objects as Olga's taking Hans into her bed:

His father accuses her, not without some show of justice, of being responsible for the outbreak of the child's neurosis, on account of her excessive display of affection for him and her too frequent readiness to take him into her bed.

(Freud, 1909/1955, pp. 27–28)

Freud here indicates something that was left unstated in Max's note but that was clearly understood without further discussion, namely, that the tenderness that was assumed to be responsible for Hans's overexcitement was Olga's allowing Hans to come into bed with her. The mutual understanding between Max and Freud suggests that Olga's taking Hans into bed with her was already seen as a dangerous Oedipal violation prior to the phobia's onset and thus could be singled out immediately as "no doubt" the likely cause of Hans's pathological condition.

Moreover, Max's disapproval of Olga's behavior at Gmunden is manifest in that he considered the mother's indulgence of Hans—even "only occasionally" and even when Hans seemed distressed—to be an *unfortunate* response:

When he was in bed in the evening he was usually in a very sentimental state. Once he made a remark to this effect: "Suppose I was to have no Mummy", or "Suppose you were to go away", or something of the sort; I cannot remember the exact words. Unfortunately, when he got into an elegiac mood of that kind, his mother used always to take him into bed with her.

(Freud, 1909/1955, p. 23)

That the access of Hans to the parents' bed was already on Freud's mind as a problem and something that he had discussed with Max prior to the phobia is further indicated by the fact that, when confronted with Hans's newly emerged phobia, the very first advice that Freud offers is puzzlingly specific:

I arranged with Hans's father that he should tell the boy that all this business about horses was a piece of nonsense and nothing more. The truth was, his father was to say, that he was very fond of his mother and wanted to be taken into her bed.

(Freud, 1909/1955, p. 28)

Freud immediately urges Max (not both parents) to emphasize Hans's desire to be "taken into her bed" with his mother (not to more generally seek maternal affection) as the crucial cause of his problem. That Hans "wanted" this suggests a partially unfulfilled desire, and it could only be Max who prevented such fulfillment.

Turning to the main question, the best evidence that Max was actually stopping bedtime comforting between Olga and Hans is the disparity in the frequency of Hans's cuddling when Max was there and when he was away. When Freud says that the parents had a habit of taking Hans into their bed "only occasionally," that is a general statement that covers the usual situation when Max was present. However, Olga was sympathetic with Hans's needs and unconvinced of the need to block Hans's access to her, so when Max was away there was a consequent deviation from the occasional "habit" and Hans cuddled with his mother more frequently, perhaps sometimes sleeping in her bed with her as well. In the course of the analysis, Max confirms his suspicion that during his absences in the summer Hans would "often" cuddle or sleep with his mother in her bed, in a sharp deviation from the situation he tried to establish and he places an Oedipal spin on this information:

I: "Did you often get into bed with Mummy at Gmunden?"
HANS: "Yes."

I: "And you used to think to yourself you were Daddy?"
HANS: "Yes."

(1909/1955, p. 90)

Max's questioning suggests that this is a deviation and that when Max was there, Hans did not often get into bed with Mummy, presumably due to Max's objections.

Max's intervention is apparent from Freud's strong emphasis in his commentary that the etiological burden for Hans's neurosis rests squarely on his coming into bed with his mother more frequently during the summer than before due specifically to the father's absence—implying that he knows that the father was controlling such access when he was present. Moreover, for Freud, this failure of the father's regulation of the mother–son relationship offers the needed explanation for the timing of the neurosis as a reaction to an upsurge in sexual desire that Hans experienced over the summer, which Hans had difficulty handling and consequently suppressed, causing it to transform into anxiety. Thus, Freud repeats this explanation several times:

> He had besides learnt from his experience that at Gmunden his mother could be prevailed upon, when he got into such moods, to take him into her bed .... Nor must we forget that for part of the time at Gmunden he had been alone with his mother, as his father had not been able to spend the whole of the holidays there.
>
> (Freud, 1909/1955, p. 26)

> This wish had originated during his summer holidays, when the alternating presence and absence of his father had drawn Hans's attention to the condition upon which depended the intimacy with his mother for which he longed.
>
> (Freud, 1909/1955, p. 133)

> This father of his came between him and his mother. When he was there Hans could not sleep with his mother, and when his mother wanted to take Hans into bed with her, his father used to call out. Hans had learnt from experience [i.e., at Gmunden-JW] how well-off he could be in his father's absence ... He not only prevented his being in bed with his mother, but also kept from him the knowledge he was thirsting for.
>
> (Freud, 1909/1955, p. 134)

Freud confidently asserts that Max's absence from the family's summer residence in Gmunden when he was in Vienna on business during the week provided an opportunity for Hans's unfettered access to his mother's bed that otherwise, were the father present, would not have been allowed. But why should Max's absence be a necessary condition for Hans's desired intimacy with his mother? There is nothing inherent in Max's presence that would preclude such intimacy, as is evidenced by the multiple instances in the case report in which Hans attempts to enter the marital bed for cuddling with the mother when both parents are present. It can only be that, as in the bedroom scenes described in Vienna after the phobia onset, Max actively objected to Hans coming into Olga's bed already in Gmunden several months before any hint of the phobia. The Oedipal theory seems to have already been in use as a justification for such concerns.

In a parenthetical remark by Freud on the above "Mariedl" passage, there is a further hint that the practice of actively keeping Hans out of the marital bed had already begun by the summer. Despite Hans's frequent desire to cuddle with his mother in bed, Freud observes that at the time of the Mariedl discussion, "Hans's father and mother were in the habit of taking him into their bed, though only occasionally, and there can be no doubt that lying beside them had aroused erotic feelings in him" (1909/1955, p. 17). (Note that Strachey observes that there is some historical ambiguity due to the placement of punctuation marks as to whether this statement came from Max or from Freud, but I believe this is clearly Freud talking.) This confirms that Hans was seeking time to cuddle in bed with his mother prior to the phobia onset, and it expresses the Oedipal theory that such cuddling in bed was inherently sexual that drove Max's concerns. Moreover, Freud's detailed knowledge of the Grafs' bedtime practices with regard to Hans long before he wrote his commentary strongly suggests that Freud had been conferring with Max over time and approved of limiting Hans's access to the parents' bed months prior to the phobia. Freud's mildly disapproving tone—the parents have a "habit" of taking Hans into their bed, "though only occasionally" violating Freud and Max's agreement—reflects that the two had likely conferred and disapproved of the cuddling, and agreed to limit Hans's access to the marital bed to the extent possible given Olga's objections. This explains why Max could mention in the letter to Freud without further explanation his hypothesis that "No doubt the ground was prepared by sexual overexcitation due to his mother's tenderness" (1909/1955, p. 22). There is no other affectionate practice between Olga and Hans mentioned anywhere in the case history at which Max's disapproval is directed. On the basis of a prior understanding, Max could assume that Freud would immediately understand to what he was referring, and Freud's response manifests that mutual understanding.

In sum, the evidence indicates that Max's practice of prohibiting Hans from coming into the marital bed was ongoing in the months before the outbreak of Hans's phobia, and likely reflected an understanding between Max and Freud. This interference with Hans's attachment reactions likely started when Hans was given his own bedroom separate from his parents' bedroom in their new apartment in Vienna just before the summer. It continued at the summer house in Gmunden just a few months before the phobia's onset, although during that period it was intermittent because of the father's frequent absences in Vienna. This conflict was renewed in full force when the family returned to Vienna, just four months before the onset of Hans's phobia.

Freud interprets this sequence as one in which there was an increase in Hans's sexual desire for his mother due to their greater intimacy at Gmunden during the father's absence, followed by frustration of these intensified desires upon return to Vienna and the father's continual presence, with Hans consequently developing fantasies of getting rid of his father to regain the situation he enjoyed at Gmunden. From an attachment-theoretic perspective, one might see things a bit differently. Hans had his attachment soothing needs intermittently satisfied at Gmunden. Upon the family's return to Vienna, the father's actions consistently frustrated Hans's attachment needs and amplified his attachment distress by blocking Hans from cuddling with his mother, leaving Hans with heightened anxiety and vulnerability to the development of an anxiety disorder.

Freud's Theoretical Sexualization of Attachment

What would explain or justify Max's consistent disruption and prevention of the affectionate cuddling between Hans and his mother? The basic theoretical rationale for Max's approach to Hans's desire to be cuddled—but not the entire rationale, as we shall see in later chapters—is what I will call the *theoretical sexualization of attachment*. (I will eventually drop the "theoretical" qualifier because this is the only type of sexualization of attachment that concerns me here.) Freud's theoretical sexualization of attachment provides the basic explanation for the exercise of Oedipal power/knowledge to protect the Grafs' marital bed documented above. In this section, I document this distinctive feature of Freud's theorizing across his theoretical works.

By the *theoretical sexualization of attachment* I refer to Freud's well-known libidinal theoretical construal of the child's instinct for seeking mother–child closeness and access, physical affection, and soothing when anxious that John Bowlby labels "attachment." Freud's theory of these child behaviors as sexually motivated is directly contrary to Bowlby's account of attachment as an independent nonsexual naturally selected mechanism. I accept Bowlby's view that cuddling in bed was a natural part of the mother's and Hans's attachment relationship and that in wanting to allow Hans into her bed to be cuddled when he was anxious, Hans's mother was responding with normal caring and appropriate attachment soothing in her maternal role as Hans's "safe haven" and "secure base."

The similarity of sexual and attachment strivings makes the sexual reinterpretation of attachment behavior particularly easy. Many characteristics of childhood attachment relationships might equally well be found in a list of behaviors characteristic of sexual bonding, such as longing for the object, desire for proximity to the object, fear of losing the object, and pleasure in skin contact and cuddling with the object. Touching, seeing, holding, cuddling, and so on are all goals common to both instinctual systems' target behaviors. Just as Bowlby emphasizes that seeking skin contact and physical cuddling and soothing when anxious is a cardinal goal of attachment-related behaviors, Freud emphasizes that the pleasure of skin contact between child and parent is a component instinctual sexual pleasure: "I should like to emphasize the importance of pleasure derived from cutaneous contact as a component in this new aim of Hans's" (1909/1955, p. 111).

Thus, anxious attachment and intense libidinal longing might look quite similar in a child. This is why Bowlby can contrast his theory with Freud's by listing attachment-related and sexual interpretations of the very same behavior:

> Hans's insistent desire to remain with his mother is seen, not in terms of anxious attachment, but as the expression of his love for his

mother, held to have been genitally sexual in character, having reached an extreme 'pitch of intensity'. The dream that his mother had gone away and left him is held to have been, not an expression of Hans's fear that his mother would carry out a threat to desert the family, but an expression of his fear of the punishment due to him for his incestuous wishes .... Mother's displays of affection to Hans and her allowing him to come into bed with her are seen, not simply as a natural and comforting expression of motherly feeling, but as actions that might have encouraged, in a rather unfortunate way, Hans's oedipal wishes.

(1973, p. 287)

It should be emphasized that the sexualization of attachment refers here strictly to the mistaken imposition of a sexualized theoretical interpretation on nonsexual attachment-related behavior such as Hans's seeking to cuddle with his mother when he was anxious. It does *not* refer to any actual clinical intrusion of sexual desire or arousal into attachment behaviors, although that may sometimes occur. So, the "sexualization of attachment" in Hans's case does *not* imply that in fact Hans's cuddling with his mother was literally sexually motivated, sexually arousing, or sexually motivating for either of them. This is not to say that there were no sexual desires or pleasures involved at all, but only that there is no evidence that the behavior, which is prototypical attachment-motivated behavior, was essentially or primarily motivated sexually as Freud claims (for a detailed analysis of Freud's argument for the sexual theory, see Wakefield, 2022). Despite the lack of evidence, the Oedipal/sexual construal has greatly influenced the psychoanalytic literature, with subsequent commentators sometimes drawing far-reaching conclusions from it about the mother's seductiveness or Hans's premature sexual arousal.

It must be kept in mind that when Freud interprets various child or parental behaviors as sexual, he means that they are literally sexual in that, based on his libido theory of sexual motivation, they share the very same sexual motivational energy based on the same underlying biochemical process that standard sexual motives possess. In other words, contrary to standard ways of making Freud's claim seem more plausible and less radical, Freud is not merely changing the meaning of "sexual" to encompass everything that is pleasurable or sensual. He means by "sexual" anything that is in fact specifically sexual as we understand the concept, even if its sexual nature is not immediately obvious. This is analogous to discovering that, say, snow is really a form of water because at a theoretical level they share an essential chemical property and can transform into one another. Similarly, Freud believes that he has discovered that maternal–child affection is really a form of sexuality and shares an underlying motivational system with standard sexual activity, so that standard forms of attachment-related motivations are in fact libidinally motivated. Thus, maternal physical affection is a form of incestuous sexual stimulation: "Lying in bed with his father or mother was a source of erotic feelings in Hans just as it is in every other child" (1909/1955, p. 17); "The sexual aim … had originated in relation to his mother …. and a new pleasure had now become the most important for him—that of sleeping beside his mother" (1909/1955, pp. 110–111).

Freud's adoption of the hypothesis that parent–child attachment is inherently sexual in nature served to protect his sexual theory of the neuroses. Having traced his patients' symptoms back to their early relations with their parents including their attachment bonds, it seemed that Freud had discovered that sex was not at the root of the neuroses after all. Instead of accepting that discovery, Freud construed the pleasures of a child's early attachment experiences as themselves sexual, bringing them within the orbit of his sexual theory. Freud's construal of attachment behaviors in sexual terms was intended to serve Freud's larger theoretical aspirations by protecting his sexual theory of the neuroses. However, Freud's insistence that what appears to be non-sexual affection is in fact a muted form of sexuality also had the effect of casting suspicion on maternal–child tenderness and placing parent–child affection in a new light that provides the justification for Max's interventions.

In passages scattered throughout his work, Freud makes explicit and defends against potential objections his claim that mother–child affection is sexual. For example, in Freud's earliest comprehensive theoretical presentation of his sexuality theory, *Three Essays on the Theory of Sexuality* (1905/1953), he specifically considers "infantile anxiety," which consists of what we would now, from an attachment-theory perspective, generally ascribe to separation anxiety or situational attachment distress. These very early pre-Oedipal anxieties were considered by Bowlby to be potential counterexamples to Freud's Oedipal theory of neurosis. Freud explains such anxiety as an expression of (sexual) love for the caretaker:

INFANTILE ANXIETY Children themselves behave from an early age as though their dependence on the people looking after them were in the nature of sexual love. Anxiety in children is originally nothing other than an expression of the fact that they are feeling the loss of the person they love. It is for this reason that they are frightened of every stranger. They are afraid in the dark because in the dark they cannot see the person they love; and their fear is soothed if they can take hold of that person's hand in the dark .... [I]t is only children with a sexual instinct that is excessive or has developed prematurely or has become vociferous owing to too much petting who are inclined to be timid. In this respect a child, by turning his libido into anxiety when he cannot satisfy it, behaves like an adult. On the other hand an adult who has become neurotic owing to his libido being unsatisfied behaves in his anxiety like a child.

(1905/1953, p. 224)

If one leaves aside the sexual "libido" attribution, Freud's description of the fears and love of the child is compatible with both common sense and attachment theory. Bowlby could equally say that "anxiety in children is originally nothing other than an expression of the fact that they are feeling the loss of the person they love." However, Bowlby would have in mind the anxiety that results from the autonomous attachment instinct when the parent is not available, having nothing to do with sexuality. Bowlby would also agree that fear of strangers and fear of the dark can be understood as forms of attachment-related anxiety and that the soothing of separation anxiety takes place with bodily contact such as holding a hand or cuddling. Thus, he could agree with Freud that "what he was afraid of was not the dark, but the absence of someone he loved; and he could feel sure of being soothed as soon as he had evidence of that person's presence" (1905/1953, p. 224, n. 1). The difference between Bowlby and Freud is that Freud makes the leap to the conclusion that this form of love is "in the nature of sexual love." To underscore the point that the entire description is to be interpreted as pertaining specifically to sexual love, in 1920 Freud added this note: "One of the most important results of psychoanalytic research is this discovery that neurotic anxiety arises out of libido" (1905/1953, p. 224, n. 1 [added 1920]), where "libido" is defined specifically as sexual motivation ("The fact of the existence of sexual needs in human beings and animals is expressed in biology by the assumption of a 'sexual instinct' … science makes use of the word 'libido'" [1905/1953, p. 135]).

Elsewhere in *Three Essays*, Freud describes what he calls the "diphasic choice of object," in which there are two periods of sexual expression, the Oedipal and pubertal, separated by a period of repression in the latency period. Freud argues that affection during the Oedipal period is sexual and, after being submerged during latency, emerges again during puberty as a muted form of sexuality that combines with overt sensuality to form the complex sexuality of adulthood:

> DIPHASIC CHOICE OF OBJECT It may be regarded as typical of the choice of an object that the process is diphasic, that is, that it occurs in two waves. The first of these begins between the ages of two and five, and is brought to a halt or to a retreat by the latency period; it is characterized by the infantile nature of the sexual aims. The second wave sets in with puberty and determines the final outcome of sexual life …. Their [i.e., infantile] sexual aims have become mitigated and they now represent what may be described as the 'affectionate current' of sexual life. Only psycho-analytic investigation can show that behind this affection, admiration and respect there lie concealed the old sexual longings of the infantile component instincts.
>
> (1905/1953, p. 200)

Freud here acknowledges that Oedipal affection includes components that are not manifestly sexual in appearance. However, he interprets them as muted forms of sexuality. In a later article, Freud (1912/1957) identifies an affectionate strand of sexuality and notes that not only the child's but the parent's affection is erotic:

> The affectionate current … is directed to the members of the family and those who look after the child. From the very beginning it carries along with it contributions from the sexual instincts …. The 'affection' shown by the child's parents … seldom fails to betray its erotic nature.
>
> (1912/1957, pp. 180–181)

In a 1923 encyclopedia article, Freud reiterates his basic view that parent–child affection is essentially sexual:

The social instincts belong to a class of instinctual impulses which ... have not abandoned their directly sexual aims, but they are held back by internal resistances from attaining them; they rest content with certain approximations to satisfaction and for that very reason lead to especially firm and permanent attachments between human beings. To this class belong in particular the affectionate relations between parents and children, which were originally fully sexual.

(Freud, 1923/1955, p. 258)

Freud well understood that his denial of the traditional and standard view that there is a form of love between parent and child independent of sexuality was one of the most challenging features of his theory of childhood sexuality. He repeatedly addressed potential objections and offered arguments for the sexual nature of parent–child love, emphasizing the reciprocal nature of the erotic connection between mother and child. For example, again in *Three Essays*, Freud writes:

There may perhaps be an inclination to dispute the possibility of identifying a child's affection and esteem for those who look after him with sexual love. I think, however, that a closer psychological examination may make it possible to establish this identity beyond any doubt. A child's intercourse with anyone responsible for his care affords him an unending source of sexual excitation and satisfaction from his erotogenic zones. This is especially so since the person in charge of him, who, after all, is as a rule his mother, herself regards him with feelings that are derived from her own sexual life: she strokes him, kisses him, rocks him and quite clearly treats him as a substitute for a complete sexual object.

(1905/1953, p. 223)

Freud also attempts to address the reaction of horror that parents may have to the notion that the physical affection they show their children is in fact sexually motivated:

A mother would probably be horrified if she were made aware that all her marks of affection were rousing her child's sexual instinct and preparing for its later intensity. She regards what she does as asexual, 'pure' love, since, after all, she carefully avoids applying more excitations to the child's genitals than are unavoidable in nursery care. As we know, however, the sexual instinct is not aroused only by direct excitation of the genital zone. What we call affection will unfailingly show its effects one day on the genital zones as well. Moreover, if the mother understood more of the high importance of the part played by instincts in mental life as a whole—in all its ethical and psychical achievements—she would spare herself any self-reproaches even after her enlightenment. She is only fulfilling her task in teaching the child to love. After all, he is meant to grow up into a strong and capable person with vigorous sexual needs and to accomplish during his life all the things that human beings are urged to do by their instincts.

(1905/1953, p. 223)

Of course, simply imposing a sexual interpretation on the entire domain of attachment-related affectionate behaviors that is usually taken to be essentially nonsexual, including a mother's stroking, kissing, and rocking of her child, is not evidence and certainly does not place Freud's interpretation "beyond any doubt." The above passage begs that question.

Freud again considers the objection to the sexualization of parent–child affection in his *Introductory Lectures* (1917/1963):

It will also be objected that the little boy's conduct arises from egoistic motives and gives no grounds for postulating an erotic complex: the child's mother attends to all his needs, so that he has an interest in preventing her from looking after anyone else. This also is true; but it will soon become clear that in this situation as in similar ones the egoistic interest is merely affording a point of support to which the erotic trend is attached. The little boy may show the most undisguised sexual curiosity about his mother, he may insist upon sleeping beside her at night, he may force his presence on her while she is dressing or may even make actual attempts at seducing her, as his mother will often notice and report with amusement—all of which puts beyond doubt the erotic nature of his tie with his mother.

(1917/1963, pp. 332–333)

Freud's argument here defending his "postulating an erotic complex" and the existence of an "erotic trend" against a common-sense egoistic theory of child attachment would equally be a defense against Bowlby's attachment-theoretic account. Note that the examples of what are claimed to be the child's sexual behaviors are basic to attachment, such as wanting to sleep in bed with one's mother or wanting to be in the same room with her, and seem to come straight out of the Hans case.

In a further passage in *Introductory Lectures*, Freud argues that, even if the objector should show that Freud was wrong about early oral and anal pleasures being sexual, the Oedipal period is surely sexual because the phallic zone is already involved:

> On the whole you will have gained very little for what you want to assert—the sexual purity of children—even if you succeed in convincing me that it would be better to regard the activities of infants-in-arms as non-sexual. For the sexual life of children is already free from all these doubts from the third year of life onwards: at about that time the genitals already begin to stir, a period of infantile masturbation—of genital satisfaction, therefore—sets in, regularly perhaps. The mental and social phenomena of sexual life need no longer be absent; the choice of an object, an affectionate preference for particular people, a decision, even, in favour of one of the two sexes, jealousy—all these have been established by impartial observations made independently of psycho-analysis and before its time, and they can be confirmed by any observer who cares to see them.
>
> (1917/1963, pp. 325–326)

It is true that children at the Oedipal age do have genital sensations that are presumably sexual. To this extent, Freud is surely correct that children and parents experience some sexual or proto-sexual pleasures in their interactions. Yet, the phenomena Freud describes of affection, preference for some people over others, and even jealousy, do not necessarily warrant a specifically sexual stamp, and certainly are phenomena that would occur as well within an attachment framework.

It is notable that Freud continued to hold to his basic position that attachment-related behaviors and anxiety are sexually driven at their core even as his theory of anxiety changed radically over the years. Early in his career, Freud thought that the anxiety children feel when separated from a caregiver resulted from frustrated libidinal desire, with the anxiety being a direct transformation of suppressed libido. Freud eventually modified his theory in *Inhibitions, Symptoms, and Anxiety* (1926/1959), postulating that anxiety is a danger signal that may or may not itself be a transformation of libido. But, he thought that children's separation anxiety was a danger signal due to increasing undischarged libido, thus ultimately a sexual issue concerning the relationship to the caregiver at its core:

> Only a few of the manifestations of anxiety in children are comprehensible to us, and we must confine our attention to them. They occur, for instance, when a child is alone, or in the dark, or when it finds itself with an unknown person instead of one to whom it is used—such as its mother. These three instances can be reduced to a single condition—namely, that of missing someone who is loved and longed for. But here, I think, we have the key to an understanding of anxiety …. anxiety appears as a reaction to the felt loss of the object.
>
> (1926/1959, pp. 136–137)

Freud's statements here seem to verge on an object-relational Bowlby-like understanding of separation anxiety in which the disrupted proximity to the mother is the immediate cause of the anxiety. However, instead of anticipating Bowlby and object relations theory and acknowledging the intrinsic attachment motivation that is satisfied simply by being in proximity to the mother, Freud goes on to sexualize the missing of the mother in terms of increasing undischarged libido and the memory of the mother's immediate satisfaction of needs:

> But a moment's reflection takes us beyond this question of loss of object. The reason why the infant in arms wants to perceive the presence of its mother is only because it already knows by experience that she satisfies all its needs without delay. The situation, then, which it regards as a 'danger' and against which it wants to be safeguarded is that of non-satisfaction, of a growing tension due to need, against which it is helpless.
>
> (1926/1959, p. 137)

Freud insists that the danger is ultimately sexual and the anxiety signal is "caused by the accumulation of amounts of [libidinal] stimulation which require to be disposed of" (Freud 1926/1959, p. 138). He thus rejects the notion of intrinsic nonsexual object-relational striving. Freud's theory of sexuality thus covers the domain of parent–child affection and love in an all-encompassing way and sexualizes the domain of behavior later covered by attachment theory.

On a historical note, Freud's sexualization of attachment is a critical point of divergence between Oedipal theory and the earlier nineteenth-century anti-masturbation crusade. The sexualization of maternal–child physical affection is a genuinely novel and momentous move by Freud that has no analog in earlier masturbation-crusade theory, which considered any evidence of sexuality in a child as a deviation from the normal state of "pure" child love and affection. Moreover, the anti-masturbation crusade deployed a concept of sexuality that was quite familiarly adult in its genital and physical stimulatory nature, even when applied to the child. Freud's shift to the libido theory with its endless transformations of sexuality allowed for the existence of unexpectedly subtle and novel forms of sexual arousal, thereby providing subtle and novel targets of control and power/knowledge.

Bowlby's Bewildering Failure to Address Max's Disruption of Hans's Attachment Behavior

Perhaps one can understand Freud's ignoring of Max's actions given his sexual theory of Hans's relationship to his mother. Freud does not dwell on the father's blocking of Hans's access to his mother because Freud is supportive of Max's efforts. He sees them as a sensible way of regulating the intensity of Hans's Oedipal desire, approvingly noting that the father's efforts rendered Hans's desire to be in bed with his mother "innocuous" (1909/1955, p. 140)—although even from Freud's perspective, we shall see in the next chapter, one can pose some puzzles.

In contrast, Bowlby's failure to focus on this issue is bewildering. Max's persistent disruption of Hans's access to his mother's affection in his soothing-seeking behavior is an obvious candidate for a causal factor in Hans's escalating anxiety according to Bowlby's own theory. Recall that one of Bowlby's points against Freud's interpretation is that, whereas Freud sees the mother's cuddling with Hans in bed in the morning as dangerously potentiating Oedipal desires, in fact the mother's behavior is a normal and natural act of maternal soothing. Freud's mistake, Bowlby argues (as we saw above), is that

> Mother's displays of affection to Hans and her allowing him to come
> into bed with her are seen, not simply as a natural and comforting

expression of motherly feeling, but as actions that might have encouraged, in a rather unfortunate way, Hans's oedipal wishes.

(Bowlby, 1973, p. 287)

This observation that Freud is systematically misinterpreting Hans's attachment behavior as sexually motivated is the key to properly under-standing the Hans case, in my view. What is puzzling is that once Bowlby took note of Freud's misconstrual of attachment behavior as sexual, it should have immediately become apparent that the father's disruption of Hans's ability to approach his mother when anxious due to the sexual interpretation is precisely the kind of disruption of the attachment relation-ship that causes situational attachment distress. And, it should have been immediately obvious that, repeated over time, such disruption in the long run can cause heightened anxiety and even potentially trigger separation anxiety, anxious attachment, and anxiety conditions as secondary effects. Yet, Bowlby does not even mention it as a possible causal factor in Hans's increased anxiety. In this matter, Bowlby, like Freud, seems intent on reading the Hans case in a way that supports his prior theoretical claims about anxious attachment, and so latches onto the possibility of threat-induced anxious attachment without systematically testing this hypothesis against Hans's and his mother's overall reported behavior.

Instead, ignoring the limitations imposed on the mother's actual avail-ability to Hans, Bowlby focuses almost exclusively on the mother's threats of abandonment as the central cause of his anxiety condition. As we saw in the last chapter, this focus is selected despite a paucity of evi-dence regarding the frequency, recency, and impact of such threats. Bowlby bases his attachment-theoretic explanation of Hans's vulnerability to developing an anxiety condition on the one fact that Hans's mother has at some previous time threatened to leave when Hans misbehaved, a point that emerges in the discussions between Hans and his father. So, we know that the mother at some point *threatened a disruption* to the attachment relationship although she did not carry out the threat.

Yet, in the father's actions we have an ongoing repeated *actual disrup-tion* of one of Hans's attachment relationship's most basic functions, inflicted at times when Hans himself says that he is afraid or anxious. One would presume that actual disruption of an attachment relationship over several months at times of the child's anxiety when the child is seeking comforting is generally much more potent as a cause of anxiety than an abstract verbal threat to disrupt the attachment relationship when disciplining a child. Bowlby quotes researchers who conclude that children's separation fears are generally reality based, and in Max's behavior we have a disruptive reality. A threat may serve to shake one's confidence, but in this case Hans was experiencing the actual unavailability of his attachment figure when he needed her. The availability and responsiveness that comprise an adequate attachment relationship from the child's perspective are understood by Bowlby in strong terms that imply genuine accessibility not available to Hans when his father intervened. Bowlby understands the attachment figure's presence or availability as implying "ready accessibility":

> Not only must an attachment figure be accessible but he, or she, must be willing to respond in an appropriate way; in regard to someone who is afraid this means willingness to act as comforter and protector. Only when an attachment figure is both accessible and potentially responsive can he, or she, be said to be truly available.
>
> (1973, pp. 201–202)

In this context, it is worth reconsidering a key piece of evidence Bowlby cited for Hans being anxiously attached. We saw in the last chapter that Bowlby makes much of an upsetting dream that Hans reported just at the time of the outbreak of his phobia: "Hans (aged four and three-quarters) woke up one morning in tears. Asked why he was crying, he said to his mother: 'When I was asleep I thought you were gone and I had no Mummy to coax with'" (1909/1955, p. 23).[1] Bowlby attends only to Hans's worry that his mother would be gone because that supports his account of Hans's anxiety in terms of his mother's threat to leave. However, Hans also specifically lamented that his mother would not be available for comforting him. As we saw in Chapter 3, Bowlby himself explains that concerns about a parent being gone of the sort that Hans at one point expresses that might indicate chronic anxious attachment can have a different more immediate meaning when uttered at a time of distress about an attachment figure not being accessible for comforting when anxious, a situation that we know confronted Hans:

> whenever our attachment behaviour is aroused ... but for some reason we are unable to find or reach our attachment figure, ... we might say,

'I was afraid you were gone', or 'I was frightened when I could not find you', or 'Your long absence made me anxious'.

(1973, p. 92)

In other words, the fear of an attachment figure being gone is exacerbated by lack of ready access after a fright, and blocked access to an attachment figure causes anxiety similar to being frightened by an external threat. This suggests that Hans's anxiety dream about his mother being gone and thus not having a Mummy to coax with might well be a reaction not to (or not only to) threats the mother may have uttered in the past but also to the father's active blocking of Hans's access to his mother when he was anxious and needed her comforting. Hans could be expressing his anxious anticipation that his mother would again be unavailable—in effect, gone—when he needs her.

Bowlby (1973) repeatedly asserts that blocked availability of an attachment figure causes anxiety and especially exacerbates other fears: "it is no less natural to feel afraid when lines of communication with base are in jeopardy than when something occurs in front of us that alarms us and leads us to retreat" (p. 94); "any possibility of defection by the attachment figure can give rise to acute anxiety in the attached. And should he be experiencing alarm from another source at the same time, it is evident that he is likely to feel the most intense fear" (p. 95); "An individual's increased tendency to respond to situations with fear can be a result of ... uncertainty about the availability of his attachment figure(s)" (p. 196); "when an individual is confident that an attachment figure will be available to him whenever he desires it, that person will be much less prone to either intense or chronic fear" (p. 202).

This is a lucid description of Hans's situation and a partial explanation of his disposition to respond with intense anxiety to the horse accident. None of these passages is specifically about anxious attachment in which one has a problematic working model; they all address situational attachment distress as well or primarily. Hans's father's behavior has created doubts in Hans that his mother will be available for comforting when needed. During this very period, Hans is terrified by the horse accident and needs to go to her more than ever. He is not a clingy child in general, and the intensity of his anxiety—emphasized by the father in a note to Freud—can plausibly be attributed to the combination of the two factors of the horse accident and his increased uncertainty about the availability of his attachment figure.

In contrast to uncertainties about the effect of the abandonment threat or threats, we know that the father's disruption of Hans's attachment relationship to his mother was ongoing at the time of the formation of Hans's phobia, that Hans was repeatedly distressed by it, explicitly expressed that he was anxious, and tried to evade his father's prohibitions and argue with his father about it. In nonetheless emphasizing almost exclusively the mother's earlier threats as his causal hypothesis over other possible factors, Bowlby sadly became the first in a long line of "pre-Oedipal trauma" theorists to—mistakenly, I will argue—identify the mother's behavior as the predominant cause of an attachment disruption between her and Hans and thus the major cause of Hans's anxiety condition. In fact, the primary cause, other than the horse accident itself, likely lies with Hans's father's Oedipal-theory-driven disruption of his wife's natural attachment response to Hans's distress.

Separation Anxiety or Situational Attachment Distress?

So, is Hans anxiously attached, as Bowlby claimed? Despite the existence of ongoing situational attachment distress, could it be argued that as a secondary factor Hans is also mildly anxiously attached? The multiple factors uncovered in the reexamination of the case history and in his family background as revealed in the Archives interviews (see Chapter 3) suggest a vulnerability to anxious attachment, and one could interpret certain aspects of Hans's behavior as evidence of a mild degree of separation anxiety.

However, Max's chronic disruption of Hans's natural desire to seek physical contact with his mother places a new and ambiguous spin on whether Hans suffered from anxious attachment. The fact that Max was blocking Hans from being able to access his mother when he needed comforting was clearly causing situational attachment distress and preventing Hans from regulating his various fears (of horses, of being alone in his new bedroom, etc.). As Bowlby suggests, the inability to access his mother would be enough to amplify, maintain, and dysregulate Hans's other fears, and his inability for anxiety regulation through soothing would itself be experienced as heightened anxiety. So, postulating anxious attachment seems superfluous. And, we saw that Hans's behavior does not overall indicate anxious attachment. On the other hand, if one insists on interpreting some of Hans's behavior as evidence of mild separation anxiety, then, rather than the mother's threat to leave when Hans was naughty, we have now identified a more plausible and temporally well-situated etiology for Hans to develop some degree of anxious attachment, namely, the actual repeated disruption and prohibition of Hans's attachment behavior in the months prior to the phobia. The ongoing attachment disruption renders anxious attachment a likely secondary effect at best.

It is challenging to distinguish anxious attachment from situational attachment-related adaptive distress reactions when circumstances are repeated over time because they can look the same in the short run. In anxious or insecure attachment, unlike situational attachment distress, the working model that regulates the attachment system's response enduringly incorporates the fear that the mother will be unavailable or unresponsive or withdraw after accessed, altering typical attachment reactions by the child. Attachment theory is not precise about the malleability of the working model and thus there is no clear generalization about how rapidly circumstantial attachment disruptions will transform into more enduring alterations of the working model that can produce chronic separation anxiety. However, several months of attachment disruption with scolding, humiliating explanations of what "big boys" do, and threats of heightened anxiety from one's father might conceivably cause one to adjust one's working model to some extent.

I argued in Chapter 3 that the case record and Archives interviews overall provide insufficient evidence to infer a substantial degree of anxious or insecure attachment in Hans. When allowed access to his mother, Hans appears to react appropriately and is soothed, and he is capable of non-anxious independence and exploration on his own, suggesting an adequate working model. In contrast, there is conclusive textual evidence that Hans experienced repeated situational attachment distress due to his father's actions that blocked Hans's access to his mother as a "safe haven" for comforting and protection and increased his general anxiety level, so that what might otherwise have been an intense normal fear reaction to a stressful event such as the horse accident was more likely to become elevated into an anxiety pathology. I conclude that the claim of anxious attachment remains unproven, but even if Hans suffered from some mild level of anxious attachment prior to the phobia, most likely it was an epiphenomenon of the chronic attachment disruption that Max inflicted on Hans. Etiologically, it is Max's application of Oedipal theory to the protection of the marital bed by prohibiting mother–son affection that must be given causal primacy over mild anxious attachment, if indeed the latter did exist.

Did Oedipal Power/Knowledge Create the Oedipal Feeling Constellation in Hans?

I have argued that the application of Oedipal power/knowledge was a factor in the causation of Hans's anxiety and his phobia. I want to go further and suggest that the application of Oedipal power/knowledge in the Hans case may have created a semblance of the very data that is supposed to support the Oedipal theory.

In the Hans case history, there is an elaborate attempt to demonstrate that the central features of the Oedipus complex exist in Hans. These include, above all, four features: intense desire for contact with the mother, jealousy of the father, anger at the father and desire for the father to be gone, and fear of the father's anger. For convenience, we can call these feelings the "Oedipal constellation" of feelings, without any assumption as to whether these feelings are in fact due to the Oedipus complex, for as non-Freudian psychoanalytic theories make clear, these same feelings could be generated in various ways.

One way that the Oedipal constellation of feelings could be generated in Hans, I suggest, is by Freud and Max blocking Hans's access to his mother's cuddling when he is anxious. It is easy to see precisely how Hans might come to experience the Oedipal constellation of feelings under these circumstances. In being denied access to his mother when he needs her while his father languishes in bed with her, Hans would inevitably feel both jealous of his father (as he does of his sister Hanna due to his mother's attentions being focused on her) and angry at his father for this seemingly arbitrary prohibition. This anger would especially be focused on his father given that his mother is portrayed as consistently receptive to cuddling with Hans. Yet, Hans loves and depends on his father and so would likely suppress his anger. Certainly, this frustration of his attachment needs would increase his need and desire for closeness to his mother. And, as is quite explicit in the case history, Hans can only interpret his father's bewildering behavior as expressing disapproval of or anger at Hans for seeking to be with his mother, which it is. Of course, following Freud's lead, Hans's father explains his intervention to Hans as a purely medical intervention, that Hans will not feel his phobic fear if he ceases

cuddling with his mother. The case history makes clear that this explanation makes no sense to Hans, who understandably places the predictable
reduction of his immediate anxiety over a theoretical prediction about his
"nonsense" that seems dubious. Hans's conclusion that his father is angry
at him for trying to cuddle with his mother—and thus that he should
potentially fear his father's reactions—is made crystal clear in an interchange late in the case history in which Hans rejects outright his father's
rationalizations:

> I: So you'd like to go to Mummy?
> HANS: Yes.
> I: What do I really scold you for? ...
> HANS: Because you're cross.
> I: But that's not true.
> HANS: Yes, it is true. You're cross. I know you are. It must be true.
>
> (1909/1955, pp. 82–83)

Moreover, as Freud emphasizes, in Gmunden the summer before the
phobia's onset, Hans's father spent much of the week in Vienna and
thus Hans was able to have access to his mother without the father there
to stop him—or her, for that matter, for Hans's mother never accepted
these prohibitions. Thus, it is true that Hans would have come to see the
father's being away as one path to gaining the soothing he wanted from
his mother, and in all likelihood he did entertain a fantasy of his father
being away. However, Freud's escalation of this quite understandable
and rational desire into a desire that the father be dead has no persuasive evidential base in the case history. In the one instance in which the
father provokes Hans into a fantasy of this happening due to an injury
to the father, Hans portrays the father as simply being away temporarily
and as returning after a while, leaving Hans time to escape from his
presumably angry father after having some of the desired time with his
mother:

> I: So you want me to fall down?
> HANS: Yes ... then I'll be able to be alone with Mummy for a little bit
> at all events. When you come up into our flat I'll be able to run
> away quick so that you don't see.
>
> (1909/1955, p. 82)

Admittedly, all of this would sound terribly Oedipal if one did not know that the entire fantasy emerged in response to the father systematically interfering in Hans's natural attachment behavior in approaching his mother for soothing. I conclude that the application of Oedipal power/knowledge to limit attachment soothing between mother and son can explain the constellation of Oedipal emotions to which Freud points as evidence—spurious evidence, I am suggesting—for the Oedipal theory.

Conclusion: Oedipal Theory as the Cause of Hans's Anxiety

The analysis above shows that Max's practice of denying Hans access to his mother for attachment soothing was going on for the several months leading up to the onset of Hans's phobia and was a regular occurrence that caused Hans distress. This anxiety-provoking practice was justified by a theoretical rationale grounded in Freud's Oedipal theory that interpreted standard attachment behaviors in sexual terms. It is plausible that Max's continuous disruption of Hans's attachment-related soothing-seeking behavior and the blocking of his access to his attachment figure would, as Bowlby claims, create a marked disposition to experience increased anxiety and potentially to develop an anxiety disorder.

I conclude that, strange as it may sound, Oedipal theory itself—not the hypothesized Oedipus complex but the Oedipal theory and its acceptance by Max and Freud—via the application of resulting Oedipal power/knowledge within Hans's family, had a role in causing Hans's phobia. The resulting triangular situation of Hans and his mother attempting to engage in normal attachment-related soothing behavior while the father attempted to block it could have generated the very feelings among family members that Freud mistook as feelings associated with the Oedipus complex.

Note

1 Strachey's term "coaxing," which I often render as "cuddling," is a translation of the German word "*Schmeicheln*." The term is used by Hans, Max, and Freud to describe Olga and Hans's affectionate interactions at bedtime that Max tries to stop. Both Max in the German version and Strachey in his translation explain that it means "to caress" ("liebkosen"), different from today's standard meaning, "to flatter." Etymological dictionaries indicate that in the Viennese dialect of German spoken at the time of the Hans case, "*Schmeicheln*" commonly indicated the kind of gentle affectionate stroking and petting one would do with a young child or a pet animal (Shealagh Weber and David Abrams, personal communication).

References

Bowlby, J. (1973). *Attachment and loss (Vol. 2): Separation: Anxiety and anger.* New York, NY: Basic Books.

Freud, S. (1953). Three essays on the theory of sexuality. In J. Strachey (Ed. & Trans.), *The standard edition of the complete psychological works of Sigmund Freud* (Vol. 7, pp. 123–246). London, UK: Hogarth Press. (Original work published 1905.)

Freud, S. (1955). Analysis of a phobia in a five-year-old boy. In J. Strachey (Ed. & Trans.), *The standard edition of the complete psychological works of Sigmund Freud* (Vol. *10*, pp. 1–150). London, UK: Hogarth Press. (Original work published 1909.)

Freud, S. (1955). Two encyclopaedia articles. In J. Strachey (Ed. & Trans.), *The standard edition of the complete psychological works of Sigmund Freud* (Vol. *18*, pp. 233–260). London, UK: Hogarth Press. (Original work published 1923.)

Freud, S. (1957). On the universal tendency to debasement in the sphere of love (contributions to the psychology of love II). *The standard edition of the complete psychological works of Sigmund Freud* (Vol. *11*, pp. 177–190). London, UK: Hogarth Press. (Original work published 1912.)

Freud, S. (1959). Inhibitions, symptoms and anxiety. In J. Strachey (Ed. & Trans), *The standard edition of the complete psychological works of Sigmund Freud* (Vol. *20*, pp. 75–176). London, UK: Hogarth Press. (Original work published 1926.)

Freud, S. (1963). Introductory lectures on psycho-analysis, part 3. In J. Strachey (Ed. & Trans.), *The standard edition of the complete psychological works of Sigmund Freud* (Vol. *16*). London, UK: Hogarth Press. (Original work published 1917.)

Wakefield, J. C. (2007). Attachment and sibling rivalry in Little Hans: The 'phantasy of the two giraffes' reconsidered. *Journal of the American Psychoanalytic Association, 55*, 821–849.

Wakefield, J. C. (2022). *Freud's argument for the Oedipus complex: A philosophy of science analysis of the case of Little Hans.* New York: Routledge.

Chapter 5

Bowlby Versus the Spoiling Theory

Understanding the Prohibitory Nature of Oedipal Power/Knowledge

In the last chapter, I showed that Oedipal theory was used by Hans's father, Max, as a rationale to protect the Grafs' marital bed from incursions by their child, Hans. When Hans was anxious and sought cuddling from his mother, Olga, she welcomed him, but Max would prohibit his coming into their bed, although Olga would sometimes succeed in providing at least brief comforting to Hans. In this chapter, I explore in further depth the theoretical underpinnings of this prohibitory application of Oedipal power/knowledge.

Why Prohibit Hans from Cuddling with His Mother?

It is not entirely obvious how one gets from the Freudian theoretical belief that the child's desire to be with the mother is sexual in nature to the conclusion that the child's access to the mother must be restricted. Even if one assumes with Freud that Hans has Oedipal sexual desires for his mother, his theory also claims that this is a natural and essential part of normal development. So, why block Hans's access to his mother for cuddling? The obvious answer is that in this case something has either gone wrong or could go wrong so the normal rules don't apply. In particular, one might assume that, given Hans's anxiety condition resulting from excessive libido, Hans needs to be protected from the intense arousal that he is assumed to experience when he cuddles with his mother.

This answer is not as conclusive as it looks. To approach the question in a different way, let me pose a puzzle lurking in Freud's view. Freud says that Hans's time alone with his mother at Gmunden, during which he cuddled with her more than would have been permitted by Max, had the effect of increasing Hans's sexual arousal and the intensity of his sexual

DOI: 10.4324/9780203817124-5

desire for his mother. Yet, no anxiety condition or other problem occurred at Gmunden despite his free access to his mother. If sleeping with his mother at Gmunden so increased Hans's libido, why did he not develop an anxiety disorder or some other neurosis at that time? If the answer is that by cuddling with his mother, Hans sufficiently satisfied his libidinal longings to forestall neurosogenesis, then why prohibit him from cuddling with his mother in Vienna?

At one point, Freud suggests that Hans dealt with his increased libido at Gmunden by masturbating, which Freud takes to be a normal way for a child to siphon off sexual energy: "we may presume that Hans, who was now four and three-quarters, had been indulging in this pleasure every evening for at least a year" (1909/1955, p. 27). However, Freud's presumption seems unlikely if Hans was frequently sleeping in the same bed with his mother during the time at Gmunden, because when he was in bed alone is the only time and place Hans was reported to masturbate in the case report. That aside, Freud's presumption is explicitly contradicted by Hans in the course of the analysis: "I: 'Did you put your hand to your widdler at Gmunden, when you were in bed?' He: 'No. Not then; I slept so well at Gmunden that I never thought of it at all'" (1909/1955, pp. 61–62). So, Hans was not making up for increased libido by masturbating. Apparently, unfettered access to his mother seems to have lowered Hans's libido and anxiety, not amplified it.

Then, Freud explains, when Hans returned to Vienna, his father was again continuously present and regularly blocked him from cuddling with his mother. The result was a surfeit of sexual need with no outlet and a consequent increase in masturbation to relieve the arousal, and ultimately the development of a neurosis. If so, the question arises: why not let Hans freely satisfy his need for his mother's cuddling as he had done at Gmunden, thus discharging his increased libido and thereby preventing any neurosis, while allowing Olga to mother Hans in the way she wants? When Freud observes that it was the closeness to his mother at Gmunden followed by the abrupt cessation of that degree of closeness in Vienna that caused Hans's anxiety, why not choose to reintroduce the former benign closeness rather than maintaining the problematic cessation?

There is also the question of why Max immediately blames Olga for Hans's problem. In his report to Freud of the outbreak of Hans's horse phobia, Max simultaneously professes utter bewilderment as to what precisely could be the cause of the problem and utter certainty that it somehow must be due to Hans's relationship to his mother:

No doubt the ground was prepared by sexual over-excitation due to his mother's tenderness; but I am not able to specify the actual exciting cause ... I cannot see what to make of it. ... [I]s the whole thing simply connected with his mother?

(1909/1955, p. 22)

Freud diverts Max from an overtly accusatory stance by observing that arousing her child's sexual needs is a role that Olga, like all mothers, is predestined to play. He analogizes her inadvertent role to the mother who properly avoids touching her son's penis when powdering him after the bath and thereby inadvertently frustrates his libidinal needs. Yet, the emphasis in the treatment is on preventing cuddling between Hans and his mother, so some sort of blame or causal attribution seems implicit. How can this be explained?

I think there are two ways to resolve these puzzles. One way—the way taken by most recent commentators on the case—is to find that Olga has some form of sexually or physically abusive pathology that endangers Hans and justifies keeping Olga away from intimate interaction with her son and blaming her for his problems. The second way, which will be my approach, is to argue that Olga is in fact a good enough mother—a position I have already defended in Chapter 3—and to claim that behind the prohibitory attitude toward Hans's desires for his mother's cuddling there instead lie further theoretical doctrines that interact with the Oedipal theory to bias Freud's and Max's response toward the prohibitory and away from the liberatory approach.

In terms of organization, the way I will address these two possible solutions is as follows. In this chapter, I will initially critique the "pathology" solution by considering Doris Silverman's (2001) claim, representative of the sort of view put forward by many trauma-oriented writers, that Freud himself judged Olga to be pathologically overly affectionate to a pathogenic degree. I will explain why Silverman's analysis, based on textual evidence, is not correct. After this first skirmish, I will set aside the "pathology" approach as unlikely and devote the rest of this chapter to formulating what I see as the deeper theoretical doctrine behind Freud's reaction and Max's prohibitions—namely, a "spoiling theory" that holds that full gratification, rather than being enduringly satiating, amplifies the intensity of desire and so is itself pathogenic. Then, later, in Chapter 7, I will circle back to take care of unfinished polemical business

by systematically critiquing recent arguments that Olga is severely pathological. I will explain why I think that such arguments are not only wrong
but are so arbitrarily theory-driven and lacking in evidential grounding
that they reveal problems with psychoanalysis as a discipline as well as
some misogynistic biases rationalized by trauma theory.

Was Olga Pathologically Overaffectionate to Hans?: Reply to Doris Silverman

To the question of why Hans should be kept from his mother's cuddling,
there is an easy answer that has been adopted by most recent commentators: Olga was *excessively* affectionate to Hans to a pathogenic degree that
represented a psychological disturbance on her part. If so, then prohibiting
mother–son cuddling would make sense.

If Olga was indeed pathogenically overly affectionate or sexual in her
cuddling with Hans, one would expect Freud to observe this somewhere
in the case record. This is precisely what Doris Silverman (2001) claims:
"Freud acknowledged and minimized what he called the mother's over-
affectionate behavior toward Little Hans" (p. 351). That is, Silverman says
that Freud told us what he really believed—that Olga was pathogenically
seductive with Hans—but then downplayed that point in his subsequent
discussion. Silverman's view echoes accusations by other writers that
Olga was inappropriately seductive with Hans. However, she additionally
offers textual evidence that Freud explicitly recognized this fact, citing
Freud's reference in one passage to the mother's "excessive display of
affection" (1909/1955, p. 28). In this section, I examine Silverman's
reading of that passage and argue that in fact Freud did not believe and
never said that Olga was excessively affectionate toward Hans. Silverman's claim and thus her understanding of the overall case, I will argue, is
based on a mistaken interpretation of that key passage.

Regarding cuddling, it is worth recalling that Bowlby cites the research literature as telling us that Hans's mother's willingness to comfort Hans by cuddling with him to calm his fear is a common approach by mothers to childhood
fears. Bowlby notes that two out of three children Hans's age have recurrent
fears and that "In general, mothers tend to favour a mixture of explanation and
simple cuddling; and these usually at least have a soothing effect, even if they
do not always drive the fear away" (Bowlby, 1973, p. 195). So, we are looking
for a distinctively excessive affection beyond the standard response.

In raising the issue of Freud's minimizing Olga's pathological interactions with Hans, Silverman is correct that a single mention of something as central to Hans's analysis as his mother's excessive affection would be quite odd. When Freud has an etiological point to make, he generally makes it repeatedly. In the Hans case history, for example, Freud repeatedly identified Hans's pathogenically intensified sexual affection for his mother as the fundamental etiological variable. According to Freud, Hans's "increased affection for his mother" caused him to experience "enormously intensified" affection at "such a high pitch of intensity" that his "state of intensified sexual excitement" grew "greater than he could control" and Hans "was overwhelmed by an intensification of his libido" (see Freud, 1909/1955, pp. 24–25, p. 28, p. 110, p. 118, p. 132, p. 133, p. 136, p. 139, p. 140). In light of such repetitious emphasis on the increased intensity of Hans's desires as the crucial etiological variable, the one apparent reference early in the case history to the mother's excessive affection toward Hans does call for explanation, for if this was Freud's view of pathogenesis then it is indeed mysterious why he did not repeat the point, and Silverman's hypothesis that in his later discussion he misled his readers would have to be considered.

However, the explanation for this anomaly is not that Freud mentioned the truth of the mother's overaffection and then turned away from what he really thought. Rather, the passage Silverman cites does not mean what Silverman takes it to mean. Freud never acknowledged Olga's overaffection to begin with, so there was nothing for him to deceptively ignore later in his Discussion, and Silverman's interpretation does not get off the ground.

To explain Silverman's error, I need to back up a bit to place the passage she cites in context. Prior to the "excessive display" passage, Freud disputes and rejects the standard medical view that masturbation is likely responsible for Hans's anxieties. In this polemical spirit, Freud then goes on to dispute another etiological claim that had been provided by Hans's father, that the problem was due to Hans's mother. Max's note to Freud reporting the onset of Hans's phobia reads in part as follows:

My dear Professor, I am sending you a little more about Hans ....
during the last few days he has developed a nervous disorder ...

No doubt the ground was prepared by sexual over-excitation due to his mother's tenderness; but I am not able to specify the actual exciting cause. He is afraid *a horse will bite him in the street*, and this fear seems somehow to be connected with his having been frightened by a large penis ....

I cannot see what to make of it. Has he seen an exhibitionist somewhere? Or is the whole thing simply connected with his mother? ...

(1909/1955, p. 22)

Although Max is clearly in some sense blaming the mother in saying that the problem arose "due to" her tenderness, a close reading reveals that he is not specifically claiming that she was overly affectionate in some pathological sense. He only says that Hans became sexually overexcited due to his mother's tenderness, and perhaps he is implying that she is blameworthy because she did not follow his Oedipally driven instructions not to cuddle in bed with Hans.

After reproducing the father's note, Freud, in his running commentary, warns the reader not to take the father's explanatory attempts at face value, suggesting that he will be disagreeing with Max later: "We will not follow Hans's father either in his easily comprehensible anxieties or in his first attempts at finding an explanation; we will begin by examining the material before us" (p. 22). Later in his commentary, after Freud rejects the medical explanation of Hans's anxiety in terms of his masturbation, Freud finally returns to the father's explanation in terms of the mother's affection and rejects that proposed explanation as well in any sense that implies that her excessive affection was the cause of Hans's problem:

We must say a word, too, on behalf of Hans's excellent and devoted mother. His father accuses her, not without some show of justice, of being responsible for the outbreak of the child's neurosis, on account of her excessive display of affection for him and her too frequent readiness to take him into her bed. We might as easily blame her for having precipitated the process of repression by her energetic rejection of his advances ('that'd be piggish' [p. 19]). But she had a pre-destined part to play, and her position was a hard one.

(pp. 27–28)

Silverman claims that Freud is here *endorsing* the father's blame of the mother. A more plausible reading of the second sentence of this passage is that Freud is simply *repeating* the father's accusation (as Freud interprets it; in fact, we have seen that the father's accusation is more subtle) that he, Freud, is about to dispute. This is Freud's standard rhetorical technique, to state as vividly as possible an objection that he is about to answer. For example, in the immediately preceding passage disputing the standard explanation of Hans's anxiety in terms of masturbation, Freud first creates a quote for his imagined interlocutor: "Hans admitted that every night before going to sleep he amused himself with playing with his penis. 'Ah!' the family doctor will be inclined to say, 'now we have it. The child masturbated: hence his pathological anxiety'" (p. 27). After compellingly formulating the objection, Freud then disputes it.

When Freud challenges the content of Max's letter, he approaches the task in a similar way rhetorically. Freud says that the father accuses the mother of being responsible for Hans's anxiety because she is excessively affectionate and too easily takes Hans into bed with her. This, Freud says, is the father's accusation, it is not Freud's conclusion. Freud's formulation of the father's view, and especially his mention of the mother taking Hans into bed, must be based partly on his knowledge of the parents' disagreement over bedtime issues regarding cuddling that are not mentioned in the father's letter.

Freud's next two sentences show that he rejects the father's accusations. Freud compares blaming the mother's supposedly excessive affection to blaming her for refusing to touch Hans's penis when powdering him, which is surely a totally normal, appropriate, and prudent parental behavior even if it may frustrate Hans. Indeed, in "Three Essays" (1905/1953), Freud uses this very example to illustrate how the virtuous mother properly behaves: "She regards what she does as asexual, 'pure' love, since, after all, she carefully avoids applying more excitations to the child's genitals than are unavoidable in nursery care" (1905/1953, p. 223). Nonetheless, according to Freud, the virtuous mother inevitably, normally, and necessarily arouses Oedipal sexual desires. This would cause her guilt if she knew it, but her guilt can be relieved by an understanding of her inevitable role in her child's sexual development:

> A mother would probably be horrified if she were made aware that all her marks of affection were rousing her child's sexual instinct ... [I]f the mother understood more ... she would spare herself any self-reproaches .... She is only fulfilling her task in teaching the child to love.
>
> (1905/1953, p. 223)

Even if Hans's mother's avoidance of touching his genitals after the bath was frustrating to Hans and a cause of Hans repressing his sexual desires and triggering symptoms, it was not inappropriate and no blame is warranted.

The essence of Freud's riposte to Hans's father's accusation of the mother's overaffection is modeled on the discussion in the "Three Essays." Freud dismisses the father's accusation with the answer that Hans's mother "had a predestined part to play." She was destined in the course of normal mothering to arouse Hans's sexual desires, and no excessive or untoward behaviors need be involved, any more than it was inappropriate to frustrate Hans by not touching his genitals after the bath.

Of course, Freud does believe that truly excessive maternal affection can lead to problems of fixation on the mother and neediness and spoiling later in life, as he noted in "Three Essays":

> It is true that an excess of parental affection does harm by causing precocious sexual maturity and also because, by spoiling the child, it makes him incapable in later life of temporarily doing without love or of being content with a smaller amount of it.
>
> (1905/1953, p. 223)

However, Freud never suggests this is an issue in the Hans case, and there is no information in the Freud Archives interviews that points to the mother's seductive or excessive attentions. Instead, Freud's comment on the mother's "predestined" role reflects the normal mother's proper role in bringing about normal sexual development in her son, for which her triggering of sexual feelings in her son is essential: "After all, he is meant to grow up into a strong and capable person with vigorous sexual needs and to accomplish during his life all the things that human beings are urged to do by their instincts" (p. 223).

One might object to my above reading on the grounds that Freud's phrase, "not without some show of justice," in regard to the father's accusation against the mother, suggests that Freud to some extent endorses the father's explanation of Hans's phobia as caused by the mother. However, as in the Strachey translation, "*show* of justice," the original German (*nicht ohne einen Schein von Recht*) even more clearly indicates that the ostensible justice in the accusation is merely the "appearance" or "semblance" (to take two standard translations of *Schein*) of justice, indicating that although Max's accusation has some superficial plausibility, it is wrong. There also might be a nuance of poking fun at Max here for an exaggerated sense of indignation about the mother's inevitable motherly role. There is some scientific justice in placing the mother within the causal analysis, but this is not because she displayed excessive or inappropriate affection in any absolute sense. As in the *Three Essays*, Freud holds that "if she understood more ... she would spare herself any self-reproaches" (p. 223), and so would Max spare her his accusations.

I conclude that nowhere in the case history does Freud himself endorse the view that the mother was overly affectionate or inappropriately seductive in allowing Hans into her bed. So, contra Silverman, Freud does not make the point that Olga is overly affectionate and then deceitfully minimize this point; he never asserts any such point to begin with. He is clear and consistent throughout the case report that the problem is not maternal overaffection but rather Hans's overexcitement resulting from the interaction of Hans's intensifying needs due partly to his constitution and partly circumstances, in the context of his mother's inherently normal responses. The problem is more interactional than one of malignant actions on the part of one party.

A surprising conclusion that emerges out of this analysis is that, although Freud and Bowlby obviously have radically different views of the meaning of Hans cuddling in bed with his mother, in one important respect their views converge. Recall that Bowlby states the contrast between his own view and Freud's when it comes to the mother's cuddling of Hans in the following rather carefully chosen words:

> Mother's displays of affection to Hans and her allowing him to come into bed with her are seen, not simply as a natural and comforting expression of motherly feeling, but as actions that might have encouraged, in a rather unfortunate way, Hans's oedipal wishes.
>
> (1973, p. 287)

Bowlby perceptively avoids suggesting that Freud thought that the mother suffered from some problem of overaffection in expressing her natural and comforting motherly feelings. Rather, he portrays the claimed Oedipal intensification as an "unfortunate" by-product that was "encouraged" by the mother's natural actions. I believe that Bowlby succeeds in accurately portraying the nuances of Freud's view here, in a way that Silverman fails to do.

It bears emphasis that the fact that Hans's mother is blamed for his problems despite doing nothing intrinsically wrong is not itself a historical innovation distinctively associated with the Oedipal theory. I distinguished above between excessive affection in an objective pathological and potentially pathogenic sense, and excessive affection in a moral sense of inadequate restraint given an interactional situation in which normal-range affection is undesirable. Mothers were commonly morally blamed for their children's problems throughout the nineteenth-century masturbation crusade, based on the inference that they must have exercised insufficient vigilance or parental guidance and thus allowed their children either to masturbate or to be sexually provoked by some other individual. Blaming the mother was not in itself new. Nor, as we shall see in a later chapter, has it gone out of fashion even today. The innovation with Freud's Oedipal theory as manifested in the Hans case is not so much blaming of the mother per se but rather the way that parental guilt is now induced over normal parent–child affection and intimacy and used to justify major interventions into the mother–son attachment relationship.

Explanatory Limitations of the Oedipus Complex

If this initial verdict against Silverman's accusations holds up when we later examine similar arguments by other recent writers, as I will argue it does, and Olga is not guilty of the misdeeds of which the literature amply accuses her, this leaves unresolved the original problem of why Max and Freud take a prohibitory approach to Olga's and Hans's cuddling. Addressing this puzzle from a new perspective requires examining the background theoretical assumptions that interact with Oedipal theory to yield the case's distinctive exercise of power in the family relationships.

The Oedipal theory taken by itself, stating that the boy sexually desires his mother, is insufficient to generate any particular power structures or conclusions about responsibility when things go wrong. In a different theoretical context, the theory might have had quite different and perhaps more liberatory consequences. The theoretical apparatus deployed in the Little Hans case that enables it to have substantial prohibitory repercussions requires at least four elements:

1   the Oedipal theory, according to which the child sexually desires the mother;

2   the sexualization of attachment in a theoretical and interpretive sense
     (described in the last chapter), in which Freud's libido theory is used
     to reinterpret a broad range of desires and behaviors associated with
     normal attachment as ultimately expressions of the child's sexual
     desire for his mother;
3   the theory that excesses of incestuous sexual arousal on the child's
     part are potential causes of psychopathology due to undischarged
     libido, and thus pose a danger;
4   and finally, a less obvious component that I will call the "spoiling
     theory," as it is specifically applied to maternal indulgence or over-
     indulgence of the child's libidinal needs. The spoiling theory is both a
     theory of what can happen when a child develops too much sexual
     desire other than the development of a psychoneurosis, and a theory
     of one way that dangerously excessive levels of sexual desire can
     come about. Basically, spoiling theory asserts that ample levels of
     gratification of unusually intense desires, rather than producing
     enduring satiation, elicit increased need for yet greater levels of grat-
     ification. I will further explain this fourth component below.

Based on the first three principles, common sense might hold, and Bowlby
implies, that if Hans desires cuddling, then his mother should provide
it. The first three principles taken by themselves do not yield any conclusion
that gratification is threatening. The Oedipal theory conjoined with the theoretical sexualization of attachment behavior yields the conclusion that
parent–child relations are sexual across the whole domain of affectionate
interactions, and the theory of psychoneuroses postulates a danger that atta-
ches to excessive arousal. However, thus far, the theory and its auxiliary
assumptions provide no guidance as to what constitutes excessive gratification or how it comes about, and thus offer no account of what actions might
help to address the potential danger.

   Although the sexualization of maternal–child affection locates the
potential pathogenic sexual influence within the maternal–child affectionate interaction, this feature remains limited in its implications. It does
not by itself explain Max Graf's immediate reaction of blaming Hans's
mother for his anxiety problems. The first three elements together—
incestuous sexual desire by the child, the sexual nature of the child's
attachment pleasures such as cuddling with the mother and being soothed
when anxious, and the potentially pathogenic effect of the child's

excessive undischarged sexual arousal—do not by themselves create a clear implication of a maternal locus of responsibility for pathogenesis. Based on these three elements alone, one might equally hold that as much maternal affection as possible is to be preferred as a preventive measure because the child's libido will then be discharged and no excess buildup will occur. Based on these elements alone, it is unclear why Max and Freud would want Hans to be kept from cuddling with his mother to the degree that cuddling, although arousing, is also gratifying.

Thus, consistent with the first three elements, the theory could be interpreted in liberatory terms that encourage an acceptance of sexuality and its expression, much like Freud's anti-Victorian claim that female orgasm is not only natural but essential to women's health, or more generally his acceptance of "perverse" sexual activities as expressions of natural component instincts. As we saw, Freud actually says something along these lines regarding masturbation in the Hans case history when he tries to explain why masturbatory pleasure in itself is not harmful:

> That the child was getting pleasure for himself by masturbating does not by any means explain his anxiety; on the contrary, it makes it more problematical than ever. States of anxiety are not produced by masturbation or by getting satisfaction in any shape.
>
> (1909/1955, p. 27)

How, then, does it happen that in the Hans case the mother takes on the role formerly reserved for lecherous nannies, uncles, fathers, prematurely sexualized siblings or playmates, and other such external influences in the nineteenth-century masturbation crusade? These were the people who, according to masturbation-crusade ideology, provided excessive premature sexual stimulation that destroyed the health of youngsters. (For a detailed discussion of this history as it relates to the development of Freud's theorizing, see my forthcoming *Foucault Versus Freud*.) Some additional component of the theory is needed to explain this outcome, and I am proposing spoiling theory as a candidate. Given that the first three elements do not imply anything about the mother's potential culpability, I will say no more about them here and focus on the spoiling theory and how it was construed within Oedipal theory and impacted Oedipal power/ knowledge. As we shall see, Bowlby (1973) also perceived the spoiling theory as a central doctrine and harmful error of Freudian psychoanalytic theory and argued against it as well, and I will focus on Bowlby's analysis in the discussion below.

The Spoiling Theory

In Hans's case, based on the first three principles, common sense might hold, and Bowlby implies, that if Hans desires cuddling, then his mother should provide it. However, given the theory that Hans's psychoneurosis is due to intensified libidinal desire, and the spoiling notion that gratification amplifies desire, Max judges that control rather than gratification is called for. Max thus decides that the only prudent thing to do is to stop Hans from cuddling with his mother to stop the amplification of his desires. Max's stopping Hans from coming into the mother's bed to prevent Hans's dangerous overstimulation is the Oedipal-theoretic equivalent of the masturbation-crusade intervention, which Max also performs, of placing Hans in a sack at night to prevent him from masturbating and amplifying his sexual desire in that way.

According to the spoiling theory, full or ample gratification of sexual need is potentially harmful. Rather than yielding beneficial satiation and security, high maternal affection that amply satisfies the child's sexual needs relative to the child's optimal developmental need based on its constitutional libidinal nature can cause intensified subsequent needs for further gratification and thus excessive sexual arousal and desire and excessive need for more gratification in the child. The result is overdependency, chronic libidinal longing, insatiable neediness, and an inability to tolerate denial of continued stimulation. In other words, too much maternal affection can cause what amounts to a sexualized version of Bowlby's notion of "anxious attachment" and what Freud labeled as "fixation" due to overgratification:

> Fixations of Preliminary Sexual Aims. APPEARANCE OF NEW AIMS. Every external or internal factor that hinders or postpones the attainment of the normal sexual aim … will evidently lend support to the tendency to linger over the preparatory activities and to turn them into new sexual aims that can take the place of the normal one.
>
> (1905/1953, pp. 155–156)

When explaining the development of children with generally anxious temperaments, Freud offers three explanations: "it is only children with a sexual instinct that is excessive or has developed prematurely or has become vociferous owing to too much petting who are inclined to be timid" (1905/1953, p. 224). It is the third option, that a child who is not constitutionally excessively libidinal but who has been subjected to too much physical affection can become anxious, that constitutes spoiling. One might argue that this image of the child as becoming more needy to the point of pathological dependency due to being sexually gratified is straight out of masturbation-crusade horror stories about what happens to children who touch their genitals, although the idea that satisfying a child's needs will spoil them has broader cultural roots.

The impact of the spoiling theory on parents' attempts to judge proper childrearing behavior in the Oedipal family is enormously magnified by the fact that children's libidinal natures vary greatly and are not obvious. Thus, parents cannot necessarily reliably judge their child's libidinal constitutional nature or how it might vary over time. Oedipal parents are faced with the challenge that ample versus moderate gratification causes increased desire rather than satiation, but what is ample versus moderate is very difficult to judge and differs for each child and over time, yielding what amounts to an ever-present danger from affectionate gratification of the child's need for comforting.

I have suggested that the incorporation of the spoiling theory as a fourth critical element in the overall Oedipal-theoretic context turns the Oedipal theory into a weapon that can be used to blame and control the mother rather than a liberatory mechanism for the mother–child pair. From a broader historical perspective, it is due to the acceptance of the spoiling theory that Oedipal theory importantly diverges from the earlier masturbation crusade in being specifically attentive to dangers in the maternal role rather than in child behavior.

As a general theory (not specifically sexual), the spoiling perspective holds that excessive parental indulgence of a child's needs does not satisfy and exhaust them but rather creates a dependency and greater chronic need for such gratification. When it is combined with Oedipal theory, it yields what is essentially a "sexual addiction" approach to pathogenesis, with the "pusher" of the addictive sexual experience being the mother. The masturbation crusade had no comparable inherent role for the parent in pathogenesis, other than as derelict parents who are so distracted as to fail to catch the child in the masturbatory act or so overly free with the household's boundaries as to allow an uncle or nanny to take liberties with the child that stimulate masturbatory activity.

The spoiling theory's distinctive impact on power results from its conjunction in Freud's hands with the libido theory. The view that abundant gratification causes excessive dependency, conjoined with the transformation of mother–son affection into sexuality via the libido theory and the assumption of the child's spontaneous incestuous sexual desire, together yield the conclusion that ample affection from the mother, rather than healthily and fully satisfyingly the child's needs, pathogenically oversatisfies and potentially sexually spoils the child. The spoiling theory warns of problematic sexual arousal caused by parental affection that is too gratifying and not carefully balanced with the nature of the child. It also describes a potential pathological outcome for the child that is much more subtle and more global than a psychoneurosis. In essence, spoiling theory postulates a danger that without careful regulation of parent–child affection, the child may be vulnerable to what in effect is a form of sexual addiction to the mother.

Given the child's decidedly incestuous desires, the mother's affections are presumably the child's main source of direct sexual gratification. Consequently, the mother's affection represents the *primary* danger to the child, other than the child's own constitution with its natural level of libido. The optimal locus of control efforts thus lie with control of the mother. And, as we shall see, the spoiling theory allows for subtle interactions in which mother's behavior does not have to be manifestly extreme to be potentially pathogenic. Nothing like this line of reasoning that routinely directs suspicion for pathogenesis on to the parents existed prior to Oedipal theory.

Bowlby on the Mystery of Freud's Acceptance of the Spoiling Theory

An implication of the combined Oedipal and spoiling theories is that the mother's affection can easily become a pathogenic source of overstimulation and overgratification for the child, even when such a danger is not obvious. This result is central to understanding how Oedipal power/knowledge restructures family relations. But does Freud actually embrace such a view?

Bowlby (1973) reviewed an "array of hypotheses that have been proposed to account for why a particular individual is prone to a high degree of overdependency or separation anxiety, the terms by which anxious attachment is usually known" (p. 237). Although several alternative hypotheses existed that attempted to explain overdependency in terms of temperament and early experience, Bowlby concluded that the spoiling hypothesis was Freud's lifelong view:

> The ... hypothesis, that an excess of parental affection spoils a child by making him exceptionally demanding and intolerant of frustration, is one that was very widely held during the first half of this century and that still dies hard. Freud not only committed himself to it at an early stage of his work but held to it firmly and consistently until the end .... [T]his view has had a deep and lasting influence on psychoanalytic theory.
>
> (1973, p. 238)

Observing that the spoiling theme not only runs through the case of Little Hans but was mentioned earlier by Freud in *Three Essays* (1905/1953), Bowlby draws attention to Freud's ambivalence about maternal physical affection due to his concern about overgratification: "After commending the mother who strokes, rocks, and kisses her child and thereby teaches him to love, he nevertheless warns against excess" (1973, p. 239). Bowlby refers to Freud's words in the *Three Essays*:

> [A]n excess of parental affection does harm by causing precocious sexual maturity and also because, by spoiling the child, it makes him incapable in later life of temporarily doing without love or of being content with a smaller amount of it.
>
> (1905/1953, p. 223)

Reviewing the evidence pertaining to needy or anxious attachment, Bowlby argues that, contra Freud, anxious attachment results from threats to the attachment bond, such as separation, threats of abandonment, and parental quarrels that suggest a risk of losing the parent. It is not caused by overgratification, and it is not inherently a sexual phenomenon. He observes that the lack of evidence for the spoiling theory leaves us with the mystery of why the spoiling theory was so widely accepted:

> Despite its wide popularity, no evidence of substance has ever been presented to support the theory that anxious attachment is a result of

an excess of parental affection. As already indicated, all the evidence points the other way. The question arises, therefore, why Freud (and many others also) should have favoured the theory.

(1973, p. 239)

Bowlby thus asks: "How came it, then, that Freud should have adopted the theory of spoiling?" (1973, p. 223). He answers his question as follows:

Apart from the likelihood that he was more influenced than he realized by the accepted opinion of his day, there is some evidence that he was misled by the show of affection and over-protection that is so frequently present either as an over-compensation for a parent's unconscious hostility to a child or as part of the parent's own desire to cling to the child. This explanation is suggested by a passage in *Three Essays*, immediately following that quoted earlier, in which he refers to "neuropathic parents, who are inclined as a rule to display excessive affection, [as] precisely those who are most likely by their caresses to arouse the child's disposition to neurotic illness."

(1973, p. 223)

Bowlby argues that in virtually all cases where a child is overdependent, rather than there being an "excess of parental affection," there is in fact a lack of adequate affection manifested typically in actual or threatened withdrawal of love from the child. He also allows that some cases of overdependency are brought about by a parent who clings to the child and, in a reversal of roles, sees the child as the parent's caretaker (i.e., it is the parent who is overdependent and anxious about separation, and the child responds to this feeling). According to Bowlby, plentiful maternal accessibility and affection lead to secure attachment, not neediness. There is simply no such thing as "spoiling" within this domain, because the more secure the early attachment relationship and thus the better the "secure base" and "safe haven" provided by the parent, the more—not less—capable is the child of later exploring the environment on his own independently of the parent's support. Bowlby (1973) presents considerable evidence that this view is the correct one and concludes:

To some it may seem a trifle absurd to go to such lengths to demonstrate that uncertainty regarding the availability of an attachment figure commonly results in anxious attachment. Yet, so long as terms such as "overdependent" and "spoiled" are in use to describe the individuals in question and a theory is current that attributes their condition to an excess of gratification during their early years, children and especially adults who manifest this type of behavior will meet with scant sympathy or understanding. Once it is recognized that the condition is one of anxiety over the accessibility and responsiveness of attachment figures, and that it develops as a result of bitter experience, there is good prospect not only of helping those who have grown up insecure but of preventing others from doing so.

(1973, p. 244)

Consistent with Bowlby's observation, Little Hans got no sympathy for his neediness, which I argued in the last chapter was proximally magnified by Max's active rejection of Hans's attempts to be physically close with his mother. Due to the Oedipal theory, Hans was caught in a vicious cycle. The more anxious and therefore needy of physical affection he became, the more he naturally sought solace and soothing from his mother's embrace. But the more he sought such solace, the more he was interpreted as sexually needy and— due to the theory that it was sexual over-stimulation by the mother's embrace that caused the neediness—the more vigorously his attempts to gain soothing were rejected. Hans finally tries to cut through this craziness by protesting with admirable common sense, "When I'm not in bed with you, then I'm frightened. When I'm not frightened any more, I shan't come any more" (1909/1955, p. 44). But his fear was taken as a manifestation of anxiety generated by sexual desire for his mother; surely a little boy who wants parental affection for the sexual gratification it affords and to which he is addicted is unlikely to get a sympathetic response to his entreaties. Hans's treatment underscores Bowlby's point that Oedipal theory represents an extraordinarily unsympathetic—and possibly inadvertently cruel—way to approach the child's desire for closeness to his mother.

Unlike Oedipal theory, the spoiling theory was anchored in the commonsense beliefs of the time. One might also suspect that Freud's disposition to accept the spoiling theory of mother–son intimacy has its source as well in Freud's insistence on the specifically sexual nature of mother–son affection. For, if such affection is an instance of the sexual gratification of a lover by his beloved, one might expect this to be addicting and to lead to a desire for more, as intense sexual love frequently does. Ultimately, the answer to Bowlby's question about the spoiling theory's appeal is likely to be intertwined with the nature of the Oedipal theory's appeal. The answer regarding the theories' appeal may be sought at least partly, I will argue, in the role they played in restructuring family power. They offer a joint theoretical context that implies danger in maternal affection, thus restructuring family life.

The Subtlety of Spoiling

The way that the spoiling theory is deployed in the family is quite subtle, especially if we take Hans's case as the benchmark. This subtlety is important because it addresses the puzzle raised earlier about the case: Hans's mother's behavior does not appear particularly deviant, abusive, or seductive, despite the fact that some commentators have found her so (those claims are addressed in Chapter 7). So why, based on Hans's cuddling with her in bed, is her responding to Hans's anxiety with motherly affection seen as triggering his neurosis and as needing to be controlled against her own wishes?

As we have now seen, Oedipal theory allows that the processes that can lead to what amounts in a practical sense to overgratification and to an intensification of the child's libido are such that there need be no deviant maternal behavior. It is possible for the mother to be perfectly normal in her responses and for her still to cause her son's overgratification if the child's constitutional sexual intensity and circumstantial sensitivity are such that his gratification brings about spoiling and thus greater neediness. This is reflected in Freud's comment, quoted above, on "Hans's excellent and devoted mother" who was simply playing her "predestined" parental role that is inevitably frustrating to the child, like not touching his penis when powdering him. Freud's point is that Olga's behavior can be objectively appropriate yet Hans can be frustrated.

So, how can one's actions be entirely appropriate and at the same time problematic? The answer is implied in Freud's explanation that "she had a predestined part to play, *and her position was a hard one*" (emphasis added). If we look beyond a sheerly developmental point, this suggests that it was not anything she did per se in discharging her predestined obligations that was wrong, but rather it was the performance of her appropriate role in the specific circumstances in which she found herself that made "her position … a hard one" and was at fault for the result.

A year later, Freud again vindicates Olga and fills in the gap in his explanation, portraying the problem as essentially relational or situational. In the Minutes of the Vienna Psychoanalytic Society (Nunberg & Federn, 1967), Freud states: "[N]ot *that* many mistakes were made, and those that did occur did not have *that* much to do with the neurosis .... [N]eurosis is essentially a matter of constitution" (p. 235). Olga's affection is exonerated and, more importantly, Freud explains that Hans's libidinal constitution created a situation in which Olga interacting in a normal way with Hans nonetheless created problematic levels of sexual desire in Hans. This explains the hard position in which the mother found herself in expressing her predestined and normal affectionate response.

The assertion by Freud that Hans's neurosis was essentially "a matter of constitution" is perhaps surprising given Freud's painstaking arguments against any hereditary theory of neurosogenesis. Having switched from an environmental theory that sexual abuse in childhood causes neurosis to his Oedipal theory of the genesis of neurosis in instinctual development, Freud wanted to emphasize the role of variations in constitutional libidinal intensity in neurosogenesis. His point here was not to deny the role of parenting or other circumstances in neurosogenesis but to imply that parenting derives its role in interaction with the child's libidinal constitution, and that constitution sometimes can be an overriding factor. The mother's level of affection may not be pathological but still may be part of an interactional causal process. Hans's mother's normal-range level of affection for Hans was enough, due to Hans's constitutionally highly libidinal nature and the circumstantial vicissitudes of his summer at Gmunden and subsequent time in Vienna, to trigger a neurosis. Being an excellent mother and yet causing a son's anxiety condition are consistent, given the interactionist explanation that depends on Hans's constitution. From this perspective, the father's persistent efforts to keep Hans and his mother from cuddling can be seen as his way of heading off the interactional problem by lowering the mother's affection below the normal range to allow a less pathogenic interaction with Hans's high libido.

The constitutional aspect to which Freud refers includes the intensity, bodily distribution, and adhesiveness (i.e., degree of capacity to displace sexual desires from one object to another or to successfully mourn and shift them when they are not gratified) of Hans's libido. Freud makes clear that it is not *purely* constitutional on Hans's side, which would raise the "hereditarily neurotic" specter. A number of events that occurred around the time of the phobia's formation contributed to Hans's increased libidinal need, according to Freud. These circumstantial factors include, for example, the father's absence from Gmunden, yielding Hans's greater closeness with his mother, followed by the return to Vienna with lessened closeness due to the father's continued presence; multiple friends in Gmunden followed by lack of friends in Vienna due to the family's move to a new apartment; Hans's move into his own bedroom; Hans's memories of being separated from his mother during her confinement a year earlier; subsequent to Hanna's birth, an "outburst of sexual pleasure and sexual curiosity" as Hans "watched the way in which the infant was looked after" and "the memory-traces of his own earliest experiences of pleasure were revived in him" (1909/1955, p. 113); and other contiguous events that similarly lowered Hans's overall level of libidinal satisfaction (see Chapter 3 and Wakefield, 2007). Hans's various experiences called for additional affectionate attention by his mother, and she stood ready to supply it. But, according to the spoiling theory, a motherly response rendered Hans ripe for overgratification because the mother's normal-range responsivity might be an excessive reaction relative to Hans's needs.

Thus, the father considers himself justified in trying to suppress his wife's responsiveness to Hans's needs, even if nothing she does is out of line with normal response. The mother remains blameworthy in Max's eyes because she does not adequately acknowledge Hans's libidinal level and restrain her natural affection to dampen the intensity of the son's expressed needs. In other words, she is blameworthy because she resists accepting and being guided by Oedipal theory and instead trusts her son's expressions of need. The crucial point within Oedipal theorizing is that what constitutes a pathogenic level or kind of maternal affection depends on the constitution and circumstances of the child, not necessarily on the inherent excesses or deviance of the mother's actions. This explains why Max's active interference in the mother-son relationship is not criticized by Freud as excessive or misguided, even though Freud thinks the mother is acting normally. It is not misguided because control of motherly stimulation, even if that stimulation is within normal range, is essential to the Oedipal approach to the family in which normal levels of affection may be pathogenic depending on the constitution and situation of the child. Such is the subtlety of sexual spoiling of the child.

What all this points to is the sinister quality of the suspicions that constitute Oedipal power/knowledge. It is not merely overtly, clearly discernible overgratification that is the culprit. It is also what otherwise would be judged normal responsiveness—not spoiling in the usual sense—that may play this role. There is here a fateful divergence between etiological theory and practices of intervention. For in the Hans case, although constitution and circumstances are judged by Freud to be the primary etiological culprits, the mother's and Hans's relationship is the target of control in the family's Oedipal power/ knowledge intervention. Constitution and life's earlier vicissitudes are not generally subject to manipulation, so the mother–son relationship is the primary target of intervention.

It is now generally accepted in light of Bowlby's theory of attachment that physical soothing, skin contact, and associated pleasures are natural expressions of a nonsexual evolutionarily shaped attachment bond between mother and son, with a variety of biological and psychological functions. Freud's theoretical construction within the affectionate nonsexual interaction of mother and child of the danger of premature sexual stimulation interfered with the workings of the attachment bond. However, it also created the opportunity for the father to justify managing mother–child intimacy and wield control over the marital bed supported by medical authority. Incidentally or not, it also increased his opportunities for intimacy with his wife undistracted by children in a modern marriage that is judged, in part, by sexual fulfillment (see Chapter 8).

We saw in Chapter 4 and above that, in a manner similar to his comment that Hans's mother was not blameworthy because she was playing her predestined role, Freud attempted to exonerate mothers in general from what might otherwise appear in his theory to be sexual abuse of their children by routine physical contact:

> A mother would probably be horrified if she were made aware that all her marks of affection were rousing her child's sexual instinct .... [I]f the mother understood more of the high importance of the part played by instincts in mental life ... she would spare herself any self-reproaches even after her enlightenment. She is only fulfilling her task in teaching the child to love.
>
> (1905/1953, p. 223)

However, this reassurance turns out to be empty because, according to Oedipal theory plus the spoiling theory, mothers can ruin their children for life simply by responding naturally to what appear to be reasonable demands for affection.: "an excess of parental affection ... makes him incapable in later life of temporarily doing without love" (1905/1953, p. 223). Freud makes clear that parents are walking a tightrope with respect to arousal of their child:

> [T]he parents' affection for their child may awaken his sexual instinct prematurely (i.e. before the somatic conditions of puberty are present) to such a degree that the mental excitation breaks through in an unmistakable fashion to the genital system. If, on the other hand, they are fortunate enough to avoid this, then their affection can perform its task of directing the child in his choice of a sexual object when he reaches maturity. No doubt the simplest course for the child would be to choose as his sexual objects the same persons whom, since his childhood, he has loved with what may be described as damped-down libido .... Society must defend itself against the danger that the interests which it needs for the establishment of higher social units may be swallowed up by the family; and for this reason ... it seeks by all possible means to loosen their connection with their family ....
>
> (1905/1953, pp. 225)

The mother has here taken the place of the Victorian outsider who might abuse and thereby prematurely awaken a child's sexuality. Even the normal child and mother are at risk. Normal behavior on the part of the child and mother, if mismatched in various ways due to unknown constitutional factors and environmental vicissitudes, can yield neurosis or spoiling. One must be "fortunate" to avoid overstimulation, and the dire consequences call for erring on the side of caution. However careful one is, things can go either way—constructive development towards a good marital life or deterioration into an overly dependent individual still attached to the parents in adulthood. Given that idiosyncratic parental judgments can easily be wrong, there is a need for family management techniques designed to ensure safety and to keep the child's sexual arousal to a minimum through such measures as reduced cuddling and separate sleeping arrangements.

Freud notes that the dangers present in unregulated affection are worrisome not just for the child, but for society itself. Society must defend itself, and the bulwark of that defense is the parents' self-monitoring and prudent restraint. The ultimate loosening of the child's connection to family on which the child's love life and society's self-perpetuation depend can be undermined by too much affection early on, for the "simplest" pathway for the child is to stay in love with its parents. It thus takes active and thoughtful management of the mother–son relationship not just by parents but also by society and its medical authorities to avoid the danger of overdependency and incestuous sexual fixation, so as to ensure society's perpetuation.

This analysis places Freud's extensive defense in his Discussion section of Hans's normality and lack of hereditary taint in a new light. Freud is primarily arguing this point to allow the generalization of his Oedipal theory to all children as a universal and normal psychosexual development stage, contrary to the masturbation-crusade account of childhood as normally nonsexual: "what little Hans shows us will turn out to be typical of the sexual development of children in general" (1909/1955, p. 7). Freud argues that Hans's sexual precocity is simply a normal variation that may not be uncommon among intellectually precocious, physically vital, curious boys such as Hans. Thus, incestuous desires in childhood are part of normal development and must be managed by parental responses, not excluded from expression or otherwise directly controlled.

However, from the perspective of Oedipal power/knowledge, Freud's argument that Hans is normal universalizes the appropriate setting for the exercise of such power and requires that the regulation of mother–son intimacy must be at the heart of the normal modern family's raising of a son. Freud gives us the bad news that the price of parenthood is constant vigilance, a point that at the time fit with the history of surveillance of the child during the masturbation crusade. Thus, Hans's phobia may actually have benefited him because it alerted his parents to the fact that his libidinal economy was not being properly managed and his relationship with his mother not properly regulated:

> In bringing up children we aim only at being left in peace and having no difficulties, in short, at training up a model child, and we pay very little attention to whether such a course of development is for the child's good as well. I can therefore quite imagine that it may have been to Hans's advantage to have produced this phobia. For it directed his parents' attention to the unavoidable difficulties by which a child is confronted when in the course of his cultural training he is called upon to overcome the innate instinctual components of his mind; and his trouble brought his father to his assistance.
>
> (1909/1955, pp. 141–144)

These new medical/scientific justifications for restraining the mother's potentially damaging affection towards her son and thus for reserving the parental bed for the parents pose novel challenges that are more subtle than previous restrictions on familial sexuality, such as the nineteenth-century masturbation crusade's focus on detecting manifestations of child sexuality. Normal childhood development must involve an affectionate relationship with a caregiver, so one cannot prohibit maternal affection entirely. One can at best regulate it so that the child's inherent sexuality is neither amplified to a pathological degree nor so deprived as to cause an alternative pathology. Thus, Western parents—and virtually only Western parents—worry about how early to move their young child to his or her own bed and room and how much crying to allow before responding (see Chapter 9 on cosleeping). The relationship between mother and son becomes a challenging emotional balancing act judged by everyone. Nothing remotely like this new family power structure existed prior to the Oedipal theory.

Conclusion

Bowlby (1973), we saw, pointed out that the scientific evidence is decidedly against the notion that ample affection creates dependency or over-arousal in a child. Bowlby thus found himself bewildered as to how the notion of neurosogenically "spoiling" a child through overly affectionate behavior, and specifically Freud's deployment of the idea of the danger of maternal over-stimulation within the Oedipal theory, could possibly garner the broad allegiance it did. Yet this questionable assumption is at the heart of the way the Oedipal theory is deployed in the Hans case analysis. It is a view that, sustained by the Oedipal theory, has diffused throughout our culture and remains an implicit consideration in shaping parent–child relations.

Later, in Chapter 8, I examine the social context of changes in the nature of marriage at the time of the emergence of the Oedipal theory to seek a "functional" understanding of what the Oedipus complex did for, and to, the family that possibly might account for its appeal. In Chapter 9, I explore one area of evidence, the Western disapproval of cosleeping of child and parent in the same bed, for my hypothesis about the broader social reach of Oedipal power/knowledge.

However, before considering these broader social implications, there is a more immediate question about how Oedipal power/knowledge played out in Hans's family dynamics, which I consider in the next chapter, Chapter 6. Foucault suggests that power always creates resistance. I will argue that at the founding of Oedipal power/knowledge in the middle-class family as represented in the Hans case, Olga Honig saw through the fallacies in Freud's theory and did attempt to resist Oedipal power/knowledge as wielded by Max and Freud. She did this to the degree and in a manner that she could within the patriarchal constraints of her time and situation.

References

Bowlby, J. (1973). *Attachment and loss (Vol. 2): Separation: Anxiety and anger.* London, UK: Hogarth Press.

Freud, S. (1953). Three essays on the theory of sexuality. In J. Strachey (Ed. & Trans.), *The standard edition of the complete psychological works of Sigmund Freud* (Vol. 7, pp. 123–246). London, UK: Hogarth Press. (Original work published 1905.)

Freud, S. (1955). Analysis of a phobia in a five-year-old boy. In J. Strachey (Ed. & Trans.), *The standard edition of the complete psychological works of Sigmund Freud* (Vol. 10, pp. 1–150). London, UK: Hogarth Press. (Original work published 1909.)

Nunberg, H., & Federn, E. (1967). *Minutes of the Vienna Psychoanalytic Society (Vol. 2): 1908–1910.* New York, NY: International Universities Press.

Silverman, D. K. (2001). Sexuality and attachment: A passionate relationship or a marriage of convenience? *Psychoanalytic Quarterly, 70,* 325–358.

Spitz, R. A. (1952). Authority and masturbation: Some remarks on a bibliographical investigation. *The Psychoanalytic Quarterly, 21(4),* 490–527.

Wakefield, J. C. (2007). Little Hans and attachment theory: Bowlby's hypothesis reconsidered in light of new evidence from the Freud Archives. *The Psychoanalytic Study of the Child, 62,* 61–91.

Wakefield, J. C. (forthcoming). *Foucault versus Freud: Oedipal theory and the deployment of sexuality.* New York: Routledge.

Chapter 6

Olga Honig's Resistance to Oedipal Power/Knowledge

My central hypothesis, developed in the last two chapters, is that what the Oedipal theory is "about" in power terms in the Hans case is the regulation of the relationship between mother and son. Hans's father, Max Graf, wields the theory to regulate the mother–son relationship by creating a sense of sexual danger about Hans and his mother Olga Honig Graf's natural attachment-related physical contact. This hypothesis was challenging to evaluate because the struggle between Hans's father and mother over Hans and Olga's mother–son affection is not the explicit subject of the case record and is largely implicit. Nonetheless, sufficient information exists in the case history to confidently excavate Max's imposition of Oedipal power/knowledge on Olga and Hans, preventing them from their usual cuddling in bed. This interference allows Max to exclude Hans from the marital bed and thus reserve the marital bed to himself and his wife, and Max's acceptance of Freud's Oedipal-theoretic sexualization of attachment allows him to rationalize these actions.

However, it turns out that the case history does not just portray a simple matter of Max and Freud effortlessly applying Oedipal theory to Hans and a consenting and submissive Olga. A close examination reveals evidence that Olga was subtly resisting their efforts to impose the prohibitions derived from the then-novel Oedipal theory on her affectionate relations with her son. This sort of resistance is not immediately obvious, but it is to be expected. In *History of Sexuality*, Foucault (1978) observes: "Where there is power, there is resistance" (1978, p. 95). If one initially exercises a novel form of theory-based power, some resistance to the attempt to alter individuals' actions and relationships is virtually inevitable, at least until the theory becomes widely accepted, routinized, implicit, and psychosocially syntonic. Resistance in this broad sense would include any action that does not acquiesce in or cooperate with the alterations in relationships demanded by the new form of power.

DOI: 10.4324/9780203817124-6

I shall argue that such resistance is evident in Olga's reactions at the dawn of Oedipal power/knowledge, in the first recorded instance of the exercise of such power within a family. When Hans and Olga are denied the ability to cuddle when Hans is anxious and needs soothing, Hans protests, but he has little ability to affect things. It is from Olga, in defense of her pre-Oedipal-theory natural feelings regarding her motherly relationship to Hans, that we might expect to see some sort of resistance, and, I shall argue, we do.

It must be acknowledged that on the surface, there is no such resistance detectable. To my knowledge, no one has ever suggested any such resistance by Olga, who appears to go along more or less passively with the Oedipal program, albeit with some occasional misgivings about denying Hans his desired soothing and cuddling. Indeed, this aspect of the case is even more difficult to reconstruct than the exercise of Oedipal power/knowledge itself because it is even less a focus of the case report and is purposely hidden by Olga, and so remains almost invisible. Consequently, such conflict must be inferred by attending to anomalous details that require explanations that are never given. I shall argue that, despite these limitations and the inferential risks they entail, the case offers compelling evidence to support my reading.

Contextual Factors Pushing for Olga's Acquiescence

If Olga did put up any resistance at all to Oedipal power/knowledge, it was a heroic thing to do given the circumstances. Despite the changing nature of marriage towards greater egalitarianism, she lived at a time of real albeit gradually receding patriarchy. We saw in the review of the Archives interviews in Chapter 2 that Max and Freud discussed by themselves major issues that impacted on Olga's life, from whether Max should marry Olga and whether the problematic marriage could be saved by having children to whether to raise Hans as a Jew. It appears that some decisions were made by them and seemingly imposed on Olga against her will. This appears especially to be the case regarding the decision to have a second child, an issue about which Olga had strong negative feelings and for which she never forgave Freud.

Beyond the issue of gendered family power and the especially imposing power of the duo of Max and Freud, there were several more specific circumstantial reasons for Olga to be, or to at least appear to be, cooperative and restrained. Her husband was a member of Freud's inner circle, so his increasing success might depend to some extent on his continued good relations with Freud. Moreover, Max's dedication to Freud meant that challenging Oedipal power/knowledge would put the couple even more seriously at odds than they already were (see Chapter 2). Most importantly, their son, Hans, was suffering, and Olga was no doubt grateful that help was being offered by a distinguished physician.

We also know from the case history that Olga had been a patient of Freud's at some earlier point, and so there was the complex relationship and bond of patient and analyst. Moreover, as we saw in Chapter 2, it is likely that Olga became a charity patient of Freud's when her mother would no longer pay for her treatment, and so there was also an unspoken element of a debt to be paid.

Additionally, as Max reports, beyond any professional interactions, there was a friendship between Freud and the Grafs that included frequent socializing as well as Freud regularly eating dinner at the Grafs' home and talking with them about psychoanalysis. The Grafs were already helping Freud by keeping a diary of Hans's sexual development, so accepting his guidance when a problem arose seemed a natural thing to do. All of these factors weighed against rocking the boat when it came to accepting the application of Oedipal theory to Hans and the family.

Olga's Sympathy to Adler as a Reason for Resistance

Against the above considerations that argued for Olga's acquiescence in Max's intrusive application of Oedipal theory to her family were quite powerful factors potentiating doubts. Some of these reasons had to do with psychoanalytic politics, and others concerned Olga's experiences in her earlier analysis with Freud.

First, regarding psychoanalytic politics, in 1908, at the time of the Hans case, the major theoretical confrontation between Freud and Adler was taking place. That was the very year that Alfred Adler presented a culminating paper expressing his views to Freud's "Wednesday Society" of psychoanalytic followers, of which Adler had long been a member and from which he was soon to depart. Adler postulated an aggressive instinct and argued that feelings of superiority versus inferiority and the "inferiority complex" rather than sexual desires and the Oedipus complex are the primary etiological factors in neurosogenesis. Within a few years,

Adler and Freud split formally, with Adler and a group of his supporters leaving Freud's circle. At about that time, Max also left the circle. As to Freud, whereas in 1908 he could not see how Adler's ideas could be incorporated into psychoanalysis, he eventually came to see the importance of an aggressive instinct (or "Death instinct") and acknowledged Adler's contribution in a note added in 1923 to the Hans case history.

Olga is described as brilliant, and she appears to have been steeped in psychoanalytic theory and certainly had a mind of her own about psychoanalysis, as the descriptions of her in the Archives interviews indicate (see Chapter 2). The divergences between Adler and Freud were highly contentious among psychoanalytic followers in the years before the 1908 paper and they certainly would have been discussed by the Grafs and Freud at their regular dinners. As we saw in Chapter 2, Olga eventually rejected Freud entirely and went to Adler's side and maintained a close friendship with him for years afterward. It is thus likely that Olga was already veering away from Freud's theory and toward Adler's theory at the time of the Hans case. Her resistance to Oedipal power/knowledge's restructuring of her relationship to Hans in terms of the sexual theory likely had a skeptical theoretical component based on her shifting psychoanalytic views and the major schism that she was witnessing.

The Deeper Sources of Olga's Resistance in Her Earlier Analysis with Freud

One can surmise that Olga's doubts about Freudian theory had additional deeply personal roots that went beyond her acceptance of Adler's views. We saw that Max mentions in his Archives interview that Olga lost her father when she was still an infant and had two older brothers who suicided by shooting themselves, and we know from Freud's comment in the case history that she had earlier been his patient. David Abrams and others have inferred from this information that Olga is the "19-year-old girl with almost pure obsessional ideas" who entered analysis with Freud in summer, 1897, and who we know had precisely those features according to a letter at the time from Freud to his friend Wilhelm Fliess sent on June 22, 1897:

> During the summer I had to take on two new cases, which are going very well. The latest is a girl of nineteen with almost pure obsessional

ideas, who greatly interests me. According to my hypothesis, obsessional ideas date back to a later psychical age, and so *a priori* do not point back to the father, who treats the child the more carefully the older it is, but to her slightly older brothers and sisters in whose eyes the child has not become a woman. Now in this case the Almighty was kind enough to remove the father by death before the child was eleven months old, but two brothers, of whom one was three years older than my patient, shot themselves.

(Freud, 1897/1985b, p. 254)

Additional evidence that this letter refers to Olga lies in the fact that Freud mentions to Fliess that at the beginning of the summer Breuer sent him a patient (Freud, 1897/1985a, p. 249), and in Max's Archives interviews (Graf, 1952) it is noted that Olga was initially under Breuer's treatment. (Actually, the name is truncated in the interview due to an interruption and is only recorded as "Breu ..., " but "Breuer" seems the likely intention.)

This discovery of the timing of Olga's treatment by Freud has dramatic implications for her relationship to Freud and his sexual theories. One can well imagine the nature of Freud's interpretations of Olga's problems at the early stage of his theoretical development when she saw him. At that time, Freud firmly believed in his "seduction theory" of psychoneuroses that postulated a cause in actual sexual abuse in early childhood. His letter to Fliess offered this theory of the case. Thus, when Freud says that the father died early "but" two brothers, one three years older than Olga, shot themselves, he is offering an implicit explanation that it is her deceased older brother who committed sexual acts with Olga. This would explain why Olga's mother cut off her funding for analysis with Freud. Yet, Olga continued with Freud.

It is difficult to imagine how Olga must have felt when, having her neurosis blamed by Freud on her dead brother's heinous sexual acts with her and paying the price of alienating her family for sticking with Freud, she then watched Freud's theories change to the point that Freud simply gave up the seduction theory altogether. This proved that her earlier "resistances" to such interpretations—which Freud at that stage in his development overcame with quite aggressive interpretive impositions—as well as her mother's objections were correct after all. One must assume that Olga's reaction to the Oedipal theory of Hans's phobia as well as her ultimately turning against Freud and embracing Adler's approach is not unrelated to her earlier experiences, especially the dire consequences of believing Freud's sexual interpretations the first time around.

We know that Olga retained her interest in psychoanalysis in later years, because Herbert in his interview says that at that time, in 1959, "She is full of psychoanalysis and studying now ... she is completely, is quite experienced, I mean, and reads about it" (Graf, 1959). However, unlike Herbert who was an enthusiastic Freudian, Olga was now an Adlerian and appears still to have felt traumatized by Freud's interference in her family and her life. In her note to Eissler declining to be interviewed, she says:

> I have nothing to do with Freud. It cost me a sleepless night, still something very precious that we still have. I am afraid there will be more nights like this and I do not want to write or talk about him. Yesterday I told you that he caused us a lot of damage.
>
> (Graf, 1953)

(As an aside, I note the totally speculative possibility that Olga's case could have been one of the cases that undermined Freud's confidence in his seduction theory. Freud reported taking on Olga as a patient in June, and in September Freud sent his momentous letter to Fliess announcing that he no longer believed in his seduction theory, a change that "has been slowly dawning on me in the last few months" (Freud, 1897/1985c, p. 264). In other words, the initial period of Olga's treatment coincides with the period during which Freud came to doubt the seduction theory. Olga's father died when she was an infant, so Freud immediately turned to her two older brothers, both of whom had suicided, as potential perpetrators of abuse. It is possible that as Freud found out more about the circumstances, he was forced to conclude that no such seduction could have occurred. Perhaps Olga's mother cut off the support of Freud's treatment of Olga because she was sure that Freud's accusation of sibling abuse was false. Given the timing, it seems possible that Olga was one of the pivotal cases in which Freud's seduction hypothesis proved to be untenable due to the circumstances.)

Olga's Struggle with Max Over Cuddling with Hans

How do we know that Olga was indeed skeptical and tried to resist the Oedipal juggernaut that encompassed her family life and disrupted her intimate relations with her son? I will argue that her resistance is revealed in a series of small but puzzling details in the case record that previously have been ignored but are best explained in terms of Olga's rejection of Oedipal power/knowledge.

Olga's first and most direct act of resistance is in her insistence on being able to comfort and cuddle with Hans over the objections of her husband. In an earlier chapter, I described in detail the ongoing struggle in Hans's family over mother–son intimacy, driven by Oedipal theory but also likely motivated by Max's Laius-complex issues of sexual-emotional jealousy of Hans (Miller, 1985) and sexual access and conflict between the parents. The specific locus of this struggle is the couple's marital bed, and the struggle is over whether Hans is allowed to enter the bed to cuddle with his mother. This struggle had been going on for some time and formed part of the fabric of family life antedating and during Hans's phobia. On Max's side, his attempts to control Olga's relationship with Hans were supported by the Oedipal theory's implication that mother–son intimacy is sexual and dangerous.

The major and most frequent way that Olga resisted Max's exercise of Oedipal power/knowledge was to insist on allowing Hans to come into bed with her in the morning or sometimes in the evening when he felt anxious despite Max's objections, even if just for a few minutes. Apparently, she did not always prevail over Max's prohibitions, but sometimes she did.

Olga's resistance to Oedipal power/knowledge in this form started well before the treatment of Hans's phobia began. This is because, as we saw in Chapter 4, the application of Oedipal power/knowledge had already begun some months before the onset of Hans's phobia, by the time of the summer stay in Gmunden. A major rejection of Max's prohibitions consisted simply of the fact that when Max was away from Gmunden in Vienna during the week for work, Olga would allow Hans to come into her bed to cuddle or perhaps to sleep, and perhaps also insisted on doing so even when Max was present if Hans expressed significant anxiety: "Unfortunately, when he got into an elegiac mood of that kind, his mother used always to take him into bed with her" (1909/1955, p. 23). Given that Olga was well aware of Max's attitude that Hans should be kept out of the marital bed, this was an act of resistance. Indeed, as we saw in Chapter 4, Freud ultimately dated the origin of Hans's problems to this period in which his libidinal satisfactions had intensified due to his mother's actions.

However, back in Vienna, although we have many reports of Hans attempting to come into the parents' bed and being turned away by his father, the case evidence for Olga's side in this struggle is not as immediately apparent as Max's prohibitions. The true situation emerges only in the analysis of Hans's "giraffe fantasy." Recall that Hans comes into his parents' bed in the middle of the night on March 27, and after he falls asleep is taken back to his own room. The next day the parents interrogate him as to what caused him to come into their room, and he reports to them a dream or fantasy he had about two giraffes:

> *In the night there was a big giraffe in the room and a crumpled one; and the big one called out because I took the crumpled one away from it. Then it stopped calling out; and then I sat down on top of the crumpled one.*
>
> (1909/1955, p. 37)

In the course of identifying the day residue that he thinks explains the meaning of Hans's giraffe fantasy, Max describes a typical interaction between his wife, Hans, and himself during this period:

> The big giraffe is myself, or rather my big penis (the long neck), and the crumpled giraffe is my wife, or rather her genital organ ….
>
> The whole thing is a reproduction of a scene which has been gone through almost every morning for the last few days. Hans always comes in to us in the early morning, and my wife cannot resist taking him into bed with her for a few minutes. Thereupon I always begin to warn her not to take him into bed with her ("the big one called out because I'd taken the crumpled one away from it"); and she answers now and then, rather irritated, no doubt, that it's all nonsense, that after all one minute is of no importance, and so on. Then Hans stays with her a little while. ("Then the big giraffe stopped calling out; and then I sat down on top of the crumpled one.")
>
> Thus the solution of this matrimonial scene transposed into giraffe life is this: he was seized in the night with a longing for his mother, for her caresses, for her genital organ, and came into our bedroom for that reason.
>
> (Freud, 1909/1955, p. 39)

Freud endorses this solution: "That same day his father discovered the solution of the giraffe phantasy" (1909/1955, p. 39). By adding the phrase, "for her genital organ," to the description of Hans's longing for his mother in the night, Max manages to turn a description of ordinary attachment behavior into a sexualized description that invokes dangers of excessive incestuous stimulation. The repeated scene Max describes is a prototypical one in the Oedipal family's life. Hans wants to come into bed with his mother for comforting, and Olga wants to satisfy his desire. They are stopped by Max, who is motivated and supported by the Oedipal theory and perhaps also inclined for other reasons to protect his marital bed from the intrusion of a child.

In the scene that repeats almost every morning, Olga welcomes Hans into her bed, but Max warns Olga of the Oedipal dangers. To her credit, Olga angrily insists that a small dose of sensual reassurance will not ruin the boy. This is a compromise that reduces the time that she would otherwise spend with Hans, but it strengthens her argument. Max, seeing the situation through his Oedipal theoretical lens, interprets Olga's acceptance of the need to satisfy Hans's desire for comforting as dangerous because it will over-gratify him, spoil him, and sustain his neurosis. When Olga nonetheless defiantly takes Hans into her bed, Max portrays this as the result of a characterological weakness of succumbing to temptation ("she cannot resist taking him into bed with her"). Yet, it appears that Olga's defiant act in responding to Hans's entreaties is due not to weakness but to the fact that her considered opinion about Hans's needs is not congruent with her husband's. Simply put, she has the integrity to defend what she believes is right against the tyranny of Freud's theory. The Oedipal theory of natural incestuous sexual desires on the part of children in this instance is used for control rather than, say, liberating the mother–son pair to enjoy the natural erotic affinity revealed by the theory. Olga resists and defies this oppressive application of Oedipal power/knowledge.

Discovery of the Phobia's "Precipitating Event" of a Horse Accident: Failure of Communication or Passive Resistance to Oedipal Power/Knowledge?

The easiest form of passive resistance is failure of communication. In the example below of Olga's inferred resistance to Oedipal power/knowledge, I argue that the couple was not communicating even when the circumstances urgently and obviously called for communication. This and another example later suggest that these instances of communication failure indicate something more than mere bad communication. Olga appears to be engaging in passive resistance to Max's exercise of Oedipal power/knowledge.

The case history's most remarkable instance of Olga's seemingly inexplicable failure to communicate concerns the emergence in the case record of the information that Hans witnessed an accident in which a horse pulling a bus fell down in the street. This was what Freud was eventually to dismiss as the "precipitating event" that triggered Hans's horse phobia. However, for most of the time Max was sending Freud transcripts of his sessions with Hans, they had no knowledge of any such experience. Freud must have been shocked when this crucial piece of information emerged quite late into the case record.

On April 5, still mystified as to what might have triggered the horse phobia in Hans in early January despite three months of analytic efforts, Max reports the following interchange with Hans:

HANS: "I think when furniture-horses are dragging a heavy van they'll
      fall down .... I'm most afraid too when a bus comes along."
I: "Why? Because it's so big?"
HANS: "No. Because once a horse in a bus fell down."
I: "When?"
HANS: "Once when I went out with Mummy in spite of my 'nonsense',
      when I bought the waistcoat."

          (This was subsequently confirmed by his mother.)

I: "What did you think when the horse fell down?"
HANS: "Now it'll always be like this. All horses in buses'll fall down."
      ...
I: "You had your nonsense already at that time?"
HANS: "No. I only got it then. When the horse in the bus fell down, it
      gave me such a fright, really! That was when I got the nonsense."
      ...
I: "Why did it give you such a fright?"
HANS: "Because the horse went like this with its feet." (He lay down
      on the ground and showed me how it kicked about.) "It gave me
      a fright because it made a row with its feet."

I: "Where did you go with Mummy that day?"

HANS: "First to the Skating Rink, then to a cafe, then to buy a waist-coat, then to the pastry-cook's with Mummy, and then home in the evening; we went back through the Stadtpark."(All of this was confirmed by my wife, as well as the fact that the anxiety broke out immediately afterwards.)

(Freud, 1909/1955, pp. 49–50)

Freud comments on this belated discovery in his Discussion section as follows:

It was at this stage of the analysis that he recalled the event, insig-nificant in itself, which immediately preceded the outbreak of the ill-ness and may no doubt be regarded as the precipitating cause of its outbreak. He went for a walk with his mother, and saw a bus-horse fall down and kick about with its feet [p. 49]. This made a great impression on him. He was terrified, and thought the horse was dead; and from that time on he thought that all horses would fall down.

(Freud, 1909/1955, p. 125)

Whether this precipitating event is indeed "insignificant" has been the topic of vigorous scholarly dispute. In an influential behaviorist reading of the case, Wolpe and Rachman (1960) elevated this incident of the horse falling down into the central cause of Hans's phobia via one-trial learning, challenging Freud's psychoanalytic interpretation. Recall as well that Max's first question in reporting the phobia to Freud was the identity of the triggering event ("an exhibitionist?", he wondered).

Whether ultimately causative or not, the event of Hans witnessing the horse accident is surely of immense and obvious prima facie importance in examining the case. Thus, it is remarkable that the event was not earlier reported by Olga before it emerged incidentally from Hans. Indeed, it seems entirely possible that except for a serendipitous conversational direction, this incident might never have emerged. At the time of the incident, Hans was out walking with his mother. She witnessed first-hand both the frightening incident and Hans's response. She was involved in the subsequent treatment of the phobia and the adjustments to family life necessary to work around it. She was the only adult to know of this inci-dent. Regarding the details of Hans's account of this event, Max notes:

"This was subsequently confirmed by his mother," including "the fact that the anxiety broke out immediately afterwards." It is not possible that Olga, a sophisticate about psychological theory, did not immediately recognize the relevance of the horse accident to Hans's condition and its importance to the analysis of Hans being undertaken by Max and Freud.

Yet, *for three months* this event of Hans being terrified by a horse falling down in the street, and the fact that Hans's horse anxiety began immediately after this event, went unreported by Olga to Max even as Max and Freud frantically searched for any clue as to the horse phobia's cause. Olga failed to voluntarily mention the incident to Max and actually had to be asked directly about the incident after it had already emerged in Hans's revelation before she acknowledged it, more like reluctantly playing twenty questions than a mother aiding in an urgent analysis of her son's phobia.

How are we to explain this lapse of communication regarding such manifestly relevant information? It is inexplicable as a mere oversight. It can only be a form of purposeful resistance to sharing the information. One can understand that almost any parent might be resistant to reporting that something bad happened to a child "on my watch." However, this failure to communicate also appears to constitute the mother's camouflaged rejection of, and passive resistance to, the imposition of Oedipal power/knowledge on her relationship to Hans via the analysis. Perhaps she feared what analysis might emerge of the incident. Perhaps she did not think it was really that important, despite what her husband and Freud might think. Perhaps she was cowed by the double-patriarchy of Max and Freud arrayed against her and what it might mean for even more control over her relationship with Hans, and thus chose to refrain from both open conflict and active contribution. Irrespective of the precise reason, which we cannot know, it was an act of resistance and sabotage.

The Giraffe-Fantasy Interrogation

If the failure to communicate the occurrence of the horse accident and Hans's reaction to it to Max and Freud were a totally isolated incident of communication failure, we might dismiss it as a random odd event. However, it turns out that there is another prima facie puzzling lapse of communication in the case record, suggesting a couple cooperating on the surface but acting at cross purposes at some deeper level. To set the

context and better understand this second puzzling communicational incident, I first return to the part of the case study concerned with Hans's
giraffe fantasy and delve more deeply into the meaning of this incident.

Hans's father reports the events of the night of the giraffe fantasy as
follows:

> During the night of 27th-28th Hans surprised us by getting out of bed
> while it was quite dark and coming into our bed. His room is sepa-
> rated from our bedroom by another small room. We asked him why:
> whether he had been afraid, perhaps. "No," he said; "I'll tell you to-
> morrow." He went to sleep in our bed and was then carried back to
> his own. Next day I questioned him closely to discover why he had
> come in to us during the night; and after some reluctance the follow-
> ing dialogue took place, which I immediately took down in
> shorthand.
>
> (Freud, 1909/1955, pp. 36–37)

Hans is asked by his parents why he wants to come into their bed. Hans
puts off his parents by saying that he will tell them the reason tomorrow—
perhaps hoping that the topic will be forgotten by then. Hans's evasive-
ness is not hard to understand. He has by now learned that his reports,
especially of fear or longing for his mother, were taken by his father to be
evidence that he wanted his Mummy excessively and perhaps was masturbating, both of which brought new efforts at control. Hans was also
aware that these sorts of questions about why he came into the parents'
bedroom were aimed not at reassuring him but at interrogating the contents of his mental states, fantasies, and dreams and prompting endless
discussion of their meanings. Like a classical analyst asking with seeming
neutrality about the reasons for a patient's lateness to a session, the Grafs'
seemingly unbiased questions are transparently judgmental of Hans. It is
no wonder, then, that Hans is an initially unwilling witness, perceiving
that although his analysis is purportedly about control of his fear, in reality
it is about control of his relationship with his mother.

The fact that his parents are asking him whether he was afraid makes
Hans particularly cautious. The peculiar power of the Oedipal form of
control of mother–son intimacy was that the more Hans felt anxious, and
thus the more Hans wanted and needed his mother's comfort, the more it
was inferred that Hans was sexually overexcited by his mother, and thus

the more Max, out of concern for Hans's health, felt he had to intervene and prevent Hans from satisfying his desires for maternal soothing. As the analysis proceeds, Hans manages to master the twisted logic of a theory that coldheartedly holds that fear on the part of a child offers a reason to eject the child from the mother's embrace:

> On April 5th Hans came into our bedroom again, and was sent back to his own bed. I said to him: "As long as you come into our room in the mornings, your fear of horses won't get better." He was defiant, however, and replied: "I shall come in all the same, even if I am afraid." So he will not let himself be forbidden to see his mother.
>
> (Freud, 1909/1955, p. 47)

Max construes Hans's insistence on seeking to cuddle with his mother when he is afraid as an act of defiance ("He was defiant … [H]e will not let himself be forbidden to see his mother"). And indeed, from Max's perspective, the continued affection between mother and son constituted a prolonged and medically dangerous act of defiance. Moreover, in wanting to be cuddled by his mother Hans is seen as expressing his sexual competition with his father and specifically, according to Freud, his insecurity about the father's larger widdler being more appealing to his mother than Hans's own smaller widdler ("a fear that his mother did not like him, because his widdler was not comparable to his father's" [1909/1955, p. 40]). That in going to his mother Hans is not only showing erotic defiance of his father's prohibition but sexually triumphing over and humiliating him is made clear in Freud's summary of the giraffe fantasy's emotional meaning:

> the whole thing was a phantasy of defiance connected with his satisfaction at the triumph over his father's resistance. 'Call out as much as you like! But Mummy takes me into bed all the same, and Mummy belongs to me!'.
>
> (1909/1955, pp. 39–40)

Some subsequent commentators have argued that Olga's simple attachment response of wanting to comfort her child is somehow an attack on male authority. For example, Frankiel (1992) says: "His mother's insistence [that Hans should be able to come to her] is bound to make a significant statement to the child: 'Let's not listen to Daddy. His opinion doesn't matter'" (p. 325). Oddly, Frankiel does not consider whether Max's symmetric insistence in the opposite direction that Hans not listen to Mummy is equally disrespectful to Olga. The question should be whether Max's prohibition is justified. If it is not, then Olga's "defiance" is warranted—and everything we know about child development as well as common sense suggests that Olga is appropriately responding to Hans.

Even accepting Max's interpretation of the identities of the giraffes in the fantasy (for a different interpretation, see Wakefield, 2007a), there is no evidence whatever of this level of defiant provocation in the giraffe fantasy, let alone evidence for Jerome Neu's (1995) inexplicable claim that the giraffe fantasy provides evidence that Hans wants to *get rid* of his father. There is at most evidence of Hans's defiance of Max's protests when Hans approaches the crumpled giraffe. Max is merely ignored, not exuberantly humiliated. What we have in Freud's comment is a pure projection. The dejected Laius-like father, seeing reality through the distorted Oedipal lens, experiences himself as humiliatingly displaced in the affections of his all too willing spouse by his young, skillfully seductive son, despite the father's vigorous protests.

It is no secret that the bond between mother and son, or for that matter between any parent and child, can be more intense than that between spouses, and it certainly often has higher priority in family life. Surely, fathers do sometimes see such intensity and priority as a potential challenge to their status within the family, and can feel its sting as if it were the sort of triumphant dalliance invoked by Freud. But the reality is that the defiance in the actual bedroom scene is the *mother's* defiance: she defies the father's prohibition of accepting Hans's approach, defies Oedipal power/knowledge, and dismisses it all as nonsense even as the humiliated father watches in anger and horror. The Little Hans case record is not only a record of the routine workings of Oedipal power/knowledge but also a record of the initial resistance to its imposition and to the consequent disruption of the mother–child bond that soon became so ego- and socio-syntonic that the motivation to resist was lost.

Olga does sometimes manage to "win" the bedroom conflict in the end, and the cuddling with Hans proceeds. Despite the vestiges of Victorian marital patriarchy, Olga has considerable power in this regard. In the romantic family as defined by the post-Victorian turn to emotional and sexual satisfaction as defining the good marriage (see Chapter 7), the man is always in danger of losing that upon which the meaningfulness of his existence is predicated, the love of his wife. Unlike the earlier more fully patriarchal husband, the husband eternally courting his wife must defer to her when necessary and is better off managing conflict by negotiation and compromise rather than coercion. Nevertheless, Max symbolically has his revenge. His theoretical understanding, expressed in his notes to Freud and in the case study, reduce Olga's acts of love to incestuous acts in which she is tricked by the Oedipal boy into symbolically offering up her genital organ, a view that, we shall see, many commentators adopt even today.

Turning now to the parents' interrogation of Hans as to why he came into the parents' bedroom that night, the essential nature of the answer is a foregone Oedipal conclusion at which Max arrives that Hans was "seized in the night with a longing for his mother, for her caresses, for her genital organ, and came into our bedroom for that reason" (Freud, 1909/1955, p. 39). However, to get to this foreordained end of the story within the rules of psychoanalytic interpretation, Hans must be induced to explain why he came into the bedroom and so allow his father to interpret his motives.

This brings us finally to what might be considered a further competition over the giraffe fantasy between the parents. Hans refuses to explain himself the night of his entering the parents' bedroom. The following day, the parents are relentless in their interrogation. Each of them grills Hans for extended periods of time, one after the other, absorbing a substantial part of the day. Max tells us that "Next day I questioned him closely to discover why he had come in to us during the night; and after some reluctance" (p. 36), Hans reported the giraffe dream. Max then questioned him at length about it, all of which Max recorded in shorthand. Hans, having finally shared this information with his father, mentions at the end of their discussion that, despite feeling embarrassed, he had already told the whole story to his mother that morning after she had persistently pressed him to do so:

> He proceeded: "Mummy begged me so long to tell her why I came in in the night. But I didn't want to say, because I felt ashamed with Mummy at first."
> I: "Why?"
> HE: "I didn't know."
>
> My wife had in fact examined him all the morning, till he had told her the giraffe story.
>
> (Freud, 1909/1955, p. 38)

This passage raises some puzzling questions. The major puzzle is: Why did Max interrogate Hans from scratch when Hans had already told the story that morning to his mother? Apparently, Olga did not communicate to Max the results of her lengthy discussion with Hans. If Olga thought that the fantasies revealed in the analysis of the previous night's occurrences were important enough to warrant spending the entire morning forcing the story out of Hans, then why didn't she immediately communicate to her husband the revelations she so patiently extracted from Hans? And why did Max feel a need to find the truth out himself rather than first asking his wife whether Hans had said anything to her during the morning she spent with him? This failure of coordination suggests parallel interrogational processes with different purposes that the parents pursued independently. The superficial impression of a parental team cooperating to interrogate Hans is challenged by this inexplicable anomaly, revealing instead a communicational gulf that wasted Max's and Hans's time and effort.

Given the context of marital conflict and divergence over psycho-analytic theory revealed in the Archives interviews, a possible answer to this puzzle is that Olga, although participating and paying lip service to the analysis, in fact thinks that the analysis, or at least its Oedipal heart, is nonsense (see below). Moreover, she is angry over the support provided by the theory for the intrusion into her bond with Hans. Her interrogation is probably as much defensive as genuinely inquisitive. She wants to be sure that there is nothing she needs to worry about in Hans's answer, nothing in the dream's contents that can be construed as damning of her intimacy with her son that Freud and her husband could use against her. On Max's part, because he sees Olga as part of the problem, he probably does not really trust her analysis of the fantasy. Moreover, he prides himself on being the agent of Freud in this matter, thus may be inclined to ignore his wife's efforts and put Hans through a possibly needless second grilling so that he can transcribe the results first-hand for "the Professor." However, at bottom there is the fact that Olga does not share with her husband what she has found and Max does not consult her.

Another puzzle is why, after he had already told his dream to his mother, did Hans at first resist telling his dream to his father? Might Hans intuit his mother's anxiety about what Max knows, as well as have his own mixed feelings about sharing his private thoughts with his father and then undergoing his father's endless questions about his feelings about his mother that were used to bar him from her bed? Or, was he just tired of talking about the dream?

In sum, this second communicational lapse—the first was the mother's failure to mention to Max the incident of the horse accident that triggered Hans's phobia—suggests a pattern. At a superficial level the analysis brought this family together to help Hans. However, under the surface, a family conflict is simmering in which Hans is coping with an oppressive and paradoxical interrogation in any way he can (and his intellectual resources in doing so are quite impressive), while Olga, oppressed by Oedipal power/knowledge that controls her natural maternal response to her son, seems to go along because she cannot overtly challenge the combined power of Freud and her husband. But, in fact, she perceives the analysis as a challenge to her relationship with Hans and she knows that anything can be grist for the Oedipal mill. So, she cooperates selectively and is reluctant to share information when she thinks there is a possibility that it might be used against her.

Oedipus Complex as Nonsense

Lapses of communication and passive resistance are one thing, and actively expressing disagreement and disparaging Oedipal theory is quite another. While attempting to appear cooperative and wanting to avoid fueling conflicts within her marriage, Olga's resistance is yet occasionally quite explicit. In her frustration, in one instance in particular Olga does allow herself to speak truth to power. For this example, I again turn to the discussion of the giraffe fantasy and focus in on a detail mentioned above. This detail is worth focusing on because, I believe, it is the one moment in the entire case history that we get to hear Olga assert what she really believes, namely, that the Oedipal theory is nonsense.

We saw that, in the course of identifying the day residue that he thinks explains the content of Hans's giraffe fantasy, Max describes a typical morning family interaction:

> Hans always comes in to us in the early morning, and my wife cannot resist taking him into bed with her for a few minutes. Thereupon I always begin to warn her not to take him into bed with her ("the big one called out because I'd taken the crumpled one away from it"); and she answers now and then, rather irritated, no doubt, that it's all

nonsense, that after all one minute is of no importance, and so on. Then Hans stays with her a little while.

(Freud, 1909/1955, p. 39)

This repeated scene is a prototypical one in the Oedipal family's life. Hans wants to come into bed with his mother, and Olga wants to satisfy his desire. They are stopped by Max, who is motivated and supported by the Oedipal theory, which turns ordinary attachment behavior into a sexualized act that entails the dangers of excessive incestuous stimulation.

This repeated scene causes Olga to speak out. She finally objects to her husband's theory-based protests by insisting that "it's all nonsense"—a harsh and provocative judgment. By the "all," we know that she is speaking of much more than just the immediate events. She means that the Oedipal theory is nonsense and that the general attempt to use an esoteric theory, like psychoanalysis, as justification for interfering with the natural act of a mother giving sensual solace to a child is nonsense. (In light of her history with Freud prior to Oedipal theory, the "all" may have an even wider intended reference.)

There is a resonance in Olga's accusation that cannot have escaped Max. Recall that "nonsense" is the term that Freud and the family use for Hans's phobia. Indeed, it was Freud who originally labeled Hans's fear of horses his "nonsense":

I arranged with Hans's father that he should tell the boy that all this business about horses was a piece of nonsense and nothing more. The truth was, his father was to say, that he was very fond of his mother and wanted to be taken into her bed.

(1909/1955, p. 28)

Subsequently, Max and even Hans himself have taken to labeling Hans's phobia his "nonsense." But in the bedroom scene, when Max, driven by the Oedipal theory, tries to stop Olga from cuddling with Hans, she turns the tables and makes clear that in her mind it is her husband and Freud that suffer from nonsense. The nonsense in this case is their Oedipal theory as well as the consequent "symptom" consisting of the limitations that they try to impose on her affection with Hans.

Freud meant by the label "nonsense" not only that the fear made no sense but also that the fear of horses is not really what the fear is about and covers over something else, namely, Hans's sexual desire for his mother and the secondary gain of his being close to her. Olga's use of "nonsense" to label Max's theory can be taken to have similar intentions. She is saying not only that the Oedipal theory is false and makes no sense, but that it is being used as a cover or rationalization for something else, namely, the exclusion of Hans from the marital bed.

If the theory is nonsense, and the way it is being applied is nonsense, then what is the implied secondary gain to Max in nonetheless embracing it and in applying it in this way? The answer is plain: the desired secondary gain is the very effect that Max is attempting to impose on Olga, namely, prevention of the natural intimacy between her and her son, including physical contact when Hans is afraid or anxious. *The reality of the application of the Oedipal theory is not liberation of childhood sexuality in mother–son intimacy but the prevention of unfettered natural attachment intimacy between mother and child in a way that liberates the marital bed for the father's exclusive use with the mother.* The sexualization of attachment has as its effect the regulation of attachment, and making Olga less intimate and responsive with Hans makes her more available to Max.

In considering Olga's labeling of the Oedipal theory as nonsense and her willingness to resist Oedipal power/knowledge, it must be remembered, as discussed above, that she had been in analysis with Freud beginning in summer 1897, when he still believed in the seduction theory that actual child sexual abuse caused all neuroses. Thus, Freud had offered the interpretation that her obsessional neurosis was due to her sexual seduction by one of her older brothers who, we know, committed suicide by shooting himself when she was a young girl. Like many of Freud's patients, Olga likely offered resistance to this outrageous theory at the time, but she came to terms with it and continued her analysis, apparently as a charity case when her family turned against the analysis and her mother would no longer pay for it (see Chapter 2, and Wakefield, 2007b). Whatever doubts Olga initially had entertained—as well as her mother's opposition—was ultimately proven correct by Freud's own abandonment of the seduction theory. Consequently, the fact that Freud's sexual theories could be nonsense—even, as in her case, very harmful nonsense that impacted family life—was part of her experience.

To her horror, Olga must have realized that in locating the sexually stimulating source of Han's pathogenically intense sexual feelings in Olga's cuddling with him, in effect Freud and Max were placing her in the position Freud had attributed to her older brother all those years before. She was, in effect, the abuser who overstimulated an innocent child. Indeed, it may be as a result of reflecting on that earlier analysis and observing the use to which Oedipal theory was being put that Olga was motivated to drift from Freud into the orbit of Adler in her analytic quest.

Bloomers, Lumf, and Oedipal Power/Knowledge

The Grafs' Oedipal-power struggle over intimacy is centered in the bedroom, but that is not its exclusive location. Given the Freudian theory of component instincts that enfolds the excremental within the sexual, Hans's parents' struggle can be observed in another setting: the W.C. (bathroom). Here, Olga again is explicit in her rejection of Oedipal power/knowledge.

Max carries out an investigation to establish the source of some comments by Hans about his mother's underwear. No doubt the topic seems of interest to Max because of its sexual connotations. However, the effect is to reveal a broadened arena in which the analysis can be used to interfere in Olga's relationship with Hans:

> After luncheon I said to him: "We'll write to the Professor again," and he dictated to me: "When I saw the yellow drawers I said 'Ugh! that makes me spit!' and threw myself down and shut my eyes and didn't look."
>
> I: "Why?"
> HANS: "Because I saw the yellow drawers; and I did the same sort of thing with the black drawers too. The black ones are the same sort of drawers, only they were black." (Interrupting himself) "I say, I am glad. I'm always so glad when I can write to the Professor."
> I: "Why did you say 'Ugh'? Were you disgusted?"
> HANS: "Yes, because I saw that. I thought I should have to do lumf."
> I: "Why?"
> HANS: "*I* don't know."
> I: "When did you see the black drawers?"
> HANS: "Once, when Anna (our maid) had been here a long time—with Mummy—she brought them home just after she'd bought them." (This statement was confirmed by my wife.)

I: "Were you disgusted then, too?"

HANS: "Yes."

I: "Have you seen Mummy in drawers like that?"

HANS: "No."

I: "When she was dressing?"

HANS: "When she bought the yellow ones I'd seen them once before already."

(This is contradicted. He saw the yellow ones for the first time when his mother bought them.)

"She's got the black ones on to-day too" (correct), "because I saw her take them off in the morning."

I: "What? She took off the black drawers in the morning?"

HANS: "In the morning when she went out she took off the black drawers, and when she came back she put the black ones on again."

Perhaps the idea of his wife changing her drawers in the middle of day before and after going out aroused other than purely analytic interest in Max. In any event, he took this information directly to his wife, pushing the whole matter to the point that even Hans was fed up with the game of analysis:

> I asked my wife about this, as it seemed to me absurd. She said it was entirely untrue. Of course she had not changed her drawers when she went out.

> I at once asked Hans about it: "You told me that Mummy had put on some black drawers, and that when she went out she took them off, and that when she came back she put them on again. But Mummy says it's not true."

> HANS: "I think perhaps I may have forgotten she didn't take them off." (Impatiently) "Oh, do let me alone."

> (Freud, 1990/1955, pp. 56–57)

Freud comments on this passage as follows:

> I have a few comments to make at this point on the business of the drawers. It was obviously mere hypocrisy on Hans's part to pretend to

be so glad of the opportunity of giving an account of the affair. In the end he threw the mask aside and was rude to his father. It was a question of things which had once afforded him a *great deal of pleasure,* but of which, now that repression had set in, he was very much ashamed, and at which he professed to be disgusted. He told some downright lies so as to disguise the circumstances in which he had seen his mother change her drawers. In reality, the putting on and taking off of her drawers belonged to the "lumf" context. His father was perfectly aware of what it was all about and of what Hans was trying to conceal.

(Freud, 1990/1955, p. 57)

The upshot of this exploration was the following interchange between Max and Olga:

I: I asked my wife whether Hans was often with her when she went to the W.C. "Yes," she said, "often. He goes on pestering me till I let him. Children are all like that."

(Freud, 1990/1955, p. 57)

Like a jealous lover, Max persists until he finally ferrets out the secret meetings between Hans and his mother in the W.C. in an implicit accusation of a violation of Oedipal regulatory power. Indeed, as Olga says, young children do often insist on accompanying an adult into the W.C., and it is often easier to let them do so than to put up with the protests and the inconvenience of a fuss at the door while one is trying to focus on one's own needs. Nevertheless, alarmed by the sexual dangers of such practices, Max becomes a sleuth who investigates lumf and widdle. In his own mind, perhaps, he is an analytic Sherlock Holmes, but in fact he is more like an Inspector Clouseau of the W.C. What is most important here is the degree of intrusive regulation by Max of the mother–son relationship that the Oedipal theory justifies in the name of medical progress, and the expanded domain of intimate life into which it allows Oedipal regulation given Freud's expansive theory of the domain of sexuality. Oedipal theory trumps convenience, parental inclination, and tradition, even in the most intimate details of life. The W.C. incident is an example of how those intimate details come under the critical scrutiny of Oedipal power/knowledge.

Hans's mother's rejection of the Oedipal theory of danger is clear. The last sentence quoted in the above passage is another instance of her resistance to the notion that her intimacy with Hans is pathogenic, and of her suggesting that a mother knows more about what is best for her children than does Freud with his sexual theories. Recall that at one point earlier in the case history, Olga asked Hans, "Do you put your hand to your widdler?," and he answered "Yes. Every evening, when I'm in bed." So, the next day, she warned Hans before his afternoon sleep not to put his hand to his widdler. The result was that when she asked Hans about it, Hans answered defiantly that "he had put it there for a short while all the same" (1909/1055, p. 24) despite his parents' prohibition. Olga responds to Max's interrogation of her in a similarly defiant vein. Not only does she take Hans into the W.C., but she does so "often" despite the expectable Oedipal objections. Hans wants to, and, she implies, this desire—and by implication her yielding to it—is perfectly normal ("All children are like that").

That Olga's behavior in regard to allowing Hans into the W.C. is indeed a defiance of Freudian Oedipal power/knowledge is eventually made explicit and official. In the *Minutes of the Vienna Psychoanalytic Society* (Nunberg & Federn, 1967), Freud states just one reservation with regard to the raising of Hans by Olga: that Hans should likely not have been allowed into the W.C. with the mother: "[N]ot *that* many mistakes were made, and those that did occur did not have *that* much to do with the neurosis. The boy should only have been refused permission to accompany his mother to the toilet" (p. 235). (Regarding Max's contribution to Hans's problem, Freud says that Max should have told Hans about the vagina and intercourse to relieve him of his confusion.) Freud's remark implicitly vindicates Olga of excessive affection in the bedroom, and Olga's act of taking Hans into the W.C. is singled out for disapproval as beyond the reach of even liberal Oedipal doctrine in its dangerousness. Olga's blunt and rather condescending response to Max in the case record in which she instructs him about the nature of children constitutes yet another subtly expressed rejection of the dictates of Oedipal theory.

Nor does Olga's taking of Hans into the toilet seem to have had the pathogenic or sexual revelatory implications that some commentators have suggested. We know from the case record that Hans had never seen his mother's or his father's genitals, so she apparently exercised a considerable degree of modesty even in that intimate situation. This would not have been difficult given the broad skirts of the day, but even today scenes of women on the toilet are common in the media without revealing any intimate anatomical detail. However, seeing his mother on the toilet may well have given Hans the material for his cheeky response to her castration threat, that then he would widdle from his bottom. In any event, it would seem apparent that the extraordinary degree of privacy in such matters that middle-class, Western families enjoy is a luxury that surely is not essential for avoiding trauma to the young. And, as Olga explains, it is not unusual for a child of Hans's age to knock on the door insistently until he is let into the toilet when the parent disappears within. I suspect that in a child with less inferred libidinal intensity, Freud would have held that even allowing entry to the toilet was not strictly an error. My own judgment is that Olga's resistance in defense of her motherly judgment was not only defiant but correct.

Were Olga's Outbursts After Sex Expressions of Her Fear of Childbearing?

In this section, I reconsider an incendiary aspect of the Grafs' intimate relationship that I considered in Chapter 2, namely, Olga's reported outbursts on some of the mornings after having sex with Max. In the Freud Archives interviews, Max cites Olga's negative emotional reaction after sex as evidence of her hysterical nature, and it could be understood that way. However, I will suggest that Olga's reaction may instead illustrate how issues of power—such as patriarchal imposition of childbearing against Olga's preference—and an individual's reaction of protest against the exercise of such power may impinge on and distort our understanding of what might initially seem clear-cut, personal pathology.

When in the Archives interviews one first reads Max's description of Olga's "outbursts" and depression the mornings after making love, one is likely to think she is reacting in a pathological manner and is highly neurotic or worse. Such ambivalence about sexual relations would also provide additional ammunition for Max's calling her "hysterical." The family testimony is consistent that she was a highly nervous and neurotic individual, so this explanation of her post-sex behavior seems to fit.

However, on reflection, the story may be a bit more complicated. It should be kept in mind that Olga wanted very much to avoid having children, and after having Hans she especially desperately wanted to avoid having further children. Observing herself in what seems to have been a fairly accurate way, she said that having more children was too much for her to handle psychologically. Moreover, as noted in Chapter 2, birth control methods available at the time were not very effective and pregnancy and childbirth posed substantial dangers to the woman.

Olga's post-coital outbursts can easily be demeaned as strictly pathological. However, Olga had seen multiple suicides in her family, and she herself suffered from severe anxiety problems. We cannot rule out that she made a rational decision not to have children based on her perceived mental capacities and family history. Moreover, in the days before truly reliable birth control, sex potentially meant pregnancy and children. Given what we know about Olga's later feelings reported in the interviews about Freud having ruined her life by influencing Max to have children, her outbursts may well have been anchored in the reality that she was being induced against her preference—forced against her will is perhaps too strong, but not by much given the patriarchal web in which she was caught—to have children. One can only imagine the desperation, rage, and possible depression of an anxiety-disordered overwhelmed individual who tells her spouse that she is psychologically unable to handle another child but is pressured into doing so anyway, with her husband aided and abetted by the physician whose medical nonsense destroyed her closeness with her family some years before. An additional factor that is purely speculative is that Olga may have entertained hopes of professional achievement that having children would make difficult. She is described as brilliant and talented, and two of her sisters achieved personal successes, one as a pianist and the other as an actress.

The truth may be that Freud and Max made a major miscalculation and that her outbursts were a manifestation of her justified anguish and outrage. Her outbursts were quite possibly a form of protest, perhaps carrying the hope that her pain would yield some understanding and sympathy.

This view of Olga's outbursts after sex finds indirect support in comments by Freud in his article on the sexual theories of children published just prior to the Hans case (Freud, 1908/1959). This article's main clinical example is known to be based on the Hans case. Freud discusses the young child's sadistic theory of coition that is based on a perception of the sexual act, with its moaning and physical configuration that appears to the child to be the violent imposition of the father on the mother. This is the theory of sex that Freud attributes to Hans in the case history.

When Freud in the earlier article considers how children come to adopt the sadistic theory of coition, he offers the following comments:

> Not infrequently, too, the child is in a position to support this view by accidental observations which he understands in part correctly, but also in part incorrectly and indeed in a reversed sense. In many marriages the wife does in fact recoil from her husband's embraces, which bring her no pleasure, but the risk of a fresh pregnancy. And so the child who is believed to be asleep (or who is pretending to be asleep) may receive an impression from his mother which he can only interpret as meaning that she is defending herself against an act of violence. At other times the whole marriage offers an observant child the spectacle of an unceasing quarrel, expressed in loud words and unfriendly gestures; so that he need not be surprised if the quarrel is carried on at night as well ...
>
> (1908/1959, pp. 221–222)

Freud mentions that sexual conflict may originate in a wife's resistance and lack of pleasure due to her fear of the risk of pregnancy. Given the revelations in the Archives interviews about the Grafs' intense sexual and general marital conflicts, and what we know of Olga's reluctance to have children and Max's diametrically opposed intention to save the marriage by having children, this passage in the 1908 paper could easily be a description of how the sexual tensions in the Grafs' marriage played out at night. It is thus tempting to infer that, just as the general statements about children's sexual theories in the article appear to be mostly derived from the one case of Hans, so the general statement about a common pattern of parental sexual relationships is in fact derived from or consistent with Freud's knowledge of the Grafs' marriage. The description of a child who witnesses the scene when he is believed or pretending to be asleep could easily be a speculative reference to Hans, for the Grafs did have Hans in their bedroom for his early years until shortly before the occurrence of his phobia.

Recall that Hans's parents insisted to Freud that despite Hans's presence in their bedroom, Hans had never witnessed intercourse, and the evidence (e.g., Hans's never having seen their "widdlers") supports them. Yet, Freud goes along reluctantly and hints that he does not accept their claim:

Hans's father was unable to confirm my suspicion that there was some recollection stirring in the child's mind of having observed a scene of sexual intercourse between his parents in their bedroom. So let us be content with what we have discovered.

(1909/1955, pp. 135–136)

The description in the 1908 paper may be Freud's rejoinder, detailing what he believed, despite the parents' disclaimers, was likely the source of the sadistic theory of coition he attributed to Hans. If this is right and the 1908 description reflects some knowledge on Freud's part, then Olga's outbursts may have had an understandable rationale in her fear of pregnancy. If so, they were not the wholly irrational, pathological expressions that Max's interview account suggests, but protests against being forced to risk bearing children contrary to her deep desires.

Olga's Insistence that Having More Children Is Her Decision, Not God's

A last example of Olga's resistance is not so much to Oedipal power/knowledge as it is to patriarchal power more generally. Olga resisted having Hans and Hanna, and apparently was determined not to have more children. In this instance, she apparently was quite forthright in expressing her preference and was willing to do so despite the patriarchal bias that the husband had a powerful voice in the decision. Indeed, we know from passages in the case history that Hans knew about his parents' conflict over having children and was aware of the difference of opinion between his parents over who has the power to decide about having children:

> I: "When Mummy was having Hanna, was she loaded full up too?"
> HANS: "Mummy'll be loaded full up again when she has another one, when another one begins to grow, when another one's inside her."
> I: "And you'd like that?"
> HANS: "Yes."
> I: "You said you didn't want Mummy to have another baby."
> HANS: "Well, then she won't be loaded up again. Mummy said if Mummy didn't want one, God didn't want one either. If Mummy doesn't want one she won't have one."

(Hans naturally asked yesterday if there were any more babies inside Mummy. I told him not, and said that if God did not wish it none would grow inside her. Hans: "But Mummy told me if *she* didn't want it no more'd grow, and you say if *God* doesn't want it." So I told him it was as I had said, upon which he observed: "You were there, though, weren't you? You know better, for certain." He then proceeded to cross-question his mother, and she reconciled the two statements by declaring that if she didn't want it God didn't want it either.)

(1909/1955, p. 91; note that I have adjusted this text in accordance with a note on p. 91 by Strachey, with which Freud agreed when consulted in 1923, that the original as reprinted contains an error in the father's transcription.)

The conflict between the parents becomes apparent to Hans in their disparate assertions to Hans, who is unfairly made a pawn in their dispute and is used in a very indirect challenge by Olga to the patriarchal power being imposed on her regarding childbearing. Hans says that his Mummy told him that she would not have more children if she did not want to, asserting her own power over such a decision. But, Hans also reports, his father told him that his mother would not have more if God did not wish it, indicating, it would seem, that the chance would be taken and then the outcome left to God. Hans demands a resolution of this conflict; who has the power over deciding whether his mother will have more children, Mummy or God? Max says that he is correct, that it is not Mummy but some other authority who will rule on this question. Olga cleverly reconciles the conflicting statements and still retains her statement that the power is hers by saying that if she does not want a child, then God will also not want her to have one. This is perhaps an expression of a wish that a "higher authority" would respect her wishes (or perhaps it is a threat of sexual abstinence). The interchange reveals the spouses' conflict over whether the wife retains the power to determine her reproductive destiny, and Olga's courage in defending her power over her own body and fate.

As a whimsical aside, we saw that the Archives interview indicates that Freud seemed to go along with Max's idea that having a child might solve the couple's marital problems, despite Olga's strong objections. It is thus ironic that, after Hans and Max see Freud for their one in-person consultation, Hans asks his father, "Does the Professor talk to God?" Freud as the conduit to God does not choose to go along with Olga's wishes, after all.

Conclusion

The deployment of Oedipal theory in the Graf family triggered a struggle over the marital bed and the father's attempt to separate and limit the affection between Olga and Hans. In this struggle, Olga offers mostly passive resistance rather than all-out warfare against the powerful duo of her husband and Freud. Disillusioned with Freud from her previous experience with his seduction theory and the damage it did to her and her family of origin, Olga labels the Oedipal theory with its attendant surveillance and control of her affection for Hans as "nonsense." When she interrogates Hans about the nature of his giraffe fantasy, or she witnesses his development of his horse phobia directly after seeing a horse accident when walking with her, she knows that any information she communicates to Max may be used to support the Oedipal theory that maternal affection is dangerous for Hans (after all, she was with Hans when it happened), and consequently she does not communicate even the most relevant information to Max.

One might commonsensically think that the information about the horse accident would go against the Oedipal theory. However, Olga, as a former patient of Freud's and one familiar with the disputes within psychoanalytic circles, knows that Freud will simply fold this event into his Oedipal interpretation. This is exactly what in fact he does (see Wakefield, 2022).

Throughout the case and throughout the Grafs' marital life, the degree to which Olga's desires and needs are taken into account in major decisions is questionable. When it comes to events covered in the case history and the interviews, the patriarchal duo of Max and Freud assume the power to manipulate things to their satisfaction. Freud, as consultant to Max about his marriage as well as the supervisor of Max's treatment of Hans, appears to have more of a say on some crucial decisions about Max and Olga's marriage than does Olga herself. Thus, one must speculatively wonder whether some problematic aspects of Olga's behavior —such as the angry outbursts after sex discussed in an earlier chapter— may have been related to her frustrations regarding imposed risks of childbearing and demands of childrearing that she would have preferred not to accept.

When it comes to her rejection of the Oedipal theory, we know that she was familiar with the harmful errors to which Freud is prone because she was treated during the seduction theory period. In this case, her objections may well have been based on her own rational assessment—and an assessment that was pretty much correct—of the evidential weakness of this new theory that was being imposed enthusiastically by her husband in a way that was aversively reshaping her functioning as a mother. Given her position, her resistance against Oedipal power/knowledge on behalf of her relationship with Hans must be considered heroic.

The situation is made more complex by the fact that, here at the birth of this new form of family power in which mother–son affection becomes an object of suspicion, the Oedipal theory is not yet internalized by Olga. She experienced first-hand as a girl the harm that Freud's sexual theories could visit on family life. She is not about to be fooled twice, and wishes simply to respond to her child's needs. In effect, the case catches that unique moment of transition at the inception of the Oedipal theory at which it is being imposed on a mother and reveals its patriarchal lineage and the inevitable, if transient, resistance in response.

References

Foucault, M. (1978). *History of sexuality, Vol. 1: An introduction* (R. Hurley, Trans.). New York: Panthcon.

Frankiel, R. V. (1992). Analysed and unanalysed themes in the treatment of Little Hans. *International Review of Psycho-Analysis, 19*, 323–333.

Freud, S. (1985a). Letter from Freud to Fliess, May 31, 1897. In J. M. Masson (Ed. & Trans.), *The complete letters of Sigmund Freud to Wilhelm Fliess, 1887–1904* (pp. 249–250). Cambridge, MA: Harvard University Press. (Original work 1897.)

Freud, S. (1985b). Letter from Freud to Fliess, June 22, 1897. In J. M. Masson (Ed. & Trans.), *The complete letters of Sigmund Freud to Wilhelm Fliess, 1887–1904* (pp. 253–254). Cambridge, MA: Harvard University Press. (Original work 1897.)

Freud, S. (1985c). Letter from Freud to Fliess, September 21, 1897. In J. M. Masson (Ed. & Trans.), *The complete letters of Sigmund Freud to Wilhelm Fliess, 1887–1904* (pp. 264–266). Cambridge, MA: Harvard University Press. (Original work 1897.)

Freud, S. (1955). Analysis of a phobia in a five-year-old boy. In J. Strachey (Ed. and Trans.), *The standard edition of the complete psychological works of Sigmund Freud* (Vol. *10*, pp. 1–150). London, UK: Hogarth Press. (Original work published 1909).

Freud, S. (1959). On the sexual theories of children. In J. Strachey (Ed. and Trans.), *The standard edition of the complete psychological works of Sigmund*

Freud (Vol. *9*, pp. 205–226). London, UK: Hogarth Press. (Original work published 1908).

Graf, H. (1959). *Interview [of Herbert Graf] by Kurt Eissler.* Box R1, Sigmund Freud Papers, Sigmund Freud Collection, Manuscript Division, Library of Congress, Washington, DC.

Graf, L. (1960). *Interview [of Lise Graf] by Kurt Eissler.* Sigmund Freud Papers. Sigmund Freud Collection, Manuscript Division, Library of Congress, Washington, DC.

Graf, M. (1952). *Interview [of Max Graf] by Kurt Eissler.* Box 112, Sigmund Freud Papers, Sigmund Freud Collection, Manuscript Division, Library of Congress, Washington, DC.

Graf, O. (1953). *Letter to Kurt Eissler*, August 8, 1953. Sigmund Freud Papers. Sigmund Freud Collection, Manuscript Division, Library of Congress, Washington, DC.

Miller, A. (1985). *Thou shall not be aware: Society's betrayal of the child.* London, UK: Pluto Press.

Neu, J. (1995). "Does the Professor talk to God?" Learning from Little Hans. *Philosophy, Psychiatry & Psychology, 2,* 137–158.

Nunberg, H., & Federn, E. (1967). *Minutes of the Vienna Psychoanalytic Society (Vol. 2): 1908–1910.* New York, NY: International Universities Press.

Wakefield, J. C. (2007a). Attachment and sibling rivalry in Little Hans: The 'phantasy of the two giraffes' reconsidered. *Journal of the American Psychoanalytic Association, 55,* 821–849.

Wakefield, J. C. (2007b). Max Graf's "Reminiscences of Professor Sigmund Freud" revisited: New evidence from the Freud Archives. *Psychoanalytic Quarterly, 76,* 149–192.

Wakefield, J. C. (2022). *Freud's argument for the Oedipus complex: A philosophy of science analysis of the case of Little Hans.* New York, NY: Routledge.

Wolpe, J., & Rachman, S. (1960). Psychoanalytic 'Evidence': A Critique Based on Freud's Case of Little Hans. *The Journal of Nervous and Mental Disease, 130,* 135–148.

Chapter 7

Trauma Theory and the Perpetuation of Mother-Bashing

Did Olga Honig's Abusive Parenting Cause Hans's Phobia?

Except for Bowlby and Freud, I have paid scant attention in this book to the mainstream psychoanalytic scholarly literature on the Hans case. This literature too often consists of theory-driven speculation without a serious attempt at evidential evaluation of competing hypotheses, and so tends to be scientifically vacuous. However, in this chapter, I consider a spate of recent articles that attempt to explain Hans's phobia not in terms of Oedipal fantasies or subtle attachment distresses but in terms of gross early trauma experienced by Hans at the hands of his purportedly highly pathological and abusive mother, Olga Honig Graf. This will complete a polemical thread that I left unfinished in Chapter 5 of addressing the arguments in papers that blame Hans's phobia on the pathology of his mother.

Preliminary Comments on Olga's Relationship to Hans

Based on the case evidence and Freud Archives interviews, Olga certainly had many problems and faults and issues. They include high neuroticism and intense emotionality, high social anxiety or avoidant personality, likely obsessive personality, reluctance to be a mother especially to her second child and allowing her feelings of resentment about being pushed into a second pregnancy to interfere with the quality of care she provided to Hanna, resentment of Max's exclusive focus on work and nightly socializing to serve his ambitions while her talents languished and she stayed at home due to her social dysphoria, ambivalence about sex with Max possibly due to her ambivalence about having children, tendency to make extreme threats when trying to discipline children, and acceptance of contemporaneous beliefs about the harmfulness of masturbation and the appropriateness of child spanking. We also know that at least early in her

DOI: 10.4324/9780203817124-7

marriage she was capable of expressing her anger at Max in a show of temper.

Despite these considerable challenges, I argued in Chapter 3 that the evidence of the case history—in terms both of her responses to Hans's distress and Hans's reactions to her comforting—as well as the additional evidence in the Archives interview provided by her ex-husband, Max, indicate that she likely was a "good enough" mother to Hans to allow his normal development and that Hans was at least approximately securely attached to her, perhaps with some mild overtones of anxiety. Hans's anxieties at the time of the onset of his phobia most plausibly came predominantly from real and chronic disruptions of his attachment relation to his mother perpetrated by his father in the name of Oedipal theory, as well as Hans's anxiety especially upon awakening in the morning about being alone in his own bedroom into which he had recently been moved.

Both on Hans's part and his mother's part, the evidence considered in previous chapters does not support an extreme abusive hypothesis and instead suggests a not-perfect but "good enough" and reasonably secure mother–son relationship. Prior to and even after the onset of the phobia, Hans is portrayed in the case history as being generally cheerful, inquisitive, and exploratory, and not as generally clingy or needy. He readily makes friends and happily goes off and plays with them and explores on his own, and he plays happily with the nanny as well. When Hans feels anxious and is comforted by his mother, this generally successfully calms him down, which is uncharacteristic of insecure attachment of the kind that would be caused by an abusive mother. In the case history, both Hans's father and Freud portray Olga as being affectionate toward Hans, and Max in his interview says she had a good attitude toward Hans and that, although self-absorbed, she did not neglect him.

Indeed, Olga's reported behavior is far from neglectful. As we saw in earlier chapters, she is happy to let Hans come into her bed for cuddling in the morning when he is anxious and seeks soothing in the months after being moved to his own room and defends his right to do so against her husband's objections, she bathes both Hans and his sister when she might easily have left this to a nursemaid, she personally takes Hans out on a walk to see what is bothering him when his anxiety is first reported by the nursemaid ("On January 8th my wife decided to go out with him herself, so as to see what was wrong with him" [1909/1955, p. 24]), she spends the entire morning talking to him trying understand what is bothering him after the night in which he has his disturbing giraffe dream ("My wife had in fact examined him all the morning, till he had told her the giraffe story" [1909/1955, p. 38]), she offers Hans helpful advice about how to deal with his fear of horses ("He managed all this, looking hurriedly away whenever any horses came along, for he was evidently feeling nervous. In looking away he was following a piece of advice given him by his mother" [1909/1955, p. 33]), and she writes multiple times to Freud to thank him when Hans's symptoms finally subside ("In the course of the next few days Hans's mother wrote to me more than once to express her joy at the little boy's recovery" [1909/1955, p. 99]). Olga's response to Hans as described in the case history appears to be by and large exactly what Bowlby (1973) suggests, namely, a "natural and comforting expression of motherly feeling" (p. 287), with some isolated exceptions. Of note, after her divorce from Max, Olga subsequently remarried and stayed married to her husband for many years until death did them part, suggesting a capacity for emotional stability despite her emotionally intense nature.

Nonetheless, the articles considered in this chapter focus in on the various negative qualities of Olga described above and various negative incidents and run with them, offering the alternative theory that Olga's highly pathological mothering is the primary cause of Hans's anxiety. They thus challenge my claim that Hans's mother, despite her many problems and faults, provided roughly "good enough" mothering to Hans and that the experiences that disposed him to an anxiety disorder lay elsewhere. If the claims in these papers have merit, then they also offer an alternative explanation to mine for Max forbidding Hans to come into the marital bed, which I explained in Chapter 6 as resulting from Oedipal theory conjoined with spoiling theory and not because of some negative attribution to Olga. Max could then be seen as protecting Hans from a grossly pathological and sexually and physically abusive mother.

The literature I will be examining here is inspired by a recent turn to trauma theory in psychoanalysis. The trauma emphasis emerged from the focus on the impact of real childhood events in attachment theory and other object relations theories, as well as critiques of Freud as having unjustifiably abandoned his early sexual-trauma "seduction theory" of neurosogenesis when he developed Oedipal theory (Masson, 1984). If trauma, most commonly in the form of parental sexual or physical abuse, must be found to explain Hans's phobia, then the natural place to look is to his mother. These writers scrutinize Olga and conclude that she suffered from extreme psychopathology and was a destructive mother who was harmful to Hans. This, they claim, is especially manifested in her willingness to take Hans into bed with her for cuddling, but also possibly in terms of physical abuse and other potentially traumatic practices.

Bowlby's concern about Olga's use of threats of abandonment to get Hans to behave does not take center stage here, for these writers are looking for much more direct and lurid forms of parental abuse to justify their attribution of trauma. Ironically, although Bowlby's focus on real events in parenting as pathogenic inspired the trauma analysis, Bowlby himself, we saw in Chapter 3, believed that Olga was providing Hans with normal motherly attachment responses when she cuddled with him in bed when he felt anxious. To add to the irony, we saw in Chapter 4 that Max *did* actively obstruct the attachment process but that this was ignored by Bowlby. This understanding of Olga is pushed aside by the commentators considered here, who all claim that the cuddling was part of a larger pattern in which Hans's mother pathogenically traumatized Hans by being excessively sexual and seductively affectionate due to a psychological disturbance on her part. Some claim Olga was physically abusive as well. I would like to give all of these writers' arguments a fair hearing, but the claims and innuendo are so plentiful that for each writer I must consider only a few selected arguments that seem most central to their case against Olga or most distinctive from the arguments offered by others.

John Lindon on Olga as an Overstimulating and Seductive Mother to Hans

John Lindon (1992) argues that Olga was sexually "overstimulating, seductive, intrusive," and that Hans is a victim of her "unconscious psychopathology" (p. 391):

> What do we know about Hans's mother? Though Hans slept in the parental bedroom and was exposed to parental nudity and sexual intercourse, and though he frequently accompanied his mother when she went to use the toilet, she persisted in lying, answering him that of course she had a penis. She inflicted rigorous toilet training on him. She pressured him not to touch his penis, including with this a threat to have the doctor cut it off.
>
> (p. 385)

Once placed into cultural and personal context, Lindon's list of maternal sexual failures is unpersuasive as evidence of maternal pathology, even if some of her actions were inadvisable. The repeated accusation that the mother was "overstimulating" and "seductive" is based largely on her refusing to yield to her husband's demands to avoid cuddling with Hans. The mother took Hans into bed when he sought soothing due to being anxious. In fact, there is no evidence in the case material that she actively encouraged him to come into bed with her; she responded to his expressed needs and anxieties. As we saw, Bowlby evaluated Olga's behavior in this regard as normal good mothering, not seductive overgratification. Bowlby also quoted research showing that cuddling is reported by mothers to be a common way of coping with childhood anxieties. But, Max tried to stop such cuddling. Olga clearly did not accept Max's theory and saw physical contact with her child as appropriate and good mothering, and she was right. It was in fact her husband's Oedipal-rationalized attempts to control her relationship with Hans that were "intrusive" for Hans and her.

Hans's mother never said that she had a penis. In answer to Hans's question, she said yes of course she had a widdler—in German, "*Wiwimacher*," urine maker—which she did have (her urethra) (Wakefield, 2017). Her response was evasive, a way of avoiding the discomfort of talking to a child bluntly and honestly about sex. This reluctance was not unique to her. Even after Freud repeatedly suggested he do so as part of Hans's cure, Hans's father was unable to bring himself to tell Hans the truth about sex.

From the fact that "Hans slept in their [i.e., the parents'] bedroom until 4+ years of age," Lindon infers that "Hans saw his parents nude, and likely observed sexual intercourse," and that "we can surmise that sleeping in his parents' bedroom and observing them nude" was traumatic (1992, p. 391). Leaving aside the absurdity of the inflated Victorian notion that seeing nude parents or witnessing sex causes devastating trauma, Lindon's assertions that Hans witnessed his parents' nudity and saw them engaging in sexual intercourse are contradicted by the case evidence. In fact, the parents carefully and apparently quite successfully hid their bodies and their intimacies from Hans. One thing that both Hans and his parents agree on is that Hans has never seen either of them nude, which explains Hans's unsatisfied curiosity about whether his mother has a widdler and his curiosity about his father as well. We also know from the interviews that the parents had a difficult sexual relationship in which sex was rare, making it plausible that Hans never witnessed sex. In any event, most children around the world sleep in their parents' bedrooms without apparent ill effect. It is a relatively recent phenomenon for parents to have sufficient room to have their children sleep in separate bedrooms. Lindon here misleadingly elevates a recent cultural contingency into a species-typical psychobiological necessity without any evidential rationale. Hans's move to a separate bedroom is what is species atypical and more likely the source of his anxiety than his being in his parents' bedroom, with one important caveat: his parents had a contentious relationship and he may have overheard marital arguments, which can be very upsetting and can trigger anticipatory separation anxiety.

The enemas Olga administered to Hans, apparently interpreted by Lindon as harshly rigorous toilet training, were in fact medically pre-scribed to address Hans's constipation. Such a remedy was more accepted then than now, perhaps because now enemas are partly seen in a Freudian light as sexually tainted. However, they are still often used. (I suffered through them as a child for reasons similar to Hans.)

As noted in Chapter 6, Olga's taking of Hans into the toilet with her when he protested being left alone does not have the pathogenic implica-tions that Lindon assumes without evidence. Olga is right that children of Hans's age, left alone, do often insistently knock on the bathroom door until admitted. We know from the case record that Hans had never seen his mother's (or his father's) widdler, so, abetted by the ample skirts of the day, she apparently was able to exercise a considerable degree of modesty even in that intimate situation. Even today scenes of women on the toilet are common in the media without revealing any intimate anatomical detail. But, seeing his mother sitting on the toilet to urinate presumably did give Hans the idea for his defiant and amusingly dismissive response to her castration threat, that then he would simply widdle from his bottom. This is not the response of a boy traumatized by accompanying his mother to the bathroom, and even Freud comments on the lack of apparent anxi-ety. In any event, contrary to Lindon's implied accusation, when Olga says of course she has a widdler she is not contradicting what Hans has seen. In fact, Hans knows she has a widdler of some sort precisely because he has seen her widdling.

Finally, control of masturbation, like early and rigorous toilet training, was of course a standard practice at the time of the Hans case and can hardly be attributed to the mother's psychopathology. Whether control of masturbation or rigorous toilet training did any harm when done in a culturally syntonic fashion remains an open question. Olga's urgent concern to stop Hans's masturbation, leading to her castration threat, is consistent with the beliefs of her time. The attempt to stop masturbation, in which she was joined by Max and Freud, was routinely advised by medical authorities and based on beliefs about the potential for severe pathogenicity. With respect to the mother's castration threat, one bit of historical context has eluded commentators. During the Victorian era, chronic masturbators were occasionally treated with castration to save them from the supposed ill effects of their affliction. This historical reality is no excuse for using such a threat on Hans, but it does provide a context for the mother's action other than mental abnormality. A possible misogynist bias is evident here, for Hans's father went to the extreme of placing Hans in a restraining sack at night to prevent Hans from having the ability to touch his penis, a standard form of Victorian anti-masturbation child torture, but not one of the commentators take up this act on the part of Max with the vehement accusations that they cast at Olga.

Aside from ignoring the Victorian anti-masturbation context, there is an irony in the fact that commentators are horrified by Olga's over-the-top utterance of a castration threat when Freud, perhaps misled by the historical context, maintained that castration anxiety due either to an explicit threat or an implicit inference by the boy was entirely inevitable in every child's life as part of normal psychosexual development. Oddly, the commentators are not at all moved or horrified by the fact that, rather than Dr. A. arriving to cut off Hans's penis, Dr. Freud's Oedipal theory arrived to effectively cut off Hans's access to his attachment figure, a real psychological harm.

I conclude that Lindon fails to make his case that Olga was pathologically seductive in her behavior in a way that would have caused Max and Freud to restrict Hans's access to her on those grounds. The reason why Oedipal theory led them to the conclusion that Olga should not comfort Hans physically lies elsewhere (Chapter 5).

Rita Frankiel on Hans Being Sexually Stimulated by His Mother

Rita Frankiel (1992), like Lindon, argues that "Hans was a seduced and over-stimulated child, excited by his mother but also terrified of his death wishes towards her" (p. 333). Writing about the two occasions on which Hans asks his mother whether she has a widdler (*Wiwimacher*) and she answers that yes "of course" she does, trading on the question's ambiguity (yes, of course she has an organ through which she urinates) to avoid embarrassing matters of sexual anatomy, Frankiel, like Lindon, takes the mother to task:

> To me, her replies on both of these occasions give evidence of difficulties: she misunderstands the intention of Hans' questions, and by ignoring the fact that he is really after information about how males and females differ, she both frustrates him and ties him to her. She does both by giving him a form of doubletalk in her answers, allowing him intimacies (in her bed, in the toilet, and in dressing) that excite his curiosity, but not giving him the answers he is seeking ... Hans cannot profit from his own researches because ... she is not able to acknowledge that difference.
>
> (Frankiel, 1992, pp. 324–325)

There are no grounds for these claims. First, Hans cheerfully continues his sexual researches with no evidence of the trauma or obstacles Frankiel infers. Second, Frankiel's comment patronizes Olga, who surely understands that Hans's question about widdlers is ambiguous between "penis" and "urine-maker" and chooses to respond in terms of urine makers to avoid explaining the anatomical difference between the sexes to her three-year-old son. Consistent with their time and culture, and despite Freud's urgings to the contrary, both parents avoid such conversations with Hans until, at Freud's request, Max halfheartedly raises the issue briefly toward the end of the case without going into detail. This culturally syntonic reticence was why Hans had not seen the parents naked. Third, Frankiel claims that Olga "misunderstands the intention of Hans' questions," and that Olga frustrates Hans by "ignoring the fact that he is really after information about how males and females differ." But, she must understand his intention in order to ignore it or to provide "doubletalk" designed to evade the issue. Frankiel also patronizes Hans's conceptual abilities. By his mother's "of course," Hans likely understands that she means that he already knows that she widdles, therefore she must have a widdler (i.e., an organ for widdling). That it is likely not a penis is suggested by the fact that she urinates sitting down, as Hans has observed.

Frankiel claims that Hans was harmed by "the over-stimulating environment of his mother's self-display" and a "need on the mother's part to exhibit herself" (1992, p. 326). Yet, Hans has never seen her naked despite sometimes having accompanied her to the W.C. and having slept in his parents' bedroom until shortly before the case history begins. The parents are obviously pretty good at being modest.

Frankiel shockingly asserts that "Hans asks his father to relay ... to Freud" the information that his "Mummy ... lets me see her in her short chemise, so short that I can see her widdler" (1992, p. 326), implying incestuous exhibitionism by Olga. However, first, Hans's reference is not to actual events but instead to a dream Hans reported to his father upon awakening, in which he saw his mother's widdler under her chemise—a dream that was specifically triggered by Max informing Hans the day before that women and girls, including his mother, do not have widdlers like his: "Next morning he woke up in a fright at about six o'clock. When he was asked what was the matter he said: 'I put my finger to my widdler just a very little. I saw Mummy quite naked in her chemise, and she let me see her widdler'" (p. 32). Second, Hans is not asking but rather accusing his father of sharing the embarrassing personal details of his dream with Freud upon realizing that his father's notes are being forwarded to Freud: "Hans: 'Why are you writing that down?' I: 'Because I shall send it to a Professor .... ' He: 'Oho! So you've written down as well that Mummy took off her chemise, and you'll give that to the Professor too'" [p. 38]). Frankiel's claims are themselves grossly misleading "doubletalk" about what actually happened.

Of her many misleading claims and overstatements, the low point of Frankiel's analysis occurs when Frankiel throws aside the ambiguities of claiming Olga is "seductive" and accuses Olga of overt sexual stimulation of Hans's genitals, a way of calming a child known to be practiced by nannies of the time:

> We have already shown that Hans was aroused, terrified, and enraged by his mother's seductiveness, exhibitionism, castration threats, and his responses to them. That he may have been exposed to provocations even more pronounced and extreme than have yet been mentioned was drawn to my attention in a personal communication by Dr. William Grossman, who noted that a footnote Freud included (p. 23) can be read to suggest that there was more than cuddling going on in

the Graf household. There, Freud stated ' ... It is one of the commonest things—psychoanalyses are full of such incidents—for children's genitals to be caressed not only in word but in deed, by fond relatives, *including even parents themselves*' (my italics).

I would take Freud to be alluding in this footnote to events that actually took place in Hans' case. We know from the text that Hans' father was handling his penis in the course of helping him urinate when they went on walks. The footnote's context could well suggest that Hans' mother was also involved in some form of seductive stroking. If so, this inference would add to the impression of seduction, in this instance verging on what we would today regard as sexual abuse.

(Frankiel, 1992, p. 330)

So, Frankiel goes beyond accusing Olga of stoking Hans's sexual desire to the accusation that she was out-and-out stroking his penis, based on a footnote of Freud's that is about a comment by Hans's aunt, but also includes a comment about how parents sometimes stroke the genitals of their children. The fact that Frankiel "would take Freud to be alluding in this footnote to events that actually took place in Hans' case" is not evidence. If we ask *why* Frankiel believes this and *what evidence* she has for this way of taking Freud's comment versus the alternative interpretation that Freud is making a general remark that does not refer to the Hans case, we find that there is no apparent evidence in the case record to support Frankiel's inclination to "take Freud" in this way. Moreover, there is evidence against this inferential leap. The father reports that when Hans asks his mother to touch his penis while being powdered after the bath, she refuses, saying that would be "piggish," clearly referring to any such touching by her. Moreover, the primary occasion of physical contact between the mother and Hans reported in the case occurs in the parental bed in the morning when the father is there as well, making such acts highly unlikely. Additionally, it seems unlikely that Freud would put such a footnote into the case record covertly referring to an act of sexual abuse when it is the father that is providing Freud with the material and Freud knows that the father will be closely reading the published record. The evidence does not support Frankiel's malign hypothesis about the mother.

Doris Silverman on Hans as Parallel to Leonardo in Being the Object of His Mother's Erotic Fixation

In Chapter 5, I addressed Doris Silverman's (2001) argument that Freud acknowledges that Olga was overly affectionate to Hans but he then ignored this point. I showed that Silverman misinterprets Freud's statement as an "acknowledgment" when in fact he is *disagreeing* with Max's blaming Olga for Hans's problem. So, the case history offers no textual basis for Silverman's claim that Freud considered Olga overly affectionate to Hans in a pathological and pathogenic sense. I will not repeat that argument here.

However, Silverman mounts a further argument that Freud thought Olga's misbehavior to blame. Silverman identifies some parallel language in Freud's Hans and Leonardo papers—Freud refers to Hans's mother's "excessive display of affection for him" and to Leonardo's mother as displaying "too much tenderness"—and infers that Freud is signaling that the other things he says about Leonardo also apply to Hans. Thus, Silverman thinks that, just as Freud says that Leonardo's mother's tenderness caused his homosexuality, so Freud is signaling that, although he did not say it, he really thinks that Hans's mother's tenderness caused Hans's anxiety neurosis. Silverman presents her "Da Vinci code" argument as follows:

> [W]hen Freud (1910) speculated about the early relationship of Leonardo da Vinci with his mother, he drew parallels between Little Hans's and little Leonardo's questions and surmises about genitals and sexuality. Freud speculated that Leonardo's mother had an "erotic fixation" (1910, p. 99), which led her to encourage "too much tenderness" (p. 99) toward the boy. The almost identical language used with regard to both mothers suggests that Freud was refraining from alluding directly to Hans's mother's inappropriate erotic desires toward her child.
>
> (2001, pp. 351–352)

However, if taken seriously, Silverman's argument would allow for endless spurious "discoveries" of such coded messages from Freud. Searches for various words and phrases in Freud's works would yield endless such attributions using similar words that have differing implications in the divergent contexts in which they occur and are not admissions of past distortions.

It is true that in the Leonardo paper, Freud does apply insights from the recently completed Hans case to his interpretation of Leonardo's "vulture" fantasy, including assumptions that girls and mothers must have penises and a link between sucking at the breast and the appeal of fellatio, citing the Hans case in footnotes on pages 87 and 95. However, these Hans-derived speculations about Leonardo's sexual theories have nothing to do with the mothers' etiological roles in their children's outcomes. No reference to the Hans case occurs on page 99 where Freud's claims about Leonardo's mother cited by Silverman appear. Silverman immediately follows her sentence about the actual Hans parallels with her sentence about the inferred parallel as if they occur together but in fact they have nothing to do with each other. Silverman simply leaps without textual justification from some explicitly stated parallels regarding childhood sexual researches to the claim of further unstated parallels regarding mothers' pathogenic behaviors.

Silverman says that "Freud speculated that Leonardo's mother had an 'erotic fixation' (1910, p. 99), which led her to encourage 'too much tenderness' (p. 99) toward the boy." This is incorrect. She may have encouraged too much tenderness, but the problem was not her erotic fixation but the boy's. Freud says that

> In all our male homosexual cases the subjects had had a very intense erotic attachment to a female person, as a rule their mother, during the first period of childhood, which is afterwards forgotten; this attachment was evoked or encouraged by too much tenderness on the part of the mother herself, and further reinforced by the small part played by the father during their childhood.
>
> (1910/1957, p. 99)

In a note, Freud reiterates that the precursor of homosexual orientation is "the fixation of the erotic needs on the mother which has been mentioned above" (1910/1957, p. 99, n. 2). Freud claims not that the mother has an erotic fixation on the son, but rather that the son has an erotic fixation on his mother.

What of Freud's comment that "this attachment was evoked or encouraged by too much tenderness on the part of the mother herself" (1910/1957, p. 99). Freud is saying that the fixation might start independently of the mother but its expression might be encouraged by a mother who is very affectionate, and the interaction between an affectionate mother and a fixated son can be pathogenic. Here, the fact that the mother shows "too much tenderness" does not necessarily imply abusive, seductive, or inherently pathogenic behavior. It can indicate a mismatch between the mother's ample but normal-range level of tenderness and the son's fixation, which gives the fixation scope to express itself, especially given the lack of a strong father figure to correct the situation. As in the Hans case, there is no implication that the mother is pathologically sexual or abusive with her child. Freud's attempt here to explain the etiology of homosexuality has little to do with understanding the dynamics of the Hans case.

Silverman argues that Freud's attribution of etiological relevance to Leonardo's mother undercuts his "predestined" view of Hans's mother's role:

> In the case of Leonardo, Freud explicitly acknowledged the power of the early mother–child relationship in shaping the child's future sexual life, instead of emphasizing his theorized position of a natural, biological unfolding of the sex drive as preordained .... His Leonardo paper ... revealed the contents he was loath to communicate in his description of Little Hans.
>
> (2001, pp. 351–352)

That is, the Leonardo paper reveals what Freud would not admit in the Hans case, that pathologically negative mothering is not predestined and has a terrible impact. In fact, in both case studies, Freud does emphasize "the power of the early mother–child relationship"—the power of the *relationship*, that is—to determine the child's outcome (e.g., anxiety neurosis, homosexuality). However, recognizing the pathogenic power of the mother–child relationship is different from attributing pathogenesis to one participant in the relationship (Wakefield, 2006a, 2006b), the mother, and Freud refrains from that leap in both instances.

The Hans and Leonardo cases are parallel to the degree that the etiologies of the respective outcomes both involve intensified libidinal desire by the boy for the mother, but they differ in almost every other way. Freud does not think that Hans's mother engaged in inappropriate behavior, but thinks that the father was wise to control Hans's access to intimate contact with her when she herself was not willing to do so because she felt the contact was good parenting (Freud approvingly says that the father's control of the mother–son interaction rendered Hans's intensified desire to cuddle with his mother "innocuous" [1909/1955, p. 140]). In Leonardo's case, there is possibly an inappropriate level of responsivity by the mother to Leonardo's fixation on her, and lack of control by a father. As noted, when discussing these features in the Leonardo analysis, Freud does not refer the reader to the Hans case as he does elsewhere in the Leonardo paper. This is for the good reason that they are quite different cases that are not parallel in these particular respects. Silverman's claim that in the Leonardo paper there is a subtle Freudian "Da Vinci code" retroactively correcting Freud's dishonest portrayal of Hans's mother and belatedly pathologizing her is sheer fiction.

Silverman attempts to solidify her argument with statements that distort the case material. For example, falsely, she says that "Little Hans reported that his mother beat him with a carpet-beater" (2001, p. 352), when in fact Hans reported only that his mother threatened to do so, and the father confirmed this. In fact, there is no evidence anywhere in the case history or in the interviews that Hans's mother ever spanked him, although she did spank Hanna. Silverman claims that Olga's behavior may have caused Hans to have an ambivalent disorganized form of attachment, yet as we saw in Chapter 3 there is not the slightest evidence of such a pattern and much evidence to the contrary. She implies that the mother "offering intense intimacy (frequently allowing Little Hans to share her bed, especially when his father was away)" (2001, p. 352) was somehow a salacious, sexually seductive act, when it is, even according to Bowlby, simply routine motherly attachment behavior. Silverman's suspicion-inducing phrasing that this occurred when the father was away—when he was there, he stopped Hans from being physically comforted by his mother—plays into the absurd jealousy-fueled sexual drama that Freud and Hans's father portray. Here and elsewhere, despite her article's excellent exploration of attachment theoretical aspects of development, Silverman confuses attachment needs with sexual striving. Silverman claims that "when [Hans] was with [his mother], she appeared to flame his emotions, thereby producing a state of extreme overexcitement," and that Hans could not self-regulate because of "his sexual overstimulation, resulting from his mother's seeming inability to be a consciously soothing, calming, nonsexual, maternal presence" (2001, pp. 352–353), claims that we saw in Chapter 3 are contradicted by the case history evidence that shows that Hans was in fact calmed down by cuddling with his mother when anxious.

In sum, in the search for a justification of a trauma explanation of Hans's anxiety, Silverman judges Olga to be seductive and sexually over-stimulating simply because she cares enough to want to comfort Hans when he is anxious and offer expectable mothering. But, when Olga is care-ful not to be seductive, such as in saying it would be "piggish" to touch Hans's private parts, or when she protects Hans's health according to the medical beliefs of the day by preventing him from masturbating, this is judged to make her a "punitive" and "harsh, critical, and judgmental" mother (2001, pp. 352–353).

Silverman concludes her attack on the mother by claiming that what Hans needed was simply more attachment soothing: "Viewed from this perspective, the nonsensual aspect of the child's emotional regulation was significantly impaired …. From my vantage point, however, Little Hans needed more calming, soothing, and affectionate reactions" (1909/1955, p. 353). On this we can agree. Yet, Silverman ignores the most obvious and persistent blockage to such soothing, namely, the father's persistent disruption of Hans's ability to seek out soothing from his mother. Throughout the case report, the father, driven by Oedipal theory, actively disrupts the mother–son attachment bond and prevents Hans from cud-dling with his mother for a while in the morning when he is anxious, thus preventing him from obtaining the soothing he needs. The father's Oedi-pal-theory-driven blockages of Hans's ability to access his safe haven are explicitly upsetting and anxiety provoking to Hans, and yet the father, propelled by Oedipal theory and contrary to attachment theory, insists that Hans is anxious *because* he wants to obtain soothing from his mother. Notably, the father's interference was ongoing before the development of Hans's anxiety issues. One need look no further for a major reason why "the nonsensual aspect of the child's emotional regulation was sig-nificantly impaired." The father chronically prevented Hans from getting from the mother the "more calming, soothing, and affectionate reactions" that he actively sought and his mother wanted to give.

Harold Blum on Hans as a Child Physically Abused by His Mother

Harold Blum (2007) argues that Hans's mother was a child abuser, and it is only the heroic action of Hans's father along with Freud that saved the child:

The severe disturbance of his mother had an adverse impact on Little Hans and his family. Her abuse of Hans's infant sister has been overlooked by generations of analysts. Trauma, child abuse, parental strife, and the preoedipal mother-child relationship emerge as important issues that intensified Hans's pathogenic oedipal conflicts and trauma. With limited, yet remarkable help from his father and Freud, Little Hans nevertheless had the ego strength and resilience to resolve his phobia, resume progressive development, and forge a successful creative career.

(Blum, 2007, p. 749)

Blum emphasizes the importance of revelations in the Graf family's Freud Archives interviews, which Blum himself, as Director of the Archives, admirably derestricted:

[T]he interviews of Max Graf (1952) and Herbert Graf (1959) provide significantly convergent data, and are consistent with other reports, (e.g., about the instability of Little Hans's mother). With the appearance of this additional follow-up material, remarkable aspects of the case that have been overlooked since its publication have been brought to light.

(Blum, 2007, p. 751)

Blum argues that Freud's emphasis on the Oedipal intrapsychic roots of Hans's problem in his own sexual fantasies is not in keeping with newer psychoanalytic thinking that places greater emphasis on the role of actual external trauma and real pre-Oedipal attachment ruptures in the etiology of neuroses. In seeking to identify early traumas to which Hans was subjected, the lack of evidence of any direct physical abuse of Hans leads Blum to focus on the indirect effect on Hans of the mother's postulated violent physical abuse of his infant sister, Hanna:

When interviewed in 1952, Max Graf stated that Olga was well behaved toward their son but rejected their daughter, possibly out of jealousy: "She never coped well with the daughter." In 1959 Herbert Graf independently confirmed that his mother could not bear a second child. Olga could be particularly more loving toward her son than toward her husband or daughter .... The postpartum rejection and infant abuse of Hanna could likely not be reconstructed in clinical psychoanalysis, but help us understand the psychology of suicide.

(Blum, 2007, p. 755)

Hans's mother did have serious psychological problems, and those problems unquestionably contributed to parental strife and had an adverse impact on the family. However, the accusation that the mother engaged in child abuse and that "her abuse of Hans's infant sister has been overlooked by generations of analysts" is evidentially dubious. The primary evidence for this dramatic assertion is one passage in the case history about Olga spanking Hanna. Blum tells us:

Hans told his father that he could not bear his sister's screaming. When his father misinformed him that she didn't scream, he responded, "When Mummy whacks her on her bare bottom, then she screams" (Freud 1909, p. 72). The implications of repeated references to his mother's beating of Hanna at less than eighteen months of age (which can be dated in the case report) have been overlooked for generations. This nonrecognition of the infant abuse of Hans's sister shows a remarkably persistent psychoanalytic blindness to the data and implications of the case report. Why was Olga's hostile aggression and violent abuse of her infant daughter not explored by Freud and the later analysts who studied the case? Freud may have been protecting a childish ex-patient who seemed to accept culturally syntonic yet abusive child-rearing practices, including punishment for masturbation.

(Blum, 2007, p. 754)

This passage, critical to Blum's narrative, deserves close scrutiny. Based on the available evidence, it is misleading to label what is described here by Hans as "abuse." When a parent hits a child on the bottom to punish or control some behavior, it is commonly called "spanking," and children commonly cry when spanked. So, Hans is saying that it bothers him when Hanna cries when she is spanked. Blum refers to "repeated references to his mother's beating of Hanna" as if this topic is salient and came up repeatedly in the case material, but in fact the quoted comment by Hans is the only reference anywhere in the case history or in the later interviews to the mother spanking Hanna. There is no other reference to spanking, beating, violence, abuse, etc., which prima facie is curious if this was a regular and salient occurrence. What Blum is observing, presumably, is that the precise wording of Hans's one comment ("When Mummy whacks her ... ") appears to imply that Hans likely is referring to multiple incidents that are not enumerated, although it is not impossible that this locution could be used by a child to refer to one salient event.

However, irrespective of the number of events to which Hans is referring, semantic slippage of another kind in Blum's reading renders Blum's inference questionable. Blum translates Hans's comment on whacking Hanna on her bottom into "his mother's *beating* of Hanna" (emphasis added). A whack or a spanking can be described as a beating (indeed, I once myself said "The case report indicates that she beat her daughter" [Wakefield, 2007a, p. 74]), but "beating" is imprecise and misleadingly suggestive here because it encompasses a larger domain of severity that goes well beyond that of whacks and spankings in length, force, and potential harm to the child, and it need not be confined to the bottom. To say that someone "beat" someone generally has the connotation of these more severe forms, although it is used of parents spanking a child as well. Blum consistently uses this more severe term, subtly altering the content of Hans's comment in a direction of greater potential severity.

Blum then pushes this initial semantic tweak much further down the slippery slope in the next sentence, in which he redescribes the "whack" or "beating" as "infant abuse." Blum subsequently refers to "Olga's hostile aggression and violent abuse of her infant daughter," thus upping the ante of Olga's transgressions to include violent physical infant abuse. Both the terms 'infant' and 'abuse' are questionable and yet exploited relentlessly for their emotional impact. First, the term 'infant' (which comes from the Latin for "incapable of speaking") is generally defined as the period ending at about one year, so it is questionable to call an eighteen-month-old toddler an infant. However, this term serves Blum's rhetorical purpose by making Olga's actions seem all the more reprehensible and potentially damaging, so he repeats 'infant' multiple times. Second, based on Hans's one-sentence case report that Olga sometimes gave Hanna a whack on her bottom, Blum refers *ten times* in a matter-of-fact way to Olga's physical "abuse" of Hanna, often with such qualifiers as "violent" (although genuine "violent" physical abuse might be expected to go beyond a whack on the bottom) and even "traumatic" (although the actual impact on Hanna of being spanked is sheerest speculation on Blum's part).

The term "child abuse" in the sense of physical abuse is a loaded one, and obviously should be used only when the evidence shows that it is clearly appropriate. What, then, qualifies as abuse? Organizations dealing with child physical abuse generally define such abuse in such a way that it is distinguished from the common practice of spanking children. Typically, abuse is defined to include intentional violent acts causing physical injury (broken bones, cuts) or physical trauma (e.g., bruises, burns) to the child. Excessively violent beatings that are excused as acts of corporal punishment of the child are also sometimes mentioned as potential incidents of abuse. In no way do the details of the case report offer sufficient support to justify attributing child abuse—let alone infant abuse—in its usual meaning to Olga. It remains true, of course, that even moderate spanking of a sensitive child can be experienced by the child in a way that has long-term psychological implications. The point is that, based on the available evidence, we just don't know the actual nature of these spanking incidents and their sequelae, so Blum's confident and repeated incendiary assertions of the mother's abusiveness are unjustified.

Having claimed without evidence that a report of spanking in the case history is in fact a report of repeated violent physical infant abuse, Blum then faces the awkward question of how this horrific observation on his part was "overlooked for generations." There is some tension in how Blum depicts the situation. The suggestion that the mother's abuse has been "overlooked" implies, implausibly, that it is there to be seen in the case record but that readers looked away or failed to notice it. Yet Blum also points out that "today we have new information about Little Hans's very disturbed mother, her family history, and her turbulent relationship with her husband and children" (2007, p. 752), suggesting that it is this new information that was unavailable to earlier commentators that allows Blum for the first time to see the text in a new way. Yet, the fact is that there is no new evidence in the derestricted interviews that points specifically in the direction of physical abuse, and Blum fails to cite any such evidence. True, the interviews yield a clearer idea about the mother's general emotional problems and her rejection of the daughter, but neither of those imply physical abuse. Consequently, Blum's claim that "with the appearance of this additional follow-up material, remarkable aspects of the case that have been overlooked since its publication have been brought to light" (2007, p. 751) cannot apply specifically to the charge of physical abuse of Hanna because no evidence in the derestricted interviews brings abuse to light. Keep in mind that the embittered interviewees shared many other quite negative things about Olga, and would likely have mentioned physical abuse if it was true. In sum, Blum's abuse accusation rests wholly on the one comment in the case history that has been known to all previous commentators, which Blum is simply interpreting in a novel and evidentially unsupported way.

Do psychoanalysts really want to endorse painting all emotionally problematic mothers with the brush of child abuse without any direct evidence? There is simply no evidence that one can reliably infer repeated violent infant abuse of the kind Blum is suggesting from the sorts of personality problems and neurotic distress that afflicted Olga. Certainly, no such inference would pass muster in a forensic context, and the DSM-5 cautions against such simplistic thinking in its introduction. Going down this path seems to play into the very worst and most stigmatizing stereotypes of the emotionally distressed. As I assume Blum knows, the evidence we have is that most mentally ill parents are not child physical abusers. Physical abuse is elevated among mentally ill cohorts, but not enormously. For example, a recent Australian epidemiological survey (Doidge et al., 2017) concluded that relative to the rate of physical abuse in the general population (reported to be about 6%), a regression analysis yielded an adjusted odds ratio for abuse among those whose parents suffered from mental illness or substance dependence of 1.58, which translates into roughly a 10% abuse rate. (To place this in perspective, having grown up "at least somewhat poor" yielded an odds ration twice as high of 3.13 for an overall rate of about 19%.) These sorts of epidemiologic studies are obviously far from evidentially ideal, but as a first approximation they do usefully underscore the fact that accusations of violent infant physical abuse of the serious sort that Blum levels against Olga cannot be taken seriously without direct evidence of the sort that Blum lacks.

Blum must address the awkward question: how is it that no one else saw physical abuse in the case's one comment about spanking Olga? Blum's answer is that failure of other observers to see what he sees "shows a remarkably persistent psychoanalytic blindness to the data and implications of the case report"—that is, everyone else came to the case with blinders that Blum has removed. He offers an ingenious two-part explanation for how this might have come about:

> Why was Olga's hostile aggression and violent abuse of her infant
> daughter not explored by Freud and the later analysts who studied the

case? Freud may have been protecting a childish ex-patient who seemed to accept culturally syntonic yet abusive child-rearing practices, including punishment for masturbation. Later analysts idealized Freud, engaging in hero worship rather than joining him in the relentless search for ever greater insight. Idealization of the heroic era of psychoanalytic discovery may have fostered a fixation to the early theory, privileging unconscious fantasy over actual trauma.

(Blum, 2007, p. 754)

So, Blum claims that Freud hid or ignored the truth of "Olga's hostile aggression and violent abuse of her infant daughter" to protect Olga, and later analysts so idealized Freud as a hero that they denied what they saw in the case record rather than becoming heroes themselves and contradicting Freud. Let's leave aside the eye-catching implication of this unlikely construction that Blum's analysis locates Blum as the first true hero regarding the Hans case. The important thing is that the evidence does not support Blum's explanation. For one thing, in the contentious and complex history of psychoanalysis, analysts regularly diverged from Freud in every way imaginable. Moreover, Freud does blame the mother when he feels it is justifiable, as in his disapproval of Olga allowing Hans into the W.C. Blum's claim that the commentators who preceded him were so blinded by their hero worship of Freud that they could not allow themselves to be heroes like Freud and pursue the truth, is dubious to say the least when applied to Bowlby, who can hardly be accused of such paralyzing hero worship of Freud, yet Bowlby never suggested abuse as an issue.

Rather than Blum being the first truly heroic figure who is able to see the truth, a more plausible explanation of Blum's novel interpretation is that Blum is taking the current renewed emphasis on trauma theory and reading it into the case in a way that he finds congenial despite a lack of evidence. This view is supported by the fact, documented above, that there is simply insufficient evidence to responsibly infer from the case material what Blum asserts as fact, that Olga physically abused Hanna. The reason Freud and subsequent commentators did not recognize this evidence is simply that the evidence is not there. The case material does not warrant the conclusion Blum draws from it.

Blum's reading ignores some textual subtleties that may have sent most interpreters on a different path. There is a reason why Strachey translated

Hans's statement as saying that his mother "whacks" Hanna whereas he translated a later statement by Max as saying that Hans might like to "beat" his mother—which Blum tendentiously translates uniformly as statements both about "beatings". In his spontaneous statement about his mother and Hanna, Hans twice uses the verb *hauen*, which is best translated as "hit" or "slap"—or perhaps Strachey's "whack" (or perhaps the Yiddishism, "shmice in tuchis"), all of which tend to connote a single or brief action ("Hans: 'Wenn man sie am nackten Popo haut, dann schreit sie.' Ich: 'Hast du sie einmal gehaut?' Hans: 'Wenn die Mammi sie auf den Popo haut, dann schreit sie'" [1909/1966, p. 307]). In describing the mother's punishment of Hanna, Hans does *not* use the common verb *schlagen*, which also can be used for "hit" or "slap" but is broader and can connote a lengthier or more violent action that qualifies as "beating" someone. It is in fact Hans's father who introduces the broader term *schlagen* into the discussion and thereby opens up the possible interpretation that the mother "beats" Hanna. Hans then mimics his father's usage in that interaction ("Ich: 'Möchtest du die Pferde so schlagen, wie die Mammi die Hanna? Das hast du ja auch gerne.' Hans: 'Den Pferden schadet es ja nichts, wenn man sie schlägt'" [1909/1966, pp. 314–315]). The father also uses this term at other times in his interactions with Hans, and Hans also uses it elsewhere, again sometimes simply following his father's usage (e.g., "Ich: 'Wen möchtest du eigentlich gerne schlagen, die Mammi, die Hanna oder mich?' Hans: 'Die Mammi.' Ich: 'Warum?' Hans: 'Ich möcht' sie halt schlagen'" [1909/1966, p. 316]). Hans well understands *schlagen* and could have used it spontaneously if he felt it was appropriate, but he never describes his mother's actions towards Hanna using this term. Hans's choice of *hauen* over *schlagen* when describing his mother's actions casts doubt on whether he meant what Blum says he meant, and Strachey's translation reflects this textual reality.

It must be kept in mind that both the mother's whacking Hanna's bottom and her attempts to control Hans's touching his penis, for which Blum also criticizes Olga, were culturally syntonic practices. With regard to spanking, as we saw, Blum himself says that the mother's practices were "culturally syntonic." With regard to masturbation, Blum says that Hans's parents "conformed to the culturally syntonic attitude that masturbation is pernicious and punishable." Indeed, the father's perception of the general acceptability of even severe spanking of children is implied when he writes to Freud at the end of the case to advise him, "In presenting the case one ought perhaps to insist upon the violence of his anxiety. Otherwise it might be said that the boy would have gone out for walks soon enough if he had been given a sound thrashing" (1909/1955, p. 100). Note that this communication to Freud at the end of the case implies that, contrary to innuendo in some of these articles, Hans was *not* spanked to get him to give up his behaviors. Of course, culturally syntonic childrearing practices can be harmful. Nonetheless, this background cultural belief system poses an obvious objection to Blum's "mother as out-of-control violent pathological infant abuser" narrative because cultural syntonicity offers an explanation of behavior that is an alternative to psychopathology.

One must also ask: if Olga was prone to violent child abuse, why did she not abuse Hans? Granted that she was more favorably disposed to Hans, and granted that of course a parent may abuse one child and not another for a variety of reasons, yet Blum's description of Olga is so extreme that it is hard to imagine that she would control her violent disposition when it came to Hans. We know she did not beat Hans because Hans reports that his mother threatened to beat him (with a carpet-beater) when he was naughty, but only threatened—she did not actually do so. A satisfactory explanation for this disparity and restraint in a supposedly uncontrollably violent Olga is not offered.

In sum, the evidence from the case record and the interviews is that Olga spanked Hanna at least once and perhaps multiple times at around the age of 18 months and threatened to spank Hans with a carpet beater but did not do so. From these premises, Blum arrives at the firm conclusion that Olga repeatedly abused Hanna in a violent, traumatizing fashion. However, in the derestricted interviews in which the interviewees do not hold back their negative reminiscences about the mother, no one mentions the mother's physical abuse of Hanna, although they do report that the mother emotionally rejected Hanna.

In my view, for Blum to put forward such serious accusations against Olga without adequate evidence and then build his interpretation on them as if they are established facts is to engage in a theory-driven form of character assassination under the guise of psychoanalytic interpretation. Given the history of patriarchal assumptions and mother-blaming within psychoanalysis, these interpretations are particularly egregious, resonating as they do with a misogynistic past. At one point, Blum offers the familiar accusation that Freud confused the reality of childhood abuse with his theory-dictated notion of childhood fantasy. Blum ought to look closer to home, for he confuses his theory-dictated trauma account with the reality that the Hans case's evidence suggests.

John Munder Ross on Hans as the Victim of His Mother's Seductiveness, Sadism, and Explosiveness

John Munder Ross (2007), like Blum, claims that the Archives interviews reveal that Hans's symptoms were due to real trauma in the form of his mother's physical abuse and seductive sexuality: "the phobia was a symbolic representation not merely of age-expectable Oedipal fantasy but of a care-taker's actual seductiveness, sadism, and explosiveness" (2007, pp. 783–784). Ross's relentless criticism of Olga is exemplified by his abstract's assertions that the interviews "describe the severe pathology of Little Hans's mother and her mistreatment of her husband and her daughter," that the Hans case "provides ample evidence of Frau Graf's sexual seduction and emotional manipulation of her son … and her beating of her infant daughter," and that "the boy's phobic symptoms can therefore be deconstructed not only as the expression of Oedipal fantasy, but as a communication of the traumatic abuse occurring in the home" (Ross, 2007, p. 779).

The claimed evidence never appears, for there is no such evidence in the interviews. Instead, Ross argues by innuendo and free-associative leaps of imagination. As we saw in Chapter 2, the interviews do reveal that Hans's mother was highly neurotic, suffering from anxiety, social phobia, obsessiveness, and intense emotionality. From this, Ross con-cludes that Olga must have been abusing Hans. Yet, individuals with such emotional challenges are not generally child abusers, and there is no hint of accusations of physical or sexual abuse of Hans in the interviews (Blum's similar accusation is discussed above). Similarly, from the fact that Olga was unhappy to have a second child and had marital problems, Ross leaps to the conclusion that the mother's relationship with Hans must also have been fraught with difficulty. No such simplistic generalization is possible in real families, and this claim is explicitly contradicted by the interview evidence in which Max reports that Olga took reasonably good care of Hans.

I have already addressed Blum's accusation that Olga "beat" her daughter in a manner constituting child abuse, and explained why there is no evidence for this claim. Ross adds an imaginative epicycle to the accusation. He suggests that Olga was spanking Hanna not at eighteen months old, the age indicated in the case record, but as early as six months old, and that witnessing this traumatized Hans:

> Given the four-year-old boy's evident protests on the potty, the row he makes, and what appears to be his unsuccessful and protracted toilet training, one cannot help speculating about Hanna's making "lumpy." That is, about her mother's premature attempts to toilet train a baby as early as six months, indeed as many Austrians and Germans tended to do in those days. A woman such as Olga Graf might well have experienced her immature infant's incapacity to comply as deliberate defiance and, it seems, punished her, "whacked" her, for this. The mother's behavior would have exacerbated her son's age-appropriate fears of being hurt.
>
> (2007, p. 792)

This is pure speculation, and it is not supported by the evidence. The case report indicates that the issue with Hans to which he reacted with frustration was not toilet training but constipation, that this was not just his mother's concern but the father's as well, and that in enforcing his bathroom times as well as giving him enemas and feeding him certain foods the family was following a doctor's advice, as Max explains:

> There has been trouble with his stools from the very first; and aperients and enemas have frequently been necessary. At one time his habitual constipation was so great that my wife called in Dr. L .... Recently the constipation has again made its appearance more frequently.
>
> (1909/1955, pp. 55–56)

The idea that Olga beat Hanna for failing to be potty trained at age six months is made up from whole cloth. Perhaps Ross realizes this is a bit much for he cautions, "Whatever the truth of this conjecture .... " (2007, p. 792).

Ross reads Olga's malign influence into every nook and cranny of the case history. For example, Ross claims that the changing nature of Hans's fears reflect the changing nature of the mother's abuse over time:

The biting horse can be understood as a direct portrayal of the mother's oral aggression and sarcasm. Hans has won a Pyrrhic victory, for what he is almost forced to desire, and to look at, is what also terrifies him: his mother's dangerous, biting vagina.

And if this is the case, and the first form of the phobia partly represents real occurrences, what about the rest of his "nonsense" … ? Hans subsequently becomes afraid not only of biting horses but also of horses falling down and making a noisy row with their feet …. What could the boy be telling his father, Freud, and now us symbolically about other stresses in his family life? For one thing, the new horse scenarios may very well portray the mother's demonstrable fits of rage—temper tantrums in which she may literally have fallen or thrown herself down and made a row with her feet, tearing up papers or perhaps spewing forth threats of abandonment and expulsion as she has done before with her son …. something has changed at home and is reflected in the changing content of the boy's phobia. Hans's mother is probably more and more out of control, her sadism less insidious and more explosive, her rage more murderous.

(2007, pp. 790, 792)

Ross here projects an incident from early in the marriage to much later in an attempt to link Olga's behavior to Hans's symptoms. In his interview, Max reports a marital quarrel during the first year of marriage in which Olga, jealous of Max's work, ripped up some papers of his. Max subsequently talked to Freud about saving the marriage by having children: "Another reason was that the woman suddenly became jealous of my writings and that she tore them up. In short, after a year, I went to Professor Freud … " (Graf, 1959). In that first marital year, Max turned out two books and innumerable newspaper articles, so Olga's irritation at his work habits might have had some basis. But Hans's phobia occurred at least five years later, and there is no evidence in the case history or the interview of such intense fights at that time, although the couple still clearly had problems.

Regarding Ross's claim that the changes in Hans's symptoms reflected changes in Olga's abusive tantrums, is it really plausible that in the course of a four-month phobia Olga altered her behavior from a biting-vagina threat to a falling-down-and-kicking threat, and that there is no hint of any of this in the case history or the interviews? In any event, Ross's assumption of the "changing content of the boy's phobia" over time is probably spurious. Freud cautions that different aspects of Hans's symptoms that emerged at different points in the analysis should not be considered new symptoms: "it was merely a question of the emergence of material that was already in existence, and not of fresh productions" (1909/1955, p. 138). Hans explains that biting, falling down, making a row with feet, and other linked fears were all derived at the same time from the same accident in which Hans saw a horse fall down in the street and kick and (he thought) potentially bite:

> HANS: " … When the horse in the bus fell down, it gave me such a fright, really! That was when I got the nonsense."
> I: "But the nonsense was that you thought a horse would bite you. And now you say you were afraid a horse would fall down."
> HANS: "Fall down and bite."
> I: "Why did it give you such a fright?"
> HANS: "Because the horse went like this with its feet." (He lay down on the ground and showed me how it kicked about.) "It gave me a fright because it made a row with its feet."
>
> (Freud, 1909/1955, p. 50)

But, if Hans's symptoms concern the mother's behavior, why did the horse accident trigger the phobia? Ross answers that the horse's behavior reminded Hans not of Oedipal issues but of his mother's traumatizing behavior. Ross claims that the horse accident "may very well portray the mother's demonstrable fits of rage" in which she literally threw herself on the ground and kicked, and

> portrayed the actual violence that was taking place within his home, disclosing, in code, the mother's fits of rage in which she hurled herself to the ground, threatened everybody around her, and actually beat her screaming and thrashing baby daughter.
>
> (Ross, 2010, p. 498)

Without a shred of evidence, Ross simply projects the features of the horse accident into his fantasy of the mother's and Hanna's behavior, then claims on the basis of his fantasy that the similarity (which he has manufactured) to the horse accident explains Hans's reactions to the horse accident. Regarding Olga supposedly thrashing about on the floor in a rageful frenzy, perhaps this is Ross's exaggeration of Max's description of events early in the marriage in which Olga was upset about having sex, likely due to her wish to avoid having children: "The circumstances of the depression, to the extent that she had them, were always after sex .... I only know that after each night of lovemaking [*Liebesnacht*], that early in the morning she would have some outburst or other" (Graf, 1959). The fact that Olga was depressed after sex and had an outburst by no means implies the kind of out-of-control rage that Ross reads into the situation. Max would not have hesitated to mention such extreme actions in the interview if they had occurred. There is no evidence anywhere in the record, for example, that the mother hurled herself to the ground in rage like a horse falling down, as Ross claims.

Nowhere in the Archives interviews does a "smoking gun" description of the physical abuse that Ross claims Olga inflicted on her children emerge, so Ross moves to the interpretive level where his imagination holds sway and lack of evidence is no obstacle. In his interview, Herbert characterizes Vienna, a city to which he has returned after many years away, in very negative terms as a decadent, dangerous, and malevolent place, and he expresses anxiety about his return. Ross interprets Herbert's negative feelings about Vienna as feelings displaced from his mother:

> Conflagration, loss of control, destruction, separation, and abandonment—are these the threats posed by a volatile mother? Herbert himself does not make the connection directly, but his associations seem to me to point in this direction. Indeed, his musings seems to reveal the same use of symbols and places in lieu of inescapable people that is seen in the boy's phobia—the use, that is, of displacement, externalization, avoidance, and generalization. These defenses may color the adult Herbert's description of the Vienna he fled so many years earlier. ... To this day he gets "jittery" when he returns to Vienna, sensing the malevolence lurking beneath its surface charm. Whatever its validity, Herbert's wholesale indictment of his countrymen, I hypothesize, has to do specifically with his mother's sadism.

(2007, pp. 785–786)

Raising a question ("are these the threats posed by a volatile mother?") is not the same as answering it, and proposing a hypothesis that "seems to me to point" in a given direction is not evidence that the hypothesis is true. Ross interprets Herbert's condemnation of Vienna as being a defensive displacement of negative associations that reflect his physical abuse by his mother. His only evidence for this hypothesis is that some of the adjectives by which Hans characterizes Vienna could characterize an abusive mother, and Vienna is where Herbert grew up and where his mother still lives. So, Ross reasons, Herbert's reaction to Vienna could be a reaction to the hypothesized abuse he suffered as a child. Ross ignores the simpler hypothesis that Herbert, being of Jewish background, is experiencing appropriate and entirely natural feelings about Vienna in reaction to what happened to Jews in Vienna during the War. These feelings in response to an all-too-real adult horror do not require explanation by the displacement of emotion from childhood experiences. Nor, we have seen, is there independent evidence of the type of abuse Ross postulates. Ross (2010) says, as if it is a demonstrated fact, that the Archives interviews contain "revelations of child abuse on the part of the boy's mother, Olga Graf" (p. 498). There is no such revelation and the overall evidence does not support any such inferential leap.

Ross makes extensive use of such innuendo. Herbert does not recall things from his childhood, so, Ross suggests, that must be due to trauma. Max tends to have strong defenses against unpleasant things, thus, Ross implies, he might be hiding child abuse. Olga appears to suffer from various mental disorders, so perhaps she is a child abuser. Olga spanked Hanna, so Ross refers outright, as if it is an established fact, to "the mother's assaults on [Hans's] baby sister" (2007, p. 793).

Ross hypothesizes that the mother's abuse was combined with seductiveness:

[T]he case history ... reveals the mother's sexual and emotional misuse of her son .... Hans's mother "coaxes with" the boy, taking him into bed in defiance of her husband's increasing protests at the impropriety of her behavior. Perhaps in contrast to her treatment of her husband, she showers "tenderness" on her little son.

(Ross, 2007, p. 787)

Placing the term "tenderness" in scare quotes is not an argument that the mother was not in fact being tender rather than sexual. Hans's mother offers Hans physical affection as do almost all good enough mothers around the world as part of a normal attachment relationship. Only through a patriarchal lens can a writer assume that the husband's sense of impropriety automatically takes priority over the mother's preference for comforting, and that the mother's action is inappropriate defiance. Bowlby, for example, disagrees. Another way of seeing it is that Max uses Freud's Oedipal theory to rationalize his desire to be left in bed in peace with his sexually reluctant wife and thus defies the mother's and Hans's normal expectations, whereas Olga has a sense of responsibility to Hans.

Ross implies that there is a seduced-and-abandoned inconsistency to Olga's actions: "She calls her sister's attention to his 'thingummy' and asks directly about his masturbation but then repeatedly admonishes him that touching his 'widdler is piggish'" (2007, p. 787). Ross is connecting dots that don't exist. It was not Olga but Hans's aunt who called attention to Hans's "thingummy" ("Aunt M. was stopping with us four weeks ago. Once while she was watching my wife giving the boy a bath she did in fact say these words to her in a low voice" [1909/1955, p. 23]). In response to Hans's question, Olga says—once, not "repeatedly"—that she doesn't touch Hans's widdler because that would be piggish "because it's not proper" (Freud, 1909/1955, p. 19). Asking Hans whether he touches his penis and then prohibiting him from doing so when he says that he does are hardly at odds, and Olga was following the standard medical advice of the day. There is nothing inconsistent or vacillating in any of this.

I want to address one final issue raised by Ross (2010) that also reflects an argument posed by Blum. As an adult living in the United States, Hanna committed suicide after the failure of a promising relationship following earlier failed relationships. (Tragically and heartrendingly, we learn that the lover sent Hanna a letter with a change of mind, but it arrived too late.) Ross poignantly invites us to "Weep for Baby Hanna" and obliquely suggests that Olga's treatment of Hanna, which Ross says that Hans tried to stop, was responsible for her death:

> we learn from these interviews, it was a birth that augured the sister's premature death some decades later when, as a lonely adult, a self-hating Baby Hanna committed suicide … Apparently, the son's pleas went unheard, and his condemned sister ended up living a miserable life until she ended it.
>
> (2010, p. 498)

Blum, too, implicates Olga: "The highly conflicted mother-daughter relationship and Hanna's traumatic experience, together with a biological
predisposition that likely ran in the family, contributed to Hanna's later
mental collapse and suicide" (Blum, 2007, p. 755).

In working on the Hans case, I, too, came to feel an affection for "Baby
Hanna," and when I read of her suicide in the interviews, I did literally
"weep for Baby Hanna." It is possible that Olga's emotional rejection of
Hanna may have played a distant role in her adult suicide by influencing
her feelings of self-worth, but we have no evidence bearing on this speculation. Although Olga, according to her ex-husband Max, emotionally
distanced herself from Hanna, she also dutifully cared for Hanna. For
example, the case history contains multiple scenes of Olga herself bathing
Hanna rather than consigning the task to a nursemaid, and she reported
her concerns about things Hans said negatively about Hanna to her husband
(e.g., Hans's comment that Hanna might fall from the oddly constructed
balcony).

As to Hanna, we know from Max's interview that, lacking an education
despite being the brighter of the two children, she went to work in an
office and married young. With a stipend from Max, she supported the
musical education of her handsome and talented husband, a former Rus-
sian army officer, with whom she appears to have been very much in love.
He developed a career in opera based on his musical training, but he
eventually divorced Hanna. He was sent to Dachau. A further relationship
of Hanna's seemed more promising but also ran into difficulties.

One can speculate about the causes of Hanna's suicide, but speculation
is not evidence. Ross and Blum note that depression and suicide ran in the
Graf family, suggesting a genetic mood component. Ross also mentions
the commonality of suicides. I hadn't known, for example, that both the
Wolf Man's sister and his psychoanalyst, Ruth Mack Brunswick, ended
their own lives, and I recently found out that Lise Graf, Herbert's first
wife who was interviewed by Eissler, also appears to have committed
suicide some years after the interview. To suggest that "we learn from
these interviews" that Olga's cruelty caused Hanna's suicide is not a reasonable inference. Surely her first husband's removal to Dachau, given
that Hanna seems to been very much in love with him, may have affected
her. We just don't know.

What we do know from the interviews is that the bizarre implication
that Hanna's suicide decades later somehow shows that Olga's abuse was

responsible for Hans's phobia as a child can be rejected. Max emphasizes that Olga treated the two children quite differently, so Olga's behavior toward Hanna says little about her behavior toward Hans.

A trauma is by definition an experience outside the bounds of expectable variations in circumstances for which we are biologically prepared, rendering it potentially overwhelming to a normal child. Ross insists of Olga's mothering of Hans, "That environment was not 'good enough', not even 'average expectable'" (2007, p. 781). Yet, contrary to Ross's claim, the actual data of the case record as well as the interviews overwhelmingly supports the conclusion that Olga's responses to Hans's needs were indeed within the normal range of "good enough" or "average expectable."

Eugene Halpert on Olga

The sort of unsupported diatribe against Hans's mother engaged in by these authors has become standard fare. For example, Eugene Halpert (2007), in an article on Hans and his father, in passing says about Hans's mother:

> The 1909 paper described scenes of maternal seduction, loss of control and rage. His mother exposed herself to him in the toilet, took him to bed with her and then told him he was bad and threatened him with castration when he masturbated. She flew into rages and beat his sister, and gave him enemas and laxatives.
>
> (p. 137)

One can only repeat that the evidence is that the mother did *not* expose herself in letting Hans come into the bathroom with her but rather remained modestly covered. Halpert's notion of "maternal seduction" is an unwarranted sexualized labeling of normal motherly comforting of an anxious child. Olga's beating of Hans's sister refers to Olga's spanking Hanna, consistent with the culturally syntonic mores of that time. The enemas and laxatives were used after consultation with a doctor regarding Hans's constipation. Olga did disapprove of Hans's masturbation and threatened him with castration to try to stop him, but this, too, was culturally syntonic at the time, at the tail end of the two-century medical anti-masturbation crusade during which masturbation was associated with dire health outcomes and in rare cases men were castrated and women clitoridectomized to stop masturbation. The only possible out-of-control rages reported in the case study or the interviews is Max's report that his ex-wife once tore up some of his papers during an argument over his work and that she had outbursts the morning after they had sex. But, both of these instances are reported from early in the marriage years before the events of the Hans case and it is sheer speculation whether such behavior occurred at the time of the case. In any event, the likely reason for the post-coital outbursts was Olga's legitimate anger over being pushed by Max and Freud into having children when, as becomes painfully clear in the interviews, she did not want them but felt compelled to go along with Max and Freud. Indeed, Freud implicitly acknowledges this issue both in his comments in an earlier paper (Freud, 1908/1959) and in his Discussion in the Hans case when he says of Hans's association to being forced to stop playing and go to the bathroom, that "this element of the neurosis becomes connected with the problem whether his mother liked having children or was compelled to have them" (1909/1955, p. 135).

As to the early argument in which Olga jealously tore up some of Max's papers, early in the marriage Olga no doubt realized that within the marriage her desire to develop her own talents, as Max was doing and as her talented siblings had done, was never to be realized and that Max would essentially ignore her to pursue his writing and socializing. The first year of their marriage Max wrote two books and in addition was turning out daily newspaper columns and pursuing professional and social contacts in the evening, whereas Olga was destined to breast feed and care for Hans after an initial miscarriage. As Ross (2007) points out, having children was simply a strategy to put her in her female place: "Freud seems to have agreed with Max's notion that children would 'change these moods of hers,' presumably by modulating her envy of his originality and productivity as a rising musicologist" (p. 782).

So, at that time, early in the marriage, she did become enraged at the situation. Blum, despite repeating unsubstantiated accusations against Olga (see above), recognizes this part of the complex misogynist truth:

> Olga Graf, given her thwarted musical talent, may well have been envious of her husband, in view of the underprivileged status and limited professional opportunities of a woman, also Jewish, in that culture …. Max Graf is reported to have expressed the opinion in the May 15, 1907, meeting of the Wednesday night society that studying

is harmful to women. He referred to Fritz Wittels's anger that women wish to study rather than have sex .... Olga's envy and anger may have been intensified by her husband's devaluation of her, his provocations, and his privileged position in their patriarchal society.

(Blum, 2007, p. 760)

Conclusion: The Dangers, Injustice, and Misogyny of Evidentially Unsupported Trauma Attributions to Mothers

The papers reviewed above are in my view a sad commentary on the state of psychoanalytic inquiry. Driven by the need to apply trauma theory, which is the current *theory du jour*, without any serious evidence or consideration of alternative hypotheses, these writers postulate a range of extreme out-of-control and horrific acts of abuse by Olga. Olga is of course not around to defend herself from these abusive interpretations. Olga experienced similar theory-driven accusations by Freud aimed at her dead older brother that alienated her from her family, then she was blamed by her theory-driven husband for being the agent of her son's Oedipal overstimulation, and now after her death she is interpretively abused again as the villain in a psychoanalytic horror story of seductive and abusive mothering.

These papers seem to me to fall prey to a basic problem with post-hoc attachment-theoretic analyses of disorder in which trauma is inferred on the basis of scanty data. Following Bowlby, such an analysis must posit actual disruptions in the attachment bond between parent and child as causes of childhood pathology. Because mothers are typically the attachment figures, this constraint tends to lead researchers to infer pathogenic malfeasance by the mother sufficient to constitute an attachment rupture, even where the evidence does not justify such an imputation. The presumption of attachment-figure psychological guilt inadvertently yields the kind of systemic misogynistic bias that we saw in Oedipal theory—"bias" because the causes of attachment issues can be much more subtle and ambiguous than that, without there necessarily having to be a clear developmental "villain." Nor is every problem an attachment problem, as Bowlby himself explained (see Chapter 3).

The above papers raise the obvious question of why the horrific chronic mothering throughout Hans's childhood that they postulate would result merely in Hans's rather typical four-month childhood animal phobia at age four which was followed by a highly successful and creative life without gross pathology and with apparent good adjustment. The kinds of gross pathology and abusiveness attributed to Olga by the reviewed papers seems out of proportion to this result; one would expect much more profound and long-lasting difficulties on Hans's part if his mother was as described above. I think the answer to this question is obvious: no such horrifically abusive parenting ever occurred.

One would have hoped that by now psychoanalysts, who after all specialize in confronting the past to avoid repeating it, would have learned to be cautious about blaming mothers without adequate evidence given the discipline's past embarrassments in this regard. These include the shameful episode of the "schizophrenogenic mother" theory, in which perceived personality flaws in mothers as dominating, rejecting, critical, and simultaneously overprotective, were confidently inferred to be the causes of severe psychotic and autistic pathology in children. (Note the resemblance to attributions of Olga's supposed critical yet seductive nature.) Research on multiple fronts destroyed the credibility of that theory (e.g., Harrington, 2012; Hartwell, 1996; Neill, 1990; Parker, 1982). However, the unwarranted attribution of the causation of children's problems to parental issues is much broader than that episode (e.g., see Chapter 11's discussion of family systems theory), as is the general tendency to shift the responsibility for other conflicts onto mothers (Rose, 2018).

So, one might hope that psychoanalysts have learned to be cautious about such theory-driven accusations. The papers reviewed above demonstrate that some psychoanalysts have not learned this lesson. The implicit misogyny of using a theoretical rationale to level excessive and unsupported etiological accusations at the mother just because she is a convenient target as caregiver, and to do this even in the case of a mildly and transiently psychoneurotic child, is alive and well.

Although the writers I have considered embrace what they consider a fresh post-Freudian approach that accepts traumatic life events as causes of neurosis, they follow directly in Freud's footsteps on the crucial dimension of the family power implications of their analyses. That is, they deploy their theory in a way that goes well beyond the evidence to create inflated suspicions and accusations aimed towards Hans's mother, marking her as the appropriate target of intervention and suggesting that her relationship to Hans must be controlled. Based on the trauma theory, they reason backward from the existence of pathology in the child to the existence of pathology or immorality on the part of the parent as the agent of some traumatic experience that brought about the child's pathology. Thus, these trauma theorists search for the most plausible sexual predator or abuser as the source of the hypothesized trauma, just as Freud had in Olga's case during his seduction theory period. Inevitably, without any real evidence to guide them, these writers all alighted upon Hans's mother's overly sexual approach to Hans as the culprit, implying regulation of mother–child affection must be the center of treatment and prevention. Ironically, they, like Freud, sexualize normal attachment relations.

What are we to make of all this unjustified mother-bashing in terms of the broader situation of psychoanalysis? If one wants to understand the excesses that have caused psychoanalysis's fall from grace in our culture because of skepticism about its truth and its moral credibility, the gratuitously vicious portrayal of Olga Graf is a good illustration. As these papers by prominent and highly respected analysts illustrate, psychoanalysis in some of its intellectual streams has become untethered from any systematic self-critical methodology for constraining and warranting interpretations. The discipline has no generally accepted systematic methodology for critically evaluating its interpretations that is taught and internalized during training, nor does it have an adequate critical evaluation apparatus at the point of journal publication. Moreover, it lacks ethical guidelines requiring an adequate evidential threshold for interpretations that might impugn a person's character or reputation. It has no systematic methodological criteria to protect against or correct false and poorly supported interpretations. In my view, the common occurrence of evidentially questionable interpretations in the papers I have examined reflects a broader problem of lack of intellectual rigor that is one factor responsible for psychoanalysis's sad fortunes of late, a situation that begs for correction if psychoanalysis is to progress.

References

Blum, H. P. (2007). Little Hans: A centennial review and reconsideration. *Journal of the American Psychoanalytic Association, 55(3)*, 749–765.

Bowlby, J. (1973). *Attachment and Loss (Vo. 2): Separation: Anxiety and anger.* London, UK: Hogarth Press.

Doidge, J. C., Delfabbro, P., Higgins, D. J., Edwards, B., Toumbourou, J. W., Vassallo, S., & Segal, L. (2017). Risk factors for child maltreatment in an Australian population-based birth cohort. *Child Abuse & Neglect, 64*, 147–160.

Frankiel, R. V. (1992). Analysed and unanalysed themes in the treatment of Little Hans. *International Review of Psycho-Analysis, 19*, 323–333.

Freud, S. (1955). Analysis of a phobia in a five-year-old boy. In J. Strachey (Ed. and Trans.), *The standard edition of the complete psychological works of Sigmund Freud*, (Vol. *10*, pp. 1–150). London, UK: Hogarth Press. (Original work published 1909).

Freud, S. (1957). Leonardo Da Vinci and a memory of his childhood. In J. Strachey (Ed. and Trans.), *The standard edition of the complete psychological works of Sigmund Freud* (Vol. *11*, pp. 57–138). London, UK: Hogarth Press. (Original work published 1910).

Freud, S. (1959). On the sexual theories of children. In J. Strachey (Ed. & Trans.), *The standard edition of the complete psychological works of Sigmund Freud* (Vol. *9*, pp. 205–226). London, UK: Hogarth Press. (Original work published 1908).

Freud, S. (1966). Analyse der phobie eines fünfjährigen knaben (4th ed.). In A. Freud (Ed.). *Gesammelte Werke* (Vol. *7*, pp. 243–432). London: Imago Publishing Co., Ltd. (Original work published 1909).

Graf, H. (1959). *Interview [of Herbert Graf] by Kurt Eissler.* Box R1, Sigmund Freud Papers, Sigmund Freud Collection, Manuscript Division, Library of Congress, Washington, DC.

Graf, M. (1952). *Interview [of Max Graf] by Kurt Eissler.* Sigmund Freud Papers, Sigmund Freud Collection, Manuscript Division, Library of Congress, Washington, DC.

Hacking, I. (1991). The making and molding of child abuse. *Critical Inquiry, 17*(2), 253–288.

Halpert, E. (2007). The Grafs: Father (Max) and son (Herbert a.k.a. Little Hans). *Psychoanalytic Study of the Child, 62,* 111–142.

Harrington, A. (2012). The fall of the schizophrenogenic mother. *Lancet, 7;379 (9823),* 1292–1293.

Hartwell, C. E. (1996). The schizophrenogenic mother concept in American psychiatry. *Psychiatry, 59*(3), 274–297.

Lindon, J. A. (1992). A reassessment of Little Hans, his parents, and his castration complex. *Journal of the American Academy of Psychoanalysis, 20,* 375–394.

Masson, J. M. (1984). *The assault on truth: Freud's suppression of the seduction theory.* New York: Farrar, Straus and Giroux.

Neill, J. (1990). Whatever became of the schizophrenogenic mother? *American Journal of Psychotherapy, 44*(4), 499–505.

Nunberg, H., & Federn, E. (1967). Minutes of the Vienna Psychoanalytic Society (Vol. *2*): *1908–1910.* New York, NY: International Universities Press.

Parker G. (1982). Re-searching the schizophrenogenic mother. *Journal of Nervous and Mental Disease, 170*(8), 452–462.

Rose, J. (2018). *Mothers: An essay on love and cruelty.* New York: Farrar, Straus, and Giroux.

Ross, J. M. (2007). Trauma and abuse in the case of Little Hans: A contemporary perspective. *Journal of the American Psychoanalytic Association, 55*(3), 779–797.

Ross, J. M. (2010). Brothers, sisters, and a return to reality. *Psychoanalytic Inquiry, 30,* 496–510.

Silverman, D. K. (2001). Sexuality and attachment: A passionate relationship or a marriage of convenience? *Psychoanalytic Quarterly, 70,* 325–358.

Wakefield, J. C. (2006a). Can relational problems be genuine medical disorders? A harmful dysfunction perspective. *The Family Psychologist, 22*(Fall), 8–14.

Wakefield, J. C. (2006b). Are there relational disorders?: A harmful dysfunction perspective: Comment on the special section. *Journal of Family Psychology, 20*, 423–427.

Wakefield, J. C. (2007a). Little Hans and attachment theory: Bowlby's hypothesis reconsidered in light of new evidence from the Freud Archives. *The Psychoanalytic Study of the Child, 62*, 61–91.

Wakefield, J. C. (2017) Concept representation in the child: What did Little Hans mean by 'widdler'? *Psychoanalytic Psychology, 34*(*3*), 352–360.

Chapter 8

The Social Context of the Oedipal Theory

Children as a Challenge to Emerging Ideals of Marital Harmony

In this chapter and the next I offer plausibility arguments for extending my analysis of Oedipal power/knowledge beyond the Hans case to our culture at large. I ask: given the lack of evidence for the Oedipus complex at least in relation to its outsized influence (Wakefield, 2022), how do we explain the Oedipal theory's inordinately widespread influence? Following Foucault (1978, 2003), I assume that the explanation for the Oedipal theory's appeal may lie in the theory's impact on family life. That is, the theory was so influential partly because its impact fit with changing middle-class family structures and values. Acceptance of the theory and the consequent impact thus served a social function.

The Challenge of Generalizing the Nature of Oedipal Power/Knowledge from the Hans Case to the Culture at Large

My analysis of the Hans case is, I believe, solidly anchored in textual evidence. However, it is a different matter to hypothesize that the Hans case reveals a form of Oedipal power/knowledge that has impacted Western, middle-class families more generally. Detailed scrutiny of a single case, no matter how prototypical, cannot be generalized to the cultural implications of the Oedipus complex without further argument. Simply leaping to the conclusion that what the Oedipal theory did to the Graf family is also what it has done to all of us, thus extending the findings from one case history published in 1909 to claimed cultural echoes a century later, is an inherently risky and initially dubious proposition.

After all, the Hans case is unique in many ways. Above all, Hans suffered from an anxiety disorder and was psychoanalyzed by his father, not a typical family experience. The account of Oedipal power/knowledge in

DOI: 10.4324/9780203817124-8

the Hans case as protection of the marital bed by emphasizing danger in mother–son affection could easily be dismissed as idiosyncratic, the result of one insecure man, charged with analyzing his son, responding opportunistically to his wife's denial of his sexual needs. So, in trying to draw broader provisional conclusions, we must ask: Was the role of the Oedipal theory as a form of power/knowledge in the Grafs' family dynamic a unique occurrence, or can it be generalized to an enduring cultural influence?

However, with regard to the unique situation of Max's analyzing Hans, it emerged in Chapter 4 that Max's way of applying the Oedipal theory to his family to restrain Olga's and Hans's relationship was *not* an artifact of his analyzing Hans or of Hans's neurosis. We discovered that, inspired by Oedipal theory, Max began well before the outbreak of Hans's neurosis to systematically exclude Hans from the bedroom based on the Oedipal-inspired idea that cuddling with his mother was potentially harmful. Thus, Oedipal power/knowledge was already part of the Grafs' family life before any emotional problems developed in Hans and prior to any analysis. Concerns about mother–son affection derived from the theory itself in a way that could apply to any family.

Moreover, the Hans findings do seem on their face to reflect broader subjective experiences. Most revealingly, if we look within ourselves, we can readily find the lurking anxiety about "excessive" physical affection between mother and son. Such background vigilance about excessive affection is, I suggest, omnipresent in our society. (Of course, father–daughter affection also often falls under suspicion, but mostly for somewhat different non-Oedipal sexual-abuse reasons that are not addressed in this study.)

A comprehensive cultural analysis bridging the gap between the Hans case and the broader culture would require a book of its own, and I do not attempt it here. Instead, I offer two approaches to supporting the hypothesized relationship between Oedipal power/knowledge and broader cultural currents. First, in this chapter, I provide some historical context regarding the ongoing changes in marital and family life that were occurring around the time of the Hans case that help to explain the Oedipal theory's impact through to our own time. I argue that ongoing changes in marriage disposed toward the theory's acceptance because the theory fit with, and advanced, shifting values about egalitarian and sexual-emotional marriage and thus had an appeal and a social function independent of its evidential support.

The cultural background discussion remains rather abstract, however. So, my second approach, undertaken in the next chapter, is to offer a concrete case study of a specific development in cultural mores and exercise of family power since Hans's time—namely, the medically sanctioned social disapproval of child–parent cosleeping in the same bed, reflecting a similar dynamic to what we saw in the Hans case—that, I argue, likely in part reflects the Oedipal theory's reshaping of our culture's family relations.

To establish a contextual reference point for my analysis, I first make some remarks about the changing nature of marriage from a Foucauldian perspective. The rest of this chapter provides a brief summary of a standard view among family historians regarding changes that were occurring to the ideals of marriage among the middle class that started earlier in the nineteenth century but culminated in pronounced changes in the late nineteenth and early twentieth century, around the time that Freud put forward the Oedipal theory, and that have stayed with us until the present. In considering the changing structure of middle-class marriage, I merely borrow from standard wisdom among family historians. The kinds of changes occurring in marriage at the time are well documented within the history-of-the-family field and I do not attempt to defend these accounts *de novo*. I simply examine what historians of the family have concluded, and identify changes with which the Oedipal theory might have been congruent or which it might have advanced, thus that might enter into an explanation of the theory's appeal.

From the Suspect Child's Bed to the Protected Parental Bed

The Little Hans case, and Freud's work in general, takes place against the backdrop of historic changes in the nature of the marital bond and in perceptions of what makes a good or bad marriage that transformed the traditional conception. Traditionally, as Foucault (1978) noted, marriage had many functions: for example, uniting family lines, reproduction, economic advancement, acquisition of property, formation of political or other alliances, and establishing lines of inheritance. Romantic and sexual fulfillment were of course considered desirable, but were not generally considered inherent to or preeminent among the essential goals of marriage.

Love and sexual attraction had always been themes in views of marriage not only because of intrinsic pleasure but because they served the ultimate procreational functions of marriage. However, during the nineteenth century, these formerly instrumental or secondary themes were being elevated into the essential meaning of a good marriage, in effect transforming marriage from primarily an economic and power-oriented family-alliance institution into a love-and-sex-based institution. These structural changes in parental relationships were taking place especially in middle-class, urban families, such as the Graf family.

Foucault (2003) portrays the nuclear family that replaced the extended family during the seventeenth to nineteenth centuries as intimately and intensely entangled—and thus suitably described in nuclear tightly bound atomic terms—via the parents' concern, guided by the medical profession, over masturbation:

> the body of the child, under surveillance, surrounded in his cradle, his bed, or his room by an entire watch-crew of parents, nurses, servants, educators, and doctors, all attentive to the least manifestations of his sex, has constituted, particularly since the eighteenth century, another 'local center' of power-knowledge.
>
> (1978, p. 98)

However, this classical masturbation-crusade configuration centered on the child's bed, which Foucault terms "the suspect bed," no longer exists. Its demise began to occur around the time that Freud was formulating his Oedipal theory, and Freud's theory has long been considered revolutionary for helping to put an end to the child's suspect bed by normalizing child sexuality. To the degree that the Oedipal theory replaced the masturbation crusade's theoretical apparatus it also altered the theory's power/knowledge in ways beyond Foucault's account (Wakefield, forthcoming).

The changes in the parent–parent family axis, although not a target of the masturbation crusade, are critical to understanding the power implications of the Oedipal theory. The care of children and the intrusion of children into the functioning of the marital dyad was a challenge to the new marital ideal. As we saw in examining the Graf family, the Oedipus complex exerted forms of power/knowledge that helped to resolve this tension by separating the child from the parental dyad in ways that allowed the parents to better pursue the new ideal of a good marriage.

As the center of the family power/knowledge configuration, the child's "suspect bed" that entangles the family in order to form the nuclear family is exchanged for an early separation of parents, who are now mutually entangled, from their children, who are kept more distant, thereby allowing for the parents' intense entanglement and the State's educational near-monopoly. What results seems not so much a nuclear family as a "molecular family" with linked but separable generational centers, with children in orbit around but distanced from the parental nucleus. In this new family, which is more like today's middle class family, the child's suspect bed has been replaced by the parents' "protected bed" that disentangles the parents from the children to allow the parents to pursue the new marital ideals of sexual and emotional intimacy, which becomes the criterion for a good marriage. Consistent with this picture, historians of the family have long described changes to marital ideals that occurred with particular intensity around the end of the nineteenth and the beginning of the twentieth centuries, to which I now turn.

The Constitution of the Emotional-Sexual Parental Dyad

In considering what family historians have to say about the evolution of marital ideals in Freud's time, there are many good books that address this period's transformation in marital ideals. I will rely here primarily on a particularly lucid and accessible source, Stephanie Coontz's *Marriage, A History: How Love Conquered Marriage* (2005). Coontz's book is essentially a review that integrates an enormous amount of disparate literature about the history of marriage. Although one might dispute some of Coontz's speculations about the origins of marriage and about the recent status of marriage since the "Ozzie-and-Harriet" era of the 1950s, I believe that what she has to say in her chapters about the nineteenth-century transformation of marriage toward an institution more concerned with the personal satisfactions of love and lust can be taken to be the "standard view" these days among the bulk of family historians. For the interested reader, many other books overlap in making a similar argument about the history of the changing nature of marriage from the seventeenth to the twentieth centuries, in which predominant considerations of economics, family status, and alliances were gradually replaced by a focus on the emotional bond and sexual interaction of the spouses. Additional references displaying this broad consensus include Lawrence Stone's (1979) well-known work and Edward Shorter's (1975) lucid survey, as well as Degler (1980), D'Emilio and Freedman (1988), Mintz and Kellogg (1988), and Mitterauer and Sieder (1982).

Coontz (2005) argues that marriage based on love and on satisfying sexual relations emerged most prominently in Western Europe starting around the beginning of the nineteenth century and culminated in the triumph of this view with an added emphasis on sexuality toward the end of the nineteenth century and the first years of the twentieth century. The love-and-sex rationale for marriage, she claims, is a historically specific occurrence rather than the natural enduring conception of marriage. Note that this historical thesis is specifically about the structure of marriage and not about love or sex in themselves. It should be sharply distinguished from the well-known—and dubious—thesis that romantic love was invented in Europe in the days of the troubadours, and other such historicist theses about love and sex.

In previous eras in Europe and America, as is still the case today in some other cultures, marriage was controlled by parents and focused on considerations of wealth, politics, inheritance, and other such issues. Love in marriage was seen as a desirable bonus, and one that might often occur after marriage, but not as an essential part of what constituted a good marriage. The Enlightenment idea of human equality eventually expressed itself as the notion that marriage should be a freely chosen association based on mutual love between equal partners, to some extent undermining the traditional marital gender hierarchy. More importantly, the rise of capitalism moved work outside of the home and the family's domain, and even outside of the community, creating a separate sphere for the family in which a new emotional intensity and private aspirations for satisfaction could thrive. Coontz links the advent of marriage-for-love to broader role changes associated with these economic shifts, such as the change from the entire family working together to the Victorian "breadwinner husband" who goes outside the household to do battle for money and returns at night to the sanctuary provided by the wife. The Grafs' middle-class household in which Hans grows up is a prototypical instance of the form of family with which Coontz is concerned.

Coontz sees the transformation of marriage during the 1800s in Europe from an economic-reproductive-kinship institution to a love-centered institution, and subsequently to a sexually-based institution as well, as historically unique:

By the end of the 1700s personal choice of partners had replaced arranged marriage as a social ideal, and individuals were encouraged to marry for love. For the first time in five thousand years, marriage came to be seen as a private relationship between two individuals rather than one link in a larger system of political and economic alliances. The measure of a successful marriage was no longer how big a financial settlement was involved, how many useful in-laws were acquired, or how many children were produced, but how well a family met the emotional needs of its individual members.

(Coontz, 2005, pp. 145–146)

Nineteenth-century marriage was thus "sentimental" marriage, in that it was based on a vision of an emotional and passionate relationship between the spouses combined with other marital commitments (e.g., care of children), a combination that we have subsequently struggled to make workable: "The Victorians were the first people in history to try to make marriage the pivotal experience in people's lives and married love the principal focus of their emotions, obligations, and satisfactions" (Coontz 2005, p. 177). I suggest that it is within the context of this difficult struggle to construct a new emotionally and sexually focused and egalitarian form of marriage that the appeal and power/knowledge of the Oedipus complex must be understood.

It is not just broader social institutional and economic changes in the abstract, but the wealth created by those changes, that provided fertile ground for the romantic-sexual marriage to grow:

Changes in material life also encouraged more affectionate relationships within the nuclear family. As the nineteenth century progressed, more middle-income people could afford houses that included a living room or parlor and separate bedrooms for parents and children. These architectural changes provided more space for joint family activities as well as greater privacy for the married couple.

(Coontz 2005, p. 173)

These observations are directly pertinent to Little Hans. His problems were correlated with the upward mobility of his family. His neurosis broke out immediately after a rapid series of affluence-dependent changes such as spending time at a summer house, moving to a new larger home, and occupying his own bedroom separate from his parents, all within the few months before the outbreak of his anxiety (Wakefield, 2007a).

As Freud Archives interviews with Max and Herbert Graf document, Hans's mother was not eager to have children and especially not more children after Hans, and forever blamed Freud for influencing her husband toward wanting more children (Wakefield, 2007b). However, note that the Grafs in fact had only two children over a period of almost five years, and no more after that, suggesting that some means of pregnancy prevention was used. In arguing for having no children or minimal children, Olga assumed that this was at least a possibility in her day. This choice of a small family and the dream of even a smaller one was much more available to Hans's mother and other bourgeois women in her era than in most previous times and places. Coontz notes that there was a dramatic rise in birth control and an astonishing lowering of birth rate by about 50% in some European countries in the late 1800s, just before the time of Hans's case: "This significant reduction in fertility, largely concentrated in the middle and business classes, relieved women of the nonstop round of bearing and nursing children and gave couples more time for domesticity" (Coontz 2005, p. 172). Birth control is not mentioned in the Hans case record, and perhaps it was unnecessary given the intense sexual conflicts that existed in the marriage, although the conflicts themselves may have arisen partly out of fear of pregnancy. However, the techniques of the time, although of uncertain efficacy, were readily available: "By the 1880s rubbers, 'womb veils' (diaphragms), chemical suppositories, douches, and vaginal sponges were widely available in Europe and North America, and abortionists openly advertised their services" (Coontz 2005, p. 193).

The change in the power over childbirth was accompanied by a broader change in the family's power dynamics as a side effect of ideals of Enlightenment equality. The man's traditional power, to the degree it was to be preserved, must result from displays of love and affection as well as rational persuasion, not mere personal assertion:

> The Victorian elevation of the love match had yet another destabilizing effect on traditional marriage. Intense emotional bonds between husband and wife undermined the gender hierarchy of the home. Although most men still believed they were the rightful heads of their households, they became more likely to exert their control through love and consent than by coercion.
>
> (Coontz 2005, p. 181)

However, Coontz also notes the continued and opposite, albeit increasingly subtle, gender expectations of male dominance:

> To "be a man," a husband had to rule his household. Victorians might laud the wife's role as a "moral monitress," but it was a withering insult to describe a household as being under "petticoat government." Now, however, unlike the past, men were expected to *inspire* rather than to extort submission.
>
> (Coontz 2005, p. 188)

This tension offers one reason why the medicalization of the family was readily embraced by men. The authority of males per se was challengeable, so male medical expertise about the healthy child and family could be used as a form of power/knowledge to exert "scientific" influence that might often happen to reinforce the male's desires. This sort of exploitation of medicalization is manifest in the Hans case. Hans's father clearly had his own reasons for not wanting Hans to come into bed with him and his wife. Yet, he could not simply assert his authority to satisfy his idiosyncratic desires. Instead, he needed some plausible grounds, such as a scientific theory of child development, to persuade his wife to disallow Hans from constantly entering the bedroom. Even with such a weapon in the father's hands in the form of the Oedipal theory, the wife resisted mightily, as we saw in earlier chapters.

The Victorians emphasized love as the basis of marriage, yet initially tended to disparage female sexuality, suggesting that female sexual inhibitions and lack of desire were useful counterbalances to male lust. However, as the turn of the century approached and passed, sexuality and love became increasingly intertwined in the notion of a good marriage, with mutual sexual satisfaction the goal. Indeed, Coontz labels the period from the end of the Victorian period at the beginning of the nineteenth century to the end of the 1920s as the shift "from sentimental to sexual marriage" (Coontz 2005, p. 196).

Freud's work falls squarely within this period in which there was a general movement of marriage towards being defined as successful when it is mutually sexually satisfying. Indeed, in a famous essay, Freud argued that, aside from the potential for pathogenesis, the sexual limitations and frustrations in the traditional marriage bed were the cause of men seeking gratification outside the marriage and thus of difficult marriages (Freud,

1912/1964). The traditional attitude that divided rank sexuality from marital purity, classically expressed by Seneca in his comment that "nothing is more impure than to love one's wife as if she were a mistress" (as quoted in Coontz, 2005, p. 17), was precisely Freud's liberatory target. Health considerations were regularly used, by Freud and others, as a rationale for social changes that encouraged sexual bonding as the cement of marriage. Freud was writing on the eve of the further shift around the 1920s to a greater emphasis on female satisfaction and female orgasm, and indeed his writings were part of the trigger for that shift in sexual attitudes.

In describing this shift, Coontz virtually ignores the role of children, even though we know that children constitute one of the greatest challenges to keeping a marriage sexually and affectionately intense. Children tend by nature to separate the spouses and to require spousal "separate domains" unless shared childrearing is instituted, given the sheer volume of care required. Moreover, they dampen sexual ardor and reduce sexual activity because they simply exhaust the mother's capacities and test her ability to remain vitally available for love and sex.

Nonetheless, the new century did bring a focus on sex:

> In the first two decades of the new century, men and women began to socialize on more equal terms, throwing off the conventions that had made nineteenth-century male-female interactions so stilted. People gained unprecedented access to information about birth control and sexuality, relieving many of the sexual tensions and fears that had plagued Victorian marriage. The old veneration of same-sex friendships and holy motherhood, which had competed with the couple bond in many people's emotional loyalties, was tossed aside as people redoubled their search for heterosexual romance .... Unlike the female social reformers of the 1890s, the New Woman of the 1900s embraced the idea that women had sexual passions.
>
> (Coontz, 2005, pp. 197–198)

In sum, in the first decades of the new century, "people rejected the notion of separate spheres and emphasized the importance of sexual satisfaction for women as well as men" (Coontz, 2005, p. 307). The Victorian notion of the asexual wife as a barrier against male lust, exemplified in physician William Acton's (1871) comment in his medical textbook that "the majority of women (happily for them) are not very much troubled by sexual feeling of any kind. What men are habitually, women are only exceptionally" (p. 112), was entirely surpassed by an ideal of mutual responsiveness. Not only Freud, but also sexologists like Havelock Ellis (1903) in what amounts to the "Kinsey report" on female sexuality of his era, wrote about the ways women's sexual needs and their orgasmic capacities had been ignored, and the mores of marriage were shifting in response. No doubt, with his wife resisting his sexual attentions, Hans's father was frustrated by his failure to participate in the emphatic marital sexuality he saw all around him. One cannot help but assume that the father's frustration made him markedly less tolerant of interruptions by children into his own "private sphere" with his wife.

Hans's father reports in a Freud Archives interview that there were serious sexual difficulties between him and his wife (Chapter 2). This perhaps reflects some of the pressures on which Coontz comments:

> But living "happily ever after" without outside constraints meant that people had to reach greater depths of emotional and physical intimacy than had been possible (or necessary) in the past. This focused even more attention on sexuality. Experts of the day believed that the success or failure of marriage was largely determined by the couple's sexual adjustment. Many even believed, as marital advice expert William Robinson claimed in 1912, that "every case of divorce had for its basis lack of sexual satisfaction." Good sex, the experts argued, was the glue needed to hold marriages together now that patriarchy had lost its force.
>
> (Coontz, 2005, p. 204)

Correspondingly. Hans's mother, given her ample anxieties (described in Chapter 2), may well have experienced the new theory that mutually satisfying sex is the test of a good marriage as a burden rather than a liberation:

> Once married, the woman was supposed to let down her sexual barriers, but this put new pressure on wives. The nineteenth-century focus on female purity had inhibited sexual openness between husband and wife, but it had also accorded women a high moral stature that made it difficult for a man to insist on sex if his wife was unwilling. The twentieth-century preoccupation with the orgasm, by

contrast, entitled a woman to more sexual consideration in love-making but increased the pressure on her to have sex whenever it was suggested.

(Coontz, 2005, p. 209)

Indeed, the man had more motive for insisting on sex. It was now a test of his marital and personal happiness and even his meaning in life, and his effectiveness as a lover was also a test of his skillful devotion to his wife's happiness. Moreover, men had fewer other legitimate outlets due to evolving marital mores that, propelled by feminist successes and fears of syphilis and other sexually transmitted diseases, curtailed the man's traditional prerogative of visiting prostitutes. In the new era, the practice of visiting prostitutes indicated not a respectful separation of lust and love but a weakness in a man's sexual bond in marriage.

Yet, in the socially idealized situation, the husband's desires must be pursued by persuasion and could not simply be imposed on his wife, for two reasons. First, the emphasis on mutual love and mutual sexual satisfaction as the basis for successful marriage meant that the husband's exercise of sheer power could play less of a role in satisfying his desires; an oppressed partner might submit but could nonetheless withhold the affection that the husband craved or not enjoy the sex that he imposed, thus denying the husband what was defined as meaningful about the experience. Second, there was a conflict between the husband's needs and the growing sense of the mother's personal responsibility in caring for her children, which took priority over responding to her husband's needs. After all, the social training for love-marriages is proper love-parenting! The mother's child-rearing responsibility was increased due to the pressure to place less reliance on relatives, servants, and nannies for childcare due to fear of sexual stimulation and the growing entanglement of the nuclear family. All of these changes formed barriers to unbridled pursuit of male satisfaction in accordance with the new ethic.

The times were therefore ripe for a medical authority who might offer the father some support in refocusing his wife's attentions on himself. The Hans case illustrates, we shall see, how the application of Freud's Oedipal theory within the family could be used to bring about precisely such a refocusing. Its appeal both to Max Graf and the broader culture is manifest; in the days of waning patriarchy, combined with the new focus on the orgasm-driven marriage, a protected marital bed would be at least of some solace to the male as he redefined his position in the marriage and subjected his manhood to novel tests defined by the new emotional/ orgasmic ideals. In the social context of evolving marital relationships, the Victorian approach of the husband seeking medical support for maintaining the wife's sexual purity and reinforcing her role as the sexually restrained protector of the family from potentially violent male lust was no longer relevant. Instead, the husband sought medical authority to maintain a free sexual sphere between the husband and wife. The Oedipal theory served as an authoritative reason for the husband to insist that the child not spend too much time in the marital bed (literally) so that the husband and wife could spend more time in it together, and husbands relied on the theory to restrict the amount of affection the wife provided the child so that she would have sufficient affection and time for responding sexually to the husband when he returned home from work.

I have argued that the social context of changing ideals of marital harmony is important to understanding the potential appeal of the Oedipal theory. Victorian medical orthodoxy held that wives had the function of restraining their husbands' lusts. Specifically, the female's lack of sexual passion except when appropriately stimulated by her husband served as a check on potentially disruptive male passion, and the woman's regulation of the household offered a calm sanctuary from the male aggressiveness of the world outside the home.

In the restructuring of marriage around the end of the nineteenth century, a radically new image of the good wife came into existence—one in which she is equal with the husband, relinquishes part of her reliance on nannies to take some degree of personal control over the emotional shaping of her children, and most of all responds with sexual passion and emotional intensity to her husband—indeed, goes beyond his needs to satisfy (or have her husband satisfy) her own long-neglected desires as detailed by early sexual researchers and theorists. This newly constructed ideal of marital harmony required some reconstructing of family life to become even an approximation to reality. Contrary to Foucault's emphasis (see Wakefield, forthcoming), these specific changes had little to do with the cohesion of the nuclear family per se, which was an accomplished fact by then. Rather, they had to do with the realization of a new conception of marital harmony between spouses within the context of the nuclear family— now, with the parent–child entanglement of the masturbation era reformulated in a distanced way, perhaps better described as the molecular family.

Foucault's analysis of the Oedipal theory focuses entirely on the promotion of cohesion of the nuclear family as it emerged from earlier extended family forms, and thereby misses the power/knowledge implications of additional social changes to ideals of marital harmony that amplify the appeal of the Oedipal theory (Wakefield, forthcoming).

The Dangers of Female Sexuality

My analysis has emphasized the resonance of Oedipal power/knowledge with Max's Laius-complex-driven sexual assertiveness in attempting to exclude Hans from the marital bed. However, Oedipal power/knowledge also resonates in other ways with aspects of Victorian views of female sexuality. The Oedipal danger of excessive motherly affection can also be understood as a transformation of Victorian ideas. Parasitic on the perceived dangers of male excessive lust, the Victorian era embraced the idea that female purity protected the family from male loss of control. In Victorian conservative medical ideology, the woman's purity and sexual reserve served as a buffer to the man's limitless wantonness. Female sexual expression—especially orgasm—was thus seen as dangerous because the delicate balance between male and female could malfunction. A wife's sexual expressiveness posed a danger to her husband's sexual restraint, in a kind of adult-to-adult version of the spoiling theory. The medical focus was on whether the wife was adequately controlled to perform her male-inhibiting function.

The Oedipal theory's presupposition of sexual spoiling of the child through excessive maternal affection is a transformation of this tradition that refocuses the target of female restraint from the father to the son. Turn-of-the-century changes in marriage brought about a change in perspective on the desirability of female marital sexual responsiveness, liberating women to experience orgasmic pleasure along with males. Indeed, they were encouraged to do so not only as a matter of claiming a right but also because the woman's active sexuality, excitement, and gratification were seen as yielding gratification for her husband, and mutual gratification was now seen as essential to a happy marriage in which the man focused his sexual longings on his wife.

However, via the Oedipal theory, the danger of female sexual expressiveness formerly seen to be a threat to the husband was transformed into a threat to the child. The object is different, but the nature of the relationship has been replicated, namely, that of a woman potentially bringing disaster into the life of a male if she is not controlled enough in her sexual inclinations to keep the male's desires subdued. Hans's mother, living in a time when just recently women sometimes had their clitorises cut off to avoid sexual chaos, projects the warning of clitoridectomy she has implicitly understood since girlhood onto Hans in the form of a castration threat—if you touch it, Dr. A. will come and cut it off. But, as Olga Honig came to understand, in fact the Oedipal theory itself did the cutting. By sexualizing the mother–child attachment bond and creating a fear of sexual overstimulation and spoiling in mother–son affection, the Oedipal theory justified cutting off the child from the attachment-bond soothing he sought from the mother in the marital bed.

Marital Re-Engineering and the Bed Time Conflict

Freud's remarkable arguments for the existence and importance of unconscious mental states (Wakefield, 2018) opened up new scientific and therapeutic vistas. However, it also opened up the potential for manipulation in which unconscious states or unacknowledged conscious states are attributed to individuals as a therapeutic tactic or a strategy of social control; for example, the recent research on "unconscious bias" illustrates how attributions of unconscious mental states can be deployed in service of social goals. The attribution of Oedipal desires to Hans appears to be one such instance in which the impact, and perhaps the function, of the attribution of incestuous desire to Hans was deployed to reduce the expression of physical affection between Olga and Hans that Max perceived as harmful to Hans and perhaps also as problematic for his troubled intimacy with his wife.

The late nineteenth century's transformation of marriage into primarily an emotional and sexual bond that is increasingly egalitarian, which was the context for Max's reaction to the affection between Olga and Hans, likely will seem familiar and natural because it remains with us today. If marital partners are not sexually satisfied or not emotionally intimate, then the marriage is considered a charade in our society. Indeed, to the degree that our culture suggests that the core meaning of one's life is interwoven with family satisfactions, lack of conjugal sexual and emotional intimacy is a threat to one's very sense of meaning. Into this marital reality, it is difficult to inject a child. Empirical research on marital happiness indicates that marital emotional intimacy, sexual activity, time spent together, subjective happiness, and all other modern indicators of a good marriage plummet immediately after having children. Most couples with children don't need research to know this. Although many of the traditional child educational and care functions of the family have been exported to other institutions, the early years of a child's life are still an enormous burden for the modern couple and greatly intrude on the couple's marital functioning.

The repeated scene in Hans's parents' bedroom of the struggle over whether Hans should be allowed to come into his parents' bed for comforting can be understood as a response to the frustrations of parenthood in our era and a negotiation of the future of family relations, as well as preparation for a more egalitarian workforce. Western culture, as we will see in Chapter 9, is virtually unique in the degree to which it expects children to be separated from their parents at young ages and at night. These novel relations between parents and children in service of transforming marital ideals and social demands required complex social restructuring. The function of the Oedipal theory—that is, the effect that made it so appealing and influential to segments of society and supported its acceptance—was precisely this restructuring of affection commitments and justification of regulation of mother–son intimacy.

References

Acton, W. (1871). *The functions and disorders of the reproductive organs in childhood, youth, adult age, and advanced life, considered in their physiological, social, and moral relations* (5th ed.). London: Churchill.

Coontz, S. (2005). *Marriage, a history: How love conquered marriage*. New York, NY: Penguin.

D'Emilio, J., & Freedman, E. B. (1988). *Intimate matters: A history of sexuality in America*. New York, NY: Harper & Row.

Degler, C. N. (1980). *At odds: Women and the family in America from the Revolution to the present*. New York, NY: Oxford University Press.

Ellis, H. (1903). Studies in the psychology of sex (Vol. 3): *Analysis of the sexual impulse. Love and pain. The sexual impulse in women*. Philadelphia, PA: F. A. Davis Co.

Foucault, M. (1978). *History of sexuality (Vol. 1): An introduction* (R. Hurley, Trans.). New York, NY: Pantheon.

Foucault, M. (2003). *Abnormal: Lectures at the College de France 1974–1975* (G. Burchell, Trans., V. Marchetti & A. Salomini, Eds.). New York, NY: Picador.

Freud, S. (1964). On the universal tendency to debasement in the sphere of love. In J. Strachey (Trans. & Ed.), *The standard edition of the complete psychological works of Sigmund Freud* (Vol. 11, pp. 179–190). London: Hogarth. (Original work published 1912).

Mintz, S., & Kellogg, S. (1988). *Domestic revolutions: A social history of American family life*. New York, NY: Macmillan.

Mitterauer, M., & Sieder, R. (1982). *The European family: Patriarchy to partnership from the Middle Ages to the present*. Chicago, IL: University of Chicago Press.

Shorter, E. (1975). *The making of the modern family*. New York, NY: Basic Books.

Stone, L. (1979). *The family, sex and marriage: In England 1500–1800*. New York, NY: Perennial.

Wakefield, J. C. (2007a). Attachment and sibling rivalry in Little Hans: The 'phantasy of the two giraffes' reconsidered. *Journal of the American Psychoanalytic Association, 55*, 821–849.

Wakefield, J. C. (2007b). Little Hans and attachment theory: Bowlby's hypothesis reconsidered in light of new evidence from the Freud Archives. *The Psychoanalytic Study of the Child, 62*, 61–91.

Wakefield, J. C. (2018). *Freud and philosophy of mind (Vol. 1): Reconstructing the argument for unconscious mental states*. New York, NY: Palgrave Macmillan.

Wakefield, J. C. (2022). *Freud's argument for the Oedipus complex: A philosophy of science analysis of the case of Little Hans*. New York, NY: Routledge.

Wakefield, J. C. (forthcoming). *Foucault versus Freud: Oedipal theory and the deployment of sexuality*. New York, NY: Routledge.

Chapter 9

Bed Time

Oedipal Power/Knowledge, Cosleeping, and the Modern Struggle Over the Child's Sharing of the Marital Bed

In this chapter I argue that Oedipal power/knowledge has reached into our era by influencing social views of family sleeping arrangements, reflecting much the same dynamic we saw in the Hans case. The Oedipal theory, I argue, has provided medical authorities with a source of support for the doctrine that parents should sleep separately from children starting at an early age. Our culture thus discourages what the literature refers to as *cosleeping* and, more broadly, *bedsharing*, which includes, like Hans, coming into the parents' bed before sleep onset or upon awakening, but also sleeping together part or all of the night either in the parents' bed or in close proximity within the same bedroom. (For convenience, I will use *cosleeping* as a generic term for all these practices.) The cultural resistance to cosleeping has many aspects and sources, but Oedipal power/knowledge as expressed in Max's protection of the marital bed from Hans applied to the culture at large appears to be one of them.

Echoes of the Hans Case in Modern Resistance to Bed Sharing with a Child

The prohibition of cosleeping and the exile of a child to a separate bedroom at an early age is a distinctive cultural practice that repeats in the culture at large the central phenomenon of the Hans case. It thus provides suggestive support for generalizing the analysis of Oedipal power/knowledge beyond the confines of the Hans case. A selective narrative review of the vast literature on this topic will reveal that the Oedipal theory enduringly influenced the degree to which parent–child bedsharing is medically discouraged in the United States. The limitations on the degree to which children can enter into the marital bedroom that American middle-class families tend to take for

DOI: 10.4324/9780203817124-9

granted as "natural" appear to have been influenced by the Oedipal theory's encouragement of control of parent–child affection.

To a remarkable degree, to this day, the appropriate response to Hans's simple human act of coming into his parents' bed seeking attachment contact and parental soothing remains highly controversial in Western developed countries. As Mileva-Seitz et al. (2016) note:

> To bed-share or not to bed-share? This seemingly innocuous question has been labeled the 'single most controversial topic related to pediatric sleep'. Bed-sharing (the practice of parent and child sharing a sleeping surface) and co-sleeping (shared sleep that includes room-sharing, bed-sharing, and everything in between) are hotly debated.
>
> (p. 4)

This debate, we shall see, distinguishes our post-Oedipal culture from the rest of the world and from our own earlier history.

Admittedly, the concern about cosleeping and bedsharing as a potential avenue for excessive affection is often set aside, especially when it is only temporary and for overriding reasons, for example, when a child has nightmares or the family has recently suffered a loss (see the discussion of intentional versus reactive bedsharing, below). Moreover, these sorts of concerns may even be derided by the sophisticated modern couple. However, even rejection of or skepticism about the implicit cultural pressures against bed-related, parent–child affection come at the cost of overcoming a reason for restraint that persists in large segments of our culture and floats in our cultural space. This potential reason does not exist in most cultures and did not exist throughout most of the history of our culture.

These echoes of the Oedipal theory, I will argue, have not yet left us, no matter who won the Freud wars. How else to explain why even today in many segments of society it is widely considered daring in a special, almost salacious way to announce that one's children share a bed with their parents? Oedipal dynamics resonate harmonically with our unique cultural obsession with separate sleeping arrangements for young children.

It is true that there are many reasons other than Oedipal fears that are offered for our society's denial of children's needs for physical affection and enforcement of separate child–parent sleeping arrangements. These recently include most saliently the threat of sudden infant death syndrome (SIDS) due to the danger of smothering the child and the danger of child sexual abuse by an aroused and opportunistic parent as the child gets a bit older. As well, there is fear of the encouragement of dependency and the impairment of the development of psychological autonomy in the child, an echo of the "spoiling theory" elaborated in Chapter 5. However, the fact that over time there occur multiple rationales supporting a distinctive cultural imposition on our intimate lives such as the discouragement of cosleeping does not undermine the power/knowledge hypothesis but comports with it. Redundancy of rationales is to be expected in such cases in which cultural appeal is the real reason for a practice.

Regarding SIDS, in order to avoid a confused picture regarding the influence of Oedipal theory, I put this issue aside and focus mostly on the literature prior to the major concern about SIDS that arose in the 1990s, and on literature that is concerned with psychosocial issues and not primarily with SIDS. However, it should be noted that the research on the danger of SIDS when bedsharing with a child has revealed that the danger is exaggerated. Problems of heightened death rates tend to occur exclusively under special circumstances, such as when a parent is smoking or drinking or taking drugs in bed with the child present, or the bedding is problematic. For example, Blair et al. (2014) found that "[R]isk associated with bed-sharing in the absence of these hazards was not significant overall ... for infants less than 3 months old ..., and was in the direction of protection for older infants" (p. 1). Similarly, Horsley et al. (2007) conclude from their review that, regarding the claim that there is an association between bed sharing and SIDS among nonsmokers, "existing data do not convincingly establish such an association" (p. 237). Revealingly, more traditional cultures in which cosleeping is routine actually tend to have much lower rates of SIDS than does the United States.

To assess the plausibility of a link between the cultural echoes of Oedipal power/knowledge and the ongoing disapproval of cosleeping, I review the literature on cosleeping of parent and child to address the following sorts of questions: Is the American practice of sleeping apart from children supported by medical authority? Is the rejection of cosleeping a common practice across cultures, or must there be some local cultural explanation of such prohibitions? Does scientific evidence support the view that cosleeping is harmful? Did the rejection of cosleeping arise or become more prominent around the same time as the Oedipal theory came into vogue? Are the reasons for rejecting cosleeping that are presented by medical professionals and ordinary people related to what plausibly might be construed as Oedipal concerns such as fear of sexual overstimulation of the child or spoiling of the child so he will be overly dependent? Are they also related to the desire for greater marital intimacy? To the degree that the answers to these questions are "yes," the analysis of Oedipal power/knowledge offered here is at least consistent with this major strand of broader cultural practice, suggesting that the analysis might be applicable beyond the confines of the Hans case. While occasionally mentioning European studies, I focus on the United States both because Freudian influence has been particularly pronounced here and because the relevant research literature on the U.S. is unusually rich. However, as Aristotle (1926) advised, I seek only the degree of precision consistent with what the subject matter allows.

Medical Authority and the Regulation of Cosleeping

Virtually all scholars of family sleeping arrangements emphasize that since early in the twentieth century, parent–child cosleeping has been against medical opinion. Crawford (1994) opens her article on parent–child sleeping arrangements by noting that

> Sleeping patterns of children and their parents have provided a topic of discussion for mental health professionals for the last 50 to 60 years. Generally, it has been believed among mental health professionals that it is healthier for children to sleep apart from their parents ....
>
> (p. 42)

Mileva-Seitz et al. (2016) similarly point out that even "Parenting and children's books in the West ... are typically dominated by a medical perspective which opposes bed-sharing" (p. 7).

Morelli et al. (1992) also report that middle-class culture at large and medical opinion in particular within the United States converge in considering parent–child sleeping in the same bed as inadvisable:

> Folk wisdom in the United States considers the early night-time separation of infants from their parents as essential for the infants' healthy psychological development. This widespread belief is reflected in the advice parents have received since the early 1900s from child-rearing experts regarding cosleeping. ... Brazelton and Ferber,

pediatricians and writers nationally known as specialists on parenting, also warned parents of the dangers of sleeping with their infants. .... [P]ediatricians generally advise parents to avoid cosleeping.

(p. 604)

Note that one of the above passages dates the anti-cosleeping ethic to the "early 1900s" whereas the other dates it back to "50 or 60" years before 1994. This is a time frame that fits with that in which the Oedipal theory was highly influential and is consistent with the influence of the Oedipal theory as one component of the movement against cosleeping.

In the decades from the middle to the late twentieth century, influential major medical authorities became increasingly explicit and absolute in their advice to parents about the inadvisability of parent–child contact in the marital bed. In one of the most influential parent-advice books ever written, Dr. Benjamin Spock (1945) wrote, "I think it's a sensible rule not to take a child into the parents' bed for any reason" (p. 101). Versions of this view were maintained over time; Spock and Rothenberg (1992) stated: "Children can sleep in a room by themselves from the time they are born .... If they start with their parents, 2 or 3 months is a good age to move them" (p. 212). In a *Newsweek* cover story, pediatrician T. Berry Brazelton (1989) asserted that "a child shouldn't fall asleep in her parent's arms" (p. 69), and maintained that parents should not be part of the child's sleep ritual. And psychiatrists Comer and Poussaint (1992) state that "it is a good idea to have your child's crib out of your bedroom by five months .... You are asking for trouble if you place him in your bed [in response to crying]" (p. 45).

Referring to Spock's (1976) book of child-care advice, Lozoff et al. (1984) note:

Pediatric health professionals often advise parents not to sleep with their children. Spock, for instance, recommends that "babies get used to falling asleep in their own beds, without company, at least by the time any 3-month colic is over," and that "it's a sensible rule not to take a child into the parents' bed for any reason," advice which is echoed in numerous other sources.

(p. 171)

Lozoff et al. (1984) surveyed Cleveland pediatricians as to their agreement or disagreement with various aspects of Spock's advice. Of around ninety

Cleveland pediatricians responding to the survey, the vast majority "showed general agreement with Spock's approaches, including disapproval of cosleeping" (p. 175). For example, here are the percentages of pediatricians who agreed with specific pieces of advice: no all-night cosleeping, 92%; no part night cosleeping, 84%; crib out of parents' room, 88%; firm handling of protests, 82%; no adult company at bed time, 79%; no adult body contact at bed time, 65%; firm handling of night waking, 59% (Table 2, p. 175). These views are reflected in the attitudes of the parents of their child patients; of 150 mothers surveyed in the Cleveland area, 71% indicated that they did not practice cosleeping during the month before the interview, and 65% disclosed that they did not provide any body contact to their child at bedtime.

Illustrating the potential power of cultural influences (such as, potentially, the influence of medical theories embraced by the white middle class), among white Cleveland-area families (N=96) in 1984, in only about 8% did the child frequently sleep in the parental bed through the night, whereas the rate was much higher among Black families, about 45% (Lozoff et al., 1984, Figure p. 176). Similar differences among American subpopulations have been found in other studies. For example, Barajas et al. (2011) observe: "Consistent with previous literature, our study found that Blacks and His-panics in the United States are more likely to bed-share than non-Hispanic whites" (p. e345). Interestingly, studies in European samples have also shown that immigrant populations, which would tend to be less influenced by Oedipal theory and corresponding medical opinion, tend to cosleep at higher rates than the native European population due to contrary cultural traditions. For example, Luijk et al. (2013) conclude:

> In Dutch mothers, the majority of mothers did not share their beds with their child, and bedsharing rates decreased from 2 to 24 months. Other ethnic groups showed higher bed-sharing rates, typified by both increa-ses in bed-sharing (the Turkish and Moroccan group) and persistence of bed-sharing over time (the Caribbean group) …. Our results suggest that mothers with a Turkish and Moroccan or Caribbean background were more influenced by cultural values, whereas bed-sharing practices were more reactive in the Dutch group.
>
> (p. 1092)

Because denial of attachment needs causes distress to the child, along with the expert discouragement of cosleeping there is advice for dealing with the resulting distress in ways other than by relenting and allowing cosleeping or otherwise attending to the child's need for physical contact. The advice of medical experts can be seen as quite extreme in terms of the lengths to which the parent should go in denial of the child's needs for parental contact and comforting, analogous to the way Hans was treated:

> Although taking your child into bed with you for a night or two may be reasonable if he is ill or very upset about something, for the most part this is not a good idea. We know for a fact that people sleep better alone in bed.
>
> (Ferber, 1985, p. 38)

> The parents have to be firm and committed to returning the child to bed ... Parents have to learn to ignore the crying until the child falls asleep. Sometimes children can cry for a couple of hours ... If parents are distressed by the crying they can go in every five minutes and quickly check the child is safe. But they should not comfort or touch the child but just tell them firmly to go to sleep.

> It is a difficult method to use for some parents as the child can become very upset. Children may vomit with crying and so parents need to be prepared to go in to clean up the child and change the bedclothes quickly and, with the minimum of fuss, put the child back to bed, and walk out. It is very important if parents opt to use this method that they be warned how the problem can be made much worse if they do give in.
>
> (Douglas, 1989, p. 128)

As a consequence, even "the rare middle-class U.S. families who do practice cosleeping often recognize that they are violating cultural norms" (Morelli et al., 1992, p. 605). As one would expect, the resistance to cosleeping is most pronounced among educated middle-class families who are aware of and sensitive to psychological and medical authorities' theorizing about proper parenting:

> The university-educated parents are the ones most likely to have taken courses in child development or psychology, where they may have been exposed to discussions of the horrors of parent-child enmeshment

brought on by child-rearing techniques like sleeping with one's child, or alternately have come to rely on advice by experts like Dr. Spock or Dr. Brazelton.

(Abbott, 1992, p. 59)

The same is not necessarily true of other American sociodemographic groups that are not as penetrated by, or as subjected to, regulation by medical authority or have alternative subcultural traditions that override medical advice. The grip of Oedipal power/knowledge is not evenly distributed among social groups. For example, Abbott (1992, p. 34) documents the high rate of cosleeping in contemporary Appalachia and quotes Verna Mae Slone, a 75-year-old Knott County, Kentucky, woman who says in her 1978 autobiography, *Common Folks*, that "I don't care what doctors say, I believe it best for the mother and child to be together" (1978, p. 60).

As the passages above indicate, in light of the pressures discouraging cosleeping, and given the natural propensities of parents and their young children to share a bed at night, a lot of distress occurs in children exiled to their own cribs and beds. Rather than taking the distress as an obvious indicator that something is likely going wrong, the distress is seen as a superfluous impediment to the goal of separate sleeping locations, to be dealt with by various means. Starting around the beginning of the twentieth century, one approach became known as the "cry it out" method, to simply allow the child to cry until they stopped crying, even if that involved enduring several uncomfortable nights of desperate child screaming. In an unfortunate and unusual instance of agreement with psychoanalytic doctrine, even behaviorists such as James Watson admonished parents against cosleeping, arguing that crying is not harmful and would extinguish by behavioral reinforcement-theoretic processes and so was best ignored. Indeed, the behaviorist approach became associated with the view that any mercy shown to the crying child by parental attention would reinforce the crying and so was problematic and to be avoided. The staunch "cry it out" and behaviorist methods were softened into what became known as the "Ferber method" or "Ferberization," in which there was a more gradual process.

As full disclosure, I should mention that in my own case, my mother, against her inclinations but under her pediatrician's and my father's pressures, separated me from the marital bed at a few months of age and endured several nights of my screaming in my room. Knowing I was agile, she placed a second crib next to mine, and sure enough I climbed from one and toppled into the other on one of the nights. My screaming was such that she went outside and looked in the window to check that I was safe, but had been prohibited from going into my room by her pediatrician, who said they were engaging in Ferberization, apparently interpreting the Ferber method as the more severe "cry it out" method. The debate about the significance, long-term impact, and acceptability of the child's distress under such circumstances continues to our day (Dewar, 2017; Narvaez, 2011, 2014; Rettew, 2014).

Although I have focused my discussion here mainly on the American experience of pressures against bedsharing, much of what I say about the pressure to avoid bedsharing applies to most European countries as well, as studies amply document. In terms of actual rates of cosleeping, the results in most European countries are similar to those in the U.S. For example, Valentin (2005) found in 100 German families he studied who had infants up to 30 months of age that: "The infants in this sample largely slept in their own bed in a separate room. Bedtime rituals were common and in general characterized by parents maintaining behavioral distance from the infants during the bedtime routine" (p. 269). As we saw above, Luijk et al. (2013) found that the majority of Dutch mothers did not share their beds with their child, and such bedsharing decreased from 2 to 24 months. Jenni et al. (2005) found in their sample of 493 Swiss children that, even with bedsharing defined quite broadly as sleeping in the parents' bed at least one night per week on average, "Less than 10% of the children shared the bed with their parents at least once per week in the first year of life" (p. 234), and for nine-month-old children the bedsharing figure was about 7%. The number of occasional (once a week or more) cosleepers increased until a maximum of 38% at four years old (Hans's age), still a minority of children. And, Ottaviano et al. (1996) found that, in a sample of 2,889 children in Rome, the percentage who were cosleeping rose from 0% at 2 months to 18% at four–six years. About half the children needed parental presence to fall asleep, which Ottaviano et al. attributed to separation anxiety at bedtime.

Lack of Empirical Evidence for Claimed Psychosocial Harm from Cosleeping

As noted in Chapter 5, considerable evidence supports Bowlby's (1973) claim, opposite to that of Oedipal theory, that greater parent–child intimacy promotes independence rather than creating addictive sexual dependence. Echoing Bowlby's dismissal of the "spoiling" theory, most researchers conclude that the evidence is against the claimed negative effects of cosleeping and if anything supports greater psychological health from cosleeping. Methodological challenges are admittedly enormous in this area. However, in terms of the feared behavioral and psychological harms suggested by Oedipal theory, the bulk of careful studies do not support such outcomes, and the few that do suggest modest negative correlates do not control for a range of potential confounding variables.

Common conclusions are represented by those of Barajas et al. (2011) that

> the findings from this study suggest that there is no association between bed-sharing between the ages of 1 and 3 years and cognitive and behavioral outcomes at 5 years of age .... There seem to be no negative associations between bedsharing in toddlerhood and children's behavior and cognition at age 5 years.
>
> (pp. e345, e347)

Similarly, Mileva-Seitz et al. (2016) conclude:

> The evidence of an association between bed-sharing and child behavioral problems is not clear. In Finland and the US, bed-sharers did not differ from solitary sleeping children on internalizing or externalizing problems or overall behavioral problems. Bed-sharing was not associated with three-year olds' symptoms of anxiety or depression in a large multiethnic cohort in the Netherlands.
>
> (p. 13)

McKenna and Gettler (2008) argue that there is no evidence that cosleeping creates a problem—in fact, the little evidence that there is tends to show the opposite, even in the psychoanalytically charged case of Oedipal-age boys:

> A study of parents of 86 children in clinics of pediatrics and child psychiatry (ages 2–13 years) on military bases (offspring of military personnel) revealed that cosleeping children received higher evaluations of their comportment from their teachers than did solitary sleeping children, and they were under-represented in psychiatric

populations compared with children who did not cosleep. The authors state: "Contrary to expectations, those children who had not had previous professional attention for emotional or behavioral problems coslept more frequently than did children who were known to have had psychiatric intervention, and lower parental ratings of adaptive functioning. The same finding occurred in a sample of boys one might consider "Oedipal victors" (e.g. 3 year old and older boys who sleep with their mothers in the absence of their fathers) – a finding which directly opposes traditional analytic thought".

(McKenna & Gettler, 2008, pp. 190–191; the quote at the end of this passage is from Forbes, Weiss, & Folen, 1992)

Clinicians have overestimated the need for infants to sleep separately in order to assure 'independence' from their parents, and recent biological data described here suggest that sleep researchers underestimate the importance of maternal proximity ….

(McKenna & Gettler, 2008, pp. 184–185)

Considerable research tends to challenge or disconfirm claims of negative outcomes of cosleeping or related practices that keep a child close to a parent at bedtime, and to support the potential benefits of child–mother contact around sleep onset (Crawford, 1994). For example, Wolf and Lozoff (1989) found that the close presence of an adult while a child is falling asleep results in reducing the need for attachment substitutes such as thumb-sucking or substitute attachment objects, and interestingly this contact during sleep onset was more important than precisely where the child slept during the night, whether in the parental bed or in close proximity. Similarly, Lewis and Janda (1988), in a retrospective study of college age individuals, found that sleeping in the parental bed during childhood, as well as other experiences including seeing others nude, was positively related to indices of adult sexual adjustment. They found in particular that males who coslept with their parents between birth and five years of age had significantly higher self-esteem, experienced less guilt and anxiety, and reported greater frequency of sex. Boys who coslept between 6 and 11 years of age also had higher self-esteem. They, as well as Crawford (1994), also found emotional benefits of cosleeping for females. These kinds of positive findings seem to generalize across cultural groups. Mosenkis (1998) studied over 1400 subjects from five different groups

(African Americans and Puerto Ricans in New York, Puerto Ricans, Dominicans, and Mexicans in Chicago) and found overall far more positive than negative adult correlates for individuals who coslept as a child, with a general finding across groups of a greater feeling of satisfaction with life.

Okami et al. (2002) longitudinally studied 205 families, with a mix of conventional and unconventional countercultural families. They found that "only 2% of the conventional families ... reported any bedsharing before age 6 years" (p. 248); the comparable figure for the countercultural families was a still-low 13%. In terms of outcomes, they concluded:

> Bedsharing in early childhood was found to be significantly asso-ciated with increased cognitive competence measured at age 6 years, but the effect size was small. At age 6 years, bedsharing in infancy and early childhood was not associated with sleep problems, sexual pathology, or any other problematic consequences. At age 18 years, bedsharing in infancy and childhood was unrelated to pathology or problematic consequences, nor was it related to beneficial con-sequences. We discuss these results in light of widespread fears of harm caused by parent-child bedsharing. We suggest that such fears are without warrant .... [O]ur data also do not support fears that bedsharing would lead to psychosexually troubled relationships later in childhood and adolescence, behavior problems and difficulties in peer and intimate relationships, or early childhood sleep problems. If anything, there are mildly positive associations in early childhood and adolescence between bedsharing and psychosexual and affect-related variables ....
>
> (pp. 248, 251)

Perhaps no study represents the paradox of cosleeping's Oedipal-generated stigma along with the lack of evidence of harm more than Oleinick, Bahn, Eisenberg, and Lilienfeld's (1966) comprehensive study of mother-repor-ted child rearing practices in which 160 child psychiatric outpatients are compared to a normal general-population control group and a hospital control group of children with non-psychiatric medical problems. In their list of variables to be explored in their questionnaire-based interviews with mothers and evaluated for potential psychiatric outcomes, Oleinick et al. have a category of "Exposure to sexual stimulation," and under this category they place the variables, "Share bedroom" and "Share bed." Yet, having classified these practices as potentially psychiatrically toxic sexual exposures rather than normal forms of affection (as was generally assumed at the time the study was done), the results for these variables were that no differences were found between outpatients and controls: "toilet training age and methods, treatment of aggression and sexual exploration, exposure to sexual stimulation (familial nudity, sharing of bathroom, sleeping in same bed or bedroom), and most methods of training and discipline were not significantly different" (1966, p. 349–350). Nor do they draw out the suggestive implications of this negative finding in their discussion. In sum, the prohibition of cosleeping cannot be anchored in solid empirical findings of harm, and in fact the literature suggests the opposite conclusion. Some other explanation is needed.

It should be clear from the above that the vast majority of research on bedsharing and cosleeping explores what are thought to be potential harmful effects. If one asks about the research on the relationship of short-term secure attachment and longer-term attachment bonding to mother–son contact during bedsharing or cosleeping, the answer is that there has been little focused study of this question. Horsley et al. (2007), reflecting the basic situation although perhaps slightly overstating the case, assert that "Our searches did not identify relevant studies, with a contemporaneous comparison, examining the effect of bed sharing in relation to bonding. The association between attachment and bed sharing has not been studied, to our knowledge" (p. 243).

The Unnaturalness and Cross-Cultural Rarity of Parent–Child Separation at Night

If there is little scientific support for the rejection of cosleeping, does it at least represent some sort of common wisdom of humankind? That is, can the prohibition on cosleeping be explained by some natural, innate human programming evidenced across cultures? To the contrary, despite the urgent medical advice to avoid cosleeping, one of the most definitive and remarkable discoveries about parent–child cosleeping is just how deviant from other cultures is the American/European practice of separating the child from the parents at an early age.

Burton and Whiting (1961), surveying the sleeping arrangements of 100 societies, observed that the "American middle class is unique in putting the baby to sleep in a room of its own" (p. 88). This has been reexamined by Abbott (1992), who summarizes some of the cross-cultural literature as follows:

> Barry and Paxson's (1971) coding of the Standard Cross-Cultural Sample revealed that in 44% of the 173 societies with information about infant sleeping locations, mothers shared their bed with their infant, while an additional 56% (N = 97) shared a room with their infant. No infants were put in rooms by themselves or with siblings. This appears to have been the pan-cultural human pattern for treatment of infants for most of human history. It has been usual for infants to sleep with their mothers, a practice that has had advantages for both the mother and the infant. Caudill and Plath's (1966) well-known study of Japanese sleeping locations describes their practices throughout the life span, making this an unusual study. They report that the Japanese age of transition away from sleeping with parents is 11, with the process not complete until 15 or 16 years.
>
> (p. 35)

Similarly, Morelli et al. (1992) report:

> Infants regularly slept with a parent until weaning in all but 1 (the United States) of the 12 communities studied by B.B. Whiting and Edwards (1988); in the U.S. community no cosleeping was observed. In a survey of 100 societies American parents were the only ones to maintain separate quarters for their babies. These findings are consistent with other work on sleeping arrangements in urban Korea (Hong & Townes, 1976) and urban and rural Italy.
>
> (p. 605)

Many others make similar remarks about the historical commonality and naturalness of cosleeping. For example, Madansky and Edelbrock state that "Parents and children sleeping together was a routine practice throughout human history and is still the norm in many cultures. This practice is not considered routine in America .... " (p. 197). Mileva-Seitz et al. (2016) state:

> Historically, humans have followed the mammalian pattern: mothers sleep in direct proximity to their young. In many cultures around the

world today, this practice persists and traditional wisdom condones and encourages it; a Korean proverb goes, "A baby must not sleep in an empty room alone, and an adult must keep watch next to it." In Tokyo, putting babies alone in a nursery is considered 'cold and cruel'.

(p. 4)

The same authors note that in America, in contrast:

Shifting cultural values put increasing emphasis on individualism, romantic love, and the sanctity of marriage … Bed-sharing began to be regarded as psychologically harmful. From the 20th century until now, putting infants to sleep on a separate surface has been the norm throughout North America, Europe, and Westernized Asian nations.

(Mileva-Seitz et al., 2016, p. 4)

Similarly, Luijk et al. (2013) observe:

Bed-sharing, the sharing of a sleeping surface by parents and children … has been the predominant sleeping strategy throughout human evolution. In modern societies, the practice is less common due to a mixture of cultural factors (e.g., parents' and professionals' beliefs that bed-sharing compromises partner intimacy and early childhood autonomy), and medical recommendations.

(p. 1092)

In their own study, Morelli et al. (1992) compared the sleeping arrangements of Mayan and middle-class U.S. parents and their infants/toddlers. They found that

all 14 of the Mayan children slept in their mothers' beds into toddlerhood. None of the 18 U.S. infants slept in bed with their mothers on a regular basis as newborns, although 15 slept near their mothers until age 3 to 6 months, when most were moved to a separate room.

(p. 604)

Across studies, where co-sleeping is defined as the child being in the same bed or same room as a parent, the percentage of cosleeping for white middle-class Americans ranges from 0% to 11% (Abbott, 1992, p. 38). In sum, "Research indicates that cosleeping is not commonly practiced by middle- to upper-class U.S. families" (Morelli et al., 1992, p. 604).

Latz et al.'s (1999) study of Japanese practices yields similar divergence from American practices. Significantly greater percentages of Japanese than US children coslept with their parents three or more times per week (59% vs. 15%), all the Japanese children that coslept with their parents slept with them through the night (vs. only 11% of US cosleepers), and most Japanese children, unlike American children, had adult body contact as they fell asleep whether or not they coslept through the night. Indeed, Brazelton (1990) reported that "the Japanese think the U.S. culture rather merciless in pushing small children toward such independence at night" (p. 7).

From these and other studies, McKenna and Gettler (2008) conclude that

> infant-parent cosleeping represents the universal, species-wide pattern of sleep for children worldwide .... In none of the cultures was the infant actually isolated at bedtime. Always the baby was placed in sensory proximity of another person, but not necessarily sleep on the same surface.
>
> (p. 208)

Consequently, there is a distinctive local explanation needed of our practice that goes beyond any general factor that applies equally to all human cultures.

One suggestive piece of indirect evidence supporting the naturalness of child bedsharing is the tendency of children, consistent with attachment theory, to spontaneously seek out physical proximity to the parents when feeling anxious or otherwise distressed or lonely. Of course, young infants cannot seek out the parents, except by crying, but older children can and do actively seek entry into the parental bed. Several studies, including Jenni et al. (2005) and Ottaviano et al. (1996), found the seemingly odd result that occasional cosleeping increased with the child's age. Jenni et al. explain that this is likely the result of an increase in occasional reactive cosleeping due to the child's ability to seek out attachment soothing:

> Independent locomotion is an essential condition for the child's proximity seeking at night. Locomotor abilities show a dramatic progress between

ages 1 and 3 years, concomitant to the increase of bed sharing in our sample. Only after the first year of life do the children become capable of getting out of their bed and going into the parents' bedroom. Taken together, specific developmental changes in separation-attachment processes, cognitive capabilities to develop self-recognition and nighttime fears, and motor locomotion may contribute to the age trend of night wakings and bed sharing during early childhood.

(p. 238)

In contrast to the genuine naturalness of a child seeking contact with his mother when anxious, the feeling that many parents have that allowing the child into the bed is dangerous and unnatural is an instance of the social or medical construction of the (supposedly) natural. Through culturally mediated theories and beliefs that are deployed by medical authorities, people come to *experience* a practice or condition as unnatural or natural, even if in fact it is not so. These feelings of naturalness and unnaturalness shape a sense of danger and judgments about health and disorder that seem obviously right to people. (For an argument that this is so in the creation of categories of child disorder, see Wakefield, 2002.)

McKenna and Gettler (2008) emphasize the arbitrariness of current medically driven Western views of child–parent cosleeping, arguing that children are captive to medical ideologies:

[M]uch of what comes to the pediatrician's attention, as problematic sleep behavior—children who have difficulty falling asleep alone at bedtime, who wake at night and ask for parental attention, or who continue to nurse at night—is problematic only in relation to our society's expectations, rather than to some more general standard of what constitutes difficult behavior in the young child …. By … implying that there is only one context within which healthy infant sleep emerges, i.e. the solitary one, pediatric sleep research is thus held captive by Western ethnocentrism …. Only in the last 100 years or so, in a relatively small number of world cultures, have parents and health professionals become concerned with *how* infants *should* be conditioned to sleep. And only in western cultures are infants thought to need to "learn" to sleep, in this case, alone and without parental contact …. .

(McKenna & Gettler, 2008, pp. 183, 185, 204)

Our notion of the natural in this area is not at all shared. Morelli et al. (1992) report that when the Mayan mothers were told that American babies and toddlers sleep alone,

> Invariably, the idea that toddlers are put to sleep in a separate room was received with shock, disapproval, and pity ... and disbelief .... The responses of the Mayan parents gave the impression that they regarded the practice of having infants and toddlers sleep in separate rooms as tantamount to child neglect.
>
> (Morelli et al., 1992, p. 608)

Interestingly, even such a standard psychoanalytic notion as the child's need for a transitional object seems not to apply as strongly in cultures with cosleeping (e.g., Hong & Townes, 1976). Transitional objects seem to be to a substantial extent specific to our culture due to sleeping arrangements.

The Link Between Cosleeping and Oedipal/Sexual/ Dependency Concerns

There is no evidential or common-sense basis for the rejection of cosleeping. What, then, are the reasons offered for this culturally distinct practice?

Again and again, issues consistent with an Oedipal influence—that is, those of sexuality, marital intimacy, and child overdependence ("spoiling") —are cited as reasons commonly offered in the American culture at large and by medical authorities for separating the child from the marital bed. These links are cited despite the fact that most researchers dispute that any such harmful effects exist. Sometimes there is an explicit reference to Oedipal-type issues, but often there is a more general discomfort or concern about bedtime intimacy.

For example, Abbott notes that the rationale for children being excluded from the marital bed is

> that they not be subjected to the parents' intimate relations and to promote the development of independence. However, research I carried out in the Basque country led me to question the validity of this belief and to reconsider the theoretical positions underlying it.
>
> (1992, p. 42)

Similarly, Morelli et al. (1992), having summarized the anti-cosleeping views of medical authorities, observe: "The concerns of such authors included ... the difficulty of breaking the habit when the child grows older (Spock, 1945), and sexual overstimulation (Spock, 1984)" (Morelli et al., 1992, p. 604).

Reviewing the literature from the period of the psychoanalytic dominance in American psychiatry and the prominence of the Oedipal theory reveals the degree to which the Oedipal account of the dangers of cosleeping beguiled the medical community. In "Child Psychiatric Patients Who Share a Bed with a Parent," Kaplan and Poznanski (1974) do a retrospective clinical chart review of child psychiatric patients who sleep in the same bed with their parents. Of course, the reason for focusing on this variable is the ingrained belief that cosleeping and bedsharing are pathogenic for Oedipal reasons. They "attempt to understand the behavior from the child's and parent's point of view" (as if there is a special explanation needed for mother–child intimacy) and formulate "clinical hypotheses" about the behavior. Reflecting the rarity of cosleeping, the authors report that, of the 700 children brought for evaluation to the outpatient department of Children's Psychiatric Hospital of the University of Michigan for the years 1966–68, only 60 (9%) reported sharing a bed with a family member (sleeping arrangements were automatically ascertained in all evaluations and recorded on a coded intake sheet, and the information was verified in chart reviews). However, when the criterion was somewhat strengthened to require that a child repeatedly slept at night in the same bed with a parent within the year preceding the psychiatric evaluation, only 27 children among the 700 met the criteria. Of the 19 boys, the vast majority (16; 84%) slept with the mother or both parents.

Kaplan and Poznanski speculate that the bedsharing behavior they identified is not only sexually stimulating for classic psychoanalytic reasons but also causes a kind of sexual addiction through precisely the mechanism attributed by Max Graf and Freud to Hans, namely, the sexual stimulation of the mother's soothing of anxiety then increases the sexual drive and thus increases the anxiety leading to a vicious circle of need for the mother's soothing and a rising arc of anxiety:

> [M]any children, although sharing a bed with a parent seems to be a source of great anxiety, insist upon doing it. The child may begin to share a bed for one reason, only to have his need for sharing a bed

intensified as a result of the sexual stimulation of the sleeping arrangement. For example, consider a child who becomes phobic as a solution to a conflict over unconscious incestuous wishes. He may begin to share a bed to reduce phobic anxiety that may result from proximity to a parent protector. With sharing a bed, the child finds that in addition to reducing phobic anxiety, he receives further sexual stimulation. With the increased sexual stimulation, the phobic anxiety and the attendant need for a parent protector that led to sharing a bed will increase. That the child has no conscious idea of the connection between the sexual stimulation of the sharing of a bed and the intensification of his phobias accounts for the paradox of his tenacious clinging to sharing a bed with a parent which is anxiety-producing in itself.

(Kaplan & Poznanski, 1974, p. 349)

Kaplan and Poznanski (1974) evaluated the "sexual preoccupations" of the children they studied. Here is what it took for a child, who is being interviewed about sleep arrangements, dreams, and so forth, to be classified as having sexual preoccupations:

During the chart review, a child was coded as having sexual concerns if he spoke about sex during the evaluation. If the child expressed wonder over where babies came from, or reported dreams of his mother in the nude, or described sleeping with his pelvis across a parent, for example, this was recorded as evidence of sexual preoccupations.

(p. 349)

It is unclear whether "concern" let alone "preoccupation" is a justifiable way of describing the child's mentioning such things. Yet, oddly enough, despite these broad criteria, of the 14 boys who slept only with the mother, just 6 (43%) were thusly "sexually preoccupied." In the unfortunate "heads I win, tails you lose" methodological approach of much psychoanalytic research, the authors address this awkward finding as follows, after noting that girls had more sexual thoughts than boys and boys from intact homes had more sexual thoughts than those from broken homes:

We may accept at face value the decrement in the expression of sexual preoccupations ... and say that these boys did not have sexual concerns. Or we may hypothesize as follows. The expression of sexual preoccupations in children who sleep with parents of the opposite sex may be inversely related to the threat of the violation of the incest taboo. Culturally, the taboo against mother-son incest is stronger than that against father-daughter incest, and thus boys from intact families who slept with their mothers were forced to repress sexual impulses more stringently than girls who slept with fathers. The decrement in the expression of sexual preoccupations from boys in intact families who slept with mother to boys from broken families who slept with mother may have occurred because the absent father made the possibility of incest more real to the child and therefore made the incest taboo more threatening.

(Kaplan & Poznanski, 1974, p. 350)

In fact, some of these children had anxieties that were anchored in real fears of things they had witnessed (e.g., parental violence), and the need for soothing likely had little to do with such convoluted sexual rationales. Nevertheless, illustrating the link between psychiatric views of bedsharing in the 1970s and the content of the Hans case, Kaplan and Poznanski (1974) conclude: that the boy is motivated by both anxiety and sexual desire to sleep with the mother; that "The child clings to sharing a bed with the parent, which is anxiety producing in itself, because he is unaware of the connection between his phobic concerns and the sexual stimulation of sharing a bed"; that "Children who shared a bed with parents of the opposite sex verbalized sexual preoccupations"; and that "A boy's sharing a bed with his mother in an intact family is symptomatic of severe marital conflict that might eventuate in divorce" (p. 355).

So, one strand of the rationale for rejection of cosleeping certainly consists of the fear of excessive intimacy, sexual overstimulation, and dependency, all of which are explicitly identified by the Oedipal theory, as well as the corresponding incursion on the parents' sexual prerogatives in the modern marriage. For example, Ferber (1985) says: "[S]leeping in your bed can make your child feel confused and anxious rather than relaxed and reassured. Even a young toddler may find this repeated experience overly stimulating" (p. 39).

Brazelton was even more explicit about the Oedipal origins of his advice. In 1990, he published a rumination on whether his previous rejection of cosleeping of parent and child needed to be rethought in light of what he had learned about Japanese practices, in which children sleep with parents until adolescence. In pondering the issue, Brazelton reported that one problem he had with cosleeping is that he "cannot shake from his mind the picture of the sexual fantasy life of young children (desiring the mother, hating the father, dreading genital mutilation) as defined by psychoanalytic theorists" (quoted in Shweder et al., 1995, p. 22).

McKenna and Gettler (2008) note the link between sexual fears and fears of cosleeping. They observe that, reflecting the spirit of the "spoiling theory's" notion that children who cuddle with a parent become addicted to the sensuality of overindulgent parental affection, it is common that "parents are warned that cosleeping creates a 'bad habit,' one that's 'difficult to break'" and that "cosleeping is said to 'confuse' the infant or child emotionally or sexually, or to induce 'over' stimulation" (p. 206). Regarding a child sharing a bed with the parent during the supposed Oedipal developmental period approximately from three to five years of age, Sperling (1971) claims that sleep disturbances among children are virtually universal due to Oedipal conflicts. She considers bedsharing to suggest that parents are excessively stimulating their child to satisfy their own needs. Even when parents only allow the child to come into their bed when the child is anxious due to having nightmares, Sperling holds that overstimulating sexual impulses is the greater danger:

> the practice of taking a child into the parental bed, as a means of restoring sleep disturbed by nightmares serves only to provide an additional source of overstimulation for the child whose disturbance of sleep itself indicates its inability to cope with its aggressive and sexual impulses.
>
> (p. 428)

In a list of historical factors influencing the emergence of the Western practice of parents sleeping separately from their infants and children, McKenna et al. (2007) mention "fear of spoiling," "fear of affection or touching," "fear of infants/children observing sex," "emphasis on romantic nature of husband-wife conjugal relationship to exclusion of children," "re-location of parental decision making to outside of home to external authorities," and "'authoritative medical' knowledge comes to dismiss acquired parental knowledge of infant" (p. 138). Shweder et al. (1995) observe that middle-class, Anglo-Americans "are disturbed by the practice of parents and children bedding down together at night and nervous about its consequences" (p. 24). Considering an example in which a husband and wife sleep apart and the wife sleeps with one of the kids, they observe that "a typical middle-class Anglo-American reader is likely to feel full of anxious concerns about issues of sexuality, excessive dependency" (p. 25). The logic of the Oedipus complex fits quite well with this trend towards separation of the marital bed from the child during sleep.

Lozoff et al. (1984) note that "cosleeping, the practice of parents and children sleeping together, was routine in our own culture until the 20th century" but is "prohibited at the present time" by most medical professionals (p. 171). Given that "in one sample of more than 100 societies, the American middle class was unique in putting the baby to sleep in a room of his own" (p. 171), the reasons offered by professionals for this view are of interest, so the authors survey the medical advice literature and cull the major reasons that are offered in objection to parent and child sharing a bed. Their findings were as follows:

> Concerns about potential ill effects are thoughtfully described by several prominent pediatricians and child psychotherapists and include the following: (1) cosleeping may interfere with a child's independence ..., (2) sleeping with parents may become a habit that is difficult to break or even an "addiction," (3) children who sleep with parents may be more likely to witness sexual intercourse, a frightening experience for some, (4) the intimate body contact involved in cosleeping may be overstimulating to children, (5) cosleeping may reflect disturbances in the mother-child relationship or in the parents' relations with each other, and (6) children who sleep with parents may develop more sleep problems.
>
> (pp. 171–172)

Similar considerations appear on a list of medical concerns about bed-sharing and cosleeping compiled by Madansky & Edelbrock (1990):

> This practice is not considered routine in America .... [C]hild health professionals commonly advise parents not to bring children into their beds, citing potential ill effects listed in the literature, including statements that cosleeping may cause or exacerbate child psychopathology, allow sexual abuse to occur, frighten or confuse children who inadvertently witness adult intercourse, overstimulate children by close but nonsexual contact, contribute to or perpetuate marital difficulties, reflect

disturbances in the parent-child relationship, reflect parental insecurity or psychopathology, interfere with the child's independence, establish a habit that is difficult to break ....

(p. 197)

What is striking about all of the above lists of fears about cosleeping is that, except for fear that children will develop sleep problems (apparently it is true that both parents and children wake up occasionally from movement when they are cosleeping), all of the other reasons—including dependency, intimate bodily contact, witnessing the "primal scene," and disturbed mother–child relationships—are consistent with the fears that arise out of the Oedipal theory about sexual overstimulation and spoiling leading to dependence on parental sensual stimulation. Given that these fears did not afflict Americans before the twentieth century and only began at about the time the Oedipal theory came into cultural prominence, and given that these fears do not afflict people in other cultures that do not have a history of Oedipal theorizing, the role of the Oedipal theory in creating or reinforcing these concerns gains in plausibility.

These views percolate out to parents. Other men seem to feel the way Max Graf did about the unnaturalness of a child coming into his mother's bed:

Loss of privacy and associated concerns about sexual intimacy were also mentioned by some U.S. mothers when discussing their decision not to sleep with their babies on a regular basis. One U.S. mother said, "My husband did not like that idea (cosleeping). He was afraid that it would be unnatural, too much intimacy." It appears that ... some U.S. families see sleeping as a time for conjugal intimacy.

(Morelli et al., 1992, p. 611)

Morelli et al. also report:

Yet some Americans express that they are simply uncomfortable with the idea ("I ... don't think that I ever want him right in the same bed as me. I don't really know why") or that it would encourage dependency ("I think that he would be more dependent ... if he was constantly with us like that"). One mother offers as a reason for separating at night from the child that "It is kind of a strain for a couple to tiptoe in (the bedroom) and be quiet."

(Morelli et al., 1992, p. 607)

Morelli et al. also note that "Previous literature has identified a stress on independence training as being connected with middle-class parents' avoidance of cosleeping (Munroe et al., 1981). Kugelmass (1959) advocated separate rooms for children on grounds that it would enable them to develop a spirit of independence" (p. 605).

Morelli et al. (1992) also observe that even "The rare middle-class U.S. families who do practice cosleeping often recognize that they are violating cultural norms" (p. 605). These attitudes shaped by cultural values were explored by Hanks and Rebelsky (1977), who reported that even among parents open to cosleeping, the dominance of Oedipal theorizing around cosleeping was enough to prevent them from, or shame them about, the practice: "in America, we typically assume that children do not sleep with their parents, and if they do, they shouldn't" (p. 277). They observe that these attitudes toward cosleeping were shaped by the "Freudian heritage" (p. 277) so that "predictably, the reason given as to why children shouldn't sleep with parents is that it arouses sexual anxiety" (p. 277).

Hanks and Rebelsky (1977) note that studies of cosleeping generally concerned psychiatrically disordered populations, thus biasing the results. Adopting a different approach, they selected twenty-seven suburban middle-class and upper middle-class educated mothers in intact first marriages and in their late 20s or early 30s, who were known to them and who had normal children—a total of fifty-three child subjects, ranging in age from two months to thirteen years—and who had participated in childbirth classes and women's support groups. In this sample, the authors found awareness of, but not adherence to the Oedipal consensus:

> In the interviews in which parents were asked directly whether cosleeping was a cultural taboo, most said that they thought it was. They perceived the cultural taboo as deriving from the assumption that it would produce sexual anxiety. These parents felt that the assumption was unfounded.
>
> (Hanks & Rebelsky, 1977, p. 280)

Twenty-three of the women reported receiving some night visits in bed from a child, however, even in this relatively "enlightened" group, when frequency of bedsharing is taken into account, only "18 of the 53 children in this sample woke up in their parents' beds at least three mornings per week" (p. 279). Consistent with an attachment construal of cosleeping, nineteen of the twenty-three women who reported cosleeping stated that the reason for the bedsharing was need for contact or security, and in some cases the need for soothing due to bad dreams or other fears, as well as occasional instances of illness, bed-wetting, and other such reasons.

The women overwhelmingly thought the effects of the bedsharing were in fact positive. Notably, "All of the children in this sample had a bedroom separate from their parents. Even the child who slept with his parents all night every night had his own room, and the parents had a separate place for love-making" (Hanks & Rebelsky, 1977, p. 279), so spousal intimacy was not obstructed. Nevertheless, despite their skepticism about the Oedipal theory, women recognized the Oedipal concerns raised by cosleeping and the taboos and salacious ideas related to it, and so the parents were reticent about the behavior, with most concealing it from their pediatrician.

This concern is no less present today. Although the rationale for the prohibition against cosleeping and bedsharing is now often framed in terms of prevention of SIDS, the feelings about it are of a nature and sufficiently intense that they seem to continue to echo the Oedipal rationale of the past. For example, Susan Stewart (2017), in connection with her book on cosleeping (*Co-sleeping: Parents, Children, and Musical Beds*) "interviewed 51 parents who co-sleep and found many would prefer not to sleep with their children. The shame and stigma associated with co-sleeping is so great that about half of the parents denied or avoided discussing it with family or their pediatrician" (Iowa State University, 2017, p. 2).

Link to Changes in the Nature of Marriage

In considering the reasons, prior to the current concern about sudden infant death syndrome, for the concerns about children entering the parents' bed, McKenna and Gettler (2008) observe that "the proliferation and expansion of the idea of 'romantic love' throughout Europe, coupled with the belief in the importance of the 'conjugal' (husband-wife) relationship probably also promoted separate sleeping quarters" (p. 207). They point out that "throughout the literature, cosleeping is described as the cause of marital discord" (p. 206) and that one of the most common reasons for excluding the child from the parental bed is that this is the way that "marriages might best be nurtured and preserved" (p. 206), even though, they note, the research suggests otherwise.

In effect, McKenna and Gettler (2008) thus suggest the same thesis that emerged from my analysis of the Hans case and the Oedipal theory, namely, that the changing nature of marriage with its increased emphasis on conjugal sexual and emotional intimacy led to pressure for excluding the child from the marital bed. My analysis suggested that this pressure fit well with and was partially resolved by the Oedipal theory's "discovery" of an entirely different and medically rationalized reason for such exclusion based on excessive sexual stimulation in mother–son physical contact, encouraging acceptance of the Oedipal theory.

Shweder et al. (1995) find a similar link of protection of the marital bed and a distinctive view of the couple. They note that "many middle class Anglo-Americans will be prepared to accept without much reflection the presupposition that the quality of a marriage can be gauged by whether or not a wife and husband sleep together … " (p. 25). They compared preferences and arrangements between middle-class, American families in Hyde Park, Chicago and high-caste families in a temple town in Orissa, India. Within the American sample, they found, "a final moral preference falls under the principle of 'the sacred couple': when it comes to cohabiting adults, emotional intimacy, interpersonal commitment, and sexual privacy require that they sleep together and alone" (Shweder et al., 1995, p. 32). This was the most powerful determinant of sleeping arrangements among the American sample except for incest avoidance. Nurturing the fragile but developing autonomy of the child through separate sleeping arrangements was also a possible reason for rejecting cosleeping, but it was found that "American informants often sacrificed the principle of autonomy while honoring the exclusive sleeping rights of the conjugal couple as required by the sacred couple principle" (Shweder et al., 1995, p. 34). In contrast, "the American sacred couple principle was violated in 78% or Oriya households" (Shweder et al., 1995, p. 37).

In their study of Japanese sleeping arrangements in which they revealed the frequent occurrence of parent–child cosleeping late into childhood and even adolescence, Caudill and Plath (1966) offer a similar rationale for the divergent sleeping arrangements between Japanese and American cultures. They theorize that this practice is due to values that support trading off the freedom of sexual activity between marital partners for greater family cohesiveness—a tradeoff western families are less willing to make given our emphasis on how important sexual satisfaction is to marriage: "[T]he frequency with which children co-sleep with parents expresses a strong cultural emphasis upon the nurturant aspects of family life and a correlative de-emphasis of its sexual aspects" (p. 344); "[S]leeping arrangements in Japanese families tend to … emphasize the interdependence more than the separateness of individuals, and to underplay (or largely ignore) the potentiality for the growth of conjugal intimacy between husband and wife in sexual and other matters in favor of a more general familial cohesion" (p. 363).

Children as Oedipal Winners and Losers

The Oedipal-theory triggered bed time conflict we saw in the Hans case remains a very real possible outcome of attitudes towards bedsharing today—attitudes to some degree derived from the implications of the Oedipal theory although generally not explicitly Oedipal in our post-Freudian climate. Indeed, although the rationale in terms of medical opinion is not explicitly Oedipal, within segments of the psychoanalytic and psychological communities, Hans's situation of struggling to enter the marital bed and cuddle with mother is still seen as the prototypical behavioral expression of the Oedipus complex's desires rather than simply attachment longing. For example, Josephs et al. (2018) recently performed a study to empirically test the validity of aspects of the Oedipal theory linked to the child's observation or fantasy of observing the "primal scene" of parental intercourse. As their experimental stimuli, they constructed two vignettes in which they portrayed what they labeled, respectively, the "Oedipal loser" and the "Oedipal victor." Both vignettes start as follows:

> Jack, a 6-year-old boy, is sleeping in his room. He wakes up and hears some funny noises coming from his parents' bedroom, so he climbs out of bed and starts walking that way. In a moment, he's standing on the doorstep of his parents' bedroom slowly pushing the door open. It makes a squeaking sound.
>
> (Josephs, et al., 2018, p. 108)

The two vignettes then continue from this common stem and diverge as follows:

> Mom and Dad are in the middle of kissing each other. As they take notice of the sound, they instantly stop hugging, and turn to Jack with

a surprised and embarrassed expression on their face. Jack is staring at them, holding the doorknob tightly in his hand. Dad puts his shirt back on and stands up. Mom looks down to check if anything is too revealing.

(Josephs, et al., 2018, p. 108)

Mom and dad are asleep in bed together. As they take notice of the sound, they wake up, and turn to Jack with quizzical expressions on their faces. Jack climbs into bed with them and squeezes himself between his mom and dad. Jack cuddles closely with his mother while pushing his father to the side. They all fall asleep together.

(Josephs, et al., 2018, p. 111)

This way of thinking about the triadic relationship is conflictual at its core. Bowlby's attachment theory represented a theoretically sophisticated return to common sense about parent–child relationships and the soothing functions of physical affection. According to the Bowlby scenario, there is no inherent conflict in the child's longing for maternal contact because it is based on an intrinsic instinctual drive for contact and not on jealousy or desire for exclusion of the father. Yet Bowlby's theory, because it attributed emotional difficulties partially to real experiences with parents rather than to Oedipal fantasies, was resisted by psychoanalysts. Bowlby had to drag the analytic world kicking and screaming to accept his insights, buttressed in his case by a mountain of empirical evidence. Ultimately, though, the Oedipal theory and attachment theory overlap in the domain of data they are claiming to explain, the intimate physical affection between mother and son. As the above vignettes and many other publications on the Oedipal theory testify, the Oedipal and attachment models continue to exist side by side.

Of course, emotional jealousy in the triadic relationship is real—Hans sometimes cried when his parents were showing affection to his exclusion, we are told in the case history—but the inflation of such human emotions into a sexualized essential state of conflict with winners and losers is unwarranted. As we have seen, with the consensus in our society still being against cosleeping, conflict is mostly created by going against what children and often parents naturally are inclined to do about bedtime arrangements. The reach of the mistakes of Oedipal theory continue to haunt us today, even if they are a submerged part of a larger process of social regulation of family affectional and sexual arrangements.

Intentional Versus Reactive Rationales for Cosleeping

It is sometimes suggested that the sheer availability of additional bedrooms to middle class families somehow explains our cultural practices of separate sleeping arrangements for parents and children. This cannot be an adequate explanation because, as we have seen, there are wealthy cultures (e.g., Japan) that choose to keep their children cosleeping until later ages, and even within our own society there are marked cultural differences among those who do have extra bedrooms. The lack of a bedroom may explain a small percentage of cosleeping; Madansky and Edelbrock (1990), for example, report that 3% of their sample (nine families) reported that they coslept every night because they had no additional bedroom, whereas 22% of the sample coslept more than once a week despite having a child's bedroom, and the remaining 75% did not cosleep even once a week. Clearly, more is going on than a sheer lack of space. Moreover, despite extra bedrooms, many studies show changes in bedsharing over time as the child gets older. Although separate bedrooms for children has been rare in most societies throughout human history except for the more affluent, what is distinctive about middle-class, Euro-American practices is not that the affluent have an extra room for the child but that there is a strong culturally anchored resistance even in the earliest years of a child's life to a fluidity in which the child either sleeps with the parents or in the parents' bedroom, or comes into their bed when he feels like it and can and often does share the parents' bed in the evening and morning.

As detailed above, bed-sharing is quite common across the world but discouraged and less usual in Euro-American culture. In this regard, it is useful to keep in mind a crucial distinction between "intentional" and "reactive" bedsharing, briefly referred to but not explored above. Although in this narrative review I did not address the methodological details of each study, it should be kept in mind that the questions used in studies of cosleeping and bedsharing vary greatly and may indicate very different types and degrees of practices. It turns out that even in populations in which all cosleeping is frowned upon and medically discouraged, many parents make an occasional exception for special circumstances. Mileva-Seitz et al. (2016) explain this distinction among such practices:

> [P]arents bed-share for many reasons. Aside from tradition, reasons to bed-share include breastfeeding facilitation, infant irritability or illness, parental ideology, parental own sleep experiences, convenience, anxiety,

child safety, parent and child emotional needs, better infant sleep, una-vailability of other beds, enjoyment, physical proximity to the infant, and better caregiving, as well as, potentially, socioeconomic factors .... Thus on one hand, bed-sharing can occur proactively, as a matter of *routine* and *intention*, whether due to cultural beliefs and practices or parenting preference ....

On the other hand, bed-sharing can be reactive, influenced by factors, including the children, that directly or indirectly lead to the initiation of bed-sharing. In Western societies, bed-sharing frequently emerges in response to problematic circumstances. Even when parents do not express intention to bed-share, many—indeed, sometimes a majority of parents in a given population—end up bed-sharing at least occa-sionally. Unlike intentional bed-sharers, reactive bed-sharers more often expressed concern about their practice. The distinction between reactive and intentional bed-sharing is crucial for the interpretation of the evidence and recommendations. Unfortunately, this distinction is mostly absent in the literature to date.

(Mileva-Seitz et al., 2016, p. 6)

Much more common than "intentional bed-sharing"—the decision by the family to have the child routinely or frequently cosleep in the same bed or room as the parents—is "reactive" bed-sharing in response to the child's anxiety, distress, nightmares, or illness. Reactive bed-sharing when a child has some special need for soothing is reasonably common even in Western developed countries that are generally low in prevalence of bed-sharing. As emerged in the above review, when bedsharing and cosleeping do occur, they generally occur relatively rarely, perhaps once a week or less, and it seems likely that this is in response to some special circumstance. For example, Madansky and Edelbrock (1990) report that the majority of those who coslept at all did so in response to special circumstances:

[O]f those who coslept ... sixty percent reported that cosleeping was for special reasons. The most commonly reported reasons were that the child awakened during the night, had a minor illness, or was afraid because of nightmares or thunderstorms. Other reasons given included having one parent out of town for the night ....

(p. 199)

Indeed, Madansky and Edelbrock report that a majority, 55%, of her parent sample said that their child had slept in their bed with them at least once during the previous 2 months, whereas only 25% said the child had slept with them more than once a week, indicating a high rate of reactive cosleeping.

This points to an interesting and somewhat disturbing feature of the Hans case that was unremarked on in earlier chapters, namely, Max's Oedipal-theory-justified attempts to keep Hans out of the marital bed even when Hans was feeling anxious. Max was concerned, and Freud made much of the fact, that Olga took Hans into bed for soothing even when he was away from home. Yet, often when a parent is away from home this might lead to a natural desire to be reassured and to have greater closeness to the parent who is present (recall that Hans explains to his father: "When you're away, I'm afraid you're not coming home" [Freud, 1909/1955, p. 44]). Furthermore, Hans's attempts to enter the parental bed were often driven by his anxiety, either from simply being alone in bed in his new separate bedroom or the anxiety he felt from his phobic anxieties or, in the middle of the night, due to vivid nightmarish dreams, such as the giraffe dream. Recall Hans's straightforward explanation when his father asks why he came into his parents' bed:

> "And why have you come today?" I asked.
> HANS: "When I'm not frightened I shan't come any more."
> I: "So you come in to me because you're frightened?"
> HANS: "When I'm not with you I'm frightened; when I'm not in bed with you, then I'm frightened. When I'm not frightened any more I shan't come any more."
> (1909/1955, pp. 43–44)

That is, Hans explains that he tries to come into the bed when he is feeling anxious, and when he is no longer anxious he will stop. This points to the fact that throughout the time of the Hans case after the Grafs had moved to their new home with a separate bedroom for Hans, there was no plan by his parents for *intentional* bedsharing or cosleeping. It was expected that Hans would routinely sleep by himself. The Oedipal drama in which Hans's bedsharing was refused or discouraged by Max occurred only in regard to potential *reactive* bedsharing or cosleeping, when Hans manifested distress and wanted to suspend the expected routine and come into the bed to get soothing due to anxiety or some other special circumstance. This is unusual and, one might say, cruel on its face. Even in our society that disapproves of cosleeping, many parents still allow exceptions for attachment soothing in instances of reactive cosleeping. Yet Oedipal theory suggests that one must be suspicious of the child as seducer as well as worried about the effect of the soothing in amplifying Oedipal sexuality and making the child's anxiety all the worse. This toxic suspicion of Hans's distress and need for attachment soothing, where it is believed that the soothing would make the distress worse in the long run, appears to have been particularly frustrating and bewildering to Hans. It shows how extreme the form of control implied by the Oedipal theory can be. The data show that, while many families accept this prohibition even on reactive bedsharing, some compromise in the light of what they presumably take to be overriding considerations of soothing a child.

Conclusion

As has become apparent, the "bed time" of this chapter's title refers not to the time at which one retires to one's bed but to the competition between father and son for how much time the child will have in the marital bed with the parents and specifically with the mother. The regulation of mother–son intimacy in the form of limitations in the time that a child can cuddle with his mother in the marital bed, facilitated and rationalized by Oedipal theory and by the exile of the young child to another room, allows the father to share the bed with his wife undisturbed by a child.

In Chapter 8, I examined the shifting cultural values concerning sex and marriage that were occurring at the time of Freud's development of the Oedipal theory. That analysis revealed that the Oedipal theory entered the broader cultural context at a time when society was rethinking marital and familial roles, including emerging egalitarian principles between spouses, and this context provided potential appeal for the theory external to its evidential substantiation. In this chapter, I furthered my review of the cultural implications of the Oedipal theory by exploring one way in which the Oedipal theory subsequently came to influence the culture at large through the specific domain of family sleeping arrangements.

It emerged in earlier chapters that a central point of contention during the deployment of the Oedipus complex in the Graf family was the struggle over whether Hans could come into the parents' bed to cuddle with his mother when he felt the need to do so. Oedipal theory interprets the child's desire to enter the marital bed in sexual rather than attachment terms. Accordingly, Max's resistance to Hans's bedsharing, although motivated by broader issues of sexual conflict between the parents, was directly justified in Max's eyes by the Oedipal theory and the alleged danger of sexual overstimulation if Olga cuddled with Hans.

In this chapter, I explored a possible relationship between these early Oedipal struggles in one family and broader cultural effects of the Oedipal theory on bourgeois family life. Specifically, I considered the closest modern equivalent of the bedsharing struggle in the Graf family: child cosleeping with the parents. The reviewed literature, while focused on cosleeping, also to some extent covers related practices, such as the child bedsharing with parents for more limited periods of time, the child being in bodily contact with the parent during sleep onset but then sleeping alone, the child sleeping only partially with the parent during the initial period of sleep before being moved to the child's room, or the child sleeping in the same room in close proximity to the parent but not in the same bed.

In reviewing the literature, I did not attempt to offer a systematic review of the extensive research on cosleeping and related practices. Nonetheless, the reviewed literature reveals both: (1) that there was a major push by the medical community to prevent parent/child cosleeping; and (2) that the evidence in support of this vigorously asserted prohibition is startlingly lacking. The fact that the available evidence did not explain the vigorously asserted professional judgment discouraging cosleeping suggests that an explanation for this injunction must be sought outside the scientific literature. Given that Euro-American bourgeois culture during the Oedipal theory's prominence was virtually unique among cultures, and even within the history of the West, in the extent to which children were separated from the parents' bed, no broad explanation based on inherent human characteristics is possible and the explanation must be sought in culturally local factors.

The literature further reveals that the reasons provided for the cosleeping prohibition both by professionals and parents are often strikingly similar to the rationales that appear in the Hans case history based on Oedipal theory. Thus, when closely examined, what emerges is a picture of medical child-rearing advice and parental belief that has remarkable fidelity to the Oedipal picture in the Hans case. Fears of dependency, sexual overstimulation, a pathological parent–child relationship, and even addiction to the sensual pleasures of bodily contact are lurking in the anxiety over cosleeping and bedsharing. These fears are virtually unique to the period of Oedipal ascendancy and closely reflect its implications and the way it is deployed in the Hans case history. I conclude, then, that the lineage of modern prohibitions on parent–child cosleeping, prior to newly developed rationales such as the prevention of SIDS, can be plausibly traced back in whole or in part to the success of the Oedipal theory.

No review of this kind can establish with scientific certainty that a cultural practice is the expansion of a form of power/knowledge derived from a specific theory. Despite the limits of the argument, based on the best evidence I could identify, I have made what I believe is a convincing case for the plausibility of the claim that the Oedipal theory had a broad cultural impact on the relationships in middle-class, Euro-American families that reproduces the way it was invoked by Max Graf in the Hans case to keep Hans out of the marital bed. I believe that the evidence I have surveyed strongly suggests that the received wisdom about child rearing and bedsharing for decades has been, if not explicitly Oedipal, tacitly Oedipal in precisely the way that was manifested in the Hans case. If so, then our cultural practices in regulating attachment soothing and affection between mother and son to some degree have been anchored in the sheer power/ knowledge of a false theory, in fact serving the cultural momentum toward the sexual-emotional marital bond but rationalized as protecting the child from the danger of mother–son physical affection.

References

Abbott, S. (1992). Holding on and pushing away: Comparative perspectives on an eastern Kentucky child-rearing practice. *Ethos, 20(1)*, 33–65.

Aristotle. (1926). *The Nichomachean ethics* (H. Rackham, Trans.). London: Heinemann.

Barajas, R. G., Martin, A., Brooks-Gunn, J., & Hale, L. (2011). Mother-child bed-sharing in toddlerhood and cognitive and behavioral outcomes. *Pediatrics, 128*, (e339–347).

Barry, H. III, & Paxson, L. M. (1971). Infancy and early childhood: Cross-cultural codes. *Ethology, 10*, 466–508.

Brazelton, T. B. (1990). Parent-infant cosleeping revisited. *Ab Initio, 2(1)*, 1, 7.

Blair, P. S., Sidebotham, P., Pease, A., & Fleming, P.J. (2014). Bed-sharing in the absence of hazardous circumstances: Is there a risk of sudden infant death syndrome? An analysis from two case-control studies conducted in the UK. *PLoS One, 9(9)*, e107799.

Bowlby, J. (1973). *Attachment and loss (Vol. 2): Separation: Anxiety and anger.* London, UK: Hogarth Press.

Brazelton, T. B. (1989, February 13). Working parents. *Newsweek*, 66–77.

Burton, R. V. & Whiting, J. W. M. (1961). The absent father and cross-sex identity. *Merill-Palmer Quarterly of Behavior and Development, 7*, 85–95.

Caudill, W. & Plath, D. W. (1966). Who sleeps by whom? Parent-child involvement in urban Japanese families. *Psychiatry, 29*, 344–366.

Comer, J. P., & Poussaint, A. F. (1992). *Raising black children: Two leading psychiatrists confront the educational, social and emotional problems facing Black children.* New York, NY: Plume Publishers.

Crawford, C. J. (1994). Parenting practices in the Basque country: Implications of infant and childhood sleeping location for personality development. *Ethos, 22(1)*, 42–82.

Dewar, G. (2017, July). The Ferber method: What is it, and how does it affect babies? *Parenting Science*. Retrieved from: https://www.parentingscience.com/Ferber-method.html.

Douglas, J. (1989). *Behaviour problems in young children: Assessment and management.* London, UK: Routledge.

Ferber, R. (1985). *Solve your child's sleep problems.* New York, NY: Simon & Schuster.

Forbes, J. F., Weiss, D. S., & Folen, R. A. (1992). The co-sleeping habits of military children. *Military Medicine, 157*, 196–200.

Freud, S. (1955). Analysis of a phobia in a five-year-old boy. In J. Strachey (Ed. and Trans.), *The standard edition of the complete psychological works of Sigmund Freud*, (Vol. *10*, pp. 1–150). London, UK: Hogarth Press. (Original work published 1909).

Hanks, C. C. & Rebelsky, F. G. (1977). Mommy and the midnight visitor: A study of occasional co-sleeping. *Psychiatry, 40(3)*, 277–280.

Hong, M., & Townes, B. D. (1976). Infants' attachment to inanimate objects: A cross-cultural study. *Journal of the American Academy of Child Psychiatry, 15(1)*, 49–61.

Horsley, T., Clifford, T., Barrowman, N., Bennett, S., Yazdi, F., Sampson, M., Moher, D., Dingwall, O., Schachter, H., & Cote, A. (2007). Benefits and harms associated with the practice of bed sharing: A systematic review. *Archives of Pediatric Adolescent Medicine, 161*, 237–245.

Iowa State University (2017, April). Musical beds: Iowa State professor finds co-sleeping is more common than some parents admit. *Iowa State University, News Service*. Retrieved from: https://www.news.iastate.edu/news/2017/04/12/musicalbeds.

Jenni, O. G., Fuhrer, H. Z., Iglowstein, I., Molinari, L., & Largo, R. H. (2005). A longitudinal study of bed sharing and sleep problems among Swiss children in the first 10 years of life. *Pediatrics, 115*, 233–240.

Josephs, L., Katzander, N., & Goncharova, A., (2018). Imagining parental sexuality: The experimental study of Freud's primal scene. *Psychoanalytic Psychology, 35(1)*, 106–114.

Kaplan, S. L. & Poznanski, E. (1974). Child psychiatric patients who share a bed with a parents. *Journal of the American Academy of Child Psychiatry, 13*, 344–356.

Kugelmass, N. (1959). *Complete child care.* New York, NY: Holt, Rinehart, & Winston.

Latz, S., Wolf, A. W., & Lozoff, B. (1999). Cosleeping in context: Sleep practices and problems in young children in Japan and the United States. *Archives of Pediatrics and Adolescent Medicine, 153,* 339–346.

Lewis, R. J. & Janda, L. H. (1988). The relationship between adult sexual adjustment and childhood experiences regarding exposure to nudity, sleeping in the parental bed, and parental attitudes toward sexuality. *Archives of Sexual Behavior, 17(4),* 349–362.

Lozoff, B., Wolf, A. W., & Davis, N. S. (1984). Co-sleeping win urban families with young children in the United States. *Pediatrics, 74(2):* 171–182.

Luijk, M. P., Mileva-Seitz, V. R., Jansen, P. W., Van, I. M. H., Jaddoe, V. W., Raat, H., Hofman, A., ... & Tiemeier, H. (2013). Ethnic differences in prevalence and determinants of mother-child bed-sharing in early childhood. *Sleep Medicine, 14,* 1092–1099.

Madansky, D., & Edelbrock, C. (1990). Cosleeping in a community sample of 2- and 3-year-old children. *Pediatrics, 86,* 197–203.

McKenna, J. J., Ball, H. L., & Gettler (2007). Mother-infant cosleeping, breast-feeding and sudden infant death syndrome: What biological anthropology has discovered about normal infant sleep and pediatric sleep medicine. *Yearbook of Physical Anthropology, 50,* 133–161.

McKenna, J. J. & Gettler, T. (2008). Cultural influences on infant and childhood sleep biology, and the science that studies it: Toward a more inclusive paradigm II. In C. L. Marcus, J. L. Carroll, D. F. Donnelly, G. M. Loughlin (Eds.), *Sleep in children: Developmental changes in sleep patterns* (2nd ed., pp. 183–222). New York, NY: Informa Healthcare USA, Inc.

Mileva-Seitz, V. R., Bakermans-Kranenburg, M. J., Battaini, C., & Luijk, M. P. (2016). Parent-child bed-sharing: The good, the bad, and the burden of evidence. *Sleep Medicine Review, 32,* 4–27.

Morelli, G. A., Rogoff, B., Oppenheim, D., & Goldsmith, D. (1992). Cultural variation in infants' sleeping arrangements: Questions of independence. *Developmental Psychology, 28,* 604–613.

Mosenkis, J. (1998). *The effect of childhood cosleeping on later life development.* Unpublished master's thesis, University of Chicago, Chicago, IL.

Munroe, R.L., Munroe, R.H., & Whiting, J.W.M. (1981). Male sex role resolutions. In R. H. Muroe, R. L. Munroe, & B.B. Whiting (Eds.), *Handbook of cross-cultural human development* (pp. 611–632). New York, NY: Garland.

Narvaez, D. F. (2011, December). Dangers of "crying it out". *Psychology Today.* Retrieved from: https://www.psychologytoday.com/us/blog/moral-landscapes/201112/dangers-crying-it-out.

Narvaez, D. F. (2014, July). Parents misled by cry-it-out sleep training reports. *Psychology Today.* Retrieved from: https://www.psychologytoday.com/us/blog/moral-landscapes/201407/parents-misled-cry-it-out-sleep-training-reports.

Okami, P., Weisner, T., & Olmstead, R. (2002). Outcome correlates of parent-child bedsharing: An eighteen-year longitudinal study. *Journal of Developmental and Behavioral Pediatrics, 23,* 244–253.

Oleinick, M. S., Bahn, A. K., Eisenberg, L., & Lilienfeld, A M. (1966). Early socialization experiences and intrafamilial environment: A study of psychiatric outpatient and control group children. *Archives of General Psychiatry, 15*, 344–353.

Ottaviano, S., Giannotti, F., Cortesi, F., Bruni, O., & Ottaviano, C. (1996). Sleep characteristics in healthy children from birth to 6 years of age in the urban area of Rome. *Sleep, 19(1)*, 1–3.

Rettew, D. (2014, July). Infant sleep and the crying-it-out debate. *Psychology Today*. Retrieved from: https://www.psychologytoday.com/us/blog/abcs-child-psychiatry/201407/infant-sleep-and-the-crying-it-out-debate.

Shweder, R. A., Jensen, L. A., & Goldstein, W. M. (1995). Who sleeps by whom revisited: A method for extracting the moral goods implicit in practice. In Goodnow, J. J., Miller, P. J., & Kessel, F. (Eds.) *Cultural practices as contexts for development* (pp. 21–39). San Francisco, CA: Jossey-Bass Publishers.

Sloane, M. S. (1978). *Common folks*. Pippa Passes, KY: Appalachian Learning Laboratory.

Sperling, M. (1971). Sleep disturbances in children. In J. G. Howells (ed.), *Modern perspectives in international child psychiatry* (pp. 418–454). New York, NY: Brunner/Mazel.

Spock, B. J. (1945). *The common sense book of child and baby care*. New York, NY: Duell, Sloan, & Pearce.

Spock, B. J. (1976). *Baby and child care*. New York, NY: Pocket Books.

Spock, B. J. (1984). Mommy, can I sleep in your bed? *Parents Magazine*, December 1984, p. 129.

Spock, B. J., & Rothenberg, M. B. (1992). *Dr. Spock's Baby and Child Care* (6th ed.). New York, NY: Dutton Publishers.

Stewart, S. (2017). *Co-sleeping: Parents, children, and musical beds*. New York, NY: Rowman & Littlefield.

Valentin, S. R. (2005). Commentary: Sleep in German infants – the "cult" of independence. *Pediatrics, 115(1Suppl)*, 269–271.

Wakefield, J. C. (2002). Values and the validity of diagnostic criteria: Disvalued versus disordered conditions of childhood and adolescence. In J. Z. Sadler (Ed.), *Descriptions & prescriptions: Values, mental disorders, and the DSMs* (pp. 148–164). Baltimore, MD: John Hopkins University Press.

Whiting, B. B., & Edwards, C. (1988). *Children of different worlds: The formation of social behavior*. Cambridge, MA: Harvard University Press.

Wolf, A. W., & Lozoff, B. (1989). Object attachment, thumbsucking, and the passage to sleep. *Journal of the American Academy of Child & Adolescent Psychiatry, 28(2)*, 287–292.

Chapter 10

Family Systems, Lacan, DSM, and Looping

Four Alternative Perspectives on Little Hans

The study in this book of Oedipal power/knowledge applied a Foucauldian framework to the case of Little Hans in a way that challenges the accounts of Freud and Bowlby. I did not attend to the many other psychoanalytic and nonpsychoanalytic approaches to understanding the Hans case. Just within psychoanalysis, the Hans case has been reinterpreted by virtually every major psychoanalytic school as a rite of theoretical passage (Midgley, 2006). In this chapter, I briefly consider a few diverse alternative perspectives on the case, including family systems theory, Lacanian psychoanalytic theory, the American Psychiatric Association's *Diagnostic and Statistical Manual of Mental Disorders* (2013, *DSM-5*), and Ian Hacking's "looping" notion. I will be mostly concerned to see whether any of these other views pose a challenge in terms of explanatory power to my account of Oedipal power/knowledge. In my view, the Foucauldian perspective offers insights into the Hans case's nature and the Oedipal theory's influence that might be supplemented by, but not replaced by, these other perspectives.

Foucauldian Power/Knowledge Versus Family Systems Theory

Family systems theory (e.g., Ackerman, 1958; Haley, 1963; Jackson, 1957) is a clinical theory of the nature and causes of psychiatric symptoms that occur to individuals within a family system. It is functionalist in the sense that it sees symptoms as developed and maintained because they perform a function within the family system. It is a "systems" theory in that it conceptualizes the family as a complex system with implicit rules and processes that maintain its existence, its boundaries, and its successful functioning. Individuals' symptoms are claimed to be an expression of the

DOI: 10.4324/9780203817124-10

family system's needs and processes rather than the expression of individual dynamics. Symptoms can thus best be understood by the functions they perform within the family system's dynamics, such as maintaining homeostasis and family self-regulation, holding a family together through concerns about one symptomatic member, or by diverting attention from certain kinds of conflicts that threaten the family.

The Foucauldian perspective is also functionalist in the sense that it holds that scientific theories of individual pathology like Hans's can have unexpected functions within family power dynamics and in society at large, and these functions explain why the theory is embraced. The functionalist approach to the role of individual symptoms in family dynamics provided by family systems theory has some affinities to Foucauldian functionalism (for a comparison, see Flaskas & Humphreys, 1993), but the two approaches are vastly different for two reasons. First, family systems theory is a functionalist theory of individuals' symptoms and perhaps of the family's view of the individual member's symptoms, but not of scientific or medical theories as such. Indeed, Foucault would likely be more inclined to analyze the function of family systems theory itself than the individual symptoms it tries to explain. Second, in family theory, it is not generally power that is the feature being regulated but rather other family functions such as the family system's homeostasis and thus its regulation and existence as a system. The individual family member's symptoms, not a scientific theory brought to bear on the individual, is claimed to perform these regulatory functions. Indeed, family systems theory's power implications—for example, in sometimes suggesting causation of intra-family violence as a symptom of family regulatory processes rather than the outcome of an individual's pathology or immorality—have been questioned and become quite controversial from a power perspective.

The classic application of family systems theory to the Hans case was Gordon Strean's (1967) analysis in the family systems field's most distinguished journal, *Family Process*. Based on the standard view within family systems theory, Strean, both a psychoanalyst and family therapist, interpreted the Hans case from a classical "family homeostasis" theoretical perspective. He claimed that within the dynamics of the Grafs' family system, Hans's phobia possessed the function of maintaining the system's homeostasis—in fact, that Hans's symptoms held the family together. Noting that "the case of Little Hans has remained a classic" (1967, p. 227),

Strean first summarized Freud's Oedipal-theoretic approach to the case report as follows:

> Little Hans was told that his phobia emanated from his oedipal wishes – his strong erotic attachment to his mother coupled with his wish to displace his father and penetrate mother with his own "widdler." Because Hans was convinced that his sexual desires towards mother and competitive drives towards father were taboo, he had to pay a penalty, namely, castration at the hands of his father. Unable to cope with his strong ambivalence towards his father, Hans repressed the hateful feelings, displaced them on to horses and then feared the horses' hostile retaliation rather than that of his father.
>
> Hans' recovery, according to Freud, was due to the boy's assimilation and integration of his father's interpretations which were mainly focused on Hans' oedipal difficulties. Recognizing that his father would not punish him for his libidinal and aggressive wishes, Hans was free to resume his energetic life outdoors and enter areas where he previously feared to tread.
>
> (1967, p. 227)

Strean then outlined an alternative (or supplementary) family systems approach to an individual's symptoms, and explained how to apply it to the Hans case, as follows:

> The family, as currently viewed by many professionals, is a social system with several interacting parts …. When the family is viewed as a social system, it is contended that a change in one family member will modify the role interactions and transactions of the others.
>
> [T]he patient with symptoms is not only serving a complex function for the family through his expression of pathology, he is also satisfying the needs of family members by serving what Ackerman has referred to as a "scapegoat function" (1958). As the displayed expression of family conflict, the patient is "holding the family together and providing a focus for its discontent" (Haley, 1963). Further, theorists on family dynamics suggest that when the family member with the presenting problem improves, other family members exhibit distress and the dissolution of

the family unit is threatened …. The family oriented practitioner assessing the case of *Little Hans* would therefore examine it not only from the vantage point of the presenting problem; he would hold as axiomatic that the behavior of one individual in a family exerts influence upon other family members and that a change in one member's behavior provokes responses in the others.

(1967, pp. 229–230)

Strean emphasized the transactional, mutual causality evidenced in the case. For example, the child's problems both are caused by, and cause problems in, the parents:

Children's developmental problems activate unresolved childhood conflicts of their parents so that when a parent seeks assistance from a therapist in relation to his child, he is also presenting a part of himself which seeks help. When Hans' father went to Freud, he may have been unconsciously communicating that "I, Hans' father, have oedipal difficulties of my own which I can't resolve. They are being stimulated constantly by my son. Please help me!"

(1967, p. 230)

Like many other family systems theorists, Strean seems prone to extreme claims about the family-systems sources of symptoms without any scientific evidence of etiology. Elsewhere, he goes so far as to claim that it has been demonstrated that both childrens' problems and chronic marital complaints are always the result of unconscious parental/partner wishes and reinforcement of the problem behavior:

Psychoanalytic practitioners and theorists have been able to demonstrate, for example, that every chronic marital complaint is an unconscious wish of the complainer. The husband who constantly complains that his wife is cold and unresponsive unconsciously wants such a wife—a warm and responsive wife would scare him—and that is why he stays married to the woman about whom he constantly complains. Similarly, parents who consistently complain that their children are too aggressive, or oversexed, or too tomboyish or too effeminate, unconsciously provoke and sustain such behavior in their children. Close examination of parent-child interaction inevitably demonstrates that parents subtly reward their children for the very behavior they consciously repudiate.

(Strean, 1986, p. 20)

While this is sometimes true, the "axiomatic" principle that the identified patient is "serving a complex function for the family through his expression of pathology" is an ideological preference by theoreticians, not an established universal scientific formula. Human misery comes in forms too diverse to be captured in any one such formula, and adherence to a formula can harm people who do not in fact fit the formula. Of course, once symptoms exist, a family will adapt to them, and the consequent adjustments may make it seem that the function of the symptoms within the family is to produce such adjustments, even when it is not true. Such effects do not meet the logical and evidential requirements of the claim that the function of the symptoms is to have certain effects on the family.

A child's symptoms may hold a family together, but they can often drive the family apart. Even if a child's symptoms do enable the family to continue to exist, that effect on the family might be an accidental side effect due, say, to the parents' reluctance to separate when it might harm an emotionally troubled and vulnerable child. The effect of holding the family together might not be the ongoing cause of the maintenance of the symptoms.

There is a logical leap from "The symptom has the effect of holding the family together" (assuming that is the case) to "The function of the symptom is to hold the family together" because the latter requires that the effect of holding the family together must be at least partially explanatory of why the symptom exists in the first place or why it is maintained once it comes into existence. For example, if a child has cancer and the child's parents would otherwise have ended their marriage but stay together in light of the dire circumstances and the need to work together in those circumstances, then the child's illness has the effect of keeping the family together and may also cause reorganization of the family structure so as to create a new form of family homeostasis. That does not mean that the function of the child's cancer is to maintain family homeostasis, for the cancer did not come about and is not maintained for that reason.

Strean relies on one crucial piece of evidence to support his family-systems account of the Hans case. Strean claims that Hans's symptoms were an expression of his parents' problems and were essential to family homeostasis; the symptoms, he holds, had the defensive function of holding the Graf family together and ensuring its continued existence as a family structure. Following out the logic of his position, Strean points to the case history's mention of the parents' subsequent divorce as a confirmation of this account. Throwing caution to the wind when it comes to the risk of committing the "post hoc ergo propter hoc" fallacy, Strean repeatedly asserts that the improvement of Hans's symptoms triggered the dissolution of his parents' marriage and the end of the family system, confirming the family systems theory account of the role that the symptoms had played:

> As family therapists have demonstrated, when the family member with the presenting problem improves, other family members exhibit distress and/or the family unit can possibly be threatened with dissolution. Hans' phobia was the displayed expression of family conflict and held the family together, preserving its equilibrium. When Hans, the family member with the presenting problem, improved, the parents' marriage soon after was dissolved.
>
> (1967, p. 232)

The problem with this argument is that in fact the homeostasis theory *fails* Strean's test in the Hans case. In 1967, when Strean published his article, the timing of the separation and divorce of Hans's parents was still unknown and Strean simply assumed that the separation must have occurred soon after Hans's phobia was cured. However, the Freud Archives interviews reveal that the family in fact stayed together for another thirteen years or so after Hans's symptoms were alleviated. The father reports that he stayed in the difficult marriage for so long because of concerns about the effects of a divorce on the children. So, Hans's brief phobia was not at all a necessary condition for keeping the couple together. Strean's "dissolution of the marriage" claim on which he rests his case is disconfirmed.

Based on his false "dissolution" assumption, Strean elaborates on the specific way that the treatment of Hans was instrumental in the couple's post-analysis separation, namely, by bringing the boy and father closer together to the exclusion of the mother:

> The mutual avoidance pattern of both parents towards each other reinforced Father's attachment to his son wherein Hans became his

father's wife. As mother became further alienated from her husband and son (and eventually bowed out entirely), Hans and his father drew closer. Father evolved into both a mother and father for Hans, was ascribed strong omnipotence by the latter, and the patient was cured through love. Hans, in his submission to father, complied with his father's prescription that was received from Freud, namely, that "the phobia is nonsense and ridiculous to keep.

(1967, p. 232)

Again, the problem with this description is that it is a theory-driven fantasy that does not describe what actually happened. There was no fresh withdrawal of the partners based on the growing closeness of Hans to his father and his withdrawal from his mother. Instead, as we saw in earlier chapters, the father actively attempted to separate Hans from his mother, and both the mother and Hans fought this separation bitterly and often defied the father's wishes. Hans stayed close to both of them, and the parents' conflicts went on as before.

Strean astutely perceives that there must have been a sexual problem between the parents, which we now know from the Archives interviews was indeed the case. However, he attributes the couple's sexual problems specifically to the father's naivete and lack of sexual aggressiveness. Instead, the Archives interviews make clear that the father desired sex and seems occasionally to have insisted on it—yielding the resultant children—despite the mother's pronounced reluctance. The sexual problems appear to be due instead to the mother's aversive reaction to sex, likely because of fears of pregnancy. In any event, the parents' sexual problems appear to have been enduring from early in the marriage whereas Hans's phobia lasted four months, so it is difficult to justify an inference that the parents' sexual problems caused the child's symptoms as a functional diversion. The nature and timing of the Grafs' marital conflicts does not offer persuasive support for a family systems account of Hans's phobia as a stand-alone account.

The family systems view does not address the Oedipal theory's influence. The most direct link between Hans's phobic symptoms and family processes is the imposition on the family of the Oedipal theory by the father some time before the onset of Hans's symptoms. This created fertile ground for anxiety in a boy who was being blocked by his father from attachment soothing by his mother due to Oedipal-theory generated concerns.

Lacan on the Oedipus Complex as Wish-Fulfillment Fantasy

Building on Freud's ideas, the influential French psychoanalyst Jacques Lacan formulated a distinct and novel perspective on the Oedipus complex and the Hans case, which he presented at length in his seminars in 1955–56 and 1956–57 that were later published (Lacan, 1993, 1994). There is a distant affinity between one aspect of Lacan's view of the Oedipus complex and my account of how the Oedipal theory has been used to alter family power specifically to control the mother and distance her from her son. In this section, I consider Lacan's views, note the affinity, and explain why I do not pursue Lacan's perspective further.

First, some caveats. Lacan's views on these matters evolved over time and had many strands, so I forewarn the reader that I am selecting a few aspects that are most relevant to my concerns in this book and compressing them artificially into one view. Also, I deal only with the superficial structure of Lacan's challenging thinking and rely heavily on the guidance of Lacan's interpreters. I make no attempt to do justice to the depth and complexity of the full theory that lies behind Lacan's view of the Oedipus complex, which would require a book of its own.

Freud claims that a son sexually desires his mother and thus wants to have his mother to himself, and as a consequence comes to fear castration by his father. It is above all castration anxiety that, if not properly resolved, can lead to neurotic problems in the child, according to Freud. Lacan rejects this Freudian account of the Oedipus complex. Rather, according to Lacan, the child at first basks in the mother's satisfaction with him due to his fulfilling her need for a substitute penis (the idea that the child is perceived by the mother as a substitute penis was earlier put forward by Freud). As Midgley (2006) summarizes:

> But in Lacan's account of this earliest stage of life (which earlier he had described in terms of the "mirror stage"), one is already involved with a triangular structure, which he calls the first "time" of the oedipus complex, and the child is never alone with the mother in a truly "preoedipal" state. At this early stage, however, the third term is not the father, but rather the "imaginary phallus"—that which stands for what the mother really desires, a role that the infant child is only too happy to fulfill. Insofar as the infant can "be" the

phallus for his mother, both infant and mother can remain in this "game of imaginary lure."

(p. 551)

However, at some point, this mutual fantasy-supported ideal state starts to come apart. The child becomes afraid when he realizes the dangers of his mother's intense need for the satisfaction he provides and of the possibility he will be either engulfed or abandoned. In Hans's case, this disruption occurs, for example, when Hans's sister is born and replaces him to some extent in his mother's attentions, or when his mother threatens Hans with the doctor cutting off his widdler if he continues to touch it and Hans experiences this as his mother's rejection of his penis. Hans is then faced with a raft of questions, such as: what does his mother really want from him? What is she willing to do to get it? What does Hans have to do to keep her wanting him but at the same time prevent her from wanting him too much? At some point, according to Lacan, Hans comes to understand the mother as desiring a penis but not having one, thus sees his own position as dangerous because the mother's impossible desire expressed through him may engulf him, perhaps—in his child's mind—literally through cannibalistic oral incorporation. He becomes overwhelmed by fear of the mother and her needs/desires.

This is where Lacan's version of the Oedipal drama takes an interestingly distinctive turn. Having come to fear (rather than only sexually desire, as in Freud's account) the mother, the child is not traumatized by fear of the father's wrath (as Freud suggests) but rather needs the father's strength as a protective bulwark against the mother. It is the father's intervention—what amounts to the father's Laius complex, his objection to the over-closeness of the mother and the son—that is the major factor that separates the child from the phallus-desiring mother and thus allows the child's anxiety to decrease. Indeed, the child will be prone for his own peace of mind to inflate the father's strength and potential wrath in separating the child from the mother. Thus, castration anxiety is not so much a fear that is a consequence of the son's desire for the mother as it is a wish fulfillment fantasy of having a strong father who will aggressively protect the child from the potentially engulfing mother.

Paul Verhaeghe (2009), in a book reconsidering the Oedipal theory from a Lacanian perspective, expresses the essence of Lacan's theory as follows: "The child is in need of a strong father who will protect him by prohibiting access to the mother ... " (p. 62). Verhaeghe notes that the father would like to be what Lacan calls the "father of the law," that is, as Lacan puts it, "the one who has the rightful possession of the mother—and in peace, in principle, is therefore envied and admired by the son" (Lacan, 1993, p. 204, as cited in Verhaeghe, 2009, p. 10). However, whether or not the father attains this goal, the son will fantasize such an outcome because he needs the "father of the law" to place limits on the mother.

Lacan claims that Hans construes his mother's scolding of him for touching himself as a rejection of his penis per se and that this renders Hans "fundamentally other than what is desired ... rejected outside of the imaginary field" (Lacan, 1994, as cited and translated in Newman, 2001, p. 119). Lacan describes Hans's "fundamental disappointment ... that the mother's interest, more or less accentuated depending on the case, is the phallus. After this recognition he also realises that the mother is deprived, that she herself lacks precisely this object" (Lacan, 1994, as cited and translated in Rodriguez, 1999, p. 125). So, the mother desires the phallus, but rejects Hans's phallus.

Rodriguez (1999) explains Lacan's view as follows:

> What is threatening to Hans is not the father (as Freud had assumed), but a desire of the mother that appears to Hans as unsatisfied and not subjected to the law. As such, it assumes terrifying imaginary figurations, dominated by oral cannibalism, that is, the fantasy of the devouring mother that lies behind the symptom (fear of horses *biting*).
>
> (p. 128)

Verhaeghe makes clear that it is not the content but what the Oedipal theory does for us that is crucial in Lacan's account: "[T]he kernel of the matter ... is situated in the *function* of the oedipal structure rather than in the specific roles of the parental protagonists and their alleged importance, be it mother or father" (p. 3). The function has to do with protection from the mother:

> Either it [the child] follows the desire of the mother, or it refuses to do so and dies. ... But this mother might be all too fully present, and mothering might be experienced as smothering .... Lacan's theory

stresses … the infant's anxiety about being reduced to a mere object of enjoyment by the (m)Other" …. This explains the necessary function of the father in Lacanian theory; the introduction of a third party puts an end to the lack of choice … [The relationship to the mother] contains a threat, and it is precisely to protect against this threat that the authoritarian father is constructed …. The child is in need of a strong father who will protect him by prohibiting access to the mother ….

(Verhaeghe, 2009, pp. 40–42, 46, 62)

As Mitchell (2009) explains Lacan's account of the infant's dilemma: "the human being is both sexually driven (has a sexual drive) and is utterly helpless (the prematurity of our birth necessitates our prolonged infantile dependence). We desire the very person from whom we are most in danger—our mother" (pp. viii–ix).

Thus, Lacan offers what can be construed as an alternative account of the appeal of Freud's (mistaken) Oedipal theory—namely, that its postulation of the son's fear of an angry castrating father in fact provided an image of precisely the kind of strong fearful father for which sons pine. Patients—and adults more generally—find this image of the imagined Oedipal fierce father reassuring because it provides a defense against the patient's true fear of the mother. And, fathers themselves may derive satisfaction from believing, even as their actual power wanes, that they are feared so terribly.

Verhaeghe (2009) lucidly summarizes Lacan's view of the function of Freud's Oedipal theory:

Freud's case studies testify to the fact that many neurotics need a strong father figure. The well-known family romance is a kind of imaginary upgrade of the father, providing him with more authority …

Lacan considers the classic Oedipus complex to be Freud's own wishful dream …. The neurotic subject dreams up for himself a strong father with whom he can start a reassuring fight, reassuring because it allows him to leave behind another fight and another threat. The latter are associated with the mother … Lacan brings the following correction: the Oedipus complex, in its classic version, is Freud's own dream, and the oedipal father is a construction made by the hysterical subject.

(pp. 32–33)

However, if Hans welcomes the father's (imagined) threats, then where do Hans's symptoms come from? Lacan suggests that Hans is constructing a feared object—the horse—because his own father is too weak to provide such an object. Consequently, his need for a strong aggressive power is projected onto the horse—along with his fears of his mother, where, for example, the feared horse's bite is an expression of the child's fear that the mother will orally incorporate (cannibalize) the child in her desire to gain the phallus. According to Lacan, the father plays a key role in ameliorating the mother's hold on the child, but his failure to provide a full solution leads to the symptom:

> '[C]astration' is always tied up with the impact, the intervention, of the real father. It may equally be deeply marked, and profoundly unbalanced, by the absence of the real father. When this atypical situation occurs, the substitution of something else for the real father is required—which creates severe forms of neurosis.
>
> (Lacan, 1994, as cited and translated in Rodriguez, 1999, p. 126)

As Midgley (2006) summarizes: "The horse that Hans fears, we might say, is not a *symbol* of the father, as Freud had suggested, but rather the child's attempt to create a *substitute* for the missing (symbolic) father that he so desperately needed" (p. 552).

The problem is that with a weak father Hans cannot move from his position within the mother-child-phallus triangle to the new situation of the father who protects him. It is this problem that creates his severe anxiety that is directed onto horses:

> For Lacan, the anxiety that Hans experiences—almost a 'nameless dread' or an existential angst—is a response to being poised between the imaginary, oedipal triangle (mother-child-phallus) and the symbolic oedipal quaternity (mother-child-phallus-symbolic father). It is the point, as Lacan puts it, in his typically enigmatic style, where 'the subject is suspended between a moment where he no longer knows where he is and a future where he will never again be able to re-find himself'.
>
> (Midgley, 2006, p. 553; final quote from Lacan, 1994, as cited and translated in Evans, 1996, p. 11)

Lacan's account, as elaborated by Verhaeghe, has an affinity to my neo-Foucauldian account in one interesting respect. Like my claim that the Foucauldian function of the Oedipal theory—what makes it attractive—is that it yields control over the mother and specifically of the mother's physical affection towards her son, Lacan claims that the function of the child's projection of the castration threat onto the father is to protect against the mother:

> The installation of the incest prohibition and—more generally—the limitations on sexuality and sexual pleasure are not the result of this Oedipus complex, they are its very aim.
>
> (Verhaeghe, 2009, pp. xvii–xviii)

> [W]omen have been assumed to be the seat of a threatening passion, even a lasciviousness, that has to be damped down because otherwise it might destroy both themselves and men. This is the underlying reasoning that explains Freud's ... oedipal theory. The child is in need of a strong father who will protect him by prohibiting access to the mother .... This also explains Lacan's first oedipal theory: it is the mother who might enjoy her child in an almost deadly way and it is only via the intervention of the father that the subject is saved from her possibly lethal enjoyment.
>
> (Verhaeghe, 2009, pp. 61–62)

In sum, Lacan reverses the Freudian family Gestalt. He transforms the mother as passive recipient of the child's desires into a potentially engulfing threat to the child, the father's supposed helpless rage into his reassuring strength that is his developmental function, and the child's seeking of sexual union with the mother into his seeking protection by the father from the mother. Lacan's idea that the oedipal theory is a wish-fulfillment fantasy of the father performing his function of protecting the son against the mother's overstimulation bears a resemblance to my claim that the Oedipal theory has the function of controlling the level of mother–son intimacy.

However, Lacan claims that the child actually experiences these developmental events and projects the castration threat onto the father to inflate his father's strength in protecting him against the mother and soothe his fears, and that the acceptance of Freud's Oedipal theory is thus a kind of community wish-fulfillment fantasy. In contrast, I am arguing that the acceptance of the Oedipal theory by adults is unrelated to the truth of any developmental hypothesis about the need to control the mother, is not based on any real threat in childhood whether from the child's incestuous desires and rageful father or from an engulfing mother, and is not a wish fulfillment. Rather, acceptance of the theory is due to the historically situated role it played in marital power relations.

Lacan uses the Hans case study's details to support his functional hypotheses about the appeal of the Oedipal theory as a projection of a strong father in defense against maternal engulfing, and Verhaeghe's book elaborates this evidence. However, even leaving aside dubious constructs derived from Freud such as fear of cannibalistic oral incorporation by the mother and the mother valuing the child as a penis substitute, Lacanian hypotheses regarding the Oedipal process are not borne out by a systematic consideration of the Hans case material.

The salient fact of the case record is Hans's attempts to get closer to his mother and his frustration, not relief, at the father's interference and prohibitions. Moreover, Olga was not one to overwhelm Hans with her affections; she was mainly reactive, providing her soothing when Hans sought it out or was obviously in need. Of course, this need not stop Hans from projecting her desires, but it suggests that there was no special, overt, engulfing process going on that might explain Hans's neurosis. Moreover, the question arises of why Hans would construct a feared object—a biting horse—that, rather than separating him from his supposedly feared mother, caused him naturally to run to her to seek attachment-related soothing of his anxiety. One would think that on Lacan's view this would be counter-productive. Was Hans perhaps going to his mother only in order to provoke the law-giving father to intervene, restoring a sense of safety? The idea that Hans is seeking his mother to manipulate his father finds no support in the text of the case; Hans often and explicitly rejects fatherly interventions as unwanted precisely because they interfere with his contact with his mother. Hans's actions appear to be consistent with his genuine desire to obtain affection from his mother when he needs it, and expressive of his genuine frustration with his father's interference in this natural process. There is no evidence of Hans experiencing relief of his symptoms from his father's Oedipal-theory-induced prevention of his closeness with his mother.

What is supposed to be the source of Hans's problem? According to Verhaeghe following Lacan, it lies with the weakness of the father: "The

man just can't assume the position of the father" (p. 10). Many others—
not only Lacanians—have picked up on the theme of the "weak father" as
the problem in the Hans case. Certainly, it is true that Max Graf was shy
about conflict and not a domineering type of individual (Wakefield, 2007).
However, rather than being ineffectual, Freud implies that Hans's father
was successful at keeping Hans out of his mother's bed at Gmunden
during the summer before the neurosis hit, at least when he was not tra-
veling. That is presumably the reason that Hans first expressed anxious
longing for his mother at that time. Freud speculates that it is Hans's discovery that he could be closer with his mother when the father was away
that triggered Hans's increasing libidinal attachment to her and his Oedipal fantasies of his father going away. Problems arose when, back in
Vienna, the father was constantly present and asserted his authority in
keeping the boy from his mother. This is precisely the opposite of what
one would expect on the Lacanian hypothesis that Hans is seeking safety
in a strong male figure's intervention.

It is true that the father is portrayed at the time of the giraffe fantasy as
having reluctantly yielded to Hans's and the mother's wishes for time
together to cuddle when Hans is anxious—surely a sane and compassionate act. It is also an acknowledgment of the post-Victorian male's less-
than-absolute power in the family. Verhaeghe appears to see the father's
compassionate act of sometimes allowing Hans and Olga to cuddle as
evidence of Max's not being a "real man." Verhaeghe mercilessly chides
the father because he visited his own mother every Sunday in Lainz with
Hans but without his wife. However, the innuendo is misleading; the
Archives interviews reveal that Max's wife refused to accompany him
despite his entreaties due to her social phobia and a specific conflict or
antipathy between Olga and Max's mother. Rather than Max being
relieved that his wife did not accompany him on social outings, he complains about Olga's social anxieties, in the interviews, as making for a bad
marriage. Verhaeghe notes that Hans says he would like to take mama to
Lainz—which Verhaeghe uses as evidence of how much of a wimp Max
is, for even his young son can see the inappropriateness of not bringing
mom along on these outings. But in fact, what Hans's statement reveals—
contrary to Lacan's and Verhaeghe's lavish constructions—is that Hans
had no particular fear of being overwhelmed by his mother due to the
weakness of his father, and no desire to be protected from his mother by
the strength of his father. If Hans had such feelings, he would have been

relieved that his father had the strength to abandon his mother for a few hours and take Hans alone to Lainz.

Verhaeghe points out that Hans insists, despite his father's denials, that his father is angry at him, taking this as support for the Lacanian theory that the child needs and must project a strong, angry father. A simpler hypothesis is that Hans correctly perceived that his father was angry whenever Hans tried to join his mother in bed, as manifested in the father's interference, and Hans was simply willing to say out loud what was obvious but his father preferred not to admit. The same superiority of Hans's reality testing when confronted by his father's defensiveness is evidenced in the one meeting Hans and his father had with Freud. The father at first refuses to admit that he has ever hit Hans, then is forced under Hans's cross-examination to acknowledge that he hit Hans that very morning! The evidence favors the simpler hypothesis that the father's actual behavior, not Hans's fantasied projection, yielded Hans's view that his father was angry.

If Hans's father's weakness, and Hans's consequent need to project a stronger and more feared object to make him feel safe, was the cause of Hans's horse phobia, then how did Hans manage to become better? Verhaeghe suggests that Freud's and the father's Oedipal interpretations to Hans, which emphasized Hans's fear of the father, somehow remade the father himself into a stronger figure (perhaps because he felt feared), thus providing the object Hans needed and leading to Hans's cure. This is an utterly ad hoc hypothesis with no evidential basis; the case record offers no support for such a transformation of the father, whose demeanor and approach are constant throughout. For example, we learn from the Minutes of the Vienna Psychoanalytic Society that, even months after Hans's phobia was resolved, against Freud's advice the father still refused to tell Hans about the source of babies in the sexual act and thus failed to illuminate for Hans the link of the child to his father. Yet according to Verhaeghe, "for me, this [the explanation of the true nature of the origin of babies and of the link of son to father via the sexual act] is the crux of the matter" (p. 12). If the father remained unwilling to address the crux of the matter, then what is the evidence that he transformed like Clark Kent into Superman in a way that manifested greater strength than before and saved his child from the fearsome mother? In any event, one might wonder whether such a convoluted explanation is needed for a child's gradually getting over a transient fear of a large animal after a frightening experience in childhood.

The Lacanian view is that the mother, due to her self-perception of her flawed nature (she doesn't have a penis) and her sexual use of the child as substitute for her desired penis, causes the child to be in a position involving deep anxieties, dangers, and contradictions or tensions, which a strong oedipal father can help to resolve. According to this account, the father's and society's restrictions on intimate physical contact between child and mother can be construed as reassuringly solving a real developmental problem for the child. To this extent, the Lacanian view resonates with my neo-Foucauldian account, because both hold that the function of the Oedipal theory can be understood as restraining mother–son intimacy. The difference is that whereas I argue that such restrictions are in the service of restructuring family power and likely harmful to the child, the Lacanian view sees these changes as directly addressing the primary threat to the child's mental health. However, as we saw in Chapter 9, such restrictions are virtually unknown in other cultures, yet the children in those cultures are not more rampantly neurotic than our own children.

In contrast to the Lacanian account, I have argued that the Oedipal-theory-derived restrictions on mother–child intimacy in our society create a serious developmental problem for the child who is seeking natural attachment soothing. In claiming that the Oedipal theory is a wish-fulfillment fantasy of the child's need to be protected from the mother, Lacan offers an evidentially unsupported rationalization of an oppressive Oedipal-driven intervention into mother–son affection. Juliet Mitchell, in a preface to Verhaeghe's book, expresses the Lacanian-proposed fear of maternal desire as follows: "We are helplessly dependent upon someone who is, and who must be, as lacking as we are and therefore as rapaciously desiring" (Mitchell, 2009, p. xi). Consequently, Lacan placed his emphasis in his early theorizing "not on the infant's incestuous love for the mother but on its need for the 'fascist' father to protect it from its mother's devouring 'crocodile' (pre-historic) love" (Mitchell, 2009, p. x). No father jealous of his son's place in the mother's embrace or irritated by the son's need for soothing in the marital bed could ask for any more extreme and satisfying rationalization of his jealous, self-indulgent, and harmful interference in attachment intimacy.

Did Little Hans Have a DSM Disorder?

How would Hans's condition be understood from the perspective of contemporary psychiatry's *Diagnostic and Statistical Manual of Mental*

Disorders (American Psychiatric Association, 2013; *DSM-5*)? Did Hans suffer from a specific phobia in the full psychiatric sense that satisfies *DSM* diagnostic criteria?

The *DSM-IV-TR Casebook* (Spitzer et al., 2002) presented the Hans case as an exemplar of specific phobia according to *DSM-IV* diagnostic criteria, which remained essentially the same in *DSM-5*. The authors of the *Casebook* state:

> There can be little doubt that Hans has a phobia. He has a persistent excessive fear of and compelling desire to avoid horses. Since the dreaded object does not involve a fear of having a panic attack, of being in situations or public places from which escape is impossible, or being in social situations with the possibility of public humiliation or embarrassment, this is a Specific Phobia.
>
> (Spitzer et al., 2002, pp. 518–519)

Remarkably, the authors of the *Casebook* were incorrect; Hans does not satisfy the *DSM*'s criteria for phobia. Hans suffered from a horse fear for a total of about four months from early January to early May of 1908. Hans's condition thus fails the duration test in both *DSM-IV-TR* and *DSM-5*. To prevent mistaken diagnosis of transient childhood fears as mental disorders, the *DSM-IV-TR* criteria for children's phobias required that they must last at least 6 months: "F. In individuals under age 18 years, the duration is at least 6 months" (American Psychiatric Association, 2000, p. 449), whereas adult phobias needed only to be "persistent" with the threshold left unstated. However, in *DSM-5*, to better protect against spurious diagnoses of transient fears in adults, the same six-month duration requirement is applied to all adult and child-specific phobias, albeit with the qualifier "typically" allowing some flexibility: "E. The fear, anxiety, or avoidance is persistent, typically lasting for 6 months or more" (American Psychiatric Association, 2013, p. 197). Thus, Hans did not have a specific phobia according to *DSM-IV-TR*, and *DSM-5* also eliminates or at least casts doubt on Hans's four months of fear of horses as qualifying for diagnosis with specific phobia, with some ambiguity due to the "typically" qualifier.

This is not surprising. Bowlby (1973) has made the case that transient fears of the sort that afflicted Hans—especially fears of the dark, of strangers, and of large animals like horses—are a normal part of a child's life and are not necessarily mental disorders. Even the psychoanalyst Kurt

Eissler, when he interviewed Max Graf, raised the question whether Hans really had a disorder versus a normal transient childhood fear. If there was no disorder, it makes the imposition of Oedipal power/knowledge all the more a social rather than medically required intervention, although of course Hans's anxiety still deserved attention. Such non-disordered conditions are the "Z Codes" in *DSM-5*.

The *Casebook* goes beyond the diagnosis of specific phobia to suggest, as Bowlby (1973) had suggested (see Chapter 3), that Hans had a separation anxiety disorder, based on his manifest symptoms of separation anxiety.

> Hans has nightmares about being separated from his mother ("When I was asleep I thought you [his mother] were gone and I had no Mummy to cuddle with."). In the evenings, when anticipating going to bed, he is extremely distressed, perhaps to the point of panic, and cannot be separated from his mother. Finally, he has an unrealistic fear that his parents will "go away and leave him." These are all expressions of excessive anxiety concerning separation from his parents, and together support the additional diagnosis of Separation Anxiety Disorder.
>
> (2002, p. 519)

This may look convincing on the surface, but a close examination reveals that Hans's symptoms do not in fact satisfy DSM-5 diagnostic criteria for separation anxiety disorder, which are carefully formulated to distinguish genuine separation anxiety disorder from common childhood expressions of anxiety. The criteria require "Developmentally inappropriate and excessive fear or anxiety concerning separation from those to whom the individual is attached, as evidenced by at least three" of a list of symptoms and "lasting at least 4 weeks." First, the passage suggests that Hans's dream with anxiety about his mother satisfies symptom criterion 7: "Repeated nightmares involving the theme of separation" (American Psychiatric Association, 2013, DSM-5, p. 191). However, the described dream is the only one reported in the entire case history in which Hans expresses concern about separation, so the requirement that there be "repeated" such nightmares is not satisfied. Second, the passage claims that Hans would not sleep apart from his mother and so satisfies symptom criterion 5, "Persistent and excessive fear of or reluctance about being alone or without major attachment figures at home ..., " or perhaps 6, "Persistent reluctance or refusal ... to go to sleep without being near a major attachment figure" (p. 191). The problem here is that it is just not true that Hans would not sleep alone or needed his mother close by to go to sleep. As I documented in Chapter 3, the case history indicates that Hans was often anxious at night about his horse fears but he was effectively calmed by his mother's soothing and went dutifully off to sleep in his own room. Finally, the passage suggests that Hans satisfies symptom criterion 2, "Persistent and excessive worry about losing major attachment figures ... " (p. 191). As explored in Chapter 3, this is based on precisely one comment by Hans to his father that due to a threat his mother made when disciplining him he is afraid his father or mother might not be there. However, his behavior shows an independent child who is not chronically worried about being abandoned. One might argue about this criterion, but the claim that Hans satisfies three of these criteria at levels that can be considered persistent or repeated over four weeks is not plausible.

Moreover, I have argued in earlier chapters that what may appear to be Hans's separation anxiety is in fact realistic situational attachment distress due to his father's interference with his ability to obtain comforting from his attachment figure, his mother. The key is that the diagnosis of separation anxiety disorder requires "Developmentally inappropriate and excessive fear or anxiety concerning separation" (p. 190) as evidenced by several out of a list of specific symptoms. Hans's anxiety due to his father's actions is entirely developmentally appropriate and, in the context of having his path to his attachment figure when he is anxious blocked by his father, not excessive. In sum, it is doubtful that Hans reached the threshold for having a separation anxiety disorder by DSM-5 standards.

Loopy about Looping

Ian Hacking's (1986, 1995a, 1995b, 1999, 2007) notion of "looping" offers a perspective on psychopathological states (and some other socially defined roles and conditions) that has been much discussed recently and which, it might be suggested, could be brought to bear on the Hans case. The basic idea of looping is simple: when theories postulate categories of types of people, this can, by a feedback process in which people come to be influenced by the postulated categories and the expectations that go along with them, cause people to grow into the role and create new forms of human behavior and experience that instantiate the postulated categories. Hacking describes "the looping effect of human kinds" as follows: "We tend to behave in ways that are expected of us, especially by authority figures—doctors, for example .... People classified in a certain way tend to conform to or grow into the ways that they are described" (1995b, p. 21). Hacking elevates this process into a basic divide between the human sciences, which commonly have looping effects, and the physical sciences, which generally do not.

The elaboration of the concept of looping is part of Hacking's larger program to try to forge a fruitful path between realism and constructivism that embraces the degree of truth in both positions (Murphy, 2001). This program can be seen as an attempt to vindicate certain elements of Foucault's project in a philosophically defensible way (Hacking was given Foucault's Chair at the College de France after Foucault's death).

Unlike entities described by physics and chemistry, the human sciences create labels and categories that interact with and influence the very things— namely, people—that are being classified and theorized about. Resuscitating and updating an old philosophy-of-science argument that the social sciences are different from the physical sciences because people can reflexively choose to follow or not follow proposed laws, Hacking has argued that theories may, in a sense, construct and constitute forms of life and forms of power even if one retains an overall realist framework. Categories that emerge at a certain time, such as child abuser, homosexual, and multiple personality disorder (to mention three that Hacking has used as examples), can define genuine new forms of life that did not exist before. The creation of social science categories can influence people to behave the way the category is described as behaving, and thus can lead to the actual creation of people who fit under the category. This is because people's awareness and acceptance of social and psychological theory and categories migrate into the mind and body and actually create the sorts of conditions and dispositions postulated by the theory. Consequently, the theory ends up being supported by evidence that the theory itself wholly or partially created.

If one conceptualizes the Oedipus complex as a result of looping interpreted in strong ontological terms (see below), then perhaps one might see Hans as coming to be genuinely Oedipal in the various ways Freud describes as a result of being indoctrinated into the theory by his father. Rather than just going along verbally with his father's suggestions, perhaps Hans changes as a person into an Oedipal form of life genuinely feeling what the Oedipal theory says he is feeling. Even if this is so, looping does not address why this particular theory and its way of creating new forms of human life was so appealing as to be embraced by many bourgeois parents and adopted by much of society at large. In other words, the looping account of how there can be a genuine Oedipus complex does not substitute for, but rather provides a compatible supplement to, my neo-Foucauldian account of why this theory was appealing due to its implied power/knowlede.

Several critiques have persuasively argued that Hacking's analyses don't have the deep ontological implications that are sometimes attributed to them (e.g., Boyd, 1991; Cooper, 2004; Tsou, 2007). Hacking's view has changed to become more cautious in response to these criticisms, so has proven to be a moving target for analysis. Hacking has hedged his ontological bets by attempting to explain that by looping he is referring not to the fact that a certain kind of thing did not exist before the corresponding social category was developed (although he does state his opinion on this), but rather to the fact that a way of life and sense of identity experienced and lived as a way to be a human being came into existence. Regarding multiple personality disorder, for example, Hacking poses his "looping" claim in the following terms:

Distinguish two sentences:

(A) There were no multiple personalities in 1955; there were many in 1985.
(B) In 1955 this was not a way to be a person, people did not experience themselves in this way, they did not interact with their friends, their families, their employers, their counsellors, in this way; but in 1985 this was a way to be a person, to experience oneself, to live in society
In my opinion, both are true, but A is too brief and contentious. Our topic is B.

To see that A and B are different, an *enthusiast* for what is now called Dissociative Identity Disorder will say that A is false, because people with several 'alter personalities' undoubtedly existed in 1955, but were not diagnosed. A *sceptic* will also say that A is false, but for exactly the opposite reason: multiple personality has always been a specious diagnosis, and there were no real multiples in 1985 either. The first statement, A, leads immediately to heated but pointless debates about the reality of multiple personality, on which I have spilt too much ink and to which I shall never again return. But open-minded opponents could peacefully agree to B. When I speak of making up people, it is B that I have in mind, and it is through B that the looping effect occurs.

(Hacking, 2007 p. 299)

So, to the degree that this distinction is clear, it seems that "making up people" involves influencing people to experience a novel way "to be a person, to experience oneself, to live in society" and relate to others. Some aspects of psychopathological experience may be at least partly due to such feedback loops. Yet, it would seem that this sort of novel experience can occur for myriad reasons. When Hacking says, "The multiple personality of the 1980s was, in my judgement, a kind of person unknown in the history of the human race. That is not an idea that we can comfortably express....careful philosophical language is not prepared for it" (2007, p. 299), it is not clear why this is so difficult an idea to express, and Hacking himself observes that it is an idea familiar enough to novelists and social historians. What, after all, could be more mundane than that people's roles and labels change with the times, and that the way they experience the world and themselves, even how they experience their deepest natures, changes as well?

Although Hacking has tended to back away from any explicit radical ontological implications of looping, the constructivist might appropriate the concept and argue that looping allows us to say that there really are Oedipal children. The very creation of the theoretical category of "Oedipal child" by Freud, it might be argued, has influenced how we interact with children and thus what they experience. The very category of "Oedipal child" has altered family life in a way that has created children that fit the category as theoretically described. For example, based on looping theory it could be argued that by theorizing about Oedipal children who are sexually attracted to their mothers, we create the conditions of attention, sexual anticipation, arousal, and so on that actually lead children to develop incestuous sexual wishes towards their mothers, analogously to the way that common experiences of attending to a sensitive or painful bodily part can cause the part to seem to become all the more sensitized or painful.

There are several problems with this idea as an alternative to the neo-Foucauldian account of the Hans case. First, as suggested above, it does not explain why the Oedipal theory emerged and was accepted in the first place, or what its social function might be, which is the focus of the Foucauldian account. Second, evidence for a prominent role for looping in the Hans case is lacking. Hans does not seem to be reconstituted or reconstructed as an Oedipal child behaving sexually towards his mother and angrily or with fear towards his father. He does not seem reshaped by the Oedipal child's "role." Rather, the case evidence suggests that Hans suffers from the oppression of being treated as if he is an Oedipal child even as he continues to be the way he always was, namely, desirous of attachment soothing but in no particular way Oedipal. It is perhaps easy to inflate a bundle of familiar causal, psychological, and practical issues in imposing a theory on a child into deeper ontological implications of a social category. However, Hans simply does not appear from the evidence to take on the role that the looping account would require of him, and it seems misleading to look to his ontology rather than his theory-driven oppression to understand what is happening to him. Indeed, to say that he has in fact become an Oedipal child who experiences Oedipal feelings and desires makes it sound ego-syntonic and thus is to distract attention from the oppressive nature of imposing a category on him that forces him to act in ways that go against his true "form of life."

A further problem is that even if Hans were induced to act more like an Oedipal child, this would not actually make him an Oedipal child in a theoretical sense. Although a human reaction to being categorized might induce a person to act as members of the category are expected to act (e.g., Hans might act more physically with his mother in what might appear to be a sexual kind of way due to hints of a verbal or non-verbal sort from his father and Freud as to what is expected of the phallic child), or even to be internally motivationally more like members of the category (e.g., Hans might actually experience sexual impulses towards his mother that he would not have experienced otherwise), that specific induction of experiences is different from actually becoming a member of the category "Oedipal child." The Oedipus complex, after all, is a developmental principle that is supposed to be universal and that includes an account of how various experiences are generated developmentally. To be an Oedipal child is to be sexualized for the reasons postulated in the theory, not because of looping, which can at best produce faux Oedipal children.

Even if looping does not create the Oedipal child in any interesting ontological sense, one still might say, consistent with Hacking's weaker formulation, that with the power/knowledge functions of the introduction of the Oedipal theory into the family, a different way of being a family came into existence through looping. This way of being was characterized by a radically altered relationship between mother, son, and father, including more restrained physical affection between mother and son. The Oedipal theory thus brought into existence a type of family which might be called the Oedipal family. Yet, even this observation does not explain why the theory and the new form of family life that went along with it should be so widely acceptable. Looping theory provides a mechanism that is at best an adjunct to neo-Foucauldian theory in illuminating the advent of the Oedipal family and its novel form of power/knowledge.

References

American Psychiatric Association. (2000). *Diagnostic and statistical manual of mental disorders, fourth edition – text revision (DSM-IV-TR)*. Washington, DC: American Psychiatric Association.

American Psychiatric Association. (2013). *Diagnostic and statistical manual of mental disorders, fifth edition (DSM-5)*. Arlington, VA: American Psychiatric Association.

Ackerman, N. W. (1958). *The psychodynamics of family life*. New York, NY: Basic Books.

Bowlby, J. (1973). Attachment and Loss (Vol. *2*): *Separation: Anxiety and anger*. London: Hogarth Press.

Boyd, R. (1991). Realism, anti-foundationalism and the enthusiasm for natural kinds. *Philosophical Studies, 61*, 127–148.

Cooper, R. 2004. Why Hacking is wrong about human kinds. *British Journal for the Philosophy of Science, 55*, 73–85.

Evans, D. (1996). *An Introductory Dictionary of Lacanian Psychoanalysis*. London, UK: Routledge.

Flaskas, C., & Humphreys, C. (1993). Theorizing about power: Intersecting the ideas of Foucault with the "problem" of power in family therapy. *Family Process, 32(1)*, 35–47.

Hacking, I. (1986). Making up people. In T. Heller, M. Sosna, & D. Wellbury (Eds.), *Reconstructing individualism* (pp. 222–236). Palo Alto, CA: Stanford University Press.

Hacking, I. (1995a). The looping effects of human kinds. In D. Sperber, D. Premack, & A. J. Premack (Eds.), *Causal cognition: A multidisciplinary debate*. Oxford, UK: Clarendon Press.

Hacking, I. (1995b). *Rewriting the soul: Multiple personality and the sciences of memory*. Princeton, NJ: Princeton University Press.

Hacking, I. (1999). *The social construction of what?*. Cambridge, MA: Harvard University Press.

Hacking, I. (2007). Kinds of people; Moving targets. In P. J. Marshall (Ed.), *Proceedings of the British Academy, Volume 151, 2006 lectures* (pp. 285–318). Oxford, UK: Oxford University Press.

Haley, J. (1963). *Strategies of psychotherapy*. New York, NY: Grune and Stratto.

Jackson, D. D. (1957). The question of family homeostasis. *Psychiatric Quarterly, 31*, 79–90.

Lacan, J. (1993). *The seminar (Book 3): The psychoses, 1955–56*. (R. Griggs, Trans). New York, NY: Norton.

Lacan, J. (1994). *Le seminaire, (Livre IV): La relation d'object, 1956–1957*. Paris: Éditions le Seuil.

Midgley, N. (2006). Re-reading "Little Hans": Freud's case study and the question of competing paradigms in psychoanalysis. *Journal of the American Psychoanalytic Association, 54*(2), 537–559.

Mitchell, J. (2009). Foreword. In P. Verhaeghe, *New studies of old villains: A radical reconsideration of the Oedipus complex* (pp. vii–xvi). New York, NY: Other Press.

Murphy, D. (2001). Hacking's reconciliation: Putting the biological and sociological together in the explanation of mental illness. *Philosophy of the Social Sciences, 31*, 139–162.

Rodriguez, L. (1999). *Psychoanalysis with children*. London: Free Association Books.

Spitzer, R. L., Gibbon, M., Skodol, A. E., Williams, J. B. W., & First, M. B. (2002). DSM-IV-TR casebook: A learning companion to the diagnostic and statistical manual of mental disorders (4th ed.) *Text Revision*. Arlington, VA: American Psychiatric Publishing.

Strean, H. S. (1967) A family therapist looks at "Little Hans". *Family Process, 6*, 227–234.

Strean, H. S. (1986). Psychoanalytic theory. In F. Turner (Ed.), *Social work treatment: Interlocking theoretical approaches*, 3rd ed. (pp. 19–45). New York, NY: Free Press.

Tsou, J. Y. (2007). Hacking on the looping effects of psychiatric classifications: What is an interactive and indifferent kind?. *International Studies in the Philosophy of Science, 21*(3), 329–344.

Verhaeghe, Paul. (2009). *New studies of old villains: A radical reconsideration of the Oedipus complex*. New York, NY: Other Press.

Wakefield, J. C. (2007). Max Graf's "Reminiscences of Professor Sigmund Freud" revisited: New evidence from the Freud Archives. *Psychoanalytic Quarterly, 76*, 149–192.

Chapter 11

Final Thoughts

Oedipal Power/Knowledge and the Future of Psychoanalysis

I have argued that the Oedipal theory, applied by Freud's follower Max Graf to his family with the aim of preventing his son Hans from developing a neurosis, actually had the opposite effect of causing Hans to become vulnerable to developing a neurosis. Relying on the Oedipal theory's sexual misconstrual of normal attachment-related affectionate behavior between mother and son combined with the Oedipal theory's claim that Oedipal sexual desire is the root of all neurosis, Max restricted the usual affection between his wife Olga and his son Hans to prevent neurosogenesis. This disruption of Hans's soothing by his mother caused Hans to be anxious and disposed him to the development of a phobia when a stressor occurred in the form of his witnessing a horse accident. Whereas Freud took Hans's development of a phobia as evidence for the truth of his Oedipal theory, in fact it was evidence that the theory itself can be harmful. Whereas Freud saw certain features of the family's interaction—for example, Hans's attempts to be with his mother, Hans's rivalry with his father, Hans's fear of his father—as evidence for the Oedipal theory, in fact these were the consequences of the father's application of the theory in a way that unduly restricted Hans's relationship to his mother.

This analysis allowed me to offer fresh solutions to two historical puzzles. The first puzzle is why Hans, normally a cheerful, sociable, and resilient boy, was nevertheless vulnerable to developing a severe phobia after witnessing a horse fall down in the street. I offered a novel neo-Foucauldian solution: Inspired by Oedipal theory, Hans's father persistently disrupted Hans's affection with his mother out of a misguided Oedipal-theory-based fear that it would arouse sexual desire, and his exercise of Oedipal "power/knowledge" inadvertently created anxiety in Hans that paved the way for the phobia.

DOI: 10.4324/9780203817124-11

The second puzzle is the larger historical and cultural puzzle as to why Freud's Oedipal theory was so widely accepted despite lack of evidence for the theory from its inception (as documented in my parallel volume, *Freud's Argument for the Oedipus Complex* [Wakefield, 2022]). Generalizing the insights gained into the Hans case, I argued that the Oedipal theory was appealing because it fit with changing social values and family structures. In misinterpreting normal mother–son attachment affection as sexual, the theory made mother–son affection appear dangerous and thus rationalized its restriction, providing grounds for patriarchal control over intimacy and yielding greater separation of the parental dyad from their children.

In both the Hans case and our culture at large, the Oedipal theory's reorganization of family affection emerged most saliently in the decreased "bed time"—the amount of time in the marital bed—allowed to the child. My analysis reveals the hidden mechanisms of power exerted by the Oedipal theory and details the surprising impact it has had on our most intimate relationships.

Answers to Three Foucauldian Questions

In this book, I have taken a neo-Foucauldian approach to understanding the impact and influence of Freud's Oedipal theory. This means that I have considered Oedipal theory not only as a structure of claimed knowledge but also, when it is accepted and applied as in the Graf family, as a social intervention that reshapes power relations. The three power/knowledge-related questions with which I started were: (1) What was the impact of the Oedipal theory on the Graf family's relationships? (2) What was the impact of Oedipal theory on our broader culture? (3) Why was the Oedipal theory so influential and so widely accepted, that is, what was its appeal or its function in our changing society?

I argued that the answers to these three questions are roughly the same. By theoretically sexualizing attachment behavior, the Oedipal theory has the impact of creating a sense of danger in mother–child physical affection due to the fear of arousing harmful sexual desire in the child. This sense of danger causes a rearrangement of family regulation by justifying limitations on mother–child intimacy, such as providing separate sleeping quarters for children at a young age. This has the further effect of protecting the marital bed from children, allowing for parental privacy. This impact is evidenced in the Hans case history in the struggle over Hans coming into the parents' bed. Hans's exile from his parents' bed is a precursor of our Oedipal culture's disapproval of cosleeping. This partial ejection of the child from the intimate orbit of the parents was the social function and appeal of the Oedipal theory because it fit with the changing nature of marriage into an emotional-sexual bond. In sum, despite lack of evidential support, Oedipal theory was widely accepted because its application provided opportunities for novel regulation of parent–child relations and for enforcing novel forms of restraint of the affection between mother and son, consistent with the direction in which marital relations were being restructured early in the twentieth century.

Foucault (1978) has described a multi-century phenomenon of the use of theories of sexuality in the formation of power/knowledge in the medical sciences that he calls the "deployment of sexuality." My analysis of the Oedipal theory places it, as Foucault claims, squarely within this overall use of sexual theories for the exercise of power in reshaping family life. However, my formulation of Oedipal theory's power/knowledge diverges quite dramatically from the specifics of Foucault's own account of Oedipal theory. A proper treatment and evaluation of Foucault's critique of Freud generally and his analysis of the Oedipal theory in particular is beyond the scope of this study, and will be presented in a forthcoming volume, *Foucault Versus Freud*.

Foucault's concept of power/knowledge refers to the impact that acceptance of the theory has on power relations and the functions its acceptance serves in advancing social changes in power relations. Power/knowledge exists whether or not a theory is true. To that extent, the analysis I have offered of Oedipal power/knowledge—namely, that it serves to make physical affection between mother and son dangerous and therefore fits with social movement toward more separation between children and parents and increasing marital emotional-sexual intensity—may be correct whether Oedipal theory itself is true or false. Believers and disbelievers in Oedipal theory can consider and evaluate my reading of the power/knowledge that impacts the Graf family when Oedipal theory is imposed on it.

If a theory is evidentially unsupported and yet is widely accepted to a degree not explainable by its support, this invites a power/knowledge analysis because the theory's power/knowledge can not only describe the theory's impact but also explain why the theory was accepted in the absence of sufficient evidential support. This is the situation with regard to

Oedipal theory. Elsewhere, in a series of papers and a book (Wakefield, 2007, 2008, 2017, 2022), I consider the evidence presented by Freud for the Oedipal theory in the Hans case from a philosophy of science perspective and find it inadequate to explain the wide acceptance of the theory. However, that analysis of the evidential base for the Oedipal theory goes beyond the scope of this book.

I argued that the primary manifestation of Oedipal power/knowledge in the Hans case is the repeated interference by Max Graf with the desires of his wife Olga Honig Graf and his son Hans (Herbert) Graf to do what parents and children all over the world do as a natural and expectable act, to physically cuddle and have skin contact perhaps in bed, especially when the child is feeling anxious and needs comforting. This exercise of power by Max is not subtle and is explicitly portrayed as a repeated event and an ongoing issue in the case history. This act of power is driven by Max's acceptance of Oedipal theory and its doctrines about the incestuous desires of a boy for his mother undergirded by the spoiling theory that indulging such needs for contact does not sate them but instead creates increasing intensity and need, and increasing symptomatology. From a neo-Foucauldian power/knowledge perspective, my claim is that this is what the Hans case is about.

A methodological implication of my analysis is that a theory's power/knowledge cannot be understood independently of a detailed understanding of the logic of a theory. Understanding the logical structure of Freud's theory including the auxiliary "spoiling" hypothesis, according to which full satiation of an intense desire may bring about intensified desire, turned out to be crucial to understanding how to decipher the theory's power/knowledge implications. Foucauldian critiques of theory are often presented independently of traditional philosophy-of-science logical reconstruction of the theory in question, but the current investigation suggests that this divorce of the two methodologies may lead to error. The nuances of Freud's theory, excavated by logical reconstruction, revealed and explained the likely marital-power impact of the Oedipal theory. Logical reconstruction and power/knowledge analysis should go hand in hand, for if one does not attend to logical structure, then power/knowledge analysis is in danger of being rendered facile.

The Causes of Hans's Phobia

Although the power/knowledge analysis can remain neutral on the truth of Oedipal theory, I have also argued for an alternative non-Oedipal attachment theoretic approach to understanding Hans's disposition to develop phobic anxiety that is different from Bowlby's analysis in terms of insecure attachment due to maternal threats, which was shown in Chapter 3 to be inconsistent with the case evidence. In this section and the next, I spell out my alternative account.

I note that there remains a question as to whether Hans's four-month animal phobia—an expectable experience at his age—needs much of an explanation at all beyond his frightening experience seeing the horse fall down. Indeed, when Kurt Eissler in his Archives interview of Max Graf asks whether Max thought of his child's condition as a neurosis, Max answers "no" (Graf, 1952). Notably, the condition's brevity means that it is questionable whether it qualifies as a DSM-5 phobia (see Chapter 10).

However, both Bowlby and Freud believed that the intense anxiety Hans developed as a result of his experience of witnessing the horse accident requires or at least invites some further understanding of his background disposition to react so intensely to such a stressor, especially in a boy who has shown no long-term tendency toward anxiety. After all, they would argue, most children who saw such a scene would not develop a phobia, so what more is at work here given that Hans's constitution, according to the parents' reports, does not seem a particularly anxious one?

If we attempt an etiological reconstruction of what led Hans to develop his intense fear, there seem to be three factors potentially at work, none involving Oedipal desires. All of these etiological processes were identified at the end of Chapter 3 as potential factors emerging out of Bowlby's multi-theoretical view of phobia uniting attachment and behaviorist elements. I think that these evidentially defensible factors jointly offer a persuasive explanation, with each one entering into the explanation with varying degrees of causal-role involvement.

1   *Normal anxiety in response to a real external danger.* The real sense of danger Hans experienced during the horse accident undoubtedly played a causal role in phobogenesis: "When the horse in the bus fell down, it gave me such a fright, really!" (Freud, 1909/1955, p. 50). However, that real danger was over in a few minutes and the danger to Hans was minimal. In many later instances in which he was intensely afraid there was no real danger at all. Real danger might make one marginally more careful around horses, but not terrified of them to the point of refusing to

go out on the street. So, real danger cannot explain Hans's subsequent phobic level of intense anxiety.

2   *One-trial behavioral fear conditioning in response to an overwhelming external stressor or danger.* Wolpe and Rachman (1960) are surely correct that witnessing a large horse fall down in the street kicking its legs was a traumatic experience for Hans in the sense that it caused one-trial learning of an enduring, extremely high level of fear of horses, specifically that horses might fall down and kick or bite. The phobia started immediately after witnessing the horse fall down: "That was when I got the nonsense" (Freud, 1909/1955, p. 50). Examination of precisely what kinds of stimuli triggered high anxiety revealed that it was consistently situations that suggested to Hans the possibility of the horse falling down (e.g., horses pulling heavy loads, horses turning a corner pulling a wagon, horses prancing in a brisk way). Hans's reported ideation suggests the kind of irrational generalization that takes place in such traumatic circumstances: "I: 'What did you think when the horse fell down?' Hans: 'Now it'll always be like this. All horses in buses'll fall down'" (1909/1955, p. 49). Bowlby acknowledges that this process of one-trial fear conditioning can proceed quite independently of attachment considerations, but he emphasizes that if the two are both present, they are likely to interact to create much greater anxiety.

So, Hans witnessing the horse accident is an obvious major causal factor. The question is what, other than some preparatory memories related to horses, may have predisposed Hans to an extreme anxiety reaction when confronted with such a stressor. Freud baldly asserts in his case Discussion that Hans's witnessing of the horse accident was insufficient by itself to be traumatic and explain Hans's subsequent intense fear ("In itself the impression of the accident which he happened to witness carried no 'traumatic force'" [p. 136]). For Freud, this is a necessary defense of his sexual theory of the neuroses against the objection that had dogged him from the start, from the early critique by Lowenfeld (1895; Freud, 1895/1962) through Breuer's reasons for diverging from Freud and on to precursors of Wolpe and Rachman's (1960) behaviorist critique. The objection was that terrifying experiences, whether on the battlefield, in a train wreck, or due to some other threatening incident, can cause neurotic symptoms without any sexual component. Bowlby, we saw, accepted the "fright theory" of some phobias as well. However, like Freud, Bowlby is inclined to postulate additional background factors that potentiate the reaction to a frightening experience so as to turn it into a phobia.

3   *Normal attachment anxiety or "situational attachment distress."* When a child feels anxious and is trying to gain access to his or her attachment figure for comforting and finds the figure is unavailable because the pathway to the figure is blocked, the child will experience normal situational attachment anxiety. The focus on this overlooked, but salient and powerful, predisposing factor, which Hans was experiencing frequently in the months leading up to the phobia in the form of Max blocking Hans's access to his mother's attachment soothing, is a distinctive contribution of my analysis. Remarkably, this blatant and distressing exercise of power by Max is never mentioned as a problem by any of the commentators I have reviewed. The only ones who take it seriously are Hans and his mother.

Bowlby, searching for an explanation of why some become phobic after a fright while some do not, emphasizes that the combination of the initial fear of some stressor plus the situational attachment anxiety when the attachment figure cannot be reached for comforting are additive and can produce a severe reaction: "Since not all children become persistently afraid after a particularly alarming experience, specific conditions are presumably responsible. Of possible candidates, compound situations of which one component is being alone seems especially likely" (1973, p. 197). This fits Hans's situation precisely, because starting a few months before Hans saw the horse accident and continuing through his phobic period, Hans's father, driven by Oedipal-theoretic assumptions, was prohibiting Hans from coming into the parents' bed where he habitually went for comforting by his mother in the morning or evening when he felt anxious. Given that one of the functions of such comforting is to help the child regulate anxiety, disruption of the child's ability to obtain contact with his mother is likely to greatly potentiate the anxiety that resulted from the initial anxiety-provoking event and the one-trial learned fear that resulted from the event. Although Hans was with his mother when the horse accident occurred, Bowlby's "compound" analysis can be extended to Hans's situation afterward as he experienced fear when alone without access to his mother to modulate his fear:

> when an individual is confident that an attachment figure will be available to him whenever he desires it, that person will be much less

prone to either intense or chronic fear than will an individual who for any reason has no such confidence.

(1973, p. 202)

The combination of Hans's witnessing the terrifying horse accident and his disposition to anxiety being raised by Max's disruption of Han's ability to obtain soothing from his mother provides a plausible explanation for Hans's disposition to develop an intense anxiety reaction. Max's theory-driven disruption of Olga and Hans's attachment relationship likely also caused Hans's anxiety to be maintained at a heightened level for longer than otherwise would have been the case. This is because blocking Hans's path to anxiety reduction through cuddling with his mother not only raises situational attachment distress but, according to Bowlby, amplifies other ongoing fears.

To this extent, Hans's phobia was an iatrogenic illness. Oedipal theory, not the Oedipus complex, was partly to blame for causing Hans to fall ill. Moreover, the father's intervention in blocking Hans's access to his mother created in Hans the very emotions—heightened frustrated desire for his mother, fear of and anger toward his father—that mimic supposed Oedipal feelings and thus provide spurious "evidence" for Hans's Oedipus complex. The "mother bashers" reviewed in Chapter 7 accuse Olga of child abuse on all sorts of evidentially dubious grounds, but one might legitimately say that Max's actions in repeatedly keeping an anxious child from obtaining the comforting he needed from his willing and concerned mother was a real if inadvertent, theory-driven form of child abuse.

So, Why Was Hans Disposed to Develop a Phobia?

Freud is likely quite correct in his repeated assertion that it was the contrast between Hans's increased access to his mother during the summer at Gmunden when his father was often absent working in Vienna and his lessened access to his mother when the family returned to Vienna and was together again that was pivotal to Hans's phobia development. However, this was true not for the Oedipal-theoretic reasons Freud provides—incestuous-libidinal intensification followed by suppression and symptom formation—but for the following more mundane attachment-related reasons.

Max's demand that Hans not cuddle with his mother likely started when Hans was moved into his own bedroom, about six months before the phobia's onset. However, this situation lasted only a short time, after which there was a partial respite from Max's disruption of Hans's bond to his mother during the summer, when the family took a vacation house in Gmunden and Max was away from the family working in Vienna during the week. Consequently, Hans was alone with his mother, who had no qualms about cuddling with Hans or allowing him to sleep in her bed. This was followed by an abrupt reimposition of the father's prohibitions when the family was reunited in Vienna at the end of the summer, roughly four months prior to phobia onset. It appears that Max, driven by Oedipal theory and perhaps personal desires to keep Hans out of the marital bed, was relentless in scolding Hans and in shaming him for wanting to be comforted by his mother. We know from the case study that, based on the father's scolding of Hans and the prohibitions he imposed, Hans concluded that his father must be angry at him for wanting to be close to his mother ("I: 'Why [do I scold you]? He: 'Because you are cross.' I: 'But that's not true.' Hans: 'Yes, it *is* true. You're cross. I know you are. It must be true" [Freud, 1909/1955, pp. 82–83]), increasing his anxiety and desperation.

This attachment-access disruption provided fertile ground for an anxiety condition to develop once a frightening incident occurred, as it did in the form of Hans witnessing a horse accident in which a horse fell down in the street. The father's actions in persistently blocking natural son–mother attachment interactions pushed the situation outside of the boundaries of a "good enough" or "average expectable" environment and plausibly disposed Hans to be less capable of adaptively handling a serious stressor when it did occur or of getting over the subsequent anxiety. Bowlby describes the situation perfectly in the abstract as one in which an actual danger situation—the horse accident—has a pathological effect because it interacts with a simultaneous disruption of the child's ability to regulate and reduce the consequent anxiety through comforting from his attachment figure. But, Bowlby failed to see how this description perfectly applied to the Hans case.

Once the phobia was under way, Max's Oedipal-theory-driven actions in blocking Hans's access to his mother likely amplified and helped to maintain the phobic reaction. We know that once Hans's phobia developed, Max went so far as to use Hans's phobia as an additional argument that even when Hans was acutely anxious he should not come into the marital bed because, based on Oedipal considerations, that would only increase Hans's anxiety. Thus, he labeled as a danger the very thing that would decrease and regulate Hans's anxiety. Hans, as the only member of the family who did not understand Oedipal theory, plainly and sensibly rejected his father's bizarre claim that being comforted by his mother when he was anxious would make him more rather than less anxious, and he insisted that he should be allowed to obtain comforting from his mother even if he was anxious. The father's prediction of higher anxiety was contradicted by Hans's actual experiences described in the case history of the times Hans did obtain comforting from his mother, which tended to help him self-regulate, as attachment theory would predict.

Recall that Bowlby, defending his "anxious attachment" view of Hans's anxiety that he claimed was due to threats by Hans's mother, says emphatically: "Thus, both the sequence of events leading up to the phobia and Hans's own statements make it clear that, *distinct from and preceding any fear of horses*, Hans was afraid that his mother might go away and leave him" (1973, p. 285). The fact that a chronic anxiety-provoking situation preceded the phobia's outbreak by some months certainly would be relevant evidence that it might have played a role in phobogenesis. However, in fact, as we have seen, the evidence for Hans specifically actually fearing that his mother might leave before the horse phobia began is weak, consisting of one vaguely recalled ambiguous comment six months before and another ambiguous statement about a dream around the time of phobia onset that may not have antedated the phobia. However, the case evidence firmly establishes that the father's disruption of Hans's access to his mother and Hans's resultant anxiety about access to his mother almost certainly started about six months before the phobia's onset and took a turn for the worse when the family returned to Vienna after Gmunden, about three or four months before the phobia's onset. It is this chronic causal factor leading up to the phobia for which the case history offers the most compelling evidence as a predisposing risk factor.

What of Olga's parenting? If we think not in terms of optimal parenting, for certainly Olga had enough difficulties to prevent her from being an optimal parent, but rather in terms of whether Olga provided adequate responsiveness to her child's needs despite her own considerable difficulties, then I think she was at least an adequate parent. The parenting provided by Olga for Hans, summarized in Chapter 3, was in the range within which a child can develop normally and nonpathologically, including securely attaching to the attachment figure. Olga was no doubt frustrating at times, but she was attentive enough and affectionate enough to allow Hans to mature normally based on biologically designed responses to an "average expectable environment" (Hartmann, 1939/1958) with "good enough mothering" (Winnicott, 1971). Such mothering need not be perfect, and some degree of child frustration is not only compatible with it but expectable and even adaptive for the older child's learning:

> The notion of an average expectable environment for promoting normal development proposes that there are species-specific ranges of environmental conditions that elicit normative developmental processes. Humans, like all other species, develop within a "normal range" when presented with such an average expectable environment .... When environments fall outside the expectable range, normal development is impeded.
>
> (Cicchetti & Valentino, 2006, p. 129)

> The good-enough mother ... as time proceeds ... adapts less and less completely, gradually, according to the infant's growing ability to deal with failure ... [S]uccess in infant care depends on the fact of devotion, not on cleverness of intellectual enlightenment.
>
> (Winnicott, 1971, p. 10)

From this perspective, Olga's simple devotion in wanting to cuddle with Hans when he needed to regulate his fears is superior to the theoretically intellectualized intervention of Max.

Some readers may object that in constructing this account of the case, I have not taken adequate care to state Freud's alternative views and to address the case evidence that he used to support his views. That is, I have not answered the question: If I am right, then precisely how and why did Freud go so wrong in presenting his case for an Oedipal account of the Hans case? This concern is absolutely correct. As noted, there was inadequate space in one focused book to present my own analysis and to look in equal detail at Freud's argument for his Oedipal interpretation of Hans's phobia. The reconstruction and evaluation of Freud's argument for his Oedipal interpretation of the case, a philosophy-of-science task, is undertaken elsewhere (Wakefield, 2022).

Why Was the Oedipus Complex So Appealing to the Culture At Large?

The Little Hans case remains the clearest and most detailed record we have of the imposition of Oedipal power/knowledge on a fin-de-siecle couple. Because this was the first such Oedipal-analyzed family, the application of the theory was not yet routinized. Consequently, the process of the imposition of the theory, what it entails for the family, and the resistances that initially occur and must be overcome are more explicit than they tend to be in later families confronted with an accepted and routine medical "fact."

The basic conclusion to emerge from my analysis of the Hans case is that Oedipal theory has a distinctive power/knowledge appeal, which consists primarily of a novel form of marital regulation of a mother's affectionate relationship with her son. Guided by the work of sexologists and physicians, at the time of the Hans case marital couples' mutual sexual gratification was coming to be seen as essential to marital happiness, rendering the child's claims on the mother's affections potentially problematic. These developments came into conflict with the simultaneous drift towards more parent–child intimacy and parental responsibility for child emotional development. The Oedipus complex allowed a medically endorsed pathway out of this emotional maze. The Oedipal theory offered a laboratory in the negotiation of parental roles in the new century's confusing emotional/sexual family. Growing middle-class affluence allowing for dedicated children's rooms and Oedipally underscored worries about the harmfulness of a child witnessing the primal scene made the child's ejection from the marital bedroom at a very young age seem the right thing to do. Oedipal power/knowledge was thus in effect a tool for redressing the imbalance between fresh ideals of marital bliss and the realities of childrearing, allowing the father to pursue his bedtime happiness and put aside his Laius-complex insecurities unhobbled by a distracted wife in love with and cuddling with her young child. The relatively sympathetic professional and middle-class reception accorded the Oedipus complex with its claimed dangerousness of mother–son physical affection fit well with these ongoing processes of the social re-engineering of marriage. This impact has resonances down to our own time (see Chapter 9).

The resulting separation of mother and son potentially allows more attention to the bond between the mother and father, although the Grafs' conflict-ridden relationship and Olga's fears of pregnancy in an era before reliable birth control seem to have kept them from benefiting very much from this dividend of Oedipal theory. In a narrower sense, the "winner" in this Oedipal shift is the post-Victorian husband/father, who tended to be less involved in child care and more interested in sexual access to his wife than in attachment-related soothing of children in the marital bed. However, the mother/wife might also be relieved of what otherwise would be broader child-related duties, for she too was embracing the new and more egalitarian pleasure-oriented view of marriage. The major loser in Oedipal power/knowledge would appear to be the child, if one accepts, following Bowlby, that his attachment needs are quite natural and their satisfaction is not addictive but essential to the child's proper development.

Reflections on Olga Honig

The analysis of the power dimensions of the Hans case places Hans's mother, Olga Honig, in a new light. As we saw in Chapter 7, the psychoanalytic literature is highly critical of her, to say the least, often blaming Hans's troubles on her pathologically bad parenting. There is no evidence to support such a view, and one wonders about attachment-theory-driven misogynist intrusions here. My analysis suggests a potential form of misogyny, but something different from the usual accusations against Oedipal theory's stylized roles of a patriarchal father and affectionate mother and its later postulation of penis envy as a central factor in female development. My analysis suggests that independently of what one thinks about the biases of Oedipal theory itself, the rearrangement of the family that it supported had a misogynistic quality in that it encouraged the regulation of a mother's natural desire to comfort her child. Regarding Olga specifically, what the evidence supports is that Olga must be considered a hero of the Hans case. Despite her limitations and the pressures on her, she attempted to be a good and even affectionate mother to Hans to the extent compatible with her mental dispositions.

Granted, Olga's behavior towards her daughter Hanna appears to be tragic and blameworthy. It was behavior, it should be said, that came about after a pregnancy she was seemingly pressured into undergoing by her husband with Freud's support, despite her vehement objections.

Why, then, a hero? A large part of power/knowledge derives from people's general acceptance of the authoritative views of experts. In Hans's family, the impact of Oedipal theory was limited by the mother's resistance to such authority. Most mothers would not have been as savvy as Olga about psychoanalysis and the weak evidential support for its sexual theorizing. When she was Freud's patient in the 1890s, accepting Freud's spurious seduction-theory interpretations of her symptoms as due to sexual abuse by family members alienated her from her family and made her a charity case, but she went along. When the Oedipal theory replaced the seduction theory and the new theory was visited by Freud and Max upon Olga and her son, this time Olga courageously rejected implausible Freudian doctrines that she thought were harmful and defended her relationship with her son. Despite expressing her resistance discreetly and mostly passively, the consequence was additional tension within her troubled marriage.

In the longer run, Olga resisted her family's decades-long pressures to conform to their Freudian-friendly views, and she actively sought insight into her problems with painful moves from one guru (Freud) to another (Adler). It is unclear whether her quest for peace was rewarded with a measure of success, although she did marry soon after divorcing Max and this time stayed married. Her story should embolden other mothers to resist the premature and often harmful imposition of psychological doctrines based on questionable evidence that can disrupt parent–child relationships.

The Non-Liberatory Nature of Oedipal Theory

Some aspects of Freud's broader theory have functioned in a liberating way. For example, the contra-Victorian idea that female sexual orgasm is a necessary part of female sexual health (although misguidedly interpreted by Freud in terms of the so-called vaginal rather than clitoral orgasm), as well as the idea of the complex nature of sexuality encompassing many divergent components, did help to move Western medicine beyond Victorianism.

However, other aspects of Freud's sex-focused theory had the anti-liberatory effect of preserving Victorianism's suspicions of sex. The Oedipus complex falls in the latter category. The sexualization of parent–child attachment relations entailed by the Oedipal theory and the consequent sense of danger attached to parent–child affection yields increased self-consciousness and self-surveillance by parents regarding the possible erotic meanings of their formerly innocent parental affections. This has the effect of limiting the natural physical soothing that takes place in the parent–child relationship.

The potential harmfulness of the deployment of the Oedipal theory is illustrated by the Hans case history. Hans underwent an enormous and painful struggle to try to make himself heard in his Oedipal family, even as he was the target of the Oedipal theory's ministrations. He was articulate and clearly expressed his entirely reasonable needs, which were ignored in the name of theory. Indeed, the theory itself, by creating a culturally syntonic sense of what is "natural" and "unnatural" in a child, dictated the illegitimacy of his feelings of distress and determined the course of action of ignoring those feelings. There is manifest harm in Hans's immediate suffering in his desperate struggle to satisfy his attachment needs in the face of his father's implacable theory-driven resistance. Whatever blessings in terms of marital-bed safety the deployment of the Oedipal theory conferred on the father, they came at a steep price for Hans. As well, there is a hint of patriarchal resurgence in the husband's new role of observer and corrector of mother–son relations.

Conclusion: Beyond the Analyst as Oracle

In illuminating what went wrong in a case that shaped Freud's clinical theory, psychotherapeutic practice, and mainstream culture for over a century, my goal is to help psychoanalysis move forward confidently and with legitimacy by freeing it of any illusions about its past. However, to embrace this opportunity and make use of this knowledge, humility is required.

I have shown that in recent trauma-theoretic analyses of the Hans case anything but humility is demonstrated. Freud provided a problematic model in this regard. Although Freud in his self-analysis may have identified with Oedipus, it is clear that he also identified with the oracle who predicted Oedipus's fate. Recall what Freud said in his one meeting with Little Hans and his father in putting forward his Oedipal interpretation:

> I then disclosed to him that he was afraid of his father, precisely because he was so fond of his mother .... Long before he was in the world, I went on, I had known that a little Hans would come who would be so fond of his mother that he would be bound to feel afraid of his father because of it; and I had told his father this.
>
> (Freud, 1909/1955, p. 42)

Freud tells Hans that he told Hans's father about Hans's fate even before Hans was born. This was precisely the role of the oracle, who told King Laius the fate of his son before the son was born. Freud is self-aware enough to know that he is playing out the oracle's role. Hans understands that Freud is claiming to have extraordinary oracular powers that go beyond those of normal human understanding. Leaving Freud's office with his father, he astutely asks: "Does the Professor talk to God, as he can tell all that beforehand?" (Freud, 1909/1955, pp. 42–43). Freud defensively acknowledges his hubris: "I should be extraordinarily proud of this recognition out of the mouth of a child, if I had not myself provoked it by my joking boastfulness" (Freud, 1909/1955, p. 43). Freud's occasional images of himself as the excavator and archeologist—who carefully explores the hidden terrain of the patient's unconscious and expects to be surprised by what he finds—is replaced here by the know-it-all oracle who gets his information from an independent source, namely, Oedipal theory, and transposes it confidently onto his patient.

This sense that the interpretation is preset, that meanings at the root of psychopathology are nomologically determined, has led to the authoritarian model of psychoanalytic intervention that has been the bane of psychoanalysis and created a well-justified backlash. By the time of this backlash, however, psychoanalysis was so identified with its specific Oedipal theoretical content rather than with its more general framework for exploring unconscious meaning (Wakefield, 2018) that it seemed that an attack on the Oedipal theory is an attack on psychoanalysis itself, a view that Freud encouraged.

Among the characters in the Hans drama, only his mother, Olga Honig, having experienced Freud's theoretical development first-hand, possessed the perception and courage to challenge the oracle. She uttered the truth-to-power words that it has taken mainstream psychoanalysis a century to only gingerly embrace—"It's all nonsense."

Really, nonsense? What of the objection that analysts since Freud have seen ample evidence that confirmed Freud's Oedipal theory? One analyst friend objects: "It is hard to believe that generations of analysts were misled by Freud and that they did not have better evidence than Freud did." But, repetition of a methodologically biased test shows nothing, as in the old joke that if one doubts the accuracy of a *New York Times* story, one can easily confirm its truth by checking another copy of the paper. No matter how many analysts reproduce the discovery of the Oedipus complex, it does not confirm the theory without some independent evidence that is more direct than analytic interpretation, any more than Freud's many successes in imposing seduction theory interpretations on patients shows the truth of that theory. Surely Grunbaum (1984) is correct that the psychoanalytic interpretive situation is generally much too methodologically contaminated in all sorts of ways to be a reliable way of confirming causal theoretical hypotheses (however, for a brilliant way that Freud tries to get around this obstacle in the Hans case, see Wakefield, 2022).

To provide such independent evidence was the express purpose of the Hans case history, and that test failed (again, for a systematic argument for this conclusion, see Wakefield, 2022). It took Freud a decade to build up the courage to publicly acknowledge that, despite all his evidential claims, he was wrong about the seduction theory. He did not have the courage to go through that humiliation again when the Hans case revealed that his Oedipal theory was just as questionable as the seduction theory.

The Oedipus complex as Freud conceived it is a developmental myth that exaggerates certain simple facts about sensual development and massively distorts the nature of attachment. Seen in its historical context, one must acknowledge that Foucault is correct that it is part of a much larger multi-century distortion of the nature of sexuality that Foucault labels the deployment of sexuality. Nevertheless, Freud's theory revealed or at least pointed to the novel complexities of the trinary relationship between mother, father, and son in the modern bourgeois nuclear-family era. Moreover, it was by identifying and renouncing the Oedipus complex's excesses that other more promising developmental theories, such as Bowlby's attachment theory, made their way into the world and drew us closer to the truth.

Sophocles's *Oedipus Rex* story is about the sins of the father being visited on the child, who is blind to his fate. The sins of Freud in defending the Oedipal theory contrary to the evidence have been similarly visited on a century of psychoanalysts, his intellectual descendants. Psychoanalysts followed Freud in blinding themselves to the evidence. For all his brilliance, Freud was unable to grasp that clinging to his beloved sexual theory of the neuroses would undermine rather than ensure the fulfillment of his desire for intellectual immortality.

If psychoanalysis has declined due to the sin of hubris, this a hopeful diagnosis. It suggests that the rebellion against the classical model in recent years was exactly what was needed to open the way to a better future for psychoanalysis. Moreover, psychoanalysis is desperately needed as a corrective to remind us of the centrality of meaning in an era in which psychiatry is dominated by a biological focus.

But, there is a price to pay for redeeming psychoanalysis. The power to interpret via unconscious meanings what the patient "really" wants demands trust by the patient and moral responsibility by the analyst. If interpretations are in error, this is not to be taken lightly. If Oedipal theory was wrong, then psychoanalysis has done on a mass scale what Freud did to Olga Honig during her treatment in the seduction-theory era; psychoanalysis has led individuals astray about the truth of their most intimate and valued relationships. Moreover, in creating a public sensitivity to Oedipal dangers of parent–child affection and intimacy that do not exist in the form they were portrayed, psychoanalysts have done to us all what Max did to Hans, inadvertently disrupting the satisfaction of the attachment needs of innumerable individuals who were never under treatment. In Freud's letter to Fliess of September 21, 1897, in which he announced that he had come to reject his seduction theory, Freud says at the end of his explanation that "it is strange, too, that no feeling of shame appeared—for which, after all, there could well be occasion" (Freud, 1897/1985, p. 265). It appears from the context that Freud was referring only to shame about having made a scientific error, not about having misled his patients. It was indeed an occasion for both forms of shame, but they were lacking. Psychoanalysis should now find the appropriate sense of shame that eluded Freud, on both the scientific and personal counts. To admit that the Oedipal theory was "nonsense" is a terrible moral as well as scientific burden, one that will take courage to face squarely and to discharge. In this regard, psychoanalysis must rise to the occasion and be better than Freud.

References

Bowlby, J. (1973). *Attachment and Loss (Vol. 2): Separation: Anxiety and anger.* London, UK: Hogarth Press.

Cicchetti, D., & Valentino, K. (2006). An ecological-transactional perspective on child maltreatment: Failure of the average expectable environment and its influence on child development. In D. Cicchetti & D. J. Cohen (Eds.), *Developmental psychopathology: Risk, disorder, and adaptation* (pp. 129–201). New York: John Wiley & Sons, Inc.

Graf, M. (1952). *Interview [of Max Graf] by Kurt Eissler. Box 112, Sigmund Freud Papers, Sigmund Freud Collection*, Manuscript Division, Library of Congress, Washington, D.C.

Foucault, M. (1978). *History of sexuality (Vol. 1): An introduction* (R. Hurley, Trans.). New York, NY: Pantheon.

Freud, S. (1955). Analysis of a phobia in a five-year-old boy. In J. Strachey (Ed. and Trans.), *The standard edition of the complete psychological works of Sigmund Freud* (Vol. *10*, pp. 1–150). London, UK: Hogarth Press. (Original work published 1909).

Freud, S. (1962). A reply to criticisms of my paper on anxiety neurosis. In J. Strachey (Ed. & Trans.), *The standard edition of the complete psychological works of Sigmund Freud* (Vol. *3*, pp. 119–139). London, UK: Hogarth Press. (Original work published 1895).

Freud, S. (1985). Letter from Freud to Fliess, September 21, 1897. In J. M. Masson (Ed. & Trans.), *The complete letters of Sigmund Freud to Wilhelm Fliess, 1887–1904* (pp. 264–266). Cambridge, MA: Harvard University Press. (Original work 1897.)

Grunbaum, A. (1984). *The foundations of psychoanalysis: A philosophical critique*. Berkeley, CA: University of California Press.

Hartmann, H. (1958). *Ego Psychology and the problem of adaptation*. New York, International Universities Press. (Original work published in 1939).

Löwenfeld, L. (1895) Über die Verknüpfung neurasthenischer und hysterischer Symptome in Anfallsform nebst Bemerkungen über die Freudsche Angstneurose, *Münchener Medicinische Wochenschrift, 42*, 282–285.

Wakefield, J. C. (2007). Attachment and sibling rivalry in Little Hans: The 'phantasy of the two giraffes' reconsidered. *Journal of the American Psychoanalytic Association, 55*, 821–849.

Wakefield, J. C. (2008). Little Hans and the thought police: The "Policeman Fantasies" as the first supervisory transference fantasies. *International Journal of Psychoanalysis, 89*, 71–88.

Wakefield, J. C. (2017). Concept representation in the child: What did Little Hans mean by 'widdler'? *Psychoanalytic Psychology, 34*(3), 352–360.

Wakefield, J. C. (2018). *Freud and philosophy of mind (Vol. 1): Reconstructing the argument for unconscious mental states*. New York, NY: Palgrave Macmillan.

Wakefield, J. C. (2022). *Freud's argument for the Oedipus complex: A philosophy of science analysis of the case of Little Hans*. New York, NY: Routledge.

Wakefield, J. C. (forthcoming). *Foucault versus Freud: Oedipal theory and the deployment of sexuality*. New York, NY: Routledge.

Winnicott, D. W. (1971). *Playing and reality*. London: Tavistock Publications.

Wolpe, J., & Rachman, S. (1960). Psychoanalytic "evidence": A critique based on Freud's case of little Hans. *Journal of Nervous and Mental Disease, 131*(2), 135–148.

Index

abandonment threat, as parental strategy 102; attachment theory and 58–63; fear of 104

Abbott, S. 231, 237, 241

Abrams, D. 140

Acton, W. 216

actual disruption, of attachment relationship 102–103

Adler, A. 29, 34–35, 139–140, 141

Ainsworth Strange Situation studies 42–43, 63

ambivalent/resistant attachment pattern 44, 53

anxiety 148, 208, 217, 268, 273, 276; attachment theory and 41, 49–52, 58, 65, 69–73; bed time and 255–256, 258; caregiver 64–65; castration 12, 48, 175, 269, 270; chronic 45, 63, 106, 297; about death 36–37, 59; disorder 39, 44, 63, 71, 72, 77, 91, 109, 162, 171, 207, 280, 281; dream 49; expression of 52, 53, 62, 94, 280; family power and 1, 4–6, 11, 15; Graf family dynamics and 18, 19, 23; heightened 46, 83, 91, 102, 105, 106, 295; infantile 94, 95; libido and 95, 99–100, 111, 112; masturbation and 115, 116, 117; Oedipal power/knowledge and 84, 104, 107; psychoanalysis future and 288, 292–297; sexual desire and 80, 89, 128, 183, 242–243, 244, 248; social 20, 22, 25, 32; trauma theory and 170, 173, 174, 183; vulnerability to 68, 83, 102

anxious attachment 20, 23, 36, 42, 53, 123, 280; Bowlby on roots of 18, 39, 41, 44–45, 126, 297; libido and 100; perspective on 105–107; and situational attachment distress compared 45–46

Aristotle 227

asexual wife, as barrier against male lust 216–217

attachment, theoretical sexualization of 8, 91–101, 121

attachment theory 1, 5, 6, 39; anxious attachment and situational attachment distress compared and 45–46; Bowlby on anxious attachment roots and 44–45; Bowlby's reinterpretation of 4, 13; as challenge to Oedipal Theory 39–44; Hans from perspective of contemporary categories of 63–65–68; Hans' disposition to anxiety and 71–73; Hans' phobia and connection with closeness to his mother 68–71; Little Hans case study and 46–48; Olga's threat to leave family and 60–63; power/knowledge and 14–15; see also Bowlby, J.

avoidant attachment patterns 43–44

Bahn, A. K. 234

Barajas, R. G. 229, 232

bed time see cosleeping

Blair, P. S. 226

Blum, H. 18, 21; on Hanna's suicide 199; on Hans as physically abused by Olga 183–192; on Olga's anger 201–202

Bowlby, J. 4, 13, 18, 22, 36, 39, 135, 198; anxiety in children and 95; on anxious attachment roots 44–45, 126, 297; on attachment 92, 252; on childhood animal phobias 65–68; on closeness-to-mother hypothesis 69;

For Product Safety Concerns and Information please contact our EU
representative GPSR@taylorandfrancis.com
Taylor & Francis Verlag GmbH, Kaufingerstraße 24, 80331 München, Germany

www.ingramcontent.com/pod-product-compliance
Lightning Source LLC
Chambersburg PA
CBHW050335270326
41926CB00016B/3462

* 9 7 8 1 0 3 2 2 2 4 0 9 1 *